ONR -

Meaningfulness and Verbal Learning

Meaningfulness and

BENTON J. UNDERWOOD

NORTHWESTERN UNIVERSITY
EVANSTON, ILLINOIS

and RUDOLPH W. SCHULZ

THE STATE UNIVERSITY OF IOWA
IOWA CITY, IOWA

Verbal Learning

CHICAGO · PHILADELPHIA · NEW YORK

J. B. LIPPINCOTT COMPANY

Preface

This is a report of research dealing with meaningfulness of verbal materials and its influence on learning. It seemed advisable to publish these studies together rather than in piecemeal fashion. The basic experiments were supported by the Office of Naval Research, through contracts N7onr-45008, and Nonr-1228(15). Not only have we received continuing financial support from this remarkable organization, but through Dr. D. D. Smith of the Personnel and Training Branch of ONR we have been encouraged to carry out the research in the manner which, in our judgment, seemed best advised.

In 1956–57 the senior author was awarded the President's Fellowship at Northwestern University for study and research. During that year the background work and preliminary theoretical analysis were accomplished, and the research initiated. The senior author is deeply grateful to Northwestern University for this year of unbroken study. We also owe a real debt to Professor Leo Postman of the University of California (Berkeley). At one time or another nearly all of the material in the book was discussed with him; he helped us over many rough spots.

Many people have been involved in the data collection. In special cases we have expressed our appreciation in the text. To all others, whose names follow, we are very grateful for the careful work contributed: Jean Barnes, Jane Chesley, Lynne Dobrin, Joyce Ferris, Anthony Finder, Patricia Frank, Judith Hidding, Diane Mair, Margaret McAllen, Michelle Melyn, Donald Nagel, Lucille Reese, Streeter Remley, Barbara Moore Runquist, and Robert Swenson.

Miss Elaine Johnson and Mrs. Fannie Robinson were responsible for the very accurate typing job.

Finally, we acknowledge with thanks permission from the following people to use certain materials: Mrs. Fletcher Pratt; Prof. Karl M. Dallenbach for *The American Journal of Psychology;* Prof. Robert B. Ammons for Southern Universities Press; Dr. Carl Murchison for the Journal Press; and Dr. John G. Darley for the American Psychological Association, Inc.

MAY, 1960   BENTON J. UNDERWOOD
                                               RUDOLPH W. SCHULZ

Contents

Meaningfulness and
Verbal Learning

Meaningfulness and
Verbal Learning

Chapter 1

Introduction

This is a study of rote verbal learning. It pursues the general line of inquiry which was initiated by Ebbinghaus and which, over the years, has consistently produced theoretical and research challenges to the students of human learning. We found these challenges in our attempts to understand how one variable, *meaningfulness*, exerted its powerful effect on rote learning in the young human adult. Our efforts to solve this engaging problem are recorded in the pages that follow.

That a single variable can engage one's research energies for a period of several years is clearly indicative of a systematic position we hold with regard to strategy for attacking research problems in psychology. We have yet to see momentous discoveries or momentous breakthroughs in our science such as have been reported to occur in the other sciences. But we can point to a gradual increase in our comprehension of the verbal-learning processes which has been brought about by systematic experimental analyses made over the years. Perhaps dramatic breakthroughs would occur if the right questions were asked. Perhaps a single study, if predicated on the *right* question, would circumvent the systematic series of experiments which has characterized much research, not only in the area of verbal learning, but in many areas of psychology. If this is so, let it be said at the outset that we have not found this happy question as far as the present work is concerned. If the virtue ascribed to systematic analyses derives as a consequence of persistent failure to find the magic and pointed question, then we not only admit our failure, but we rap our knuckles for having misunderstood our reasons for ascription of the virtue. Whatever the cause, it will be seen that the present study continues our commitment to systematic analysis as one way of attacking research problems; it is a way we find both fruitful and exciting.

In recent years we have arrived at two conclusions about verbal learning which have direct relevance to our present study of meaningfulness. We concluded first that there are very few variables which produce any marked effect on the rate of verbal learning shown by the adult subject. Of these few variables, meaningfulness is by far the most powerful. It is a rare situation in the study of behavior when the range of differences attributable to a manipulated variable is greater than that attributable to individual differences. But such is the case for meaningfulness. Indeed, for certain materials we can predict the relative rate at which an individual subject will learn various items, and the predictions are surprisingly accurate. Although there were other specific reasons (to be mentioned shortly) which determined the moment for us to undertake an analysis of meaningfulness, the realization that it was a rare variable in terms of the magnitude of its influence made the undertaking inevitable sooner or later.

The second factor which helped guide us in the present work is the conclusion that when we study the present verbal learning of the young adult, we must study simultaneously the learning which has taken place previously in his life. We can only fully understand present learning when we understand habits which the subject brings to the learning laboratory. A knowledge of certain types of habits which the subject brings *is* essentially a study of meaningfulness, for the indices of meaningfulness are derived from an elicitation of these types of habits. Sooner or later, of course, research must be directed toward the study of the origin of these habits. We must eventually study the verbal-learning processes at the moment the organism is first capable of exhibiting such processes. But until we surmount many of the problems attending such research, inferences about these early stages of verbal learning can be made with some confidence if we understand the habits which the adult subject brings with him to the laboratory.

THE PROBLEM

The central empirical problem of our work can be illustrated very simply. If we construct one list made up of items such as GJX and QZB, and another of such items as CAT and IBM, why is the second list learned so much more rapidly than the first? If a layman is asked this question, he may be insulted because of the obviousness of the answer, for he will say that the second list is learned more rapidly than the first because it is made up of more meaningful items than the first. Yet, in spite of the dimension per se being obvious, just how the characteristics or attributes which make up or are associated with this dimension, and which make it so obvious—just how they lead to such large differences in learning is not so easy to "come by." At least, we have not found it so. As will be seen, the difficulty in arriving at an accounting of how meaningfulness affects learning stems in large part from the many correlated attributes which seem to go together to make up the gross dimension. There is a great deal of untangling to be done before one can determine whether or not it is possible to say that this particular attribute or that particular attribute is *really* responsible for the differences in learning. Anyhow, that is the problem we faced after we had made some initial analyses, and much of our effort was directed toward an untangling of these attributes. The dimension of meaningfulness is not a unitary one; it is a complex dimension, and no hint of this complexity is given by the original, simple, defining operations.

THE ORIGINAL DEFINING OPERATIONS

In 1928 J. A. Glaze presented a long series of nonsense syllables to subjects with the request that they indicate for each syllable whether or not it suggested an association to them. Then these syllables were ordered along a scale defined as the percentage of the subjects who "got" an association. These were the original defining operations for the dimension which we are calling meaningfulness, and Glaze's procedure is used as a point of departure for our analyses. It should be apparent, therefore, what is meant by the term "meaningfulness." However, it may be worthwhile to disavow certain associations attached to the word. More specifically, meaningfulness as used here should not be confused with the term "meaning." As is well known, meaning has been a focal point of argumentation for generations of philosophers and, in recent years, semanticists. It will be seen that there are no ultimates in the meaning ascribed to meaningfulness by the operations of the learning laboratory, and there need not, therefore, be any cause for confusion with philosophical problems of meaning.

It is also necessary to disclaim any immediate relationship between meaningfulness and meaning as this latter term is used by Osgood (e.g., Osgood, Suci, & Tannenbaum; 1957). Osgood has engaged in multidimensional scaling of words to produce an operational specification of the meaning of concepts. It is quite possible that the dimensions isolated by these procedures may be found to have relevance to the learning of verbal materials. But even if they do, it should be clear that the present work is not concerned with such relevancies. To repeat, the Glaze procedure will be used as a reference definition for meaningfulness, and, although several procedures producing correlated measures will be identified, none strays close to the two meanings of meaning noted above.

THE ORIGIN OF OUR STUDIES

We earlier noted certain general factors which sooner or later would have committed us to the present studies. However, there were two particular developments which were responsible for starting the work when we did. About 1955 certain data suggested that meaningfulness was a critical variable determining whether or not distributed practice facilitated verbal learning. More specifically, the data at that time indicated that the higher the meaningfulness, the less likely it was that distributed practice would facilitate learning. It seemed, therefore, that the understanding of how distributed practice facilitates learning might come via an understanding of how meaningfulness influences learning. The most recent evidence now suggests that the interaction between meaningfulness and distributed practice is of much smaller magnitude than originally supposed. Nevertheless, the mistaken inference about this interaction is partly responsible for the present work on meaningfulness.

A second development which focused our interest on meaningfulness was the interpretation we made of certain retention data. In this interpretation we felt that language habits, particularly letter-sequence habits, were an important source of interference in the retention of verbal materials. Furthermore, some early analyses we made in an effort to document the importance of these letter-sequence habits showed that differences in the strength of letter-sequence habits could be viewed as another way of defining meaningfulness. Again, therefore, an understanding of meaningfulness seemed propaedeutic to the design and interpretation of other research we wished to undertake.

But if these developments initiated the studies, they certainly cannot be said to be responsible for sustaining them. First of all, our original studies on meaningfulness produced puzzles of such intrinsic interest to us that the research on meaningfulness almost became functionally autonomous; we forgot the original purposes which initiated the studies. But above all, and fortunately or unfortunately, our study of the work of previous investigators and the initial studies we did led to a theoretical notion. The more we examined various implications of the notion, the more we became convinced of its usefulness. It was the theory which determined the character of several of our studies and perhaps sustained our efforts longer in certain directions than the results of previous experiments warranted. To call our notion a theory is probably a misuse of the word. No formal theory—no elegant system —is involved. It is perhaps more accurate to say that this so-called theoretical notion played the role of an analytical device. It provided us with a new point of view for examining the results of research in which meaningfulness was manipulated.

Finally, by way of introduction, we will present the plan for reporting the studies and our evaluation of them.

THE PLAN

To a large extent our report will follow chronologically the order of events as they actually happened. First, we will summarize the work of other investigators to give a picture of the state of knowledge about meaningfulness and learning at the time we undertook our studies. Then, we will show how our early analyses led us to a theoretical position that we were to test in several studies. Finally, these studies will be reported in the order in which they were done. Roughly speaking, the first half of the book is devoted to background material, and the second half to our experimental analyses.

Although we find the historical method of reporting very compatible, and although it may have a didactic value which the nonhistorical approach does not, we realize that it has certain deficiencies. For example, we eventually had to conclude that our theoretical notion had very limited application; it "worked well" in certain types of situations, but not in others. Under the historical method of reporting, a reader is never allowed to find out just what these theoretical deficiencies are until the particular experiments demonstrating the deficiencies are reached. In a certain sense the reader may learn something which he must later unlearn. At the same time, however, there may be some interest in the readers' meeting the puzzles as we met them that they might begin by being as puzzled as we were. In any event, we shall quite faithfully order our experiments, hunches, puzzles, and so on as they occurred chronologically. When we deviate seriously from this order, we will so state this fact.

It was noted above that our first step in reporting will be to summarize the work of previous investigators. Immediately, we must say that our chronological order is broken as far as the first two chapters are concerned. That is, at the time we started our experiments we did not have the wealth of information which became available from other laboratories during the course of our experiments. For, whatever the reasons, be it the *Zeitgeist* or be it a consequence of Dr. Clyde Noble's reopening of the problem of meaningfulness in 1952 after a stagnant period of many years, the fact is that in the very recent years many investigators have taken up the same problem with which we are concerned. We have, of course, gratefully made use of these studies whenever we could; many of them are reported in the first two chapters.

REFERENCES

Glaze, J. A. The association value of non-sense syllables. *J. genet. Psychol.*, 1928, 35, 255–269.

Noble, C. E. An analysis of meaning. *Psychol. Rev.*, 1952, 59, 421–430.

Osgood, C. E., Suci, G. J., & Tannenbaum, P. H. *The measurement of meaning.* Univer. of Illinois Press, Urbana, 1957.

Chapter 2

The Definitions of Meaningfulness

The present chapter will be devoted to an exposition of the different techniques used to define the attribute of verbal units called meaningfulness. In addition, we will examine the relationships among the scales of meaningfulness resulting from the different operations. Finally, certain scaling procedures used by the present writers will be presented along with their relationships to the more classical techniques.

The results of various defining procedures are often said to yield an *association value* for a verbal unit. In the present work we use *association value* and *meaningfulness* interchangeably at the definitional level. M Furthermore, since this latter term occurs with such high frequency in our writing, it will be abbreviated as M.

In the examination of the various scaling operations, emphasis is given to the names of the investigators. The purpose for this is entirely an expository one since, in detailing the results of various learning experiments, we will find it convenient to identify the materials used by referring to the name of the investigator who did the scaling.

Glaze (1928). Although nonsense syllables had been used in learning experiments since the classical work of Ebbinghaus in 1885, Glaze's work represents the first systematic attempt to order syllables along a dimension of M. An inspection of a group of nonsense syllables will show that the dimension is an obvious one; undoubtedly, many previous investigators had noted the possibility that differences in learning could be attributed to some such dimension. Technically, of course, a nonsense syllable is a vowel between two consonants giving a three-letter combination which does not form an English word. As would be expected, this latter criterion is not a very rigid one since whether or not the combination forms a word depends upon the exhaustiveness and date of publication of the dictionary used. Noble, Stockwell, & Pryer (1957) present some evidence on this matter. Their search leads them to conclude that there are only 1,675 nonwords among all possible consonant-vowel-consonant combinations.

The list which Glaze finally presented to his subjects consisted of 2,019 syllables. No syllables were used which had the same initial and final letter, and the letter y was considered a vowel. The syllables were presented one at a time by use of a tachistoscope for a minimum of 2 sec. and a maximum of 3 sec. As the syllable was presented the experimenter spelled it. The subject was instructed to indicate in one or two words what the syllable meant to him, if anything. If the syllable meant something to him which he could not verbalize, he was to indicate this. If the syllable meant nothing to the subject, nothing was to be said.

TABLE 1. Some Nonsense Syllables and Their Glaze Association Values

(Glaze, 1928)

Association Value				
0%	CEF	QOB	XUH	ZIL
20%	CUJ	HUQ	TAH	YUX
40%	DEQ	PEX	SIF	WOH
60%	BAW	FOZ	RAH	XEM
80%	CEL	KOM	PAM	TOL
100%	BIZ	FEL	RAV	VIK

The subjects, a total of 15, were given 15 practice syllables first and then presented the 2,019 syllables at the rate of 252 per session. The association value or M of each syllable was calculated simply as the percentage of subjects who "had an association" to the syllable. The instances where the subject could not verbalize the association were included as positive cases. To the syllable PIL all 15 subjects produced an association, so this syllable is said to have an association value of 100 per cent. The syllable XUC elicited no associations for any subject; it has an association value of 0 per cent. Since there were only 15 subjects, the steps between successive values are approximately 6.7 per cent. The distribution is rectangular; the number of syllables at each step is roughly the same.

The complete list of Glaze syllables is presented in Appendix A. However, in order to establish a quick and easy "feel" for the nature of the dimension, a few representative syllables are given in Table 1.

Hull (1933). Hull used 320 syllables, most of which had appeared in Glaze's list. These 320 syllables were divided into 20 lists of 16 syllables each. The 20 male subjects worked with all 20 lists in a rotational scheme calculated to spread the effects of practice equally over all items. Each list was presented three times at a rate of 2 sec. for each syllable. On the second and third trials the subject was instructed to anticipate the syllables; thus, the procedure corresponds to simple serial learning. But, in addition, Hull asked his subjects to report to him what a syllable made them think of, if, in fact, it did make them think of anything. The subject was not to *try* to think of associations to a syllable, but if he did, he was to report it. The M index was the number of associations reported for each syllable out of the 60 possibilities to report (three trials and 20 subjects). If the same association were given on all three trials by the same subject, it was counted as three in determining M.

Hull used the above procedure because he wanted to get a measure of association value in an actual learning situation. However, viewed only as a case of scaling, Hull's procedure is puzzling. In a relatively brief period of 2 sec. the subject was expected to carry out a number of activities. He was to anticipate the next syllable, tell what the syllable made him think of, and check to determine whether or not his previous anticipation was correct. Yet, the subject was not *really* supposed to try to get an association. There was no way to know whether he did have one and didn't have time to report it, whether he didn't get one, or whether he got one but failed to report it. Furthermore, since the items were presented in a constant order on the three trials, serial position becomes a possible source of bias. This bias results from the fact that learning rate varies as a function of serial position; the better an item is learned, the greater is the amount of time for reporting an association after the item has been anticipated.

Considered over-all, Hull's procedures raise two basic questions. First, did the items have an "equal opportunity" to elicit associations, and secondly, can the results of these operations be said to be behaviorally equivalent to those used by others, e.g., to Glaze's procedures? If the answer to the first is negative, the answer to the second will also be expected to be negative. Some evidence on these issues will be presented later.

Krueger (1934). Krueger spelled each syllable twice, the two spellings requiring about 4 sec. on the average. The subject wrote the syllable as the experimenter spelled it and then made a notation (word or phrase) of the idea aroused by the syllable. The entire sequence for each syllable consumed 7 sec. Those syllables arousing the greatest frequency of response were said to have 100 per cent association value;

the values of the other syllables were based on the percentage frequency of the associations aroused by the 100 per cent syllables. A total of 2,183 syllables was used following 100 practice syllables. Although a total of 586 subjects participated, each rated only 1,200 syllables. It is not possible to tell exactly the number of subjects rating each syllable, but apparently this number was something over 250. The M values should, therefore, be very stable. The values for these syllables are also given in Appendix A. The distribution is quite skewed, with over half the syllables having M values above 75 per cent and very few having low values.

Witmer (*1935*). Glaze, Hull, and Krueger all determined M for nonsense syllables. Witmer worked with consonant syllables which consist of three consecutive consonants—no vowels occur. In fact, in the 4,534 syllables in Witmer's final list, *a, e, i, o, u, y,* and *v* were excluded. The same letter never occurred twice in a syllable and no two letters adjacent in the alphabet appeared in a syllable. Each syllable was exposed for 4 sec. on a memory drum. The subject was instructed to spell the syllable and then state in a word or phrase what it meant. If the syllable meant something but he could not verbalize its meaning within the 4-sec. interval, he was to say merely "yes." The M value was the percentage of the 25 male subjects who reported an association. Thus, XFQ turned out to have 0 per cent M (no subject reported an association), and WHP had 100 per cent M since all subjects reported an association to it. Some other illustrations are as follows: HFK, 8 per cent; FJP, 21 per cent; CZH, 29 per cent; DPG, 38 per cent; NLG, 45 per cent; CHG, 58 per cent; TBR, 71 per cent; LBR, 83 per cent; HLD, 96 per cent. The complete list is given in Appendix B.

The range of M values resulting from Witmer's procedures is the same as that resulting from Glaze's and Krueger's, namely, 0 per cent to 100 per cent. It is not to be concluded, however, that equivalent values resulting from the different procedures means equivalence in the sense that items having the same M values will be equally difficult or easy to learn. Certainly whether or not a subject can "get an association" will be a function of the time allowed him. Witmer's subjects were allowed 4 sec., whereas the Glaze subjects were given from 2 to 3 sec. It is not completely clear exactly how long Krueger's subjects were allowed, but probably somewhat longer than were Glaze's.

Thus, the fact that different time intervals were used by these three investigators has two consequences. First, it is not to be expected that a nonsense syllable and a consonant syllable with the same M value will be equivalent in learning. Second, the same nonsense syllable may have different M values along the Glaze and Krueger scales. However, this latter fact does not imply that the ordering of items along the scales will not show a high correspondence. Evidence on this question will be presented shortly.

Noble (1952). Following Witmer's work in 1935, a period of 17 years elapsed before Noble's investigations reopened and extended the issues involved in deriving an index of M for single verbal units. After preliminary tryouts, Noble selected 96 units for the final scaling. These units consisted of about 20 per cent paralogs (e.g., *neglan, tarop, gokem*), 35 per cent words having a low-frequency-of-use index in the Thorndike-Lorge (1944) tables, and 45 per cent having high-frequency values in these tables. In the aggregate these units are called dissyllables.

Noble's theoretical conception of M led him to use a somewhat different method of determining an index than those used by previous investigators. This method used by Noble will be called the *production* method. The subject was presented with a to-be-scaled dissyllable and given 60 sec. to write all the different words elicited by the dissyllable.

> You will be given a *key* word and you are to write down as many *other* words which the key word brings to mind as you can. These other words which you write down may be things, places, ideas, events, or whatever you happen to think of when you see the key word (Noble, 1952, p. 425).

Noble's preliminary work made it clear that subjects may produce chain associations. Thus, a given key word elicits a response, this response in turn becomes a stimulus for the next response, and so on. It is likely that such a group of chain associations should not be used to obtain an index of the number of words elicited directly by the key word. To minimize this danger of chain associations, and variants on such, Noble had only one key word on a sheet of paper, and this key word was repeated on every line so that the subject always returned to it before writing a new associate. Even with this precaution there was some evidence for chain associations in some of the records (e.g., the stimulus *lemur* elicited the following: *Dorothy, Hope, faith, charity*). Such associations were eliminated from the records as were other responses when it was clear that the subject had not followed instructions.

The records of 119 subjects (basic airmen) were used in the final calculations of an index of M. The order in which the words had been presented to these subjects was essentially random so that no bias should accrue as a result of differences in practice effects. The index of M was the mean number of responses given to each word during a 60-sec. period. The scale varies from a low of .99 (*gojey*) to a high of 9.61 (*kitchen*). Correlations among subgroups of subjects for the 96 items ranged from .96 to .98, indicating very high reliability of the scale values. The complete list is given in Appendix C.

Mandler (1955). This investigator also used the production method as devised by Noble but employed nonsense syllables as stimuli. A total of 100 syllables was selected so as to be representative of the entire range of M as scaled by Glaze. Each syllable was printed in the middle of a sheet, and the subject was instructed to write all words which he thought of as he looked at and pronounced the syllable. The subject wrote his associations around the stimulus syllable, and although he was warned not to give chain associations, it is not clear from the report that such associations were effectively eliminated. The 34 subjects worked in small groups. The index of M was the mean number of responses written during 30 sec. The syllables LAT and PAS elicited the greatest frequency (a mean of 5.3), and XOK the fewest (2.9). Thus, the range of values resulting from Mandler's scaling is quite restricted. Furthermore, it is to be noted that Mandler's lowest value is appreciably higher than Noble's lowest value in spite of the fact that Noble's subjects were allowed 60 sec. and Mandler's, 30 sec. Mandler suggests that the differences in the frequency might be attributed to population differences, since he had used college students and Noble had used basic airmen as subjects. This may be true, although the particular characteristics on which the populations may differ and which are critical for the production of associates is not apparent. For example, Witmer (1935) could find no relationship between the number of responses produced to consonant syllables and either intelligence or size of vocabulary. Nevertheless, Mandler may be right, and certainly the problem is a researchable one.

Noble, Stockwell, & Pryer (1957). Using 100 nonsense syllables, these investigators introduced still another method for defining M. Noble first, and then Mandler, had had subjects actually write the different associations suggested by the stimuli. In the Noble, et al. study the subjects *rated* nonsense syllables for the number of different things or ideas which they thought each syllable suggested. A portion of the instructions to the subjects will make this clear.

> This is a test to find out how many associations you have to certain combinations of letters from the alphabet. You will be given

a list of 100 3-letter syllables, and you are to rate each one as to the *number* of things or ideas it makes you think of. The ratings are made by simply placing a check mark ($\sqrt{}$) in one of the 5 spaces provided for your estimate. This is to be done for each of the 100 syllables. The 5 possible ratings are described by the words *None, Below Average, Average, Above Average,* and *Very Many.* The way in which your estimates are to be made will now be explained by several examples. Take the item TEX. Spell it. Pronounce it. This syllable probably makes you think of "Texas," "textbook," "cowboys," "wide open spaces," "oil," "Texaco," "gasoline," "Texan," "millionaires," "the Alamo," "pretty girls," and so on. You have a very large number of mental associations to TEX. For this reason, TEX would be rated in the *highest* category (*Very Many*) . . . (p. 442).

A total of 200 subjects, tested in groups of approximately 25 each, made the ratings for the syllables. Since, on the average, 30 min. were required to complete the ratings, it is apparent that the subject did not spend much time on any one syllable. The data are treated in several ways. The most simple score used, however, was the mean rating of each item. The range of these means was from 4.44 (SUB) to 1.28 (XOQ).

This completes the survey of studies which had as their primary purpose the assessment of the relative M of individual verbal units. It should be noted in passing that no single study has covered what one would suspect to be the entire range of M. That is, no investigator has subjected such verbal units as Noble's high-M words and Witmer's low-M consonant syllables to a common scaling procedure. Therefore, a continuous quantitative index is not available for the entire range of M as we conceive of it.

RELATIONSHIPS AMONG THE SCALES OF MEANINGFULNESS

In the work of the investigators reviewed above, three clearly distinct methods of assessing M have been used. Must these different operations force the maintenance of three different scales of M? Or, can a conclusion be reached that the same basic characteristic of the verbal units is being reflected in the responses of the subjects under the different methods? It is to such issues that our attention will now be directed.

Clearly different scaling procedures have been used only for nonsense syllables. First, Glaze, and then Krueger, determined whether or not a syllable aroused an association within a very limited interval of time. Hull also employed essentially this technique. Secondly, Mandler determined the number of different associations actually aroused by a syllable. Finally, Noble, Stockwell, & Pryer asked their subjects to rate the number of different associates which they thought a syllable elicited. How much commonality is there among the relative association values of syllables as determined by these three methods?

Peixotto (1948) chose 300 syllables which were common to Glaze, to Krueger, and to Hull. For these 300 syllables she reports correlations of .65 between Glaze and Krueger, .62 between Glaze and Hull, and .70 between Krueger and Hull. Mandler reports a correlation of .65 between his scale values for 100 syllables and Krueger's values for the same syllables.

Noble, Stockwell, & Pryer (1957) had used 100 syllables common to Krueger and Glaze and 21 common to Hull. Thus, intercorrelations among the methods for these 100 syllables could be determined. In addition, other correlations were determined so that a fairly complete picture of the relationships among the results of the various scaling methods emerged. This is given in Table 2.

TABLE 2. Correlations Among Meaningfulness Values
for Different Scaling Methods

(Noble, Stockwell, & Pryer, 1957)

Investigators	Number Syllables	r
Glaze vs. Hull	306	.63
Glaze vs. Krueger	100	.86
Glaze vs. Noble, Stockwell & Pryer	100	.81
Hull vs. Krueger	305	.72
Hull vs. Noble, Stockwell & Pryer	21	.55
Krueger vs. Noble, Stockwell & Pryer	100	.90

It will be noted that there is one rather marked discrepancy between the correlations given by Peixotto and those given in Table 2. Peixotto reports a correlation of .65 between the M values of Glaze and those of Krueger for 300 syllables, whereas Noble, Stockwell, & Pryer report one of .86 for 100 syllables common to the two scales. There is no obvious reason for this discrepancy, and no attempt will be made here to "run it down."

From Table 2, it would seem obvious that the Hull values do not relate with other values as highly as the other values relate among themselves. The peculiar nature of Hull's procedure has already been pointed out and is probably responsible for the relatively low correlations which occur. It may also be noted that Hull estimates the reliability of his scaling to be only .78. It seems quite justifiable to view Hull's scale values as a special breed, and no further use of them will be made in the present analyses.

As noted above, Mandler reported a correlation of .65 between his scale values and those of Krueger's. On the basis of the other correlations presented in Table 2, this is lower than might be expected. It was pointed out previously that Mandler's range of values was very limited. In addition, no reliability estimates are given, and there remains the possibility that his subjects gave excessive chain associations. There is, of course, no way of knowing whether or not these factors could account for his relatively low correlations. In any event, the discussion will proceed as if the burden of proof is on Mandler.

Looking at the correlations among M values determined by Glaze, by Krueger, and Noble, Stockwell & Pryer, we may reach the conclusion that these three investigations measured essentially the same "thing." Statistically, of course, even a nonexpert on the meaning of correlations can argue with such a conclusion. But looking at these values from several points of view seems to justify a conclusion of near perfect commonality. All the following factors would tend to reduce the statistical commonality but are irrelevant to the conceptual question of whether or not the different methods are tapping the same behavioral reactions to the syllables:

1. Differences in the size of the samples of subjects from 15 to well over 200.

2. Differences in the populations sampled.

3. Differences in the era in which the studies were conducted and consequent changes in M of some syllables due to special cultural usage. Soap manufacturers alone would seem to be responsible for a small portion of the non-common variance, e.g., DUZ, VEL, FAB. A recent trend toward the use of three-letter prefixes on auto license plates is a matter of no small concern to certain psychologists.

4. Arithmetical errors which must inevitably occur in the huge tabulating jobs which occur for such studies.

5. Failure to meet assumptions on which the use of certain correlation techniques are based.

6. Tendency for subjects, when working fast, to reverse rating scales occasionally.

7. Problems involved in chain associations when using the production method and in scoring the responses elicited by the production method. For example, how similar can two responses be and still be judged to be different responses?

For the results stemming from different techniques for scaling M, intercorrelations less than unity would indicate an interaction between methods and responses of the subjects. From the above considerations we arrive at the working conclusion that the differences in methods are not an appreciable source of variance. The fact that different response indices were used becomes irrelevant; they are measures of the same behavioral reaction to the verbal units. Indeed, there is something quite remarkable about some of the relationships noted above. In 1928, Glaze had 15 subjects indicate whether they did or did not "get" an association to nonsense syllables. In 1957, Noble, Stockwell, & Pryer took 100 of these syllables and asked each of 200 subjects to rate the number of associates which he thought the syllables suggested. In spite of a difference of nearly 30 years in time, the relationship between the indices of M in the two studies gives a correlation of .81. Or consider the fact that Krueger's values, determined in 1934, with one technique, correlate .90 with those determined by Noble, Stockwell, & Pryer in 1957 with what would appear to be superficially a quite different technique.

It is, furthermore, worth noting that different populations at a given point in time will give amazingly high correspondence in association values. Rocklyn, Hessert, & Braun (1957) used 24 of Noble's 96 dissyllables selected so as to cover the complete range of M defined by Noble. These were presented to subjects for a 60-sec. production period per item. There were three groups of 16 subjects each. One group fell between the ages of 20–29, another 30–49, and the third, 50–66. Educational level varied widely among the subjects. For all 48 subjects combined, the correlation with Noble's values for the 24 items was .96. The correlation decreased in successive age groups from .96 to .94 to .92. Noble's subjects, it may be remembered, were basic airmen at Lackland Air Force Base. Such evidence indicates an extremely stable set of responses to the verbal units in addition to high universality through broad segments of the population.

The discussion turns now to an evaluation of other dimensions of verbal units and how they relate to M as defined by the various operations outlined above.

OTHER CORRELATES OF MEANINGFULNESS

In this section three correlates of M will be discussed. It may, therefore, be considered a continuation of the previous section in the sense that three additional scaling operations for verbal units will be described.

Judgments of learning speed. The two initial studies to be reported are previously unpublished. These studies were done with two questions in mind: (1) If subjects are asked to rate how fast they think they can learn a given verbal unit relative to other units, how will these values relate to indices of M? (2) What characteristics or attributes of verbal units do subjects use in making these ratings?

The scaling was carried out with groups of subjects. The following instructions were read by the experimenter. (A copy was given to each subject who was requested to follow the reading by the experimenter):

1. Below are 10 words or word-like combinations of letters. First, look carefully at each word separately and pronounce it to yourself.

KITCHEN	QUARRY
ORDEAL	ULNA
GAMIN	REGION
NEGLAN	ZEBRA
WAGON	PALLOR

2. Below is what is called a rating scale; it has the numbers 1 through 9 on it. At one end, to your left, the label "Difficult" appears. At the other end, the word "Easy" appears. In the middle you will note the word "Average." Note that the end to your left is labeled 1, that to your right 9, with 5 in the middle.

1	2	3	4	5	6	7	8	9

Difficult   Average   Easy

3. On the next page 86 more words or word-like combinations of letters are listed. In front of each word is a blank. Your task is to assign a number from the above rating scale to each word. To do this, for each word ask yourself this question:

If this word were placed among the 10 words listed above and if I were asked to learn this list, how fast would I learn this particular word relative to each of the other 10 words?

For example, look at the first word on the next page. You might judge that it would be as difficult or more difficult to learn than any of the 10 words above in which case you would assign it a "1." If you judge that it would be as easy or easier to learn than any of the 10 words, you would assign it a "9." If you estimate that it would be easier than about half the words but more difficult than the other half, you would give it a "5." Likewise, you might assign it a 2, 3, 4, 6, 7, 8, depending upon where you think it ranks or falls in difficulty relative to these 10 words.

Please use the full range of numbers on the rating scale but do not be concerned about the number of times you use any given number. Keep this sheet in front of you so that you can refer to the 10 words and to the rating scale.

Do not spend too much time on any one word. First judgments are usually best on a task like this so work rather quickly but at the same time be sure that you make an independent judgment for each word.

The 86 words actually rated were the remaining ones from Noble's list after using the 10 for reference purposes in the instructions. They were listed in random order. The 10 items used in the instructions, used to establish the "length" of the scale, represent the entire range of the Noble scale and are approximately equally spaced along this scale.

After the subject had completed rating all the items, he was asked to turn the form over and on the back to "write the ways you arrived at your judgments for the words. That is, what did you 'use' in making your judgments? What differences did you look for among the words that helped you in making a judgment?"

A total of 116 subjects completed the forms. For each of the 86 units a mean scale value was determined, and these were correlated with the mean scale value for the production method as determined by Noble. The product-moment correlation was .90.

A comparable scaling was performed on the nonsense syllables Noble had scaled. For 90 syllables and 58 subjects, the correlation between the mean scale value and the scale value determined by Noble by having subjects rate the number of associations an item evoked, was .86.

These two studies indicate a striking relationship between the outcomes of two rather diverse sets of operations. The rating given a unit as to how fast it will be learned can be predicted almost perfectly from a knowledge of the number of associations that item elicits (or is believed to elicit). Of course, the reverse prediction is true also. Since later chapters will show a high relationship between actual speed of learning and the ratings, it is apparent that a close relationship exists between number of associations an item elicits, rated speed of learning and actual speed of learning.

The generality of relationship between rated speed of learning and other scaling operations is further demonstrated in a study by Richardson & Erlebacher (1958). One group of subjects was presented pairs of items and was asked to rate the degree of relationship—the associative connection—between the two members of each pair. A second group of subjects was asked to rate how fast they thought they could learn the second member of these pairs when the first was presented (as in paired-associate learning). Using words, nonsense syllables, and consonant syllables, paired in various combinations, these investigators found the rank-order correlation for 223 pairs for the two sets of instructions was .96.

It will be remembered that the subjects in the two earlier studies on rating of speed of learning were asked to indicate what attributes or characteristics they had used in making their ratings. The three most frequently mentioned attributes were as follows:

1. *Number of associations elicited.* These are shown by remarks in which the subject said that he rated a unit higher if it made him think of a word than if it didn't make him think of one. This attribute is also given directly when the subject said that if a word or syllable made him think of other things, he rated it higher than if it didn't.

2. *Familiarity.* This was a common direct response; the more familiar an item, the higher it was rated. This probably overlaps some with the first category in the case of nonsense syllables. That is, if a syllable (e.g., BAL) made the subject think of BALL, it would be called familiar.

3. *Pronunciability.* This description, or others which clearly meant the same, also occurred with high frequency in the subjects' reports. Typically, the subject said that if he could pronounce the unit, he rated it as easier to learn than if he could not pronounce it. A careful inspection of the complete range of nonsense syllables will make it evident that there is a clear difference among syllables, at least at the extremes, on this attribute.

The discussion of scaling techniques and results thus far has been directly relevant to only one of the three factors noted by the subjects as important in their ratings, namely, number of associations elicited. Therefore, we now ask whether or not M (as determined by number of associations and correlated methods discussed earlier) can be predicted from ratings of *familiarity* and from ratings of *pronunciability*.

Familiarity. Probably no word comes as natural for a synonym to M as does the word *familiarity*. Another name which has been applied in this context is *acquaintance*, and, as Robinson argued so convincingly in 1932 (without data), those items with which one is acquainted should be learned more easily as the situation changes. To use Robinson's words:

. . . the act of reading or reciting a given syllable may, irrespective of its associative connections, influence the facility with which that act enters into new associations (p. 118).

It should be noted that Robinson implies that it is not the *number* of associations involved which is critical for more easily learning an "old" item; it is the fact that it is *familiar* that is important. A consideration of the facts in this case is getting ahead of the plan of our exposition; the point of importance for the present is the fact that familiarity or acquaintance may well be expected to be related to other indices of M. Furthermore, this relationship can be established without considering whether or not number of associations is critical for the relationship between M and learning.

For correlational data relevant to this issue, reference is made again to Noble (1953). To 200 subjects he gave the 96 dissyllables (which he had previously rated for M by the production method) and asked them to rate each item as to its familiarity. Familiarity was defined as how frequently the subject had had contact with the word. In order that the defining operations are clear, a portion of the instructions to the subjects will be quoted:

This is a test to find out how often you have come in contact with certain words.

You will be given a list of 96 nouns and you are to rate each one as to the number of times you have experienced it by simply placing a check mark (√) in one of the five spaces provided for your rating.

The five possible ratings are described by the words NEVER, RARELY, SOMETIMES, OFTEN, and VERY OFTEN. This means that you have *seen* or *heard* or *used* the particular word (in writing or in speech) . . . (p. 90).

Noble then specified in more detail what he meant by the five categories. Finally, he told his subjects:

Do not be bothered if you are unable to give a definition of some of the words. Simply rate each one as to the number of times you have come in contact with it regardless of its meaning (p. 90).

When the index of M for the 96 items as determined by the production method and the median scale value defining familiarity for the same items were correlated, the value was .92. Thus, another set of operations, this time those said to be defining familiarity, is shown to be highly related to a scale derived by having the subject produce associates to the verbal units. It may be noted that familiarity was defined to the subjects as the frequency of contact with a word, a criterion which seems very defensible in terms of the common meaning of familiarity. It could also be presumed that the more frequent the contact, the greater is the number of *different* contexts in which a word has been used, thus leading to a large number of associates. It is therefore perhaps not surprising that the two scales correlate so highly. Nevertheless, there may be many negative cases; that is, there may be cases in which the subject has had frequent contact with the word but in the same context each time so that the number of different associates may not increase much as contact increases. Over-all, however, the correlation which Noble found argues against this interpretation as the general case. The facts point strongly to the fact that the more frequent the contact, the greater is the number of associates which that word picks up.

Pronunciability. The correlational evidence on this dimension was obtained by another group-rating procedure. These results have not been previously published. A total of 181 subjects took part in the scaling. They were presented with 178 different three-letter combinations, among which were the 100 nonsense syllables that Noble had scaled for M by having subjects rate the number of associates which they thought a syllable would elicit. The other 78 units consisted of what were considered to be more extreme examples of M, since they included common three-letter words and also consonant syllables. The ratings of pronunciability on these latter items were obtained for reasons which will become clear at a later point in the book.

The instructions were given to the subjects in printed form and as the experimenter read them aloud, the subjects followed this printed form. The instructions were:

> This is an experiment to determine the ease or difficulty of pronouncing various combinations of three letters. On the following two pages a number of such three-letter combinations are listed. You are to rate each combination as to the relative ease or relative difficulty of pronouncing it.
>
> A 9-point scale will be used for your ratings. This scale may be visualized as follows:

Easy				Average				Hard
1	2	3	4	5	6	7	8	9

Note carefully that words which are relatively easy to pronounce are given low numbers and relatively hard words are given high numbers. The scale is reproduced at the top of each succeeding page so that you will not reverse your number systems.

To carry out your ratings, you should proceed as follows. First, try to pronounce the first combination in the first column, whispering it to yourself, of course. Then try the second, then the third, and so on, for approximately the first 10 combinations. Then, skip around over the first page pronouncing to yourself approximately 10 additional combinations. The reason for this is that it will give you an idea of the range or span of pronunciability which is involved. Since each combination is to be rated relative to the others you have to get an idea of what is meant by a hard combination to pronounce and what is meant by an easy combination of letters.

After you are confident that you have tried to pronounce both hard and easy combinations, as well as combinations which would fall in between, go back to the first combination in the list. Pronounce it to yourself, then assign a number to it which you think represents its approximate location on the 9-point scale. A blank is provided after each combination for your number. Use only whole numbers 1 through 9; do not assign a combination a fractional or decimal value. If you think that the first combination, relative to the others, is among the easiest to pronounce you might assign it a 1 or perhaps a 2. If you think it is among the most difficult, you would give it an 8 or 9. If you think it is neither as difficult nor as easy as others you have seen in the list, you would give it some middle number. You are expected to use all numbers of the scale. That is, there will be combinations which may be about half way between average and hard so that you would give it a 7, perhaps. However, you do not have to use all numbers equally often.

Some of the combinations of three letters actually make common words, many do not. Do not let this influence your judgments. Your job is to pronounce each combination to yourself and make a judgment as to its relative ease or difficulty of pronouncing. Do not spend a great deal of time on any one combination; rather, say it to yourself—two or three times if necessary—then assign it a number and proceed to the next one.

After you have completed both pages look back over them to make sure you have rated all combinations.

The 178 items were randomized on the two pages. When the pages were stapled together, each preceded the other approximately an equal number of times.

The results show a product-moment correlation of .78 between Noble's scale values and the mean ratings for pronunciability for the 100 nonsense syllables. It seems reasonable to conclude that another characteristic of a verbal unit which goes along with M (defined as the number of associates) is pronunciability. Pronunciability, therefore, may be considered as a possible theoretical base in attempting to understand how M may produce its effect on learning. Finally, it may be noted that the product-moment correlation between pronunciability and ratings of speed-of-learning for 86 syllables was .92.

SUMMARY

High interrelationships have been shown to exist among the scale values for verbal units subjected to what appear to be a variety of different operations:

1. Whether or not a subject "gets" an association within a limited period of time.

2. The number of associates which an item elicits in a given period of time.

3. The number of associates which the subject thinks a given item would elicit.

4. Ratings of how fast the subject thinks he can learn a unit relative to other units.

5. Rated familiarity of the units.

6. Rated pronunciability of the units.

Thus it would appear that the theorist has several different ways by which he might conceptualize the relationship between M and rate of learning. Before examining these various alternatives, we will summarize in the next chapter the relationship between M and rate of learning.

REFERENCES

Glaze, J. A. The association value of non-sense syllables. *J. genet. Psychol.*, 1928, 35, 255–269.

Hull, C. L. The meaningfulness of 320 selected nonsense syllables. *Amer. J. Psychol.*, 1933, 45, 730–734.

Krueger, W. C. F. The relative difficulty of nonsense syllables. *J. exp. Psychol.*, 1934, 17, 145–153.

Mandler, G. Associative frequency and associative prepotency as measures of response to nonsense syllables. *Amer. J. Psychol.*, 1956, 68, 662–665.

Noble, C. E. An analysis of meaning. *Psychol. Rev.*, 1952, 59, 421–430.

Noble, C. E. The meaning-familiarity relationship. *Psychol. Rev.*, 1953, 60, 89–98.

Noble, C. E., Stockwell, F. E., & Pryer, M. W. Meaningfulness (*m'*) and association value (*a*) in paired-associate syllable learning. *Psychol. Rep.*, 1957, 3, 441–452.

Peixotto, H. E. The recognitive value of three hundred nonsense syllables. *Amer. J. Psychol.*, 1948, 61, 352–360.

Richardson, J., & Erlebacher, A. Associative connection between paired verbal items. *J. exp. Psychol.*, 1958, 56, 62–69.

Robinson, E. S. *Association theory today*. New York: Century, 1932.

Rocklyn, E. H., Hessert, R. B., & Braun, H.W. Calibrated materials for verbal learning with middle- and old-aged subjects. *Amer. J. Psychol.*, 1957, 70, 628–630.

Thorndike, E. L., & Lorge, I. *The teacher's word book of 30,000 words*. New York: Columbia Univer. Press, 1944.

Witmer, L. R. The association value of three-place consonant syllables. *J. genet. Psychol.*, 1935, 47, 337–360.

Chapter 3

Meaningfulness and Learning:
Initial Evidence

The purpose of this chapter is to exhibit the facts relating M, as discussed in the previous chapter, and rate of learning lists made up of units of known M. In certain instances logical extensions of scaled M will be assumed so that the full range of the influence of M on learning may be more nearly approximated.

THE GROSS RELATIONSHIP
Serial Learning

It seems reasonable to expect that if nonsense syllables and three-letter words were scaled with common operations, the former would be designated as having lower M than the latter. Assuming that this would be true, it is worth pointing out the results of some studies in which comparisons of learning have been made with such materials.

Davis (1930) employed six subjects who learned a total of 40 serial lists over a period of many days. Of the 40 lists, 20 were serial lists of 12 syllables, each having a Glaze value of 20 per cent or less. The other 20 lists were made up of 12 three-letter words. On one day the subject would learn one list of a given kind, on the next day a list of the other kind, and so on, so that practice effects should be distributed essentially equally over both kinds of lists.

Learning was carried to one perfect trial, i.e., until the subject correctly anticipated all items on a single trial. On the average the syllables required 9.8 trials, the words, 3.7 trials. The important points to

27

note here are not only that the word lists were learned more rapidly than the syllable lists, but also that the magnitude of the difference is very large. Within the range used (later evidence will show that it is not the complete range), a difference in learning of over 2.5 to 1 is involved. In a follow-up study, Sauer (1930), using much the same material but with 20 subjects who were less well practiced than were Davis' subjects, showed that the mean number of trials to learn the syllables was 14.05 and to learn the words, 5.67. Again, the great difference in rate of learning should be noted along with the fact that the difference in learning seems relatively independent of stage of practice.

The McGeoch study. The first really systematic attempt to investigate learning as a function of variation in scaled M was published by McGeoch in 1930. Ten-item serial lists were constructed, two each from the Glaze association values of 0, 20, 46, 53, 73 and 100. In the first part of the experiment 36 subjects learned a list from each level of M. The method of learning was complete presentation; the subject studied the list for 2 min. and then was allowed 2 min. for recall. The order of the lists differed among the subjects so that practice effects were probably fairly equally distributed over all lists. In a second phase of the experiment, 31 of the same 36 subjects learned another list from each level of M but, in this case, were allowed only 60 sec. to study the list before recalling. The data are presented in terms of the mean number of items correctly recalled (regardless of serial position) for each level for both study intervals. The functions are shown in Fig. 1.

McGeoch's results show quite clearly that there is an increase in amount learned (for a constant period of study) as M increases. However, in spite of the rather large number of subjects, the function is not smooth. It will also be noted that as many or more items were recalled after 1 min. of study as were recalled after 2 min. The learning with 1 min. is favored by practice since the lists given 2 min. of study were all learned in the first cycle of the experiment, whereas the lists given 1 min. of study were learned in the second cycle.

Noble's dissyllables. Noble (1952) constructed three 12-item serial lists using his scaled dissyllables. The items in one list had a mean value of 1.28 (low M), those in another, 4.42, and those in the third, 7.85 (high M). The subjects were college students, and a different group learned each list following practice on three other lists. Serial anticipation learning was used with a 2-sec. presentation rate. Learning was carried to one perfect trial. The relationship between the three levels of M and mean number of trials to learn is shown in

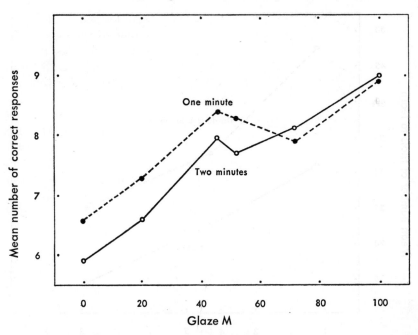

Figure 1. Immediate recall of serial lists of nonsense syllables as a function of Glaze M following 1 minute and 2 minutes of study by the method of complete presentation (McGeoch, 1930).

Fig. 2. The list consisting of items of low M required over twice as many trials to learn as did the list of high M.

The second set of data exhibited in Fig. 2 comes from a study by Dowling & Braun (1957). The mean scale values for the items at the three levels of M were exactly the same as those used by Noble. Indeed, there are only two apparent differences between the studies: (1) Dowling & Braun carried learning to a criterion of two successive perfect trials (vs. Noble's one perfect), and (2) their subjects apparently were not as well practiced as were Noble's. The results for this study, like Noble's, show a difference of about 2 to 1 in trials to learn at the extremes of M.

In a subsequent study, Braun & Heymann (1958) constructed two serial lists. One was made up of items very high on Noble's scale and the other of items very low on the same scale. Again, the high-M list was learned much more rapidly than the low-M list; this finding held for several different presentation rates and several different intertrial intervals. Such large differences in learning produced by dissyllables at

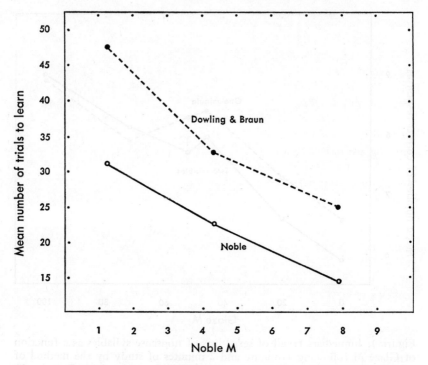

Figure 2. Serial learning of dissyllables as a function of Noble M (Noble, 1952; Dowling and Braun, 1957).

the two extremes of Noble's scale have also been found by Sarason (1958).

Other data from serial lists. Underwood & Richardson (1956) constructed two serial lists of 10 nonsense syllables each. One of the lists was made up of items in the Glaze 93–100 per cent range, and the other of items falling between 0–20 per cent. Each list was learned to one perfect trial by a different group of 100 unpracticed college students. The list made up of items of high M required 19.27 mean trials to learn, whereas the list of low M required 29.18 trials. This difference does not appear to be as great as that shown by the dissyllables in Fig. 2. Thus, this study, considered in conjunction with McGeoch's results noted earlier, suggests that a wider range of M is covered by Noble's dissyllables than is covered by Glaze's syllables. It is perhaps more accurate to state that the relationship between learning and M in the range of dissyllables is sharper than in the range of Glaze's syllables.

In McGeoch's study the change in learning associated with differences in the lower part of Glaze's scale was greater than that in the upper. This has not been a universal finding. For example, Sarason (1957), using serial lists of 17 Glaze syllables, found only a very small difference between lists made up of 27 per cent syllables and those made up of 53 per cent, whereas he found the difference between 53 per cent and 80 per cent was quite large. The results for some paired-associate lists (to be examined shortly) tend to be more in line with Sarason's findings than with McGeoch's; that is, the differences in learning associated with the low end of Glaze's scale are less than that associated with comparable scale differences in the upper range. But it should be remembered that the nature of the Glaze scale units is unknown: no assertions can be made about the phenomenal equality of the units throughout the scale.

All of the evidence on serial learning reviewed above demonstrates unequivocally that as M increases, rate of learning increases. The maximum difference in learning as a function of M would appear to be large, but the lack of a scale for the entire range of M of verbal units makes any statement of the absolute differences in learning which can be attributed to M somewhat hazardous. Nevertheless, for serial tasks of an equal number of units varying with respect to degree of M, differences in trials to learn of as much as 3 to 1 may well be expected when the total range of M is examined on a common scale.

Paired-Associate Lists

Noble's dissyllables. Kimble & Dufort (1955) sampled at 10 different points along Noble's scale of dissyllables. Items which were paired had approximately the same M value. Two separate experiments were run, varying only in that the second experiment used an almost entirely different set of pairs from those used in the first. For presentation here the results of the two experiments were combined. Samples of the pairs, with the scale value for each member of the pair, are as follows: *neglan* (1.04)—*meardon* (1.05); *pallor* (3.06)—*sequence* (3.21); *quarter* (5.98)—*region* (5.98); *army* (9.43)—*kitchen* (9.61).

A separate group of 20 subjects was used for each experiment. The words were presented at a 3:3-sec. rate with six different orders of presentation. It should be clear that the 10 pairs, each with a different M value, all appeared in a single list in each experiment. While the subjects apparently learned to one perfect trial, the measure of learning presented by these investigators is the median number of trials required to achieve the first correct anticipation.

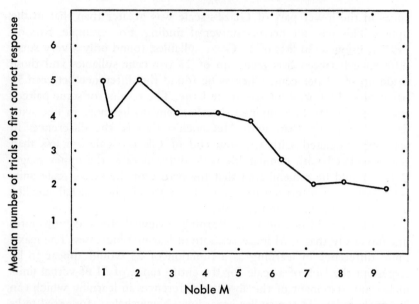

Figure 3. Paired-associate learning as a function of Noble M of dissyllable pairs (Kimble and Dufort, 1955).

The results for this study are plotted in Fig. 3. Even combining the results for the two lists does not remove the irregularity, although it is quite clear that the direct relationship between M and rate of learning holds. The pairs with low M require over twice as many trials as do the pairs with high M before the response is first correctly anticipated.

Referring to the irregularity in the Kimble-Dufort curve, we should broach certain issues at this time.

1. The points on the dimension of M are each represented by only two pairs of words. Is this an adequate sampling of items to expect a smooth function? Noble & McNeely (1957) were inclined to believe that the *particular* variations in the Kimble-Dufort curve were indeed due to an inadequate sampling of items. They felt an important issue was at stake since Kimble & Dufort attempted to make a theoretical issue out of the particular variations. Noble & McNeely performed an experiment which was very much like the Kimble-Dufort study except that 18 different lists were constructed, each list being learned by a different group of five subjects. Twenty learning trials were given. As in the Kimble-Dufort study, the value of a pair was obtained by averaging the scale values for the two members

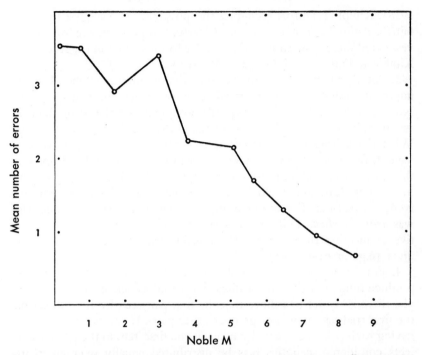

Figure 4. Paired-associate learning as a function of Noble M of dissyllable pairs (Noble and McNeely, 1957).

composing the pair. In the final accounting, pairs of like scale value were grouped, and the average scale value of the groups was used for plotting purposes. A total of 10 such groupings was used. The major results are presented in terms of mean number of overt errors made for the items in each M group. The results are shown in Fig. 4. Even with 18 different lists the function is somewhat irregular, although it does not seem that the irregularities agree with those found by Kimble & Dufort. However, different response measures are used in the two studies so that specific comparisons cannot be made with complete confidence.

2. Kimble & Dufort manipulated M *within* a list rather than *among* lists as was true with the studies reviewed earlier on serial learning. One consequence of manipulating the variable within a list is the possibility that interaction effects may emerge which would not be present if the variable were manipulated among lists. It is a fact that certain minor interaction phenomena have been found with heterogeneous lists which disappeared when homogeneous lists were used (Peters,

1936). Kimble & Dufort recognize this possibility and suggest that certain "isolation" effects may occur. Clearly, this problem needs to be investigated directly with materials similar to those used in the studies by Kimble & Dufort, and Noble & McNeely.

3. Another factor which may disturb the smoothness of the M-learning relationship stems from possible consequences of pairing items. Noble's scale (and most others) tells nothing about the M of the pair as a pair; it describes only the M of the individual members of the pair. What the pairing does (for example, different pairs of equal M may have different associative connection) can only be speculated upon at this time. Nevertheless, it does seem quite possible that variations in the M-learning function could be due, in part, to differences resulting from the pairings. For example, in the Kimble-Dufort study one pair was *army-kitchen*. This pair, it seems to us, has much higher associative connection than many other possible pairs made up of high M units (e.g., *army-heaven*).

4. Finally, it should be noted that serial position effects may still produce some variation in learning in a paired-associate list. For example, there is reason to believe that the first pair seen by the subject on the first trial has an advantage over other pairs. If this is true, only by having each pair occur equally often as the first item in the list, all subjects considered, can this bias be distributed equally over all items. Without such a procedure for a heterogeneous list, minor variations in the M-learning function may result.

Thus, all four of the above considerations may warn against attempting to make a theoretical issue out of particular fluctuations in the M-learning relationship.

Nonsense syllables. Mandler & Huttenlocher (1956) used the syllables scaled by Mandler. The scale range was divided into eight fairly equal intervals, and a pair of syllables was chosen from each interval to make eight pairs in a paired-associate list. A second list was constructed in the same manner; therefore, the learning scores for each list may be considered independent tests of the M-learning function. The response measure was the number of the second of two successive trials on which the response syllable had been anticipated correctly. In Fig. 5 the learning values for each list are plotted separately. Again, M of the pairs is seen to be related clearly and sharply to rate of learning, but the variations within and between lists underscore the cautions noted above.

The results of Mandler & Huttenlocher have been confirmed by Noble, Stockwell, & Pryer (1957). Therefore, it seems clear that

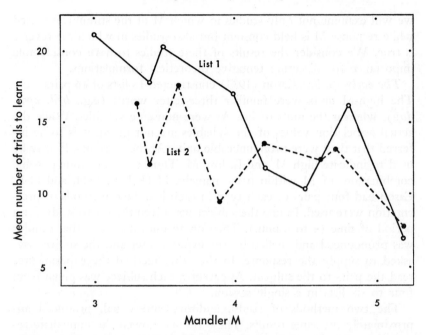

Figure 5. Paired-associate learning as a function of Mandler M of nonsense syllable pairs (Mandler and Huttenlocher, 1956).

whether the verbal units are placed in serial lists or in paired-associate lists, learning and M are directly related. There are also other bits of scattered evidence on the relationship (e.g., Postman, Adams, & Phillips, 1955; Jantz & Underwood, 1958), and all show the same general function.

Thus far it has been shown that M of verbal units can be scaled reliably and that investigators using quite different scaling methods appear to end up with almost the same ordering of the verbal units. Without exception, learning experiments using these verbal units have shown a marked positive relationship between rate of learning and M. The discussion now turns to experiments in which a somewhat more analytical approach has been used in investigating the relationship between M and learning.

MEANINGFULNESS OF STIMULUS VS. MEANINGFULNESS OF RESPONSE

In both the serial and paired-associate studies reviewed above, stimulus and response M of the units always covaried. In the present section we will examine not only studies in which M of the stimulus is varied while response M is held constant but also studies in which the reverse is true. We consider the results of these studies to have considerable importance for directing tentative theoretical formulations.

The early studies. Cason (1933) constructed 18 lists of 16 pairs each. The high-M units were familiar three-letter words (e.g., *bed, cow, dog*), whereas the units of low M were nonsense syllables. While the actual association values of the syllables are not given, it is to be inferred that they were pronounceable units. At the extremes, H may be used to indicate high M, and L, low M. Thus, there are four possible combinations of M within pairs, namely, H-H, L-L, L-H, and H-L. Cason had four pairs of each type in each list. Two methods of presentation were used. In one the subject was given the list to study for a period of time (4 to 8 min.). Then on an immediate test the stimulus was pronounced and spelled by the experimenter and the subject was asked to supply the response. In the other method the experimenter read the pairs to the subject. Apparently each subject was given from four to six lists in a single session.

The two methods of study, auditory and visual, produced approximately the same results. These results showed the immediate recall to be significantly greater for H-H than for L-L (which merely confirms the studies reviewed above), and the L-H and H-L pairs to be about the same magnitude of recall, halfway between H-H and L-L. Cason repeated the study with what he considered to be more extreme degrees of M and got the same results. Thus, on the basis of this study it would be concluded that stimulus M and response M affected rate of learning roughly to the same degree.

By way of anticipating later results, we may note that Cason's results do not in general correspond to those found by other investigators; this is true as far as the L-H and H-L conditions are concerned. There is no obvious way to account for this, but it may be noted that when a list made up of heterogeneous items is given to a subject to study, there is no control over the study time per item. The subject may spend more time on the difficult items than on the easy ones.

A classroom experiment conducted by Stoddard (1929) has relevance to the problem at hand. A total of 328 subjects in junior and senior high school was used. One half of the subjects was given a list of 50 French vocabulary pairs in which the French word was the stimulus and the English translation the response (e.g., *apprendre-learn*). The other half had these 50 pairs "turned over" so that the French word was the response and its English equivalent, the stimulus (e.g., *learn-ap-*

prendre). None of the subjects had previously studied French. They were given 20 min. in which to study the list and were told to learn from left to right. If it is granted that the English word has higher M than the French word, this study provides a test of the relative influence of M of the stimulus versus M of the response. On the recall test the subject was given the stimulus and was asked to write the response. Those subjects who learned L-H (French-English) gave an average of 15.1 correct responses. Those who learned H-L gave 8.0 correct responses. Thus, these results indicate that high M in the response is more critical than high M of the stimulus. Stoddard's results correspond quite closely to the over-all picture given in more recent studies. These recent studies may now be examined.

The recent studies. Sheffield (1946) used approximately the same type of materials as had Cason in the early study. However, Sheffield used a memory drum so that time factors were somewhat better handled than they were in Cason's study. Again, various combinations of M of stimuli and responses were included within the lists. His results show that H-H was learned most rapidly and L-L most slowly, and once again such findings confirm previous work. However, Sheffield's H-L pairs produced learning which was only slightly faster than the learning produced by the L-L pairs and his L-H pairs were only slightly inferior to the H-H pairs. Thus, contrary to Cason's findings, Sheffield's results indicate that differences in M of the stimulus produces relatively minor changes in rate of learning as compared with corresponding differences in M of the response.

Kimble & Dufort (1955) constructed lists of 10 paired associates in which the stimuli were 10 items from Noble's dissyllable list. These 10 items actually represent a rather complete range of M on Noble's scale. For response terms, three-letter words which were very common (e.g., *man, rag, tax*) were used, and the reasonable assumption is made that *as a group* these 10 common words had higher M than the 10 units from Noble's list. One group of subjects learned the list with Noble's units as stimuli and the three-letter words as responses, whereas another group learned the list with reversed positions of the two classes of items. The response measure was the mean number of trials an item was presented before first being anticipated correctly. This value for the list in which Noble's dissyllables were stimuli was 2.3 trials; for the list in which they were responses, the mean value was 3.1. This difference is highly significant statistically.

Cieutat, Stockwell & Noble (1958) have performed two experiments. In the first they used lists making up four conditions, namely, H-H,

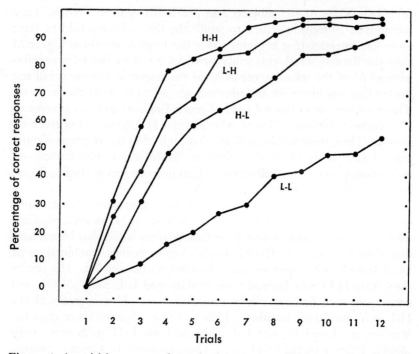

Figure 6. Acquisition curves for paired nonsense syllables as a function of combination of high (H) and low (L) stimulus and response M (estimated from Cieutat, Stockwell, and Noble, 1958).

L-L, L-H, and H-L. The units were Noble's dissyllables. The mean medium scale value of the low M items was .29, the high, 7.50. There were 10 pairs in each list. The H-L and L-H lists were composed of identical items, the positions merely being reversed. A different group of 20 subjects was used for each of the four lists, the lists being presented for 12 learning trials.

The percentage of correct responses on each trial for each list is shown in Fig. 6. With mean total correct responses over the 12 learning trials used as the response measure, the results show difficulty to increase in the order H-H, L-H, H-L, and L-L. These investigators report that the variance attributable to response variation is approximately 2.6 times that attributable to stimulus variation. But they also note certain interactions which tend to complicate the findings. More particularly, it may be noted from Fig. 6 that variation in stimulus M produces a much greater effect on learning when response M is low than when it is high. Similarly, the effects on learning of variation in response M is greater when stimulus M is low than when it is high. Such clear interactions were not apparent in the Sheffield study. The difference between the results of the two studies is attributed largely to the H-L condition. If the H-L curve in Fig. 6 were depressed appreciably, the two sets of results would correspond, and these particular interactions would be eliminated.

In their second study, Cieutat, et al. (1958) used nonsense syllables (as scaled by Noble, Stockwell, & Pryer) and three levels of M of stimuli and responses. Again the variation in response M was shown to produce a greater effect on learning than did corresponding changes in stimulus M, and the magnitude of the effect was about the same as in the first study. While the stimulus-response interaction is, therefore, significant, it is not clear from the report whether the second-order interactions discussed above occurred or not.

L'Abate (1959) used Glaze syllables to form the four conditions of stimulus and response M: H-H, H-L, L-H and L-L. Throughout 10 learning trials his results clearly show that variations in response M produced a greater difference in amount learned than did the corresponding variation in stimulus M. In a recent study by Hunt (1959), Noble's dissyllables were used to form four lists having the usual four extreme combinations of stimulus and response M. His results show that the H-H list was learned most rapidly, the L-L list most slowly. Although the L-H list was learned somewhat more slowly than the H-H list, and the H-L somewhat more rapidly than the L-L, the differences were small and statistically insignificant. This led Hunt to conclude that stimulus M was of small consequence for learning. However, in both comparisons for determining the effect of response M (H-L vs. H-H, and L-L vs. L-H), the differences were large and statistically highly significant. Therefore, Hunt's results conform to those of the other studies reviewed. Fairly comparable results have also been reported by Weiss (1958). Finally, it is worth mentioning that Morikawa (1959), using materials scaled for his Japanese subjects, reports results almost identical to Hunt's findings.

At this point it can be stated that the preponderance of the evidence indicates that a given variation in response M produces a greater difference in learning rate than does a corresponding change in stimulus M. There is no consistent evidence on the second-order interactions. The discussion turns finally to a study by Mandler & Campbell (1957) which must be examined in considerable detail.

Two studies were performed by these investigators. The verbal units were nonsense syllables scaled by Mandler. In the first experiment three lists of six pairs were formed, thus representing a total of 18 pairs. Since three levels of M were used, nine different combinations of stimuli and responses were involved; therefore, two pairs represented each combination. The two like pairs were always placed in the same list so that there were three different types of items in each of the six-item lists. One list contained two pairs each of the following combinations: H-H, M (medium M) -L; and L-M. Another had H-M, M-H, and L-L. The third had H-L, M-M, and L-H. Three different groups of 12 subjects each were presented a list until they had correctly anticipated each item at least once.

The response measure was the mean number of trials required to attain the first correct anticipation. These means are shown in Table 3.

TABLE 3. Learning as a Function of Three Levels of Stimulus Meaningfulness and Three Levels of Response Meaningfulness

The values are mean number of trials to first correct anticipation for two pairs and 12 subjects
(Mandler & Campbell, 1957)

Response Meaningfulness	Stimulus Meaningfulness			
	High	Medium	Low	Total
High	9.6	9.7	15.5	11.6
Medium	10.1	19.0	10.4	13.2
Low	19.0	17.3	10.8	15.7
Total	12.9	15.3	12.2	

Statistically speaking, both the effects of stimulus M and response M are significant. However, the interaction term is not significant, i.e., the effects of stimulus M and of response M do not differ. The totals show that with stimulus M constant, mean trials to the first correct anticipation increases as response M decreases. This would confirm previous findings. However, with response M held constant there is no progression in learning as stimulus M changes. The mean number of trials to the first correct anticipation is about the same for both low and high stimulus M. Several reversals of trend are to be noted in the body of the table. Furthermore, it should be noted that there is practically no difference in learning for H-H and L-L. All other studies reviewed in this chapter have shown a wide difference in learning between such conditions.

The question must be raised as to whether or not the results of Mandler and Campbell, which lack the discipline of those of several studies reviewed earlier, should be taken seriously as contradictions of the results of these other investigators. The following considerations are judged relevant.

1. Note was taken in the previous chapter of the fact that Mandler's scale values do not correlate very highly with the scale values determined by others for the same units. Either his method of scaling is "getting at" something different from the methods of others or the scale values have lower reliability.

2. Only two pairs of items were used to represent each combination of M. The sampling problem has been discussed earlier.

3. The same items were apparently not used for the same variation in M among stimuli and among responses. For example, the mean scale value for high stimulus M is 4.9, for high-response M, 4.7. Thus, the items could not have been identical.

4. In presenting the list, six different orders of presentation were used, but it is not stated whether or not each pair was used as the first pair of a list equally often. If this were not the case, it is possible (as noted earlier in the chapter) that some bias would result.

5. The lists differed widely in difficulty. Although it is reported that this factor is equalized for statistical analysis, it is not removed in Table 3. If it is assumed that there is a limit to the rate at which items can be learned, and that these are learned in order of difficulty as indexed by M, the learning of a given item would be affected by the rate at which other items in the list are learned. Differences in difficulty among the lists might mean that such a situation obtains. However, a rough adjustment for this by using deviation scores (deviation of the mean of a pair of items from the mean of all six items) does not smooth out the data in Table 3.

In the second experiment all 18 pairs were placed in a single list and presented for 30 trials. Over-all, the results show a decrease in amount learned as response M decreases and a like relationship when stimulus M decreases. Furthermore, the interaction between stimulus and response M is significant. However, it is clear that this significant interaction does *not* result from the fact that response M produces a greater effect than stimulus M. In fact, variations in stimulus M produced a slightly greater mean effect than did response M. The interaction effect is apparently a consequence of a series of nonsystematic "disturbances" among the separate functions.

It is thus seen that there is no high consistency between the results of these two experiments by Mandler and Campbell. The use of a single list of all 18 pairs in the second experiment (as compared with three lists of six pairs in the first) provides one possible source of discrepancy (as per point 6 above). But, it is also possible that length of list as such is a variable which modifies the M-learning relationship.

What shall be concluded? The Mandler-Campbell results are in partial contradiction to several other studies reviewed and to several experiments to be reported later in the book. A number of factors which may be responsible for these contradictions have been suggested. There is, of course, no way to assert unequivocally that these factors are indeed responsible. It must also be kept in mind that the Mandler-Campbell experiments do not themselves yield a set of clear relationships with which one might work. Therefore, we will conclude that these findings cannot be allowed to obscure the clarity of the major trends found in the other experiments.

SUMMARY

The major trends relating M and learning may be summarized in two statements:

1. When stimulus and response M covary, there is a direct relationship between M and rate of learning.

2. When stimulus and response M are varied independently, both are directly related to rate of learning, but the magnitude of the effect is greater for response M than for stimulus M.

REFERENCES

Braun, H. W., & Heymann, S. P. Meaningfulness of material, distribution of practice, and serial-position curves. *J. exp. Psychol.*, 1958, 56, 146–150.

Cason, H. Association between the familiar and the unfamiliar. *J. exp. Psychol.*, 1933, 16, 295–305.

Cieutat, V. J., Stockwell, F. E., & Noble, C. E. The interaction of ability and amount of practice with stimulus and response meaningfulness (*m, m'*) in paired-associate learning. *J. exp. Psychol.*, 1958, 56, 193–202.

Davis, F. C. The relative reliability of words and nonsense syllables. *J. exp. Psychol.*, 1930, 13, 221–234.

Dowling, R. M., & Braun, H. W. Retention and meaningfulness of material. *J. exp. Psychol.*, 1957, 54, 213–217.

Hunt, R. G. Meaningfulness and articulation of stimulus and response in paired-associate learning and stimulus recall. *J. exp. Psychol.*, 1959, 57, 262–267.

Jantz, E. M., & Underwood, B. J. R-S learning as a function of meaningfulness and degree of S-R learning. *J. exp. Psychol.*, 1958, 56, 174–179.

Kimble, G. A., & Dufort, R. H. Meaningfulness and isolation as factors in verbal learning. *J. exp. Psychol.*, 1955, 50, 361–368.

L'Abate, L. Manifest anxiety and the learning of syllables with different associative values. *Amer. J. Psychol.*, 1959, 72, 107–110.

Mandler, G., & Huttenlocher, J. The relationship between associative
frequency, associative ability and paired-associate learning. *Amer.
J. Psychol.*, 1956, 69, 424–428.

Mandler, G., & Campbell, E. H. Effect of variation in associative frequency of stimulus and response members on paired-associate
learning. *J. exp. Psychol.*, 1957, 54, 269–273.

McGeoch, J. A. The influence of associative value upon the difficulty
of non-sense-syllable lists. *J. genet. Psychol.*, 1930, 37, 421–426.

Morikawa, Y. Functions of stimulus and response in paired-associate
verbal learning. *Psychologia*, 1959, 2, 41–56.

Noble, C. E. The role of stimulus meaning (m) in serial verbal learning. *J. exp. Psychol.*, 1952, 43, 437–446.

Noble, C. E., & McNeely, D. A. The role of meaningfulness (m) in
paired-associate verbal learning. *J. exp. Psychol.*, 1957, 53, 16–22.

Noble, C. E., Stockwell, F. E., & Pryer, M. W. Meaningfulness (m')
and association value (a) in paired-associate syllable learning.
Psychol. Rep., 1957, 3, 441–452.

Peters, H. N. The relationship between familiarity of words and their
memory value. *Amer. J. Psychol.*, 1936, 48, 572–585.

Postman, L. J., Adams, P. A., & Phillips, L. W. Studies in incidental
learning: II. The effects of association value and of the method
of testing. *J. exp. Psychol.*, 1955, 49, 1–10.

Sarason, I. G. The effect of associative value and differential motivating instructions on serial learning. *Amer. J. Psychol.*, 1957, 70,
620–623.

Sarason, I. G. Effects on verbal learning of anxiety, reassurance, and
meaningfulness of material. *J. exp. Psychol.*, 1958, 56, 472–477.

Sauer, F. M. The relative variability of nonsense syllables and words.
J. exp. Psychol., 1930, 13, 235–246.

Sheffield, F. D. The role of meaningfulness of stimulus and response in
verbal learning. Ph.D. dissertation, Yale Univer., 1946.

Stoddard, G. D. An experiment in verbal learning. *J. educ. Psychol..*
1929, 20, 452–457.

Underwood, B. J., & Richardson, J. The influence of meaningfulness,
intralist similarity, and serial position on retention. *J. exp. Psychol.*,
1956, 52, 119–126.

Weiss, R. L. The role of association value and experimentally produced familiarity in paired associate learning. Ph.D. dissertation,
Univer. Buffalo, 1958.

Chapter 4

Frequency and Meaningfulness

Operational definitions of phenomena often provide useful as well as convenient starting points for theory construction. Indeed, it is often necessary to start theorizing in terms of the implications of such definitions. The various highly correlated definitions of M given in the second chapter ought, it would seem, to yield some very fruitful theoretical notions. Yet, with several highly correlated dimensions, the question of fundamentality persistently crops up. In other words, is one of these variables basic in that the others are a consequence of it? Or, is there still some other variable which lies "behind" all of these? The approach to be taken here is indicated by the last question.

At this point it will be asserted merely that *frequency of experience* is the fundamental antecedent condition leading to the secondary phenomena exhibited by the scaling procedures detailed in the second chapter. In a later chapter attempts will be made to show how frequency produces the relationship between learning and M. It may be noted that even if frequency is the variable responsible for the dimensions used to define M and for their high intercorrelations, it does not inevitably follow that frequency should be the starting point of a theoretical structure. It is quite possible that the *effects* of frequency would be more useful theoretical tools for the understanding of learning than would frequency *per se*. Nevertheless, a variety of considerations, theoretical and empirical, led to the conclusion that it is worthwhile to "push" a frequency theory as far as it will go before adding secondary propositions to the theory.

Three steps will be taken in the present chapter. First, some comments are needed about the theoretical potential of the dimensions used to define M. This may give some understanding of how we tentatively judged them to be unsatisfactory as a theoretical base, hence, how it occurred that a more fertile starting point appeared to be frequency. Secondly, an examination will be made of certain experiments which directly relate frequency and learning. Finally, an analysis of verbal units used in learning experiments will be made to see if a direct relationship between frequency and M can be inferred.

THE DIMENSIONS OF MEANINGFULNESS
Number of Associates

One definition of M has been given in terms of the number of associates elicited by a verbal unit. This has been done by having the subject actually produce the associates or by having him rate the number of associates which he thinks a stimulus will evoke. Assuming that the more quickly a stimulus elicits an associate, the greater the number of associates it will elicit, the defining operations of Glaze (number of subjects getting an association within a very limited interval) may also be included here.

Of all the definitions of M, this one provides the most compelling one as a base for a theory; its potential seems very great. To use it as a starting point for a theory would be quite consonant with most psychologists having associationistic learnings, and this would include the present authors. Others have been attracted to it (e.g., Mandler, 1954). The basis of the theory would be the notion of associative probability. In a paired-associate task the subject must learn to associate two items; he must learn to say B when A is presented. The basic postulate of the theory could state that the greater the M of these items—the greater the number of associates which they elicit—the greater the probability that associates from the two items will link up in some manner so that B is connected to A via already existent associations. The link might be made directly (at one extreme) in that an associate of A *is* B. At the other extreme the link may come via one or more mediated associations.

There are a number of reasons why a decision was made not to use an associative probability theory as a basic starting position. It should be noted that this decision does not mean a rejection of *any* use of the idea of associative probability. The notion may be very useful at least for certain aspects of verbal learning; it is here being rejected as a basic postulate to relate M and learning. Some of the considerations which led to this decision follow.

Elaborateness. A serious attempt was made to outline an associative probability theory so that it would handle the facts of paired-associate learning. The outcome, while not judged entirely unsuccessful, was an extraordinarily elaborate system. For example, the theory does not immediately mediate the fact that response M produces greater variance than does stimulus M. It is quite possible that others, more skilled in theory construction than we, can avoid this elaborateness, so this fact alone is no basis for rejecting the approach. Furthermore, it is quite possible that such an elaborate system is necessary to reflect adequately the verbal learning processes. So, all that can be said is that we became uncomfortable with this approach as the elaborateness increased.

Secondary nature. As an exclusive approach the associative-probability theory leaves no room for "raw" learning. That is, it is based entirely on the use of and strengthening of associations which already exist in the subject's repertoire. Somewhere, sometime, these associations must be initially established. Here again, it is barely possible that in dealing with M there is no new learning; that is, perhaps with college students as subjects, no really new learning occurs with verbal material. It can only be asserted that this implication of an associative-probability theory was incompatible with our orientation.

Interference paradox. When a theory is based on an associative-probability notion, one must deal with an interference paradox. Since it is known that the greater the number of responses attached to a stimulus in the laboratory, the greater the negative transfer (e.g., Bugelski, 1948), some way out of this apparent paradox would have to be found. An associative-probability theory would assert that the greater the number of associates, the greater is the likelihood that an associative connection would be made. A consideration of the interference potential could lead to a contrary assertion that the greater the number of associates, the greater the amount of interference. This paradox can probably be resolved, and there is no intent here to conclude that it cannot. For example, evidence from certain transfer situations point unmistakably toward the operation of negative or interference effects even when the over-all transfer effects are quite positive. Thus, as far as M is concerned, it may be that as the number of associates increases, the negative effects of interference increase at a less rapid rate than do the positive effects produced by an increase in associative probability.

We must conclude that while it may be quite possible to resolve this paradox in the context of an associative-probability theory, the resolution would only add to an already elaborate structure. Of course, to reject the associative-probability theory does not remove the necessity for considering the interference effects which associates may produce. The interference potential or problem remains, regardless of the theory. To reject the associative-probability theory on this score merely resolves an initial paradox implied by the basic postulate of the theory.

Direct evidence on mediation. The associative-probability theory, as conceived here, would state that the greater the number of associates elicited by items, the greater is the probability that some associative linkage could occur. As noted earlier, such linkage might be direct. That is, if B is to be attached to A, and if a strong associate of A is B, the association is direct. Studies by Key (1926) and by Underwood & Schulz (1960) show that the stronger the direct association, the more rapid is the learning. However, when consideration is given to less direct forms of linkage, i.e., to mediated links, the evidence (such as it is) is much less compelling. That such mediation can occur with enormous effect under very favorable conditions, i.e., when associations with the mediator is very strong, seems to have been demonstrated by Barnes & Underwood (1959). But when such mediators are more remote (involving more than one mediator) and less strong, the effect is much less convincing (e.g., Russell & Storms, 1955). The older studies (e.g., Peters, 1935), in which associations to be used as mediators were acquired in the laboratory, gave only a small positive effect, if any. In short, the evidence available does not warrant high optimism toward an associative-probability theory when this depends upon mediation of remote and weak associates. It would seem that this would be especially true in lists in which the experimenter, in pairing items, makes a definite attempt to eliminate the more obvious associative linkages.

Individual differences. Let us assume that the M of a group of items is determined (by the production method) separately for different individuals. It is a fact that wide individual differences can be shown to exist; i.e., some subjects will produce many associates to a given item, and others will produce few. If the number of associates elicited is the critical factor involved in the rate at which an item is learned, it would be expected that the subject who gives many associates will learn more rapidly than the subject who gives few to the same items. There are some data on this question.

Mandler & Huttenlocher (1956) asked subjects to give associates to nonsense syllables. Each syllable was presented for 30 sec. Each of these subjects also learned a paired-associate list made up of syllables different from those used in the association test. Thus, two scores were available for each subject, an association score and a learning score. The correlation between the two arrays for two separate groups of 20 subjects each did not differ significantly from zero but were in the expected direction; i.e., the greater the number of associates a subject wrote down, the faster he learned. When a partial correlation was obtained between learning and total associates elicited by the 10 syllables having highest M (holding number of associates to the syllables of low M constant), the correlations became significant. Thus, these results might be taken as suggestive of a relationship between the number of associates produced by a subject and his rate of learning.

That the above suggestive relationship lacks generality is indicated by the results of a study by Scheible (1954). Scheible determined the associative capacity of 108 college students; the Glaze technique was used. After some practice syllables established the routine of the procedure, 27 syllables, differing widely in Glaze values, were presented one at a time to each subject in an individual session. The subject was allowed 2 sec. to respond with the first "thing" the syllable made him think of. For the 27 syllables, a score was determined for each subject, a score which was the number of syllables eliciting an association within the 2-sec. interval. These scores were shown to be reliable. Furthermore, for the results of all subjects combined, the correlation between the Glaze value and Scheible's corresponding index was .79.

As the next step, Scheible divided her 108 subjects into three groups of 36 each. The groups were differentiated on the basis of the number of syllables to which they had responded with an association. The subjects in one group had given associations to 21 to 26 (out of a possible 27) of the syllables; in another the subjects had given associations to 18, 19, or 20, and in the third they had responded to from 6 to 17 of the syllables. All subjects learned three serial lists composed of the 27 syllables used in the association test, the syllables being divided into three lists of nine syllables each. The results show that M was strongly related to learning, but the three groups did not differ in trials to learn the lists. Over-all, a nonsignificant correlation of −.13 is reported between number of items to which the subject responded on the association test and the rate of learning.

The evidence available gives very little support to an expectation (which might follow from an associative-probability theory) that a subject who scores high on the indices used to define M will learn more rapidly than will a subject who scores low on these indices.

Pre-association. In an auxiliary part of a study reviewed in the previous chapter, Mandler & Campbell (1957) requested subjects to give associates to nonsense syllables just prior to learning a list made up of these syllables. The learning was compared with that of a group having given associates to items not in the list to be learned. The expectation might be that if associates are critical to learning, the group having given the associates to the items to be learned would have these more readily available to "assist" in learning. This expectation was not borne out since there was no difference in the learning rates of the two groups.

A related finding, also negative with respect to an associative-probability theory, has been reported by Riley & Phillips (1959). In one experiment these investigators gave familiarization training for 24 nonsense syllables (Glaze, 19 to 22 per cent) and did not give such training for 24 other syllables of like M. Following such training a 30-sec. production test was given for both groups of syllables. No differences appeared in number of associates produced by the two groups of syllables even though the familiarized syllables were subsequently found to be learned more rapidly than the nonfamiliarized syllables. In a second experiment the association test was delayed until after learning of familiarized and nonfamiliarized syllables. Again, the number of associates produced did not differ, although learning rate had been positively influenced by familiarization.

While positive results (differences in number of associates produced as a consequence of familiarization or learning) are not demanded by an associative-probability theory, it would make the "going" easier for such a theory if positive results had been found. The Riley-Phillips results do seem to demand another explanatory principle to account for differences in learning as a consequence of familiarization if one is to use the associative-probability theory to account for the relation between M and learning. It is our belief that such results can be accounted for by a frequency interpretation and thus bring these results into a system accounting for the effects of M on learning. How this is done will be made clear in a later chapter.

In this section points have been discussed which were responsible for our rejection of an associative-probability theory as a base for understanding the relationship between learning and M. No point, taken individually, was judged lethal to the theory, but taken in the aggregate, the points provide a block which to us seemed difficult to overcome.

Pronunciability

As was shown in the second chapter, ratings of the relative pronunciability of verbal units correlate highly with other methods of defining

M. It must also follow that pronunciability and rate of learning will be strongly related. (Data which confirm this expectation will be presented in later chapters.) The question asked here is whether or not pronunciability is a reasonable starting point for explanatory notions of how M influences learning. Certain considerations have led to a tentative negative answer.

It has been asserted that frequency of experience is taken to be the critical variable lying behind all of the correlated dimensions discussed in the second chapter. For the present it will be asserted further that one of the results of frequency, not measured directly or totally by any of these dimensions, is the consequence that the elements (letters in the case of three-letter units) making up the responses become integrated into a unitary response. The three letters XQL do not form an integrated response; the letters CAT do. Ease of pronouncing a unit is one measure of degree of integration of the letters. A syllable that is clearly pronounceable can be represented or recalled at the outset by one response; one that is not (e.g., XQL) must be represented by three responses. However, evidence to be presented in later chapters will show that integration may well occur in ways other than by a combination of letters being pronounceable.

The conclusion is that pronunciability is not judged a good starting point for a theory. Not only does it seem somewhat barren of theoretical potential but, as the evidence suggests, it is also only a special (if highly frequent) case of response integration resulting from frequency.

Familiarity

Ratings of familiarity of verbal units have been shown (Chapter 2) to correlate very highly with the number of associates elicited by these units. The instructions given to subjects in rating familiarity directed them to rate the frequency with which they had experienced the units. Thus, the operations defining familiarity tie M more directly to frequency than do any of the other operations.

A disturbing thought which may have occurred to many is the question of how it is really known that subjects do rate solely on the dimension on which they are requested to rate. A number of different instructions given to the subjects have all resulted in approximately the same rank-ordering of these items. Is it possible that there is one strong dimension running through the items which subjects "use" regardless of the instructions?

It is not possible to give any general answer to this question for the several covariant dimensions outlined in Chapter 2. For the position assumed here it would be pleasant to be able to conclude that subjects are in fact really rating in terms of the frequency with which they have experienced the units. To conclude this is, of course, just as impossible as it would be to conclude that the ratings under the various instructions are directly reflecting number of associates.

The issue of the moment concerns judgment of frequency differences. Suppose that subjects, when asked to judge such frequency differences (to define familiarity), actually rate the number of associates which they think the item will evoke. This would result in the obtained correlation but would be more indicative of reliability than of the correlation between two independently defined dimensions. There is, as noted above, no completely satisfactory way to handle this issue for data which are available. However, the evidence on the capacity of subjects to reflect environmental frequency is fairly broad and consistent, and it seems quite reasonable to believe, therefore, that when subjects are requested to judge relative frequency they do so. Some of this evidence, showing how the subjects' judgments correspond to known frequency of verbal units, will be reviewed.

Individual letters. As a starting point we will use the judgment of the frequencies of occurrence of letters in the English language. On an absolute basis, all letters have been experienced very, very frequently. Can a subject judge relative frequencies with accuracy? If we look at the extreme cases, it would seem likely that such judgments could be made. The letter *a* would certainly be judged to occur with greater frequency than would, say, *z*. The answer to the basic question concerning all letters of the alphabet comes from a study by Attneave (1953).

Attneave told his subjects that they were to imagine a newspaper clipping with 1000 letters in it. Then the subjects were asked to assign each of the 26 letters the frequency with which they believed each would occur in the clipping. They were further told that if each letter were used equally often, each would occur about 38 times in the total of 1000 letters and that, therefore, this could be considered the frequency for a letter having average frequency of use. The subjects were able to complete this task in about 10 min. The correlation between true frequency and judged frequency was .79; the low frequencies tended to be overestimated, and high frequencies, underestimated. Another group of subjects, using a somewhat different procedure, yielded a correlation of .88. Clearly, the subjects can reflect actual frequencies with considerable precision.

Words. It might be expected that subjects would err more in the judgment of frequencies of words than in the judgment of frequencies of letters. The evidence does not support such an expectation. Howes (1954) in three different studies had subjects judge the relative frequencies (by rank ordering) of words. It was shown that subjects were highly reliable in these judgments. The over-all value for all three studies of the relationship between judged frequency and actual frequency may be taken as .80. Actually, there is no way of knowing how accurately the frequency count (taken from popular magazines) represents the true frequency of experience of these college-student subjects. Therefore, it is quite possible that the true relationship between experienced frequency and judged frequency is higher than that indicated by the correlation of .80. It is worth noting also that Howes believes that the frequency with which a word is emitted is more important than the frequency with which that word is read (more important in the sense that frequency judgments correspond more closely to it). No information concerning the frequency with which words are emitted in normal conversation is available.

Bigrams and trigrams. The data to be presented in this section were obtained by the authors and have not been published elsewhere. A bigram is a two-letter sequence, and a trigram a three-letter sequence. The questions we asked concerned the accuracy of judging the relative frequency with which certain bigrams occur in words and the relative frequency with which certain trigrams occur. The source of our information about the frequency of bigrams and trigrams will be detailed in a later chapter.

For determining the accuracy in judging frequencies of bigrams, 100 *pairs* of bigrams were selected. A total of 405 different bigrams were listed in alphabetical order. All of them were known to occur as two-letter sequences within words, but the frequency with which they occurred varied widely. From a table of random numbers, successive pairs of numbers falling between 1 and 405 were used to pair the items. "Replacement" was used so that a given bigram may have been drawn more than once. The drawing continued until 100 pairs were obtained. These were mimeographed on a single sheet of paper, the order of the listing being that obtained in pairing the items.

The instruction sheet given to the subject contained the following directions:

> On the following page pairs of two-letter combinations are listed. These combinations are taken from a large number of common English words. For example, to get such two-letter com-

binations from the word "teacher," the word would be broken down into all possible forward two-letter sequences, namely: *te, ea, ac, ch, he, er*. A large number of such words were "broken up" to obtain the combinations listed on the following page.

It is apparent that certain letter combinations will occur more frequently in words than will other combinations. We are interested in the accuracy of your judgments concerning which combinations occur most frequently. For each pair on the following page you are to judge which of the two occurs most frequently in our written language. You are to encircle the one which you think occurs most frequently. For example, if the pair was: *la* and *qy*, you might decide that "la" occurs most frequently and you would indicate this by drawing a circle around it.

In making your judgments, the following procedures should be used:

1. Look at each of the two combinations carefully; then, try pronouncing each to yourself; then, make your decision as to which you think occurs most frequently. Do not spend too much time in arriving at your decision.

2. Do not be misled by letters which form initials of friends, or form abbreviations for various concerns, such as government bureaus. We are concerned with the frequency of letter combinations as they occur in English words.

3. When a two-letter combination forms a word, your judgment of frequency should include its frequency of use as an individual word as well as its frequency of use as a part of longer words.

Remember: For each pair encircle the combination which you think occurs most frequently in our written language.

For the trigram judgments, 150 pairs were assembled in exactly the same manner as for the bigrams, the items being paired randomly from a listing of 2,258 different trigrams. The instructions to the subject were the same as for the bigram judgments, except for reference to three-letter sequences rather than two-letter sequences. A total of 99 subjects completed the judgments for bigrams, 86 for the trigrams. No subject made both sets of judgments.

There were 100 pairs of bigrams. For each pair the proportion of subjects choosing each alternative was determined. If over 50 per cent of the subjects chose the bigram having the highest frequency, the aggregate choice was said to be correct. If less than 50 per cent of the subjects chose the bigram with the highest frequency, the aggregate choice was said to be incorrect. When these criteria were used, judg-

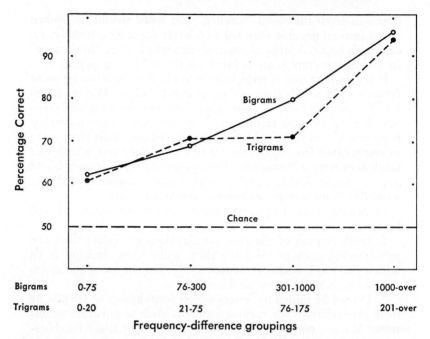

Figure 7. Percentage of correct judgments of frequency of bigrams and trigrams as a function of the difference in frequency of the members of the pair being judged.

ments were correct for 78 per cent of the pairs, and incorrect for 22 per cent.

When the trigrams were paired at random, the two members of one pair had the same frequency; therefore, correctness and incorrectness could be determined for only 149 pairs. Of these 149 pairs, the majority judgment for 73 per cent was correct and was incorrect for 27 per cent.

It would be expected, of course, that the greater the difference in frequency between members of a pair, the greater would be the number of correct judgments. That this is generally true can be seen in Fig. 7. In this figure four groupings of increasing frequency differences were formed, so that the number of pairs in each of the four groupings was roughly the same. These four groupings are indicated along the baseline; no attempt has been made to order this baseline so as to correspond to the magnitude of the frequency differences. For the pairs in each grouping, the per cent judged correctly is plotted on the ordinate. As can be seen, while there is a clear increase in per cent correct as frequency differences increase, the relationship is by no means sharp, especially for the trigrams.

As a further test of the relationship, product-moment correlations were calculated between the frequency differences of the pairs and the number of subjects choosing the bigram or trigram with the highest frequency in each pair. For the bigrams the correlation was .35, and for the trigrams, .28. Although both of these values are highly significant statistically (it is improbable that the true correlation is zero), it is obvious that the relationship is much lower than that found for judgments of word frequencies and judgments of frequencies of single letters.

If these judgments of frequencies of bigrams and trigrams follow expectations based on judgments resulting in difference thresholds, it would be anticipated that accuracy would be maximal the smaller the frequency of a member of a pair (Weber's law?). This expectation is supported. We shall present only an illustration of this fact. From the bigrams, 44 pairs were chosen in which one of the members of each pair had a frequency of 25 or less (the remaining had minimal frequencies of over 25). For these 44 items a correlation was determined between the differences in frequencies for members of the pairs and the number of subjects choosing the member of the pair having the highest frequency. The resulting value was .76, a value which compares favorably with those reported earlier for words and letters.

It should be clear that in both of these experiments, bigrams and trigrams were used regardless of whether they formed words, cut across syllables, or formed initial or terminal parts of words. Undoubtedly the lack of homogeneity for such factors may influence judgments over and above frequency *per se*. It is possible that if judgments were made between items forming a pair of items homogeneous on all such factors, the relationship between frequency and judgmental accuracy would be sharper. Nevertheless, for the present purposes, the data warrant the conclusion that subjects can judge these environmental probabilities with appreciably greater-than-chance accuracy. Thus, to relate familiarity and frequency, even with nonsense-type material, seems quite justified.

In this section arguments have been advanced to support the decision *not* to start with certain of the defining operations of M as a theoretical base. The exception has been *familiarity*, the operations for which reflect directly on frequency of experience; it is this factor which has been chosen as a more hopeful starting point for a theory to relate learning and M. The next section will be of a more positive nature, in the sense that data which relate frequency and learning directly will be examined.

FREQUENCY AND LEARNING

Before we go further with the notion of ultimately explaining the effects of M on learning by a frequency hypothesis, it will be well to see if frequency and learning have been related. Is there a direct relationship between rate of learning verbal units and the frequency with which a subject has experienced those units? To determine this requires, of course, some measure of frequency. For units forming words, the Thorndike-Lorge (1944) word counts are available. These tables give the frequency with which the 30,000 most frequent words occur in writing. Insofar as the frequency of the printed word can be taken as an index of the frequency with which a subject will have experienced a word, the relationship between frequency of experience and learning could be determined by the rate of learning of words occurring with different frequencies. Some data on this relationship are available.

Hall (1954) constructed four lists of 20 words each. One list consisted of words occurring once per million, another, 10 per million, a third, 30 per million, and a fourth, 50 to 100 times per million words of printed text. The words for a list were chosen at random from a given frequency level, subject to the restriction that each word contain seven letters. The lists were presented five times at the rate of 5 sec. per word, and then the subject was given 5 min. to write all the words he could remember.

The results (Table 4) show a direct relationship between fre-

TABLE 4. Learning as a Function of Thorndike-Lorge Word Frequency

(The values indicate mean number correct out of 20 possible)
(Hall, 1954)

Thorndike-Lorge Frequency	N	Mean Recall
1 per million	76	12.04
10 per million	52	13.31
30 per million	44	15.02
50–100 per million	55	15.04

quency and mean number recalled. Statistically speaking, the effect of frequency is significant, but it should be noted that the differences are actually quite small in an absolute sense. Or, to view this in another manner, the differences are much smaller than those resulting from variation in M among nonsense syllables as reported in the previous chapter. Also, it should be noted that the major effect occurs with low frequencies.

Jacobs (1955), as a subsidiary finding in an experiment designed for other purposes, reports a correlation of .74 between the Thorndike-Lorge values and the number of correct responses in a paired-associate list. The stimuli for this task were nonsense syllables (all of approximately the same M), and the responses were the words varying in Thorndike-Lorge frequency. The complete range of Thorndike-Lorge frequencies is involved. Thus, this study suggests a clear positive relationship between frequency and learning when the words are used as responses in a paired-associate list.

Bousfield & Cohen (1955) presented two lists of 60 words each, each word being exposed for 3 sec. Only one trial was given before the subject wrote all the words he could remember. One list consisted of items of low Thorndike-Lorge frequency (about 2.6 occurrences per million on the average), and the other of higher frequency (24 occurrences per million on the average). The high-frequency words yielded a mean recall of 25.55 items, and the low, 22.18 items. Again, while this difference is highly significant statistically, it is clear that in an absolute sense the differences in learning are not great. A subsequent study by Bousfield, Cohen, & Whitmarsh (1958) showed essentially the same results. Furthermore, this latter study, like the Hall study discussed above, indicates that the change in learning rate is much sharper for changes in frequency at the low frequency levels than it is for corresponding changes at the high frequency levels.

As far as is known, the only published results in which the small but consistent relationship between Thorndike-Lorge frequency and learning did not occur are those of Peters (1936). A series of studies were performed, all showing the same lack of relationship between frequency and learning. There were 10 words in each list which was read once to the subject at the rate of one word per sec. Then immediate recall was taken.

The essentially negative results found in this study might be attributed to certain procedural factors, but the most likely explanation may be found in the fact that in no experiment was the frequency range extended beyond the 10,000 most frequently used words. As a consequence of the findings of later studies, presented above, it seems quite clear that the frequency differences must be rather extreme when words are used before even a small relationship emerges. Yet, it could be argued that if frequency is a critical factor (as is being assumed), why doesn't a relationship appear clearly and consistently for such materials when absolute differences in frequency of words in printed text are so large? We make a tentative answer by saying that the relationship between frequency and learning may be either S-shaped or negatively accelerated and that words of the order of frequency used in these experiments fall (in terms of frequency) on the upper, nearly flat portion of the curve.

It was noted above that the absolute *differences* in frequency of words used in these experiments to relate word frequency and learning appear large, yet the corresponding differences in learning are relatively small. However, it is quite possible that absolute frequency of experience with even low-frequency words is high. Many of the words listed in the Thorndike-Lorge book as occurring once per million words appear to be very familiar. If the thesis being advanced here is correct, this would imply that such words will have been experienced many times in an absolute sense. An appropriate question might be, therefore: "How many times will the college student who serves in learning experiments have experienced in his lifetime, say, a word which occurs once per million words?" It is obvious that to obtain an accurate answer to such a question would be a very difficult task indeed. Therefore, the data to be presented are suggestive only.

This study was done by Mr. Allyn Remley, under the supervision of the senior author. Remley set about to determine the number of words read by a college freshman during a calendar year. To do this he conducted extensive interviews with 29 college freshman men in June at the end of the freshman year. All were students at Northwestern University. During the interview, the materials listed were various texts used in courses, laboratory manuals, mimeographed material, syllabii, class notes, etc., all with the intent of making an estimate of the number of words involved. For each source of printed words an estimate was made of the number of words. For example, in 16 textbooks most widely used by these 29 subjects, there was an average of 225,000 words. If the subject reported he had read a given text twice, the entry would be twice as great as the number of words in the text. If the subject said he read the entire book once and then selected sections (e.g., underlined sections) a second time, an estimate was made of how much of the total these sections constituted. Also estimated was the number of words read in a pleasure sense, e.g., newspapers, magazines, novels, mail, both during the summer and during the regular school terms. The estimates were made by getting an index of time spent in such reading and then multiplying by an average reading speed. Other sources of words were also examined (e.g., number of words one sees on sign boards in a one-hour drive), but the absolute number of words estimated from such sources was so small that for the present purposes they may be ignored.

Remley's final tabulation shows that approximately 56 per cent of all words read during the year were from academic sources, and 43 per cent from pleasure sources. For the subject calculated to have read the smallest number of words, the total was 6.5 million. (This subject was in school only two of the three quarters). The greatest number of words esitmated for any one subject was 11.3 million. The mean figure for all 29 subjects was 9.5 million.

Very roughly, then, we may say that a freshman in college reads 10 million words during that calendar year. Is this a reasonable figure? If a conservative reading rate of 200 words per min. is assumed, the total time in reading would work out to approximately 833 hr. or something over 2 hr. per day for every day in the year. This is probably not an unreasonable estimate.

If we extrapolate backwards to younger ages, with a steadily decreasing number of words per year, we might estimate that when a student arrives at college for his freshman year, he will have read 50 million words. By the time he finishes four years of college, this total should have mounted to nearly 100 million. Of course, it is to be expected that as age decreases, the number of different words read decreases, and it is also likely that as the subject progresses through college, the number of different words read increases. Nevertheless, we believe that the evidence suggests that the average college sophomore or junior may have seen a word which occurs once per million words as many as 50 times. There is also the added frequency produced by hearing words that others speak and the frequency produced by the emission of words in oral communication. We haven't the slightest idea how much these sources would add to the total frequency. Our belief is, however, that as far as emission of words in speech is concerned, the usual college student is going to use high-frequency words in disproportionate frequency to their occurrence in written discourse. Thus, a disproportionately greater frequency would be added to the already high-frequency words than would be added to the low.

The purpose of this diversion has been to suggest the possibility that words occurring in the Thorndike-Lorge list, even words with the lowest frequencies, may in fact have been experienced many times by a subject who serves in learning experiments. It is not surprising to us, therefore, that relatively small differences in learning occur when Thorndike-Lorge frequency is manipulated. If the relationship between frequency of experience and rate of learning is S-shaped or negatively accelerated, such an outcome might well be anticipated.

The implication of the above discussion is that analyses of verbal units which do not form words must be made if the effects of low absolute frequencies are to be examined. Or, to put this another way, how are frequency differences among consonant syllables, nonsense syllables, etc., to be measured so that a more reasonable test of the relationship between learning and frequency may be made? An initial attack on this problem is the purpose of the next section.

FREQUENCY AND DEFINITIONS OF MEANINGFULNESS

Earlier in the chapter it was shown that *familiarity* of verbal units could be considered a direct consequence of frequency. The question now raised is whether or not a direct relationship can be established between frequency and other operations for defining M. If such a correlation can be established, it makes more plausible the assumption that frequency of experience "lies behind" the various definitions of M. Some evidence is available on this point from the work of other investigators, and this will be covered in the remainder of this chapter. Because this work deals largely with words, it still does not handle the problem for nonsense and consonant syllables. An evaluation of the latter materials in terms of the frequency hypothesis will be given in the next chapter.

Production method. It will be remembered that Noble scaled dissyllables for M by the production method. It was also shown that this index of M and rate of learning were directly related. The first 60 units in his list—rank-ordered according to the number of associates produced—were examined with regard to the frequency with which they occur in the Thorndike-Lorge most frequently occurring group of 20,000 words (Underwood, 1959). The results are presented in Table 5. The Thorndike-Lorge count symbol is listed after each word. The symbol *AA* means that a word occurred over 100 times per million words; the symbol *A* means that it occurred between 50 and 100 times, and the numbers indicate actual frequency per million. A dash indicates that the word does not occur in the 20,000 most frequently used words. The over-all relationship is quite clear; as the number of associates elicited by an item decreases, so, also, does its frequency decrease.

TABLE 5. The Highest Ranking 60 Words in Noble's List and the Thorndike-Lorge Frequency Values

(AA indicates the word occurred over 100 times per million; A indicates the word occurred 50–100 times per million, and the words with numbers indicate the actual frequency per million. A dash indicates the word does not occur in the Thorndike-Lorge list of 20,000 most frequently used words. The words are in order of Noble's M index; that is, *kitchen* has highest M, *stoma* the lowest.)

(Underwood, 1959)

1.	kitchen	AA	16.	youngster	21	31.	quota	3	46.	vertex	—
2.	army	AA	17.	uncle	AA	32.	yeomen	11	47.	rostrum	1
3.	money	AA	18.	income	46	33.	zenith	4	48.	ovum	—
4.	dinner	AA	19.	zero	11	34.	ordeal	5	49.	tartan	1
5.	wagon	A	20.	hunger	37	35.	pigment	4	50.	endive	—
6.	office	AA	21.	region	A	36.	naphtha	1	51.	jetsam	—
7.	heaven	AA	22.	quarter	AA	37.	pallet	2	52.	lichens	7
8.	jelly	19	23.	leader	AA	38.	entrant	—	53.	percept	—
9.	jewel	41	24.	mallet	3	39.	jitney	—	54.	capstan	—
10.	insect	40	25.	kennel	6	40.	rampart	4	55.	lemur	—
11.	village	AA	26.	keeper	23	41.	argon	—	56.	nimbus	—
12.	garment	40	27.	fatigue	19	42.	sequence	6	57.	carom	—
13.	zebra	2	28.	unit	29	43.	pallor	2	58.	flotsam	—
14.	captain	AA	29.	effort	AA	44.	tankard	1	59.	grapnel	—
15.	typhoon	—	30.	quarry	11	45.	bodice	2	60.	stoma	—

Direct evidence on number of associates produced and frequency is given by Cofer & Shevitz (1952). Four high-frequency words and four low-frequency words were used. The high-frequency words had an occurrence of 100 times per million or more, and the low, one time per million. Two adjectives and two nouns were used at each frequency level. The high-frequency words were *evening, office, pretty,* and *simple,* and the low-frequency words, *cynic, bedspread, slavish,* and *obtuse.* Each word was presented for 10 min., with the subjects being asked to write all the words they could associate with each word. The high-frequency adjectives elicited an average of 50 associates, and the low ones, 42. The high-frequency nouns elicited an average of 61, and the low-frequency ones, 44.

In a somewhat similar fashion, Lepley (1950) directed subjects to rate words for frequency of use. (We have shown earlier that frequency of use is one way to define familiarity and that it correlates almost perfectly with the production method of defining M.) Then he asked them to produce as many different synonyms of the words as possible. The number of synonyms produced and frequency ratings were directly related. Such a result might be expected from the fact that it is known that high-frequency words in the Thorndike-Lorge lists have more dictionary meanings than do low-frequency words (Thorndike, 1948; Zipf, 1945).

The above data are all quite compatible with an hypothesis that relates frequency and M as defined by the production method.

Reaction time. Another method which has been used to define M is that of determining the number of subjects who "got an association" within a very short interval after a verbal unit was presented to them. This was the method used by Glaze. One implication of the method, viewed in light of the frequency hypothesis, is the expectation that the higher the frequency of a word, the less is the average free-association reaction time to that word. A study by Hall & Ugelow (1957) confirms this. They used 24 words that occur with high frequency and 24 which occur with low frequency, all words having five letters. The mean reaction time to the high-frequency words was 179 msec., and to the low, 257 msec. Thus, if the experimenter had set a criterion of, say, 200 msec. as a cutoff point in the Glaze sense—if the subject had to get an association within 200 msec.—it is clear that more subjects would get associations to high-frequency words than would get them to the low-frequency words. By the Glaze definition, this would result in the high-frequency words having higher M than the low-frequency words.

SUMMARY

In this chapter we have indicated our intention of developing an hypothesis of frequency of experience as the critical variable underlying the relationship between M and learning.

1. An evaluation of the theoretical potential of various correlated dimensions defining M was made. Primary attention was given to the reasons for rejecting an associative-probability theory approach to an understanding of the effects of M. The associative-probability theory stems directly from the production method of defining M.

2. Experiments relating word frequency and learning rate were surveyed. These experiments show a clear positive effect, but in an absolute sense the differences are small. This might be due to the high absolute frequency of even the so-called low-frequency words, and to the shape of the function relating frequency and learning.

3. Distinct relationships were shown in data relating word frequency and other techniques of defining M.

REFERENCES

Attneave, F. Psychological probability as a function of experienced frequency. *J. exp. Psychol.*, 1953, 46, 81–86.

Barnes, J. M., & Underwood, B. J. "Fate" of first-list associations in transfer theory. *J. exp. Psychol.*, 1959, 58, 97–105.

Bousfield, W. A., & Cohen, B. H. The occurrence of clustering in the recall of randomly arranged words of different frequencies of usage. *J. gen. Psychol.*, 1955, 52, 83–95.

Bousfield, W. A., Cohen, B. H., & Whitmarsh, G. A. Associative clustering in the recall of words of different taxonomic frequencies of occurrence. *Psychol. Rep.*, 1958, 4, 39–44.

Bugelski, B. R. An attempt to reconcile unlearning and reproductive inhibition explanations of proactive inhibition. *J. exp. Psychol.*, 1948, 38, 670–682.

Cofer, C. N., & Shevitz, R. Word-association as a function of word-frequency. *Amer. J. Psychol.*, 1952, 65, 75–79.

Hall, J. F. Learning as a function of word-frequency. *Amer. J. Psychol.*, 1954, 67, 138–140.

Hall, J. F., & Ugelow, A. Free association time as a function of word frequency. *Canad. J. Psychol.*, 1957, 11, 29–32.

Howes, D. On the interpretation of word frequency as a variable affecting speed of recognition. *J. exp. Psychol.*, 1954, 48, 106–112.

Jacobs, A. Formation of new associations to words selected on the basis of reaction-time-GSR combinations. *J. abnorm. soc. Psychol.*, 1955, 51, 371–377.

Key, C. B. Recall as a function of perceived relations. *Arch. Psychol.*, N. Y., 1926, 13, No. 83.

Lepley, W. M. An hypothesis concerning the generation and use of synonyms. *J. exp. Psychol.*, 1950, 40, 527–530.

Mandler, G. Response factors in human learning. *Psychol. Rev.*, 1954, 61, 235–244.

Mandler, G., & Campbell, E. H. Effect of variation in associative frequency of stimulus and response members on paired-associate learning. *J. exp. Psychol.*, 1957, 54, 269–273.

Mandler, G., & Huttenlocher, J. The relationship between associative frequency, associative ability and paired-associate learning. *Amer. J. Psychol.*, 1956, 69, 424–428.

Peters, H. N. Mediate association. *J. exp. Psychol.*, 1935, 18, 20–48.

Peters, H. N. The relationship between familiarity of words and their memory value. *Amer. J. Psychol.*, 1936, 48, 572–585.

Riley, D. A., & Phillips, L. W. The effects of syllable familiarization on rote learning, association value, and reminiscence. *J. exp. Psychol.*, 1959, 57, 372–379.

Russell, W. A., & Storms, L. H. Implicit verbal chaining in paired-associate learning. *J. exp. Psychol.*, 1955, 49, 287–293.

Scheible, H. Individual meaningfulness ratings and speed of learning with observations on retroactive and proactive inhibition. Ph.D. dissertation, Northwestern Univer., 1954.

Thorndike, E. L. On the frequency of semantic changes in modern English. *J. gen. Psychol.*, 1948, 39, 23–27.

Thorndike, E. L., & Lorge, I. *The teacher's word book of 30,000 words.* New York: Columbia Univer. Press, 1944.

Underwood, B. J. Verbal learning in the educative processes. *Harv. Educ. Rev.*, 1959, 29, 107–117.

Underwood, B. J., & Schulz, R. W. Response dominance and rate of learning paired associates. *J. gen. Psychol.*, 1960, 62, 153–158.

Zipf, G. K. The meaning-frequency relationship of words. *J. gen. Psychol.*, 1945, 33, 251–256.

Chapter 5

Word Structure and Learning Materials

The question posed in the present chapter is: "Can the dimension of M, running through consonant and nonsense syllables, be translated into frequency values?" Or: "Are nonsense and consonant syllables, themselves not forming words, represented with differential frequency in words in our language and will these frequencies correspond to M values?"

Such questions could be answered if the relative frequency with which various three-letter combinations (trigrams) occur in the language were known. The only known available tables which might meet these requirements are those given by Pratt (1939), but since little is known about the sample of words from which these values were derived, we made a decision to undertake independent counts.*

TRIGRAMS BASED ON THE THORNDIKE-LORGE WORD LIST

The problem was conceived as one of breaking down words into successive trigrams. For example, consider the word *learning*. The suc-

* Subsequent to the making of these counts, Professor Leo Postman made available to us a letter he had received from Mr. Pratt in response to an inquiry about the sample of words used in the Pratt count. This letter reads in part: "In an effort to get a sampling that would hold good for written English generally, I used 500-word extracts from all sorts of texts—newspaper articles, letters, and various types of fiction and nonfiction books. About the only thing not included was military telegraphic text, where the word and letter counts are aberrant, and compilations have to be made separately."

cessive trigrams are LEA, EAR, ARN, RNI, NIN, and ING. If such a breakdown were made for a large number of words taken from English text, and if all like trigrams were added together, the result would be a count of the relative frequency with which trigrams (when defined as any successive three letters within the bounds of a word) occur in the language.

Of first consideration, of course, was the choice of sample of words to "break up" into trigrams. Such a sample should be reasonably representative of those seen or used by subjects who serve in learning experiments. However, it appeared to be virtually impossible to know what the population of words is that would be appropriate for such subjects. In part, this is due to the problem (mentioned briefly earlier) concerning the relative effect of written vs. spoken words on language repertoire and habits. But the problem is still complicated when one views only the written language. How does non-textual written material get handled? For example, the word STOP is seen by a driver many times each day and yet would probably appear with relatively low frequency in written discourse. There seemed to be no simple way by which such issues could be resolved in a satisfactory manner; therefore, certain arbitrary decisions were made in an effort to obtain data that would, at least, provide rough answers to the questions.

It was reasoned that the number of words sampled could be multiplied greatly, without having to break down many words into trigrams, by using the Thorndike-Lorge lists in which the frequency of occurrence of words in the language is given. Thus, if the trigram ARN appears in a word that occurs 17 times per million words, this trigram could be tallied as having occurred 17 times. Then, ARN might occur 43 times per million as indicated by its occurrence in a more frequent word. In the end, all such occurrences would be added together to get a grand total of the frequency with which that trigram occurred. In effect, a million words would have been sampled, and the summed frequencies would indicate frequency per million. We will now present the details of the sampling, and hereinafter will refer to the results of this procedure as the T-L Count.*

T-L Count Sample. The 20,000 (actually 19,440) most frequently used words are listed on pages 1–208 of the Thorndike-Lorge book. There are two columns on each page with an equal number of words in each column, except for small breaks to indicate a change in the initial letters of the words. With exceptions to be noted later, the sample consisted of the five top words in each column, thus resulting in a

* We acknowledge the careful work of Mr. Rex Hanks, who made this count.

total of 2,080 words. Each word was broken down into its trigrams (always two less than the number of letters in the word), and the appropriate frequency entry was made for each trigram. With little additional effort it was possible to make a count of two-letter sequences (bigrams) and also to obtain the frequency with which each individual letter occurred. Hence, the count was designed to give the relative frequency of trigrams, bigrams, and single letters.

The five words at the top of each column were always used, except in the following instances:

1. No contractions were used.
2. No words were used for which there was no entry in the frequency column (Column G).
3. No abbreviations were included, e.g., A.D.
4. If the same word was given twice, once capitalized and once not, and if there was only a single frequency value in Column G, the word was used only once. (See the word Armada).
5. When a hyphenated word appeared, only the letters before the hyphen were used.

Whenever a word was omitted for any of the above reasons, the sixth word became a replacement if it met the criteria. If not, the seventh word was selected, and so on, so that five words were always used from each column.

After the 2,080 words were broken down into trigrams (and bigrams), all identical trigrams were placed together and their frequency values summed. In the Thorndike-Lorge listing the words which occur at least 50 times per million, but not 100 times, are designated as *A* words. Words which occur 100 or more times are labelled *AA* words. Obviously, some decision was required to change these letters into numerical multipliers. The decision was to use 50 as the multiplier for the *A* words and 100 for the *AA* words. This patently produces underestimations. But, ignoring this matter for the moment, it can be seen that for each trigram and bigram there is a frequency value resulting from these procedures which would estimate the frequency of occurrence of a trigram in a million words of text material used by Thorndike and Lorge in their counts. As will be seen later, distributions of both the frequency of trigrams and bigrams are markedly skewed. Since no good reason has been found as yet for transforming the frequency values of the individual units into percentages or some other scale, the values are presented in Appendix D as raw frequencies.

Initial evaluation. As we used the results of the T-L Count, certain relationships with learning data and with nonsense and consonant syllables were discovered which seemed promising. But it also became apparent that the systematic error present in the count could be more serious than originally supposed. This error (resulting from the use of 50 as a multiplier for *A* words and 100 for *AA* words) could not be corrected if words were obtained from the T-L tables. Although a reasonable multiplier might be guessed for the *A* words (such as 65, to reflect the skewed distribution), no such estimate seemed possible for *AA* words. Another alternative would have been to use the Lorge Magazine Count. While this count was made from a restricted sampling of text material, all frequencies are given a numerical value; thus, the problem of assigning values for *AA* and *A* words would have been avoided. However, we decided to undertake a count in which continuous passages were employed (as opposed to sampling from the T-L list of words), and we will refer to this count as the U Count.

THE U COUNT

This count of trigrams and bigrams was made from approximately 15,000 words of written passages. The 15,000 words came from 150 passages of 100 words each, the 100 words being consecutive ones in a longer selection. All words were used, including contractions (e.g., don't), and were broken down as if the apostrophe were not present. Hyphenated words were considered to be two independent words. In obtaining the 150 samples we made an attempt to get 150 different authors and 150 different topics or subjects. The passages were selected from novels, short stories, advertisements, monthly magazines, weekly magazines, newspapers, news magazines, encyclopedias, and so on.*

In the T-L Count 2,080 words were broken down, whereas in the present one 15,000 words were involved. Of course, in the latter count the sums include only the actual frequencies of the various trigrams and bigrams. Therefore, no direct comparisons are meaningful between the absolute frequencies of the two counts. In the T-L Count the frequencies refer to number per million words; in the U Count

---

* The U Count was a hand tabulation made by the senior author. As noted, approximately 15,000 words were included. However, no definitive checks were made on this. For each text sampled, a passage of 100 words was counted. Then the words were broken into trigrams, but no check was made to see if the passage did indeed include the same number of trigrams as were recorded. Minor errors are, therefore, a distinct possibility.

they refer to number per 15,000 words. An inspection of the tables in the appendix shows differences (relatively), and many of these appear to be due to the fact that high-frequency words in the T-L Count were underestimated in frequency. Nevertheless, as will be seen, there is considerable agreement between the two counts.

SOME GENERAL FACTS FROM THE COUNTS

Single-letter frequency. For each count the frequency of occurrence of individual letters was determined. The rank of each letter is shown in Table 6, along with the ranks from three other counts (Encyclopedia Americana, 1956; Lysing, 1936; Attneave, 1953).

TABLE 6. Frequency of Use (Ranks) of Individual Letters as Given in Five Different Samples

(Absolute frequencies in U Count are given in last column)

Letter	Americana	Lysing	Attneave	T-L Count	U Count	Absolute *f*
A	3	3	3	2	3	5417
B	21	20	20	19	20	1049
C	13	12	12	10	13	1893
D	10	11	10	14	11	2697
E	1	1	1	1	1	8532
F	15	15	17	17	15	1494
G	19	17	15	15	16	1433
H	8	9	9	12	9	3596
I	4	5	6	5	5	4993
J	23	24	24	24	24	119
K	22	22	22	22	22	493
L	11	10	11	9	10	2761
M	14	14	14	16	14	1751
N	7	6	4	6	6	4820
O	6	4	5	7	4	4982
P	18	19	18	13	19	1308
Q	24	25	26	25	26	61
R	9	8	7	4	8	4217
S	5	7	8	8	7	4578
T	2	2	2	3	2	5983
U	12	13	13	11	12	2085
V	20	21	21	20	21	688
W	16	16	16	21	17	1378
X	25	23	23	23	23	132
Y	17	18	19	18	18	1331
Z	26	26	25	26	25	67

As may be seen in Table 6, the correspondence among the five samples is high. Rank-order correlations among the five samples are shown in Table 7. All correlations except those involving the T-L Count are virtually unity. The somewhat lower correlations resulting from frequency values from the T-L Count confirm the belief that high-frequency words were not being given enough weight by the particular multipliers used.

Bigrams. The complete listing of the bigrams with the frequency for each as determined in the T-L and U counts are shown in Appendix D. The T-L Count produced 405 different bigrams—405 different two-letter combinations. The U Count resulted in 432 different bigrams. The five most frequent bigrams from the T-L Count are ER, RE, ST, IN, and EN. From the U Count the five most frequent are TH, HE, IN, AN, and ER. As is apparent, the overlap is far from complete, and this again is undoubtedly attributable to the underestimation of the high-frequency words in the T-L Count.

TABLE 7. Rank Correlations for Frequency of Use of Individual Letters in Five Samples *

	(2)	(3)	(4)	(5)
(1)	.99	.98	.94	.99
(2)	—	.99	.96	.99
(3)	—	—	.96	.99
(4)	—	—	—	.96

* (1) *Encyclopedia Americana,* 1956
  (2) Lysing, 1936
  (3) Attneave, 1953
  (4) T-L Count
  (5) U Count

A frequency distribution with frequency ranges for the bigrams in each count is shown in Table 8. Both distributions are markedly skewed. Again it should be noted that no direct comparison between the values in the two counts is meaningful. However, relative comparisons can be made, and an inspection of the tables shows that the agreement is fairly high. As a specific index of agreement, several rank-order correlations have been calculated between the two counts. Correlations were determined separately for bigrams starting with A, G, M, N, S, W, and X, and these correlations, shown in Table 9, vary from .81 to .94.

Trigrams: T-L Count vs. U Count. A complete listing of the trigrams is given in Appendix D. The T-L Count resulted in 2,250 different trigrams, and the U Count, in 2,844. The frequency range for the T-L Count was from 1 per million to 1,318 per million. For the U Count the range was from 1 to 1,201 per 15,000 words. The distribution of frequencies is shown in Table 10. Again it can be seen that the distributions are markedly skewed, with over 50 per cent of the trigrams falling in the lowest frequency range in the table. In the T-L

TABLE 8. Frequency Distributions of Frequencies of 405 Different Bigrams in the T-L Count and 432 in the U Count

T-L Count		U Count	
Intervals	*f*	Intervals	*f*
1– 100	175	1– 25	178
101– 200	53	26– 50	49
201– 300	28	51– 75	44
301– 400	24	76–100	18
401– 500	23	101–125	18
501– 600	20	126–150	16
601– 700	16	151–175	15
701– 800	7	176–200	14
801– 900	13	201–225	8
901–1000	8	226–250	13
1001–1100	7	251–275	6
1101–1200	3	276–300	8
1201–1300	5	301–400	12
1301–1400	3	401–500	9
1401–1500	3	501–600	7
1501–1600	2	601–700	7
1601–1700	2	701–800	4
1701–1800	1	801–over	6
1801–1900	—		
1901–2000	1		
2001–over	11		
Total	405	Total	432

TABLE 9. Rank Correlations of Frequencies of Bigrams of T-L and U Counts for Bigrams Starting with A, G, M, N, S, W, and X

First Letter	Number Different Second Letters *	Rank Correlation
A	26	.92
G	18	.83
M	15	.94
N	26	.85
S	22	.94
W	17	.87
X	12	.81

* If the frequency was zero for one sample and one or more for the other for a given bigram, zero was the value assigned the former in calculating the rank correlations. The values in the middle column indicate that for both samples considered together, this many letters were involved.

Count the five most frequent trigrams were ENT, ION, ING, TER, and TIO; in the U Count the most frequent were THE, AND, ING, HER, and ENT.

The correspondence between the two counts is appreciably less for the trigrams than for the bigrams. As an indication of this a series of rank correlations were calculated. Successive sets of 25 trigrams each were obtained by taking every tenth trigram in an alphabetical listing, a total of 13 such sets was drawn, and a rank correlation determined for each set between the frequencies in each count. The following correlations were obtained: .73, .73, .62, .56, .45, .61, .44, .34, .51, .67, .67, .77, and .35. Eight of these correlations are significant beyond the 1 per cent level of confidence, and the mean correlation (.57) would

TABLE 10. Frequency Distributions of 2250 Trigrams from the T-L Count and 2844 from the U Count

T-L Count		U Count	
Frequency Ranges	Number Trigrams	Frequency Ranges	Number Bigrams
1– 25	1295	1– 5	1486
26– 50	289	6– 10	443
51– 75	166	11– 15	278
76–100	107	16– 20	147
101–125	116	21– 25	115
126–150	65	26– 30	68
151–175	51	31– 35	60
176–200	31	36– 40	43
201–225	29	41– 45	25
226–250	21	46– 50	32
251–275	23	51– 55	19
276–300	7	56– 60	18
301–400	29	61– 65	23
401–over	21	66– 70	9
		71– 75	12
		76–100	24
		101–over	42
Total	2250	Total	2844

also be significant if interpreted as coming from a single sample of 25 cases. However, while such evidence leaves little doubt of a positive relationship between the frequencies of trigrams in the two counts, it is quite apparent that as a measure of reliability, a relationship of this magnitude is not very satisfactory. Undoubtedly the underestimation of high frequencies in the T-L Count has lowered the correlation. But the sample sizes must also be indirectly responsible. For these rank correlations, where there were 25 entries from each count, the average number of zeros in the T-L Count was 6.9. This means that out of 25 random trigrams, there were approximately seven trigrams which occurred with a frequency of at least one in the U Count but which did not appear at all in the T-L Count. It is perhaps not surprising, therefore, that the correlations are no higher than they are.

Trigrams: U Count and Pratt Count. It was noted earlier that Pratt gives tables of the frequency of occurrence of trigrams in his book on cryptography (1939). The frequencies are based on 20,000 words of text material.

Corresponding distributions of the frequencies of trigrams for the Pratt Count and U Count are shown in Table 11. A study of the distributions allows certain conclusions to be drawn concerning the nature of Pratt's sample relative to that used for the U Count. It should be

TABLE 11. Frequency Distributions of 2509 Trigrams from the Pratt Count and 2844 from the U Count

Frequency Ranges	U Number Trigrams	Pratt Number Trigrams
1– 5	1486	1381
6– 10	443	424
11– 15	278	212
16– 20	147	123
21– 25	115	76
26– 30	68	65
31– 35	60	53
36– 40	43	43
41– 45	25	27
46– 50	32	15
51– 55	19	19
56– 60	18	13
61– 65	23	10
66– 70	9	8
71– 75	12	2
76–100	24	14
101–over	42	24
Totals	2844	2509

noted first that Pratt obtained only 2,509 different trigrams from 20,-000 words as compared with 2,844 different trigrams from 15,000 words in the U Count. This difference could be produced by two factors, either separately or jointly. First, Pratt's sample of words may be more homogeneous than that used for the U Count. That is, the number of *different* words in the Pratt Count could be less than in the U Count, for this should result in fewer different trigrams. The other possibility is that the words in Pratt's sample are, on the average, shorter than those in the U Count. This would result in fewer total trigrams, although not necessarily in fewer different trigrams.

If Pratt's sample of words consisted of fewer different words (although of equal average length) than the U Count, it would be expected that in several categories (frequency ranges), especially in the upper categories, the absolute frequency of trigrams in the Pratt

Count should be greater than in the U Count. This does not happen even though Pratt's sample consisted of 5,000 more words than did the U Count. It might then be concluded that Pratt's sample consisted of as many different words as the U-Count sample but that his words were, on the average, shorter. However, this is also not likely to be the case since it is known that the less frequently a word occurs in the language, the greater the number of letters it is likely to contain. Thus, the conclusion seems inevitable that Pratt's sample, compared to that used in the U Count, consisted of fewer *different* words and that, therefore, his words were shorter on the average. This is supported by comparing frequencies of certain specific trigrams. For example, the trigram ING often occurs as a part of fairly long words. Pratt records a total of 317 instances of ING in 20,000 words whereas the U Count recorded 512 occurrences in 15,000 words. Certain other facts suggest that Pratt's sample of words came from texts having shorter sentences than those used in the U Count. For example, AND occurs 154 times in Pratt's tables, but 548 times in the U Count. Of these 548 occurrences, 437 were occurrences as a word (*not* a part of a longer word). This suggests that Pratt's text may have consisted of short sentences in which connectives occur with less frequency than they do in longer sentences.

The question now asked is how do the relative frequencies of trigrams compare for the two counts. Ten samples of 25 trigrams each were selected by taking every tenth trigram in a listing. For five of these samples, every tenth trigram having a frequency of one or more in the U Count was used (regardless of frequency in the Pratt Count); for the other five, this procedure was reversed. The rank order correlations ranged from .65 to .94, with the mean for the ten correlations being .78. The relationship between the frequencies in the two counts is respectable and considerably higher than that between the U Count and the T-L Count.

Trigrams: All Counts Combined. The values for the Pratt Count are also included in the appendix. Since it is believed that these trigrams may have some use in selecting materials for learning experiments, the question may be raised as to which sample is the "best." There is no satisfactory answer. The objection to the T-L Count is the likelihood that it underestimates the frequencies for the more frequent trigrams. But if it is true that learning rate differs but little for these higher frequencies (as the data in a previous chapter indicated), then very little bias can result. The U Count was based on a greater number of different words than the other two, but the Pratt Count is based on the largest number of words. All facts considered, it would seem that the most stable values would result if the frequencies for all three samples were summed. Theoretically the summed values would represent frequency of occurrence in 1,035,000 words. Such a total column is included in the tables in the appendix, and a distribution of frequencies based on the summed values is shown in Table 12.

TABLE 12. Distribution of Trigram Frequencies for the Three Counts Combined

Frequency Ranges	f	% of total
1– 5	1309	36.9
6– 10	400	11.4
11– 20	417	11.8
21– 30	228	6.4
31– 40	151	4.3
41– 50	130	3.7
51– 60	111	3.1
61– 70	68	1.9
71– 80	75	2.1
81– 90	46	1.3
91–100	52	1.5
100–140	183	5.2
141–180	113	3.2
181–220	60	1.6
221–260	46	1.3
261–300	38	1.1
Over 300	109	3.1
Totals	3537	99.9

Pertinent evidence concerning the overlap among the three samples is given in Table 13. Nearly 30 per cent of the trigrams appeared in

TABLE 13. Overlap in Trigram Occurrence Among the Three Counts

One Count Only	Number Trigrams	Per Cent of Total
T-L Only	310	8.8
U Only	448	12.7
Pratt Only	283	8.0
Two Counts		
T-L and U	270	7.6
T-L and Pratt	100	2.8
U and Pratt	556	15.7
All Three Counts	1570	44.4
Totals	3537	100.0

only one count, the greatest frequency of these "unique" trigrams being in the U Count (12.7 per cent of the total of 3,537 different trigrams resulting from combining all samples). Approximately 25 per cent of the trigrams occurred in two samples, and about 45 per cent were recorded in all three counts.

A word of caution may be inserted concerning the use of these trigrams in learning experiments. It would be our judgment that one should not "bank on" the frequency value of a single trigram as being accurate. Thus, to determine learning as a function of different frequency ranges, it would probably be prudent to *sample* a frequency range by choosing (at random if possible) several items from each of the specified ranges.

WORD STRUCTURE AND MEANINGFULNESS

Now that the relative frequencies with which various letter combinations occur in the language is known, we may turn toward answering the question posed at the beginning of the chapter. Can frequency be related to M of consonant and nonsense syllables? Before considering answers to this question for the trigram frequencies, certain relationships between individual letter frequency and consonant and nonsense syllables will be presented.

Letter Frequency

In 1939 Waters asked whether or not nonsense syllables of different association values "used" consonants with a frequency that differed systematically from their frequency of use in the written language. He also asked the same question about consonant syllables. The answer in both cases was affirmative. He determined that the six most frequently used consonants in the language were T, N, R, S, H, and D, and the six least frequently used were V, K, J, X, Z, and Q. Then he examined the Glaze 100 per cent syllables and 0 per cent syllables to determine the frequency with which each class of letters (high use or low use) appeared. In the 100 per cent syllables, 41 per cent of the consonants were the six most frequently used in the language, and 15 per cent were those most infrequently used. For the 0 per cent syllables, only 10 per cent of the consonants were among the six most frequent (in the language), and 56 per cent were among the six least frequent.

For the Witmer consonant syllables the same relationship appears. Waters used Witmer syllables having association values of from 92–100 per cent and, also, those from 0–4 per cent. In the former, 56 per cent of the consonants were from among the six most frequently used consonants in ordinary language and only 9 per cent from the six least frequently used. For the low-association value syllables, 8 per cent were from the most frequently used consonants and 66 per cent from the six least frequent consonants.

Water's work makes it clear that the most frequently used letters in the language are more likely to occur in syllables of high M than in syllables of low M. By the use of different techniques, the present analyses merely confirm Water's findings.

If, as M of syllables increases, the frequency of occurrence of the letters in the syllables approaches more and more closely their frequency in written English, clear changes in the correlation between frequency of consonants in syllables and frequency in the language should be present. That such is true is shown in Table 14. There are

TABLE 14. Relationships between Frequency of Consonants in Nonsense and Consonant Syllables for Various Association-Values, and Frequency of these Consonants in Written English

(The entries are rank-order correlations)

Glaze Values	*rho*	Witmer Values	*rho*
0–20	−.78	0–13	−.73
40–60	−.60	50	+.62
80–100	+.68	83–100	+.86

two parts to the table, one dealing with Witmer's syllables and the other with Glaze's syllables. Three ranges of association value have been used for each type of material. For the Glaze syllables the rank correlation between the low-association syllables and frequency of consonants in written English (as determined in U Count) is high negative. This also holds for the middle range, but for the syllables having association values from 80–100 per cent, the correlation is significantly positive. It is worth pointing out that this trend in the correlations suggests a positively accelerated relationship between M and consonant frequency. This relationship is also suggested in other analyses (to be presented shortly).

The negative to positive relationship between association value and letter frequency also holds for Witmer syllables. However, not only is the correlation for consonant syllables of 50 per cent M higher than that for the middle range of Glaze, but also the correlation at the high end is noticeably higher. Some understanding of these facts is gained by an examination of the Witmer syllables having high M. Many of the consonant syllables at the high end of the Witmer scale appear as if

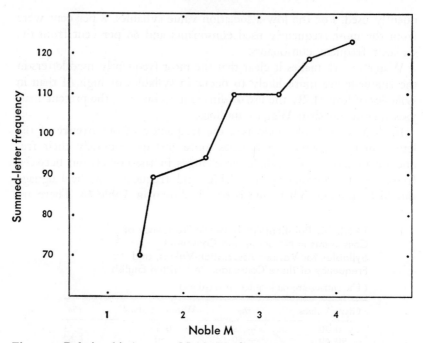

Figure 8. Relationship between Noble M of nonsense syllables and summed-letter frequency (see text for complete explanation).

they were four-letter words with the vowel missing. Some examples are: PNK, SNK, DRK, BLD, BND, GLD. Insofar as this observation holds generally and insofar as these "words" contain consonants in a frequency approximating that of the language, the correlation should be high.

For nonsense syllables, on the other hand, the situation is different. Given the first consonant and the vowel, many high frequency consonants in the third position will form words. Thus RAQ is a nonsense syllable, but RAT is obviously not. Therefore, the relatively low correlation between frequency of consonants in the language and their frequency in high M nonsense syllables is probably attributable to the fact that many high M "nonsense syllables" which would increase the correlation are automatically eliminated because they are words.

A second way of viewing the relationship between single-letter frequency and M of syllables is to see if it is possible to derive values for each letter of a syllable and then combine these values to discover if there is a relationship between them and the M values. For this analysis the 100 nonsense syllables scaled by Noble have been used.

To get a numerical value for each letter, we assigned a value of 100 to the most frequent letter in the U Count (the letter E), and then to other letters assigned values based upon their absolute frequency of occurrence relative to the absolute frequency of E. These values ranged from 1 to 100. Each letter in a syllable was then assigned its appropriate number, and the values were summed to get a total value for the syllable. Seven groupings of Noble's 100 syllables were made, such that there is an increasing level of M from the first to the last grouping. The plot of the relationship between letter sums and the M values is shown in Fig. 8. It is quite clear that the relationship is positive; as Noble's association values increase, so also do the summed values increase.

The foregoing analyses have shown that M of nonsense and consonant syllables can be understood or translated in terms of frequency of letters making up the syllables. The more frequently a letter occurs in the language, the more frequently it will occur in syllables of high M than in syllables of low M. Now, a somewhat less atomistic approach will be taken.

Trigram Frequency and Meaningfulness

Nonsense syllables. In this section we ask the question: "Is trigram frequency related to M of nonsense syllables?" For the first analysis the Glaze values have been used. For each Glaze value the proportion of syllables which also occur as trigrams was determined. Out of the 3,537 trigrams observed in all three counts combined, 695 were found to be nonsense syllables in the Glaze list. Since 1,995 Glaze syllables were used in this determination, it can be said that about 35 per cent of the Glaze syllables appeared as trigrams in one or more of the three counts.

The likelihood of a trigram appearing in the Glaze list is directly related to the Glaze association value. The essential data are shown in Fig. 9. Of those syllables having 0 per cent values, approximately 4 per cent occur as trigrams. Of those having 100 per cent values, 92 per cent occur as trigrams. It may be noted that the greatest increase in frequency of trigrams appearing as Glaze syllables occurs in the upper part of the scale.

The mean frequency with which a trigram occurs is also directly related to the Glaze values, as may be seen in Fig. 10. Although the curve is quite irregular, there seems little doubt that frequency of occurrence as a trigram in the language and M value are related.

The counts have given 3,537 different trigrams. It is not known, of

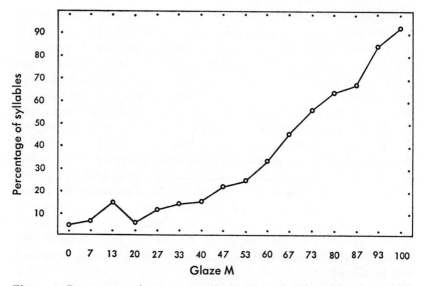

Figure 9. Percentage of nonsense syllables at each Glaze M value which occur as trigrams in words.

course, how many different trigrams actually exist in the language. If all of these were available, it would be expected that the proportion of occurrences of trigrams as nonsense syllables would increase for all association values but would increase more for the lower than for the higher values. The present data show nothing in an absolute sense; they show clearly that the more meaningful a nonsense syllable, the greater is the probability that that syllable occurs as a trigram in the language and the greater will its frequency be in the language.

As a further measure of the relationship between appearance of a trigram as a nonsense syllable and the M value of the syllable, the 100 nonsense syllables scaled by Noble were used. A biserial correlation between his association values and whether or not the syllable was also a trigram yielded a value of .79.

Consonant syllables. Since Witmer's consonant syllables are made up of three consecutive consonants, it would be expected that few of them would also occur as trigrams in the language. Indeed, the present count shows that only 4 per cent of these syllables also appear among the 3,537 trigrams. However, the data show that the higher the M of the syllable, the greater is the probability that it will occur as a trigram. The relationship is shown in Fig. 11, where Witmer values have been grouped to give stability. At the low association values, none of the

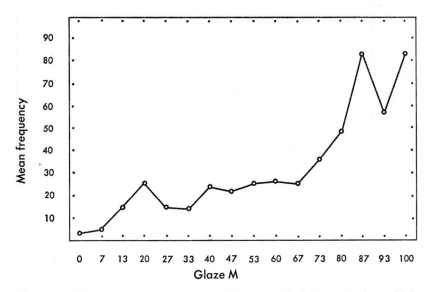

Figure 10. Frequency of nonsense syllables at each Glaze M value which occur as trigrams in words.

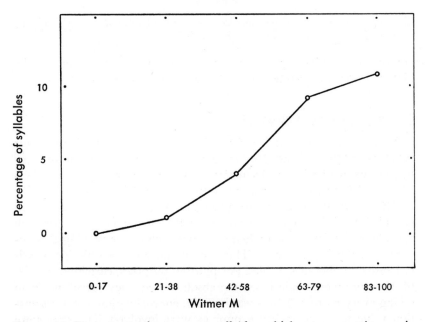

Figure 11. Percentage of consonant syllables which occur as trigrams in words as a function of Witmer M.

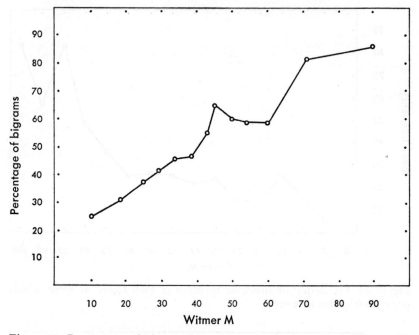

Figure 12. Percentage of bigrams in consonant syllables at each Witmer M value which also occur as bigrams in words.

consonant syllables appears among the language trigrams, but at the highest association values 11 per cent do so appear.

Bigram Frequency and Meaningfulness

As shown above, relatively few of the trigrams appear as consonant syllables in Witmer's list. Reverting to a somewhat more atomistic approach, we may ask how frequently *bigrams* appear in consonant syllables and how they are related to association value.

For this analysis every tenth syllable in Witmer's list was used. Each syllable contains, of course, two potential language bigrams. For each syllable it was determined whether or not each of the two bigrams occurred in the Total Count. Thus, the number of possible bigrams is twice the number of syllables. For plotting purposes, certain groupings of M values were made when the absolute frequency (resulting from taking every tenth syllable) was low. An approximation of the association value was made when groupings were involved. The results are shown in Fig. 12. For low association values, 25 per cent of the two-letter combinations occur as bigrams in the language; for high association values, 87 per cent occur.

SUMMARY

The purpose of the analyses presented in this chapter was to translate M values of consonant and nonsense syllables into frequency values. Frequency here refers to the frequency with which specified two and three-letter sequences occur in English words. All analyses clearly showed the relationship between M and frequency, e.g., as M increased there was a corresponding increase in the probability that the consonant or nonsense syllable also occurred as a three-letter sequence in words. Such a relationship was further elaborated in terms of frequency of single letters and frequency of bigrams.

REFERENCES

Attneave, F. Psychological probability as a function of experienced frequency. *J. exp. Psychol.*, 1953, 46, 81–86.

Encyclopedia Americana. 1956 Edition, 17, p. 285.

Lysing, H. *Secret writing, an introduction to cryptograms, ciphers, and codes.* New York: D. Kemp, 1936.

Pratt, F. *Secret and urgent.* Indianapolis: Bobbs-Merrill, 1939.

Waters, R. H. The law of acquaintance. *J. exp. Psychol.*, 1939, 24, 180–191.

Chapter 6

Frequency and the
Spew Hypothesis

The two previous chapters have been devoted to showing how frequency of experience may underlie scaled M. Without exception, all definitions of M can be translated into frequency terms, thereby leading to the principle that the higher the M of a verbal unit, the more frequently has that unit been experienced. The exposition now turns to an initial consideration of how frequency is believed to exert its influence on certain phases of the verbal-learning process.

CONSEQUENCES OF FREQUENCY

As an explanatory principle, frequency is, to say the least, a decidedly unpopular notion. Classical associationism (last systematically represented by Robinson, 1932), in which frequency (or exercise or repetition) figured prominently, was replaced by an associationism in which mere frequency was of little or no consequence for learning. Frequency of reward or frequency of drive reduction was held to be important, perhaps, but mere repetition was not. Frequency could not be avoided for it is the basic plotting variable of learning, but it was said to hold no fundamental theoretical importance. Frequency was merely a vehicle by means of which the critical processes operated in the learning situation.

The present argument, which assumes an importance for frequency *per se*, will not challenge directly the importance of reward or of drive reduction in the formation of new associations. This is not for lack of temerity but rather for lack of relevant data for the learning topic with which we are dealing. The subjects on whom most verbal-learning data have been collected are college students; they bring to the situation a great deal of learning which may well have occurred because of rewards. The problem with which the present authors are grappling is how new learning gets established on top of or through the aegis of this old learning. The rewards accruing to a college student learning a list of paired associates appear remote from the situation in which a rat gets a piece of food for making a right turn in a T-maze. But the rewards may be there, and they may be specific to a given association as well as to the situation or task in general. Most subjects, when instructed to do so, do learn a list of words. Presumably there is motivation to do so (or lack of motivation not to do so). That subjects will do this may result from a long history of learning which has often been rewarded. The present argument contributes nothing pro or con to these matters, and a disavowal can be made of any intent in this direction.

Without considering the problem of reward or any other factor which presumes to operate *via* frequency, we believe that some further understanding of the verbal learning process can be obtained by referring to certain consequences of frequency. These consequences, while not being ignored by theorists, have been given too little attention.

The term "frequency of experience" will have to retain a certain amount of ambiguity, because frequency may occur in several ways, and at the present time it is not known if the changes assumed to occur as a consequence are equivalent for the different "kinds" of frequency. Reading verbal units is one way to increase frequency; hearing is another, and talking, which involves recall, is still a third. Previous analyses have used frequency of printed words as an index of frequency of experience in general. While undoubtedly the correlation between the frequency of occurrence of a printed word and its frequency of occurrence in oral communication is high and positive, the correspondence is probably far from perfect. Furthermore, it is quite possible that the changes assumed to occur as a consequence of frequency are not equivalent for the different kinds of frequency. It was noted earlier that emitted frequency (in the sense of oral recall) may produce more change than does reading frequency. Indeed, if one wishes to interpret the studies on active recitation versus passive study within this framework, the emitted frequency does seem to be of greater importance. However, the present work gives no evidence on this matter, so when the term frequency is used, it will mean any and all of the different ways by which increases in frequency may occur.

The spew hypothesis. The general hypothesis is this: the order of availability of verbal units is directly related to the frequency with which the units have been experienced. Other things being equal, therefore, the more frequently a verbal unit has been experienced, the more quickly will this become a response in a new associative connection. Note that this does not say that the association is formed more rapidly as a function of frequency; it says merely that the more frequently experienced unit (because it is more readily available) *starts* entering into a new associative connection earlier than the less frequently experienced unit. The issue of the *rapidity* with which the new associative connection develops is a special problem.

This, then, is the spew hypothesis; the order of emission of verbal units is directly related to frequency of experience with those units. Certain restrictions must be made on the general principle when it is applied to a specific learning situation. This will be done at a later point. The next step is to consider certain data which have suggested the spew notion.

SUGGESTIVE EVIDENCE ON SPEW
Classical Free Association

What is the nature of responses elicited in the classical free-association experiment? It can be shown that in spite of some restriction presumed to be placed on the subject by the particular stimuli employed, the responses which occur most frequently to stimuli in a free-association test are those which have the highest frequency in everyday usage. Two studies will show this.

Johnson's analyses (1956). From the Kent-Rosanoff tables Johnson chose 10 stimulus words and for these words examined the responses they elicited. For each word he selected the 10 most and the 10 least frequent responses. For the most frequent responses it was found that 84 per cent occur with a frequency of 50 times or more per million in the Thorndike-Lorge list, whereas only 48 per cent of the least frequent responses had equally high ratings.

In a second test of the relationship, Johnson took all the responses given to five stimuli and sorted them into three groups according to the frequency with which they occurred. Then he took a rough median of frequency of occurrence for these words (again using the Thorndike-Lorge table). The results are shown in Table 15. Clearly, as frequency of the words increased as responses to stimuli, the greater was the associated frequency in the Thorndike-Lorge count.

TABLE 15. Frequency of Response to Five Kent Rosanoff Stimuli and Frequency of Appearance in the Thorndike-Lorge Count

(Johnson, 1956)

Kent-Rosanoff Frequency	Number of Words	Thorndike-Lorge Median *
Once	360	42
Two-Three	138	65
Four or More	152	100 plus

* Number times per million words

In concluding his article, Johnson says:

Presumably they [common words from Thorndike-Lorge] are produced more often because the availability of a word for free association depends in part on its general familiarity or response-strength regardless of any associations with specific stimulus words (p. 126).

Johnson clearly points out, however, that other factors in addition to familiarity (such as set) also operate. Yet, even when specific stimuli are used as in the Kent-Rosanoff list, it is of great importance to realize that the words which occur as responses are words which, generally speaking, the subject has experienced many, many times.

Howes' correlation (1957). Howes tackled the same problem as did Johnson. Again the responses to the Kent-Rosanoff stimuli were used, and these were correlated with frequency of use measures as given in the Lorge magazine count. Howes estimates the correlation between the two arrays to be .94 when certain words that he calls interstitial words (e.g., *the*, *and*) are omitted from consideration. Howes believes that if all factors for the frequency count and for the free-association experiment were comparable, the correlation would be unity. Thus, frequency of input and frequency of output in a relatively free responding situation are closely associated.

Freedom of Response within a Category

Cohen, Bousfield, & Whitmarsh (1957). In preparing materials for studies of learning, these investigators obtained free responses to category stimuli. That is to say, they gave subjects the names of categories and asked them to write the first *four* specific associates the category name made them think of. A total of 43 category names, such as *fish, articles of furniture, male first names, vegetables,* and so on were given. The 43 category names were presented to 400 subjects, 200 each of men and women, all college students. As a rough check on the relationship between frequency of occurrence of a member of a category and frequency of occurrence in the Thorndike-Lorge tables, we have taken the responses for some of these categories and determined the Thorndike-Lorge frequencies. More specifically, 15 categories were chosen. For each category three responses which occurred with high frequency and three which occurred with low frequency were chosen. Usually these included the three *most* frequent and three among the *least* frequent, although not always the three last ones in the ranked lists. The frequency for each response was determined if it fell among the 20,000 most frequently occurring words. The intent is to show that those responses which occurred most frequently to the category stimuli are also words which occur with higher frequency in the language than those which occurred least frequently.

The outcome of the comparisons are shown in Table 16. While some may quibble about the "unfairness" of including certain words with multiple-category usage (e.g., *wine* is a color but also a beverage), the results show that those responses given by the greatest number of subjects are also words which occur with relatively high frequency in the written language.

First names and the frequency hypothesis. Among the categories used in the above experiment was one called "male first names." The results in Table 16 apparently show that those names which occur most frequently in the written language are also those most likely to be given by a subject. Further details on the meaning of this fact is available from a study by Cromwell (1956).

The subject was given eight blank cards and asked to write the names of eight different people who had the same first name. The first name was specified by the experimenter with different subgroups being given different first names. The cards were numbered so that the order in which the names were written was available to the experimenter. Following this the subjects ranked the eight names for: (1) how well they liked the person; (2) how much contact they had had with each; (3) how long it had been since they had seen each person; (4) how well they knew each person. Cromwell was interested in the relationship between the order in which the names were written

TABLE 16. Relationship between Frequency of Response to Category Stimuli and Frequency of Occurrence of Response in the Language

(For each category three frequent and three infrequent responses are given. After each response the Thorndike-Lorge Frequency is given in parentheses. A dash indicates that the word does not occur in the 20,000 most frequently used words). (Cohen, Bousfield, & Whitmarsh, 1957)

Category Stimuli	Frequent Responses		Infrequent Responses	
Fish	trout	17	grouper	—
	bass	7	chub	1
	perch	23	crayfish	2
Furniture	chair	AA	setee	1
	table	AA	rocker	2
	bed	AA	commode	—
Part of Body	arm (s)	AA	trachea	—
	leg (s)	AA	tongue	A
	head	AA	thumb	27
Male Name	John	AA	Vinton	—
	Bob	A	Wallace	7
	Joe	38	Wesley	1
Insect	fly	AA	scorpion	3
	ant	38	chigger	—
	bee	A	aphid	—
Four-Footed Animal	dog	AA	elk	7
	cat	A	muskrat	7
	horse	AA	antelope	7
Flower	rose	AA	mayflower	2
	violet	34	goldenrod	1
	tulip	8	cornflower	1
Tree	maple	18	balsam	2
	oak	A	sassafras	1
	elm	16	ming	—
Instrument	piano	26	zither	—
	violin	11	tambourine	—
	trumpet	17	ukelele	1
Clothing	shirt	47	cape	34
	hat	AA	petticoat	8
	dress	AA	cloak	28
Bird	robin	48	snipe	2
	sparrow	22	heron	6
	canary	8	mynah	—
Metal	iron	AA	strontium	—
	copper	46	selenium	—
	steel	A	plutonium	—
Vegetable	carrot	9	endive	—
	pea	30	yam	1
	potato	A	kale	1
Fruit	apple	A	melon	5
	pear	21	raisin	7
	orange	A	blueberry	4
Color	red	AA	magenta	—
	blue	AA	wine	A
	green	AA	beige	1

originally and the rankings to the various questions. The point to be made here is that the order of recall and frequency of contact were correlated very highly (.96). This is taken to mean that frequency of contact, hence, probably frequency of name emission, is closely related to the order of output. This order effect will now be discussed in somewhat more detail.

Frequency and Order of Output

The spew hypothesis states that frequency of intake determines directly the order of output. Except for the last study, none of the data presented thus far is relevant to the order effect. For example, when investigators asked subjects to name the members of a category, the data presented merely indicated frequency of response; they did not indicate the order in which the responses were given.

The issue may be made clear with a hypothetical illustration. Suppose a subject is asked to give the first three members of a category which occur to him and he is given the category stimulus, "birds." Three subjects could write three responses each in the following order:

Subject 1	*Subject 2*	*Subject 3*
heron	eagle	thrasher
starling	owl	wren
robin	robin	robin

If these responses were added simply with an eye to total frequency, it is clear that the response "robin" has been given most frequently. But this most frequent response is not the one given first by the subjects. Is this what actually happens? The answer is unequivocally "no."

Bousfield & Barclay (1950) asked their subjects to name as many members of a class, e.g., "birds," as they could. The results leave no doubt that the *order* of emission and frequency are highly related. In a study by Brown (1915) the subjects were asked to write all the advertisements they could remember. Those advertisements recalled by the greatest number of subjects were also those recalled first.

Individual differences and frequency. To restate the hypothesis, when the subject is faced with a relatively unstructured situation, the order of output of verbal units is directly related to frequency of input. It seems inevitable that individual differences in spew order could or should be related to differences in nature of intake. No attempt will be made to review the several studies which are relevant; a summary of a number of such studies is given by Foley & MacMillan (1943). In their own study these investigators chose subjects with different professional backgrounds (students in first year law, second year law, first year medicine, second year medicine, and non-professional students). There were clear differences in the responses given by these various groups to the same stimuli, and it is inferred that the differences are a function of differences in the experiences of the subgroups, which in turn reflect different frequencies of experience with particular verbal units.

To jump a little ahead of the over-all scheme of presentation, we may note briefly that several studies have shown differences in *learning* rate of the same materials by different groups known to vary in a manner relevant to the words being learned. For example, Bousfield & Cohen (1956) show that after a single presentation of a long list of words, men and women differ systematically on the words they recall. Words considered masculine words (e.g., *aileron, fuselage, cowling*) are better recalled by men than by women, and feminine words (e.g., *chintz, crepe, faille*) are better recalled by women than by men. These differences could well be due to frequency differences in the experiences of the two sexes.

There are a number of other studies in which different learning rates for the same words were related to differences in attitude structure of the groups. For example, Havron & Cofer (1957) show that:

> . . . it is easier for Religious *Ss* to learn paired associates in which the response word is a religious one than it is for them to learn paired associates in which the response word has a political economic meaning. The reverse finding was obtained for *Ss* with strong politico-economic values (p. 98).

In all such studies it is reasonable to assume that the fundamental variable is M when this is defined as differences in frequency. They would carry more conviction, of course, if differences in frequencies of experience were known.

It shall be concluded that the data thus far fully support a statement that in a relatively free responding situation the responses which have been most frequently experienced by the subjects are given most frequently, all subjects considered. Furthermore, the order in which the responses occur is predictable from the frequency with which the words have been experienced.

The above statements can be supported in a general way by the work on determination of perceptual thresholds for words. In these experiments the subject is presented a word on a screen at very low levels of illumination. The illumination is gradually increased until the subject correctly reports the word being shown. The summary of these studies, both for aural and visual presentation, as given by Rosenzweig & Postman (1958) leaves few doubts that a fundamental variable is frequency; the more frequently a word has been experienced (as indexed by, say, Thorndike-Lorge counts), the lower the threshold.

A recent research in this area is a study by Goldiamond & Hawkins (1958). These investigators used nonsense syllables. Before determining visual thresholds for the syllables, the subject was given varying amounts of frequency of experience with the syllables. To provide this experience, a card on which a syllable was printed was shown to the subject for 8 sec. during which the subject spelled and pronounced the syllable. Five different frequencies were given, namely, 25, 10, 5, 2, and 1 exposures. Following this, "thresholds" for the syllables were determined. In actual fact the experimenter at no time flashed any of the syllables on the screen. But, by appropriate instructions, the subject was led to believe that the syllables were being shown. These investigators were interested in which syllables the subject emitted as guesses. The results are clear in showing that the more frequently the syllables had been exposed in the pre-threshold procedure, the lower was the verbal threshold; the guesses made by the subjects corresponded in order to the frequency with which the syllable had been experienced previously.

The above resume of various studies might suggest that the spew hypothesis should be called the spew principle. Indeed it could for these particular studies. However, when the translation is made to the verbal-learning situation, a small jump is involved, and it is for this reason that reference will be made to the spew hypothesis. This translation will be made after an analysis of the verbal-learning process is presented.

STAGE ANALYSIS OF VERBAL LEARNING

Logically speaking, the acquisition of a serial or paired-associate list can be divided into two stages. The first will be called *response-learning* or *response-recall* stage. It occurs temporally prior to the second stage which will be termed the *associative* or *hook-up* stage. During the response-learning phase, the subject must learn to recall the responses; we think of it as making the responses available for the second or hook-up stage. At the extremes, response learning may involve two somewhat different processes. First, if the response is already a part of the subject's repertoire as an integrated response (e.g., a common word), response recall consists merely in strengthening this response to this particular situation so that it has greater response strength than the many other responses in the repertoire which are not in the list the subject is to learn. Secondly, the response as an integrated unit may not be in the subject's repertoire (e.g., a consonant syllable such as QBZ). Consequently, the subject must connect or associate the response units (the letters Q, B, and Z) to form a larger unit. Mandler (1954) has spoken of this as response integration. Once a response has been integrated and is readily recallable as a unit, the second or associative stage can proceed; the subject may now connect the response to the particular stimulus with which it is presented in the list.

It should be noted that when a response must be integrated in the response-learning phase, the two phases of learning must occur as subphases of the response-learning phase. For example, if the response syllable is QBZ, the subject must learn to recall B before it can be connected to Q, and must learn to recall Z before it can be connected to B.

To say that we can make a logical division of verbal learning into two stages does not mean that these phases are completely non-overlapping. It is more reasonable to expect that they will overlap, and this overlap may be identified at three different points. First, for some items in a list, both stages may be virtually complete before the first stage is complete for other items. Secondly, for some items the second stage may overlap the first in the sense that some degree of association may develop between the stimulus and response (second phase) while response integration is taking place. For example, if the response is QBZ, a certain amount of associative strength may develop between the stimulus and Q, even though B and Z are not thoroughly integrated with Q. Finally, the specific stimulus to which a response is to be associated may have associative strength to this response before the list is actually presented to the subject. In this case, response learning is circumvented since the stimulus is the immediate eliciting agent. And since there is an already established connection between the stimulus and response, a portion, at least, of the second phase of learning is circumvented. If such an association obtains, it must inevitably mean that the response is integrated, and its pre-established association with the stimulus produces recall directly. Under such circumstances, "learning" rate should be extraordinarily rapid, which is indeed the case (Key, 1926; Underwood & Schulz, 1960).

It is reasonable to ask the pesky question of what the stimulus consists for response recall when it occurs in a relatively pure way, e.g., when it is not elicited by a particular stimulus in the list. To ask this question is the same as asking what the stimulus is when a subject is read a list of words and then asked to write all of them he can. There are a number of stimulus possibilities, such as the apparatus, the room, the instructions, etc. Furthermore, one response in a list may serve as a stimulus for another response so that if the first is elicited, so also will the second be elicited. For example, it has been demonstrated that inter-response similarity enhances response recall, presumably because of the associative connections existing among similar items (Underwood, Runquist, & Schulz, 1959). Because there are several possibilities for potential stimuli for response recall, it does not seem possible to specify a stimulus which serves to produce the recall of the response in the response-recall phase.

The division of verbal learning into two stages is not new; it has been made by others (e.g., Hovland & Kurtz, 1952). However, we do not believe that a full exploitation of the implications of this division has taken place, and we will use it extensively as an analytical device. As will be seen, most of the data to be presented are concerned with the first phase—response-recall.

With the above stage conception in mind, we can turn to a linking of the spew hypothesis and verbal learning.

THE SPEW HYPOTHESIS AND RESPONSE RECALL

We would like to repeat a quotation from Robinson (1932):

> . . . the act of reading or reciting a given syllable may, irrespective of its associative connections, influence the facility with which that act enters into new associations (p. 118).

Thorndike, who above all had many things to say about frequency, essentially reached the same conclusion as Robinson, although that he reached this conclusion is apparently not widely realized. It is probably fair to say that the results of his extensive experiments led Thorndike to conclude that frequency *per se*—frequency without belonging, without reward or satisfyingness—had little or no effect on the *development of an associative connection between two items*. In terms of the present analysis this means that Thorndike is saying that frequency has no effect on the second phase—the associative phase—of verbal learning. That frequency might have an effect in another sense of the term is suggested at two different points in Thorndike's writings, although no experimental work was cited in support of this position. At one point, Thorndike says:

> The repetition of a situation does, of course, cause increased familiarity with it . . . (1932, p. 63).

Insofar as the term familiarity may be used in a technical sense, it was shown in earlier chapters that familiarity and frequency are directly related.

At still another point Thorndike suggests that:

> . . . responses require much practice to reach the status of easy availability . . . (1932, p. 351).

The position taken here is that frequency *per se* is important for verbal learning because it controls the availability of responses in the first stage of verbal learning—the response-recall stage.

Assume the subject is presented a paired–associate list consisting of responses all fairly well integrated but differing in the frequency with which they have been experienced. We make the assumption that when the subject studies the responses on the first trial, whatever mechanism is responsible for spew in the free situation operates in this very restricted situation. The recall strength of the responses is directly related to the frequency with which they have been experienced, and their priority of occurrence in the response-recall stage will reflect this directly. In short, the subject will spew these responses in an order that reflects frequency; therefore, the more frequent response will be available first for the development of associative connection with a specific stimulus. Note again that the hypothesis says nothing about how rapidly the association will develop as a function of prior frequency; it says only that since the most frequent response is most available, it will start entering into the development of an associative connection with a stimulus more quickly than will one with low frequency.

The data given in a previous chapter suggested that the effect of stimulus M on learning was less than a corresponding range of response M. The spew hypothesis readily accounts for this gross difference. When an item is in the stimulus position, no response recall is involved for the stimulus; only responses are involved in response recall. The stimuli are influenced by M (frequency?) only in the associative stage. If the response-recall phase of learning could be completely eliminated, the prediction is that the effect of M on the stimulus and on the response would be equivalent, for both effects would be limited entirely to the associative stage.

The above analysis considered a situation in which the responses were previously integrated—in which response frequency was relatively high for all items. When the situation involving nonintegrated responses is considered, the analysis is somewhat more complex.

Consider a response consisting of the letters QZB. These three letters never occur as a trigram in the language, and there is probably little or no associative connection between the letters. According to the previous analysis, they must be integrated and then recalled as a unitary response.

The process of integrating letters involves the same principle of priority as does emission of an integrated response. Insofar as letters occur with different frequency, the priority of emission is determined. However, because of the great absolute frequency with which all letters have been experienced, it might be expected that priority effects would be relatively small. That certain small effects may be present, however, will be made evident in data to be presented in a later chapter.

To recapitulate, in integrating a response there is a priority of emission among first letters of the various three-letter combinations in the list, a priority in availability of the second, given the first, and in the third, given the first two. Again, the hypothesis does not indicate how the letters get linked in an associative connection; it only states how various letters have different probabilities of availability for being linked.

In the response-integration process there is another factor involved which is probably of less importance for linking the entire response to a stimulus than it is for linking a single letter with another letter. This is an interference factor. Letters have certain strong associative connections with other letters. When unusual combinations of letters must be integrated, the recall of any single letter may be accompanied by a strong tendency to emit a letter which has frequently followed it in the past history of the subject. This knotty problem will be most meaningfully handled in the context of experimental data where its extent and complexities can be assessed more easily.

One common way in which many responses, especially nonsense syllables, are integrated is via pronunciation. Pronunciation provides a single and consistent response which may be "used" in the response-recall phase. The sound is an integrating device for the syllable and can be applied quickly and consistently because of heavy frequency of use in the past. A pronounceable unit, even a combination of letters with low frequency, may allow bypassing of response integration letter by letter.

These, then, are the general notions of spew. It remains to be seen if such notions help in understanding the details of the verbal learning process.

MANIPULATED FREQUENCY

Frequency has been asserted to be the fundamental variable lying behind the various dimensions of M. It has been shown how this conception leads to certain hypotheses concerning the learning process. Correlational data of the type which led to the assertions about frequency are seductive, but they lack conclusiveness because of the age-old cause-effect problem. It will be well, therefore, before advancing further with the frequency notions, to see if the relationships between learning and M can be approximated by laboratory manipulation of frequency.

Previous Investigations

The Noble study (1954). Noble chose 16 items from the low end of his scale of dissyllables and presented these for different frequencies of from 0 to 25 times. They were presented at a 2.3-sec. rate with the subject required to pronounce each item aloud as it appeared. Following this the subject rated the 16 words on a familiarity scale, although he had not been informed ahead of time that this would be required. There was a direct relationship between scaled familiarity and frequency of original presentation. The curve of the relationship was clearly negatively accelerated, indicating that beyond a certain number of presentations, scaled familiarity did not increase much.

Noble (1955) then reasoned that if the relationship between familiarity and frequency is not an artifactual one, those items given the most familiarization training should be learned most rapidly. For this study he chose six items having very low M; the amounts of familiarization training were 0, 1, 2, 3, 4, 5, 10, and 20 trials. As in the previous study, the subject pronounced each item during familiarization training. Following this training the six items were made into a serial list and learned to two successive perfect trials. Items with different amounts of manipulated frequency apparently occurred equally often at each serial position in the lists. Obviously, different groups of subjects were used so that all eight frequency conditions were manipulated an equal number of times.

The results show that rate of learning an item is directly related to number of familiarization trials. The relationship is clearest when the items given 0, 10, and 20 familiarization trials are considered; little effect was noted with items given between 1 and 5 familiarization trials. The effect of familiarization is most apparent on the first anticipation trial, which is what *should* happen if the effect has its largest influence on the first stage of learning as the present hypothesis asserts.

Hovland and Kurtz (1952) have shown that a familiarization procedure for moderately low-association Glaze syllables facilitated somewhat the learning of serial lists made up of the familiarized syllables. This was later confirmed by Riley and Phillips (1959).

Sheffield (1946). In addition to studying the effects of stimulus M versus response M on learning, as reported earlier, Sheffield also investigated the effect of stimulus versus response familiarization in paired-associate learning. The to-be-familiarized units were nonsense syllables, and the other members of the pairs, common three-letter words. Familiarization was given in two ways, for either 10 or 20 trials. One type of familiarization training consisted of presenting the subject with a nonsense syllable and requiring him to pronounce it. Next, the subject had to find the syllable among 20 syllables on a slip of paper and pronounce it again. The syllables on the slip of paper were the stimulus or response units of the to-be-learned paired–associate list, plus "filler" syllables, arranged on the paper in different random orders on successive trials. The second method of familiarization training had the added feature that the subject was always required to make a unique response when he found the syllable on the slip of paper, e.g., to blacken a given syllable with a pencil, circle a second syllable with a green crayon, etc.

The rate of learning the paired-associate lists containing the familiarized syllables did not differ as a function of the type of familiarization procedure. However, pairs containing response terms which had been familiarized by either method were learned significantly faster than nonfamiliarized control pairs. There was no difference between 10 and 20 trials of response familiarization. For conditions in which the stimulus members of the pairs were familiarized, 10 trials of familiarization training had a slight detrimental effect on paired-associate learning while 20 trials had no effect. Thus, in this study, manipulated frequency has produced results which are, for the most part, consistent with the findings concerning the effect of stimulus M versus response

M in paired-associate learning. The failure to find at least a small amount of facilitation attributable to stimulus familiarization is the only major inconsistency (cf., Chap. 3). On the other hand, the results are in complete agreement with the spew hypothesis.

The work of Waters (1939) injects a discordant note in the review; since his studies give no support to the effect of manipulated frequency on learning, they will be examined in some detail.

Waters (1939). The first Waters' experiment was a group procedure. A group of subjects was read a list of 14 syllables (Glaze, 13.3 per cent) with instruction merely to copy them. The syllables were spelled at the rate of one letter per sec. The list was read a second time, ostensibly as a means of checking the correctness of copying, but actually to provide another repetition. Then the subject wrote the words in alphabetical order. Next, on another sheet, the subject wrote pairs of syllables (composed of the original 14) as the experimenter spelled them again. Once more the syllables were read as the subject checked them. Thus, the subject had heard the investigator spell the syllables four times and, in addition, had written them three times. Finally, the subjects were asked to learn the list of associates with recall being tested by presenting the stimuli alone. A control group merely learned the list without the familiarization training. There was no difference between the two groups in the amount learned as measured by recall; the familiarization trials apparently had no effect.

In a second experiment the subjects were handled individually and went through four conditions. The subject was instructed to spell the syllables aloud. Under one condition all 14 items in the paired-associate list (Glaze, 0 to 6.7 per cent) were spelled three times; under a second condition, only the stimulus items were spelled three times; in a third, only the response items were spelled, and in a fourth, no familiarization training was given. There was no difference in learning under the four conditions. The experiment was essentially repeated with another group of subjects, and the same negative results obtained.

In still another experiment, Waters told his subjects that the initial training had to do with speed of reading. The subject read the five-syllable list five times, again by spelling the syllables. Subjects in a control group were given no experience before learning. The groups did not differ in trials to learn.

Waters' experiments give absolutely no support to the relationship between manipulated frequency and learning. What is the difference, or differences between, say, Noble's or Sheffield's work and Waters'? First, the amount of familiarization training given in Waters' experiments was relatively small. Noble's results were clear only when rather wide differences in familiarization existed. Sheffield's subjects pronounced and saw each syllable a minimum of 20 times, whereas even Waters' most extensive familiarization involved only about half as many presentations. Second, Noble and Sheffield asked their subjects to pronounce the units (as did Hovland and Kurtz), while Waters' subjects either had the syllables spelled to them or spelled the units themselves; in no case did the subjects pronounce the units. This may not be a relevant difference, although it is suggestive in view of the strong relationship between pronunciability and M. A third factor concerns paired-associate learning when familiarization training involves both the stimuli and responses. In terms of the response-recall phase the spew hypothesis makes no prediction concerning the effect of familiarization training when it involves the stimulus members. That is to say, the hypothesis predicts neither a positive nor a negative effect; the hypothesis is not relevant for stimulus familiarization. However, Sheffield found, as we did in an experiment to be discussed in a moment, that stimulus familiarization may actually have certain detrimental effects. If stimulus familiarization had the same effect in Waters' experiments, then it might have masked positive effects accompanying response familiarization in those cases where both the stimulus and response units of a list had been familiarized.

The available data on manipulated frequency and learning are not completely clear-cut. Therefore, with the above studies as background, additional experiments were undertaken in an attempt to clarify certain issues. Four experiments will be reported; essentially these were run concurrently with those to be outlined in the next two chapters. However, for purposes of exposition, we want to establish the facts concerning manipulated frequency before proceeding to experiments in which frequency differences are inferred.

EXPERIMENT 1 *

If the hypothesized relationship between frequency and M is to remain tenable, then the following predictions, based on findings with respect to M, must be verified when frequency is manipulated via familiarization training: (1) The rate of paired-associate learning should be an increasing function of amount of familiarization training given

* This experiment was part of the junior author's dissertation submitted to Northwestern University in partial fulfillment of the requirements for the Ph.D. degree.

the response units of the list. (2) Similarly, increasing amounts of familiarization with the stimulus units should increase rate of paired-associate learning. (3) Response familiarization should facilitate learning considerably more than stimulus familiarization. Furthermore, predictions 1 and 3 also follow from the spew hypothesis; hence, failure to confirm these predictions will constitute evidence against the hypothesis.

Method

Experimental design and subjects. The attempt to verify the above predictions required manipulation of the two independent variables, locus and amount of familiarization training. The design consisted of a 2 x 4 factorial arrangement with locus and amount of familiarization as the two respective sources of classification. Four points on the amount dimension were sampled, namely, 1, 10, 20 and 40 presentations of the appropriate syllables. Thus, there were eight groups. Hereafter we will refer to these groups in terms of their treatment, e.g., Group R10, where R refers to response, and 10 to the amount of familiarization training. Subjects were randomly assigned to groups, with the restriction that 24 subjects be assigned to each group. These 192 subjects were Northwestern University undergraduates enrolled in introductory psychology courses.

Materials. The basic experimental materials consisted of 40 low-association value nonsense syllables (Glaze, Mean = 17.12 per cent). When the syllables were selected, every effort was made to keep inter-item similarity at a minimum, e.g., no two syllables were allowed to have two first letters or two last letters in common, etc. These 40 syllables were divided into five sets of eight syllables each. For expository purposes these five sets will be called A, B, C, D, and E. Set A and B were used to construct the eight-unit paired-associate test lists. Half the subjects in a given condition of the experiment had Set A as the stimulus members of their list and Set B as response members; the other half had Set B as stimuli and Set A as responses. Thus, there were two test lists, one the "turned-over" version of the other. The precaution in method was taken so that the stimulus versus response treatment comparison would be unconfounded by peculiarities of the items being treated. The purpose of the remaining three sets of syllables will be taken up momentarily.

General procedure. The experimental time for each subject consisted of two 50-min. sessions at the same hour on consecutive days.

On Day 1, the subject began by learning a practice list of 10 paired adjectives. The practice list was included in the design to reduce variability due to learning-to-learn and to permit a check on the adequacy of random assignment in providing equivalent groups. The remainder of the first session was spent on five trials of familiarization training. On Day 2, the subject received five additional trials of familiarization training, followed by a 3-min. free-recall period. The remainder of the session was devoted to the learning of the paired-associate test list for 20 anticipation trials.

All subjects received standard anticipation-method instructions before being presented the practice list. Prior to learning the test list, the subjects were reinstructed, especially in connection with the necessity of *spelling* the syllables instead of pronouncing them as they had done with the adjectives of the practice list. Both the practice and test lists were presented on a memory drum. The stimulus member was exposed alone for 2 sec. followed by a 2-sec. exposure of the stimulus and response units together. The intertrial interval was 4 sec. To prevent serial learning, each list was arranged in five different orders.

Familiarization training. The familiarization training procedure was patterned after the procedure used by Hovland and Kurtz (1952). All subjects had the same total amount of familiarization with a comparable number of units. The differences in treatment required by the experimental design were accomplished by having the syllables in Set A or B receive the amount of familiarization prescribed for a given condition while those in Sets C, D, and E were given irrelevant familiarization. This familiarization is irrelevant as far as later test-list learning is concerned, and was given so that all groups had the same total amount of prior experience with a comparable number of items and the same amount of sheer practice in familiarization. Therefore, the groups differed *only* with respect to amount of relevant familiarization. By way of illustration, let us consider a subject in group R10. The materials used to give this subject familiarization training were arranged so that either Set A or Set B (depending on whether the subject was due to learn the A-B or the B-A version of the test list) was presented 10 times. If Set B was presented 10 times, then Set A (the stimuli of the paired-associate list) was never presented. The assignment of syllable Sets C, D, and E to the various amounts of irrelevant familiarization was systematically randomized so that each set served equally often with each amount.

Syllables were printed on plain white 3 x 5 cards. They were arranged into packs so that the frequency with which a given set of syllables occurred in the pack was such that the appropriate amounts of familiarization required for each set would be obtained by presenting the pack 10 times.

During familiarization training, the experimenter sat directly across from the subject at a small table and manually presented the syllable cards at the rate of approximately 2-sec. per card. The subject *spelled* each syllable aloud as it was presented. After each presentation of the card pack, hereafter called a study trial, the experimenter shuffled the cards thoroughly while engaging the subject in conversation. On Day 1 of the experiment the subject was given three study trials followed by a test trial, two more study trials, and a final test trial. A test trial consisted of presenting the subject with a printed sheet containing the syllables with which he was being familiarized; however, one letter was omitted from each syllable. The subject was requested to write in the missing letter while spelling each syllable aloud. If an error was made, the experimenter supplied the correct letter. Day 2 of the experiment began with a test trial followed by three study trials, a test trial, two more study trials, and a final test trial. The test trials were given to determine explicitly that the desired differences in amount of familiarization were in fact occurring. In addition, it was found during pilot work that the test trials motivated the subject and helped minimize the boredom which inevitably accompanies a task of this kind. A final assessment of the differences in response strength resulting from differences in amount of familiarization was made by giving the subject a 3-min. free recall test during which he wrote as many of the syllables as he could remember.

Results

Preliminary considerations. An analysis of the practice-list performance showed the eight groups to be of comparable ability. The next step was that of determining whether the different amounts of familiarization did, in fact, produce the desired differences in response strength.

Test trial performance, in terms of mean number of correct responses per trial, was a negatively accelerated increasing function of amount of familiarization. The function relating per cent correct responses during free recall and amount of familiarization was essentially identical to the one for test trial data. Recall ranged from 70 per cent correct with 40 presentations to 3 per cent correct following 1 presentation. The differences in test-trial and free-recall performance

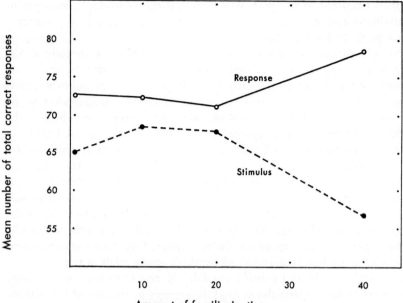

Figure 13. Experiment 1. Mean total number of correct responses on 20 trials as a joint function of locus and amount of familiarization.

as a function of amount of familiarization are significant at well beyond the 1 per cent level.

From the standpoint of the spew hypothesis, it is also of considerable interest to note that the *order* in which the syllables were recalled during free recall was related to amount of familiarization. Of the first three syllables the subject gave during free recall, 43 per cent were syllables which had been presented 40 times, 33 per cent, 20 times, 22 per cent, 10 times, and only 2 per cent, 1 time.

In short, on the basis of the test trial and free-recall results, it seems justifiable to infer that variation in amount of familiarization has produced the desired differences in response availability or strength.

Paired-associate test-list learning. It will be remembered that predictions were made concerning the course of paired-associate learning under the conditions of the present experiment; rate of learning was expected to increase as amount of familiarization of either stimuli or responses increased, and response familiarization was expected to lead to faster learning than stimulus familiarization. The remainder of the results section will be devoted to the analysis of the data to which these predictions apply.

The mean total numbers of correct responses during the 20 trials of test list learning are shown in Fig. 13 as a function of locus and amount of familiarization. It can be seen from Fig. 13 that response familiarization produced consistently better performance than stimulus familiarization. It is also noted that the amount of familiarization had very little effect until it reached 40 presentations. The performance of the R40 group, consistent with expectation, appears to have been facilitated by familiarization training. However, quite contrary to expectations based on findings in connection with M, the performance of the S40 group appears in some way to have been inhibited by familiarization. Thus, there appears to be interaction between locus and amount of familiarization. The latter contention, however, failed to be supported by statistical analysis. The only significant source of variation in total correct responses was attributable to locus of familiarization ($F = 5.47$; with $F = 3.84$ required for significance at the 5 per cent level).

The total number of trials required in accomplishing the first correct anticipation of each of the eight respective pairs in the list was the second response measure used to evaluate the treatment effects in paired-associate learning. Since learning consisted of a constant number of trials, some Ss failed to reach the criterion of one correct response with respect to some pairs. These pairs were given an arbitrary score of 20 trials. This second measure failed to reveal any treatment effects which had not already been shown by the analysis of mean total correct responses. Again the effects of the treatment were clearest with the S40 and R40 groups. The relationship between performance and amount of response familiarization was, also, in somewhat closer conformity with the expected relationship with this measure than it had been in the case of total correct responses. Locus of familiarization was again the only reliable source of variance as indicated by an F of 8.18 which is significant beyond the 1 per cent level.

The two preceding analyses have shown the effects of familiarization to be most apparent in the performance of the S40 and R40 groups. Therefore, it will be of interest to examine the performance of these groups more closely. In Fig. 14 the acquisition curves for the S40 and R40 groups are contrasted with the acquisition curve for the combined S1 and R1 groups. The S1 and R1 groups were combined in order to obtain a more stable estimate of performance under conditions where the effect of familiarization is expected to be at a minimum. Thus,

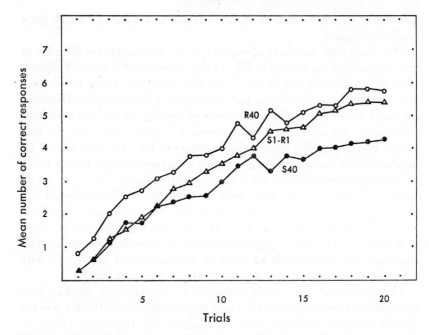

Figure 14. Experiment 1. Acquisition curves for three selected groups (see text for complete explanation).

Fig. 14 is designed to be a contrast of the extremes and should be interpreted accordingly.

First, it is seen from Fig. 14 that the performance of the R40 group was superior throughout. Moreover, this superiority tended to be greater during the first 10 to 12 trials than it was for the remaining trials. Second, it is seen that the performance of the S40 group was initially comparable to that of the S1-R1 group; but as learning continued, the S40 group became progressively more inferior to the S1-R1 group. On trial 20, the S40 group was performing at a level equivalent to that reached by the R40 group between trials 10 and 11, while the S1-R1 group reached this level between trials 12 and 13. These observations are further supported by an analysis of variance for repeated measurements. This analysis shows that the over-all differences between groups in Fig. 14 are significant but, most importantly, that the trials by treatment interaction is also highly reliable.

No specific hypothesis was entertained with regard to overt errors during test-list learning. Nevertheless, it will be of interest to determine whether the treatment affected this type of response. The mean total number of overt errors ranged from a high of 27.21 in Group R1 to a low of 22.75 in Group S20. No trends relating error frequency to locus or amount of familiarization were apparent. All *F*s were less than unity in an analysis of variance of these data.

The failure to find differences in the frequency of errors does not, however, preclude the possibility that the treatment produced differences in the types of errors which were made. Therefore overt errors were classified in terms of the following four categories: (1) stimulus recall errors: stimulus unit given as response; (2) misplaced response errors: response unit given to the wrong stimulus; (3) intrusions: an item from the irrelevant familiarization list given as a response; (4) mixed errors: any three-letter response not among the 40 syllables of the present experiment. Only errors consisting of three letters were categorized. The partial errors (i.e., errors consisting of one or two letters) were not included in the present analysis because they are sometimes difficult to classify.

Table 17 shows the frequency with which these several types of

TABLE 17. Experiment 1. Frequency (*f*) and Percentage of Overt Errors by Types During Test-List Learning Following Stimulus (S) and Response (R) Familiarization

Type of Error	Locus of Familiariza-tion	Amount of Familiarization								Total
		1		10		20		40		
		f	%	*f*	%	*f*	%	*f*	%	
Stimulus	S	5	1.1	5	1.2	7	1.8	1	.2	18
Recall	R	1	.2	2	.5	3	.7	1	.2	6
Misplaced	S	261	57.2	265	65.8	272	71.4	331	74.5	1129
Response	R	352	70.7	311	76.4	327	75.9	381	83.6	1371
Intrusions	S	15	3.3	6	1.5	9	2.4	7	1.6	37
	R	8	1.6	8	2.0	16	3.7	4	.9	36
Mixed	S	175	38.4	127	31.5	93	24.4	105	23.6	500
	R	137	27.5	86	21.1	85	19.7	70	15.4	378
Total	S	456	100.0	403	100.0	381	100.0	444	100.0	
	R	498	100.0	407	100.0	431	100.0	456	100.0	

errors occurred under the conditions of the experiment. These frequencies are also expressed as percentages of the total number of three-letter errors in each group. From Table 17 it can be seen that the percentage of misplaced responses increases slightly as amount of familiarization increases. The percentage of mixed errors in general decreased as familiarization increased. Stimulus familiarization produced more stimulus recall and mixed errors than did response familiarization while response familiarization led to a greater number of misplaced response errors. Finally, intrusions do not appear to be related to either amount or locus of familiarization.

Discussion

Locus of familiarization. It is clear from this experiment that response familiarization produced significantly better performance in paired-associate learning than stimulus familiarization. This result, consonant with the hypothesis that frequency is an antecedent of M, was predicted by the spew hypothesis. It is also of interest to note that certain of the overt-error results lend further support to a spew interpretation; the response-familiarization groups made considerably more misplaced response errors than the stimulus-familiarization groups. Such a result would be expected on the basis of the postulated increase in response availability associated with response familiarization. In addition, it was found that the response-familiarization groups made consistently fewer mixed errors, which is in line with the notion that familiarization facilitates response integration.

The present results regarding locus of familiarization are in agreement with those obtained by Sheffield (1946). An unpublished study by Weiss (1958), only recently brought to our attention, has also found response familiarization to be superior to stimulus familiarization in paired-associate learning. The Weiss procedure was very similar to ours except that he had his subjects pronounce instead of spell the syllables, no irrelevant familiarization was given, and familiarization was carried to a criterion of one errorless test trial plus five presentations. Thus we are left with Waters' (1939) experiment as the only one in which response familiarization failed to be superior to stimulus familiarization. However, the present experiment does settle at least one issue regarding Waters' experiments. It will be remembered that earlier in this chapter it was suggested that Waters' negative results may have been due to the fact that he had his subjects spell rather than pronounce during familiarization training. Since positive results have been obtained in the present experiment with the spelling procedure, it is doubtful whether Waters' negative results can be attributed to spelling.

Amount of familiarization. Unfortunately, amount of familiarization had a considerably less clear effect than locus in the present experiment. In fact, statistically, it could be concluded that the curves in Fig. 13 may be considered two parallel horizontal lines. In both cases amount was not a significant source of variation, nor was the locus by amount-of-familiarization interaction a significant one. Yet, when the performance of the S40 and R40 groups is considered, the foregoing conclusion seems a bit unrealistic. Furthermore, when the S40 and R40 groups were compared with the S1-R1 group, the differences in the performance of these groups were, in fact, statistically reliable. Therefore, perhaps it will be wise to attempt at least a tentative interpretation of these data while awaiting further verification.

In the case of response familiarization, if, as suggested previously (cf., Chap. 4), the function relating frequency and rate of learning is of the sigmoid type, then the performance of the R1, R10, and R20 groups could be viewed as representing the initial positively accelerated portion of this sigmoid function. This reasoning is further supported by Sheffield's (1946) finding that there was no difference in rate of paired-associate learning following 10 versus 20 trials of response familiarization. The studies which suggest that there is a sigmoid relationship between amount of M and difficulty in learning also provide evidence favoring this interpretation (Noble & McNeely, 1957; Noble, Stockwell, & Pryer, 1957). Thus it would be expected that a relatively large increment in frequency, such as that represented by the R40 group, would be required to produce a clear indication of facilitation. This interpretation would also account for Waters' (1939) failure to find facilitation with response familiarization, since the frequencies he employed would fall well within the range of this positively accelerated portion of the postulated curve.

It was predicted that the greater the amount of stimulus familiarization, the faster the learning. This prediction was clearly not verified. Even if one is statistically rigorous and maintains that stimulus familiarization did not produce bona fide inhibition, there is certainly no doubt that it failed to produce facilitation. Hence, these results could be taken as evidence against the hypothesis that frequency is an antecedent of M, but such a conclusion is not appealing in light of the rather considerable evidence already mustered in favor of coordination of frequency and M. Therefore, an alternative interpretation seems preferable, at least for the time being.

The method of administering familiarization may have been responsible for the inhibitory effects noted with stimulus familiarization. That is, there may have been a loss of differentiation between stimulus and response systems during the learning of the paired-associate list because the subjects in the stimulus familiarization groups became accustomed to giving the stimulus units of the list as "responses" during familiarization training. Thus, as the subject learned the response units of the list and they became more nearly equal in strength to the stimuli as "responses," he may have confused the syllables serving as response units with those serving as stimulus units in the list. One obvious implication of this notion is that the stimulus familiarization groups should have made more stimulus recall errors than the response familiarization groups during paired-associate learning. Table 17 did show this to be the case; in fact, the stimulus groups made three times as many errors of this type than did the response groups. However, the relative infrequency of this type of error and the failure to find any consistent relationship between its frequency and amount of stimulus familiarization may be taken as evidence contrary to the loss-of-differentiation hypothesis.

Fortunately, the loss-of-differentiation hypothesis is amenable to direct test. If familiarization training were given to the stimuli of a paired-associate list in which stimulus and response members belonged to completely different classes of verbal materials, then the possibility for loss of differentiation should be minimized. The next experiment to be reported employed such a list and was designed to test this hypothesis.

EXPERIMENT 2

The main purpose of this experiment, as mentioned above, was to provide an empirical test of the loss-of-differentiation hypothesis. One set of conditions in this experiment essentially duplicates the S1 and S40 conditions of Experiment 1, while a second set of conditions was designed to minimize the possibility for loss of differentiation. However, even in the former conditions certain changes in material and procedure were deliberately made so that the generality of the results of Experiment 1 to stimulus familiarization could be assessed. Therefore, if the results of Experiment 1 were due to some peculiar combination of factors specific to that experiment rather than loss of differentiation, then the present experiment may be viewed as representing two further attempts to reproduce the facilitating effect of stimulus M via manipulated frequency.

Method

Experimental design. The test of the loss-of-differentiation hypothesis presents a problem in design. The test calls for two basic lists. Both lists will have the same nonsense syllables as stimulus terms, but one list will also use syllables as response units (same class of materials as the stimuli) while the other list will use Noble's paralogs as responses (a class of materials different from that of the stimuli). To support the hypothesis, the learning of the syllable-paralog list must be more rapid than the learning of the syllable-syllable list following equal amounts of familiarization with the stimuli common to both lists. Unfortunately, however, the learning of these two lists might also be expected to differ solely on the basis of the fact that they have different response terms. To solve this problem one could, of course, undertake a long series of pilot studies and try to equate the difficulty of the paralogs and syllables. There is, however, a simpler solution to this problem. Two additional groups of subjects who learn the respective test lists following *irrelevant* familiarization training are needed. The test-list performance of these two groups establishes the amount of difference in difficulty between the lists due to the presence of different response terms. Any divergence in performance from this base difference on the part of the two groups receiving relevant familiarization can then be unambiguously attributed to the effects of stimulus familiarization. Statistically, these effects will be reflected directly in the type-of-familiarization by type-of-test-list interaction. Thus, the hypothesis will be supported if the nature of this interaction is such that with relevant familiarization the group learning the syllable-paralog list shows better performance than the group learning the syllable-syllable list, and if the magnitude of this superiority is significantly greater than the magnitude of the difference in the performance of the irrelevant familiarization groups learning these lists.

Material and procedure. The syllable-syllable and syllable-paralog lists had identical stimulus units with a mean association value of 9.12 per cent and a range from 0 per cent to 20 per cent as determined by Glaze. The response units had a mean M of 1.32 and 14.12 per cent for the paralogs and syllables, respectively, according to Noble and Glaze. There were eight pairs in each list. The eight items used for irrelevant familiarization training consisted of two nonsense and two consonant syllables plus four ordinary three-letter combinations (e.g., PME, AIS). This was done to further minimize interlist similarity between the irrelevant items and the items in the paired-associate list. Similarly, every effort was made to keep intralist similarity among items in the paired-associate lists at a minimum.

A total of 100 subjects was assigned randomly to each of the four conditions, with the restriction that 25 subjects be assigned to each condition. As in Exp. 1, the subjects were Northwestern University undergraduates most of whom had previously served in some type of verbal-learning experiment.

The 50-min. experimental session began with familiarization training which was, for the most part, identical to that used in Experiment 1. The subject spelled each item aloud as it was presented on a 3 x 5 card on study trials at a 2-sec. rate by the experimenter. Each of the eight relevant or irrelevant items was presented 40 times. Four test trials, during which the subject had to supply missing letters, were interpolated among the study trials.

Familiarization training was followed immediately by 20 anticipation trials with the appropriate paired-associate list presented on a memory drum at a 2:2-sec. rate with a 4-sec. intertrial interval. Again five orders of presentation were used to prevent serial learning. The subject pronounced the paralogs but spelled the syllables.

Results and Discussion

An analysis of the total number of correct responses during test list learning showed the F for the interaction between type of familiarization and type of list to be less than unity. The groups learning the syllable-syllable and syllable-paralog lists following relevant familiarization had 61.44 and 65.28 mean total correct responses, respectively. Following irrelevant familiarization, the means were 57.40 and 70.68 for the syllable-syllable and syllable-paralog groups. Hence, these results do not confirm the loss-of-differentiation hypothesis, and there was, in short, neither facilitation nor inhibition following relevant stimulus familiarization.

That there was some loss of differentiation in the syllable-syllable groups is indicated by the fact that stimulus units were given as responses during test-list learning 26 times following relevant familiarization and 12 times following irrelevant familiarization while only *one* such error was made by the groups learning the syllable-paralog lists. However, this loss does not appear to have inhibited performance in terms of correct responses. Furthermore, the fact that 12 stimulus-recall errors occurred following irrelevant familiarization suggests that at least part of the loss is due to intralist factors rather than entirely to familiarization training as had been supposed originally. Therefore, unless the present experiment was in someway an inadequate test of the hypothesis, it must be concluded that loss of differentiation cannot be held accountable for the inhibitory effects of stimulus familiarization in Experiment 1.

Finally, our inability to replicate the inhibition in performance on the syllable-syllable list following stimulus familiarization which was obtained in Experiment 1, suggests that this phenomenon is either an unreliable one or one which is of very restricted generality. It is also clear that, while we did not find inhibition, we certainly did not find facilitation following 40 trials of stimulus familiarization with either the syllable-syllable or syllable-paralog lists (the F for relevant vs. irrelevant familiarization was also less than unity). Hence, again we have failed to reproduce stimulus M effects via manipulated frequency.

EXPERIMENT 3

What is another way in which verbal units acquire frequency? In the preceding two experiments we have manipulated the frequency of the subject's experience with nonsense syllables by having him recite (spell) them a different number of times. In other words the syllables were spelled in response to the presentation of the syllable itself as a stimulus. We will not attempt to catalogue all of the possible alternative ways in which a unit may acquire frequency; however, one obvious second general way of acquiring frequency is to make the verbal unit a response to some physical or symbolic stimulus other than the unit itself. That is, we respond to the sight of an actual oak tree by saying, "oak tree." As a consequence the units, oak and tree, have received an increment in frequency. In studying a foreign language, say German, the student spends a good deal of his time responding to English words with their German equivalents (e.g., cat—*die Katze*, eagle—*der Adler*, etc.). To be sure he may also recite, "*die Katze*," "*die Katze*," "*die Katze*"; but, if he is to learn the referents for these words, then he must in addition learn to associate *die Katze* with cat, or a picture of a cat, and in so doing, *die Katze* will acquire frequency in a way different from the frequency acquired during recitation. The young infant just learning to speak provides a final illustration. First he will practice a response, say, "da-da," without any apparent stimulus other than his own verbalizations and those of his parents. Eventually, however, the frequency of emission of "da-da," and its more highly integrated successor "daddy," will become directly correlated with the actual presence of daddy. Parenthetically, it is probably not an accident that a child's early language learning behavior is so apparently analogous to the two-stage conception of verbal learning proposed. But, returning to the topic at hand, we see that a second important way in which verbal units acquire frequency is by way of their elicitation by stimuli with which they have become associated.

Experiment 3 and 4 were designed to investigate this second general method of manipulating frequency. This was done by giving familiarization training with paired-associate lists in which the to-be-familiarized syllables served as response terms.

When we selected the stimulus units for the familiarization lists we posed the following question: "Will familiarization be more effective when the to-be-familiarized syllables are associated with verbal stimuli than when they are associated with non-verbal stimuli during familiarization training?" To answer this, some subjects were given familiarization training with paired-associate lists whose stimulus terms consisted of nouns; other subjects received training with lists whose stimulus units consisted of nonsense forms. Then the effects of familiarization were evaluated by having all subjects learn a serial test list consisting of the familiarized syllables.

We are indebted to Mr. Robert Swenson for collecting the data of this experiment as part of his senior honors project as Northwestern University.

Method

Experimental design and lists. The experiment required four groups of subjects. The way in which each of these groups was treated is summarized in Table 18, and from this table it can be seen that familiariza-

TABLE 18. Experiment 3. Experimental Design and Test List

(See text for complete explanation)

Group	Familiarization Lists		Items In Serial Test List	
	First	Second		
RN (relevant)	Noun-XON	Noun-XON	XON	JEC
RF (relevant)	Form-XON	Form-XON	YIL	QUG
IN (irrelevant)	Noun-DIW	Noun-DIW	RUY	VAK
IF (irrelevant)	Form-DIW	Form-DIW	KIZ	MEQ

tion training was relevant for two of the groups and irrelevant for the other two. Under each type of familiarization, one group received familiarization with paired-associate lists whose stimulus units were common English nouns, and the other group learned paired-associate lists whose stimulus terms were nonsense forms. The stimulus units of the first and second familiarization lists were completely different for both noun and form lists whereas the response units (the to-be-familiarized syllables) remained the same (e.g., *heart*-XON, *eagle*-XON). However, the same nouns and forms were used for relevant and irrelevant familiarization. After familiarization training all groups learned the serial test list shown at the right of Table 18. As illustrated by the syllable XON, the test list consists of the eight syllables used as responses in the paired-associate lists of relevant familiarization groups, while syllables such as DIW were used as responses during irrelevant familiarization. The capital letters used to identify each group summarize that group's treatment, e.g., Group RN had relevant (R) familiarization with noun (N) lists.

The nouns used in the present experiment were chosen from among the 20,000 words which occur most frequently in the language according to the Thorndike-Lorge list. The Glaze value for the test-list syllables ranged from 0 per cent to 20 per cent. The irrelevant syllables were also from the 0 per cent to 20 per cent range of Glaze. The nonsense forms were devised by the writers and have not been submitted to any scaling operations; however, they were drawn to be of low M. That is, they did not correspond to any common geometric configurations such as a square, circle, or triangle, etc., nor did they suggest common objects readily. The two respective sets of nouns and forms for the first and second familiarization lists were paired randomly with the syllables to make up the paired-associate lists. The nouns and syllables were selected with an eye toward keeping intralist and interlist similarity at a minimum. All familiarization lists consisted of eight pairs.

Procedure and subjects. The 120 subjects were randomly assigned with the restriction that there be 30 subjects in each of the four groups. Approximately half the subjects had served in verbal learning experiments prior to the present one.

After the subject was read standard paired-associate learning instructions, he learned the first familiarization list. Each of the three lists in this experiment was presented for a total of 15 anticipation trials, all subjects being given a 3-min. rest period between the learning of each successive list. The serial test list was, of course, always the last list to be learned. Prior to learning this list, the subject was given instructions for serial learning which pointed out the differences between it and the paired-associate learning which the subject had just completed.

All lists were presented on a memory drum. The paired-associate lists were presented at a 2:2-sec. rate with a 4-sec. intertrial interval, and in five different orders to prevent serial learning. The serial list was presented with a 2-sec. interitem and intertrial interval, and the serial order of the items in this list was different from any of the orders used

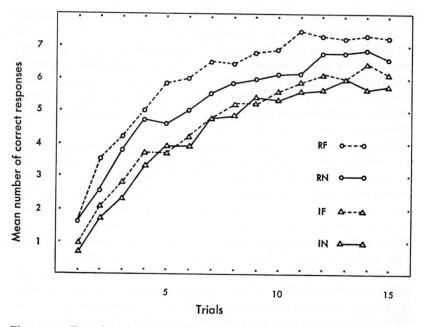

Figure 15. Experiment 3. Acquisition curves for a serial list of nonsense syllables following relevant (R) and irrelevant (I) familiarization with paired-associate lists in which the responses were the nonsense syllables and the stimuli either forms (F) or nouns (N).

to present these items in the paired-associate lists. All learning was by the spelling-anticipation method.

Results

Familiarization lists. The mean total number of correct responses, after combining first and second list familiarization list scores, was 150.70, 160.83, 142.83 and 149.23 for the RN, IN, RF, and IF groups, respectively. The differences among these means are not statistically reliable. Thus, it appears safe to conclude that the syllables have been spelled about an equal number of times under the various conditions. On the average, each syllable was spelled as a correct response 17 to 20 times, and the subjects saw (if they were awake) each syllable 32 times.

Serial test list. The learning curves for the four groups (Fig. 15) make it apparent that the treatment produced clear differences in performance on the test list. Performance was best following familiarization with lists whose stimulus units were nonsense forms. Familiarization with noun lists, while leading to considerably better performance than irrelevant familiarization, was not as effective as training with form lists. As would be desired, the two types of irrelevant treatment produced essentially no difference in test-list performance. The mean total number of correct responses for 15 trials of test-list learning was 78.80, 64.73, 89.23, and 68.93 for Groups RN, IN, RF, and IF, respectively. A statistical analysis of these data showed relevant versus irrelevant familiarization to be a highly significant source of variation ($F = 27.81$; an F of 6.87 is required at the 1 per cent level). The effect of familiarization with noun versus form lists was also significant ($F = 5.04$; the F needed at the 5 per cent level is 3.93). The F for interaction was not significant.

The mean total number of overt errors during test-list learning did not vary reliably as a function of the conditions of the present experiment. None of the Fs even approached significance. However, when overt errors are classified as to type, as shown in Table 19, differences as a function of treatment are quite evident. Again only complete three-letter errors were classified. From Table 19 it can be seen that

TABLE 19. Experiment 3. Frequency (f) and Percentage of Overt Errors by Types During Test-List Learning for Four Familiarization Groups

	Groups							
	RN		RF		IN		IF	
Error Type	f	%	f	%	f	%	f	%
Misplaced Response	250	77.6	191	78.6	101	36.1	109	33.2
Mixed	72	22.4	52	21.4	179	63.9	219	66.8
Total	322	100.0	243	100.0	280	100.0	328	100.0

with relevant familiarization about three of every four errors were *misplaced responses*. In the case of irrelevant familiarization, the reverse is approximately true, namely, three of every four errors were of the *mixed type*. On the other hand, type of familiarization list does not appear to have influenced error type, although the absolute frequency with which both types of errors were made was considerably greater for Group RN than for Group RF. The latter was also apparent for total number of overt errors; nevertheless, the over-all analysis of variance failed to identify it as a statistically reliable variation.

Discussion

This experiment has demonstrated unequivocally that familiarization training of syllables as the response terms in a paired-associate list facilitated the subsequent learning of these syllables as a serial list. The wide difference in the percentage of misplaced response versus mixed overt errors (Table 19) would appear to leave little doubt that response integration was the major vehicle for the facilitating effect of relevant familiarization. Thus, we find the results in complete agreement with, and predictable from the spew hypothesis. Furthermore, the facilitating effect of M in serial learning has been reproduced by manipulating frequency. There remains, however, one small puzzle.

What about the differential effectiveness of the familiarization lists with nonsense forms as stimuli over the lists with nouns as stimuli? Although the performance of Group RN was significantly facilitated by familiarization when compared with Group IN ($t = 3.06$; with $t = 2.58$ required for significance at the 1 per cent level), its performance was nevertheless significantly poorer than that of Group RF ($t = 2.27$; $t = 1.96$ for significance at the 5 per cent level). The degree of familiarization was comparable for the two groups; in fact, if anything, familiarization was somewhat higher for Group RN (150.70 vs. 142.83 mean total correct responses during familiarization training for Groups RN and RF, respectively). Hence, it would appear that the *nature* of the association between the nouns and the syllables is the factor which is to be held accountable for the inferior performance of Group RN. But how?

It is our guess that R-S or "backward" learning which is known to occur during paired-associate learning (e.g., Morikawa, 1959; Feldman and Underwood, 1957) interfered with the formation of the requisite serial associations during test-list learning. For example, if *XON* calls out *heart* or *eagle* due to the R-S association acquired during familiarization training, then *heart* and *eagle* will compete with *YIL* which is the response to be associated with *XON* in the serial list. In order to account for the present results, it remains, of course, to be shown why there should be more of this interference for Group RN than for Group RF. This could occur in several ways.

First, it is known that degree of R-S learning varies as a function of stimulus M with high M leading to greater R-S learning (Jantz and Underwood, 1958). Therefore, if it can be assumed that the nouns had higher M than the forms, then R-S learning would be of a higher degree for Group RN than for Group RF. As a result, more interference from R-S learning would be expected in the former than in the latter group during test-list learning. In fact, a few subjects spontaneously mentioned that some of the nouns seemed to "get in their way"; sometimes when a syllable came into the window all they could "think of" was the noun (or nouns) it had been associated with during familiarization training. Furthermore, it seems highly likely that if the nouns and forms of the present experiment were scaled for M by the production method, the nouns would be found to have higher M than the forms. At this point, it can be argued that the noun lists should have been learned faster than the form lists if their stimulus M was higher. Aside from the fact that stimulus M is not a very potent variable in paired-associate learning, it can be said that there are a number of reasons, without detailing them because it would take us too far afield, why the effect of greater stimulus M with the noun lists need not have "shown up" in the present experiment and yet be present to effect R-S learning.

A second factor which may have contributed to the production of greater interference from R-S learning for Group RN than for Group RF is the presense of greater formal similarity between nouns and syllables than between the forms and syllables. Finally, a third factor related to both the first and second factors is the fact that the nouns are highly available verbal responses, whereas the forms do not lend themselves very readily to verbalization unless the subject gives them a name or label of his own. Hence, the occurrence of the forms as competing responses is virtually precluded by the nature of the materials themselves. Obviously, the only way a final decision can be reached as to the factor or factors responsible for the differential effectiveness of these two types of familiarization training is by further research, which we have not undertaken. However, a study in which the stimulus M of the familiarization lists is deliberately manipulated by using scaled materials would appear to be an excellent starting place.

EXPERIMENT 4

The major difference between Experiments 3 and 4 is the use of a paired-associate list as the test list in Experiment 4. This permitted evaluation of the relative effectiveness of the present type of familiarization training when applied to the stimulus terms versus the response terms of the test list. Therefore, the familiarized syllables occupied the stimulus positions in the test list for half of the subjects, and the response positions for the other half. In many respects Experiment 4 was like Experiment 1, except that a different method of familiarization training was used and two instead of four points on the amount-of-familiarization dimension were studied. There were three independent variables in this experiment: (1) locus of familiarization (stimulus vs.

response terms of test list), (2) type of familiarization lists (noun vs. form stimulus units), and (3) type (or amount) of familiarization (relevant vs. irrelevant).

Method

Familiarization training in this experiment was exactly the same as in Experiment 3. The design of the present study is most easily visualized by merely considering each of the four groups of Experiment 3 (Table 18) as consisting of two subgroups. For one subgroup the familiarized syllables appeared as the stimulus units on the test list, and for the other subgroup, as the response units. It should, however, be kept in mind that a given set of two subgroups is *not* treated differently until test-list learning actually begins. Thus, there was a total of eight groups in the present experiment, and 160 subjects were randomly divided among these groups, with the restriction that 20 subjects serve in each group. The subjects in this experiment differed from those in Experiments 1, 2, and 3 in that none of them had served in a verbal learning experiment prior to their participation in the present experiment.

The paired-associate test list used in the present experiment consisted of two "versions." For the stimulus-familiarization groups the stimulus units were the nonsense syllables used under relevant familiarization conditions in Experiment 3 (cf., Table 18). The response units were low M paralogs from Noble's list with a mean M of 1.32. For the response-familiarization groups, the list was "turned over" making the paralogs the stimulus units and the relevant syllables the responses. Paralogs were used to avoid the intralist generalization tendencies noted with syllable-syllable lists in Experiment 2.

The test lists were presented in five different orders which were different from those used to present the relevant syllables during familiarization training. The test list was presented for 15 anticipation trials on a memory drum at a 2:2-sec. rate with 4-sec. intertrial interval. When the syllables were responses the subject spelled them; when the paralogs were responses he pronounced them.

Results

Familiarization lists. As in Experiment 3, the various familiarization lists were learned at essentially the same rate. No grounds for rejecting the null-hypothesis were found in an analysis of variance of these data.

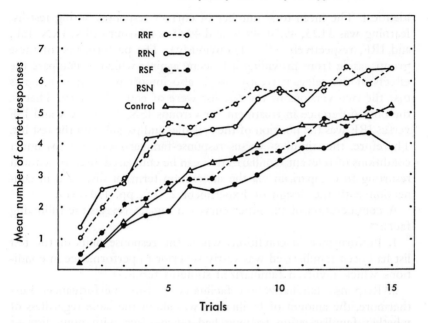

Figure 16. Experiment 4. Acquisition curves for a paired-associate list following relevant (R) and irrelevant (Control) stimulus (S) and response (R) familiarization lists in which the responses were the nonsense syllables and the stimuli either forms (F) or nouns (N).

The comparability in the performance of various stimulus- and response-familiarization subgroups provided a gratifying confirmation of random sampling theory. The largest of the four *t*s resulting from a comparison of the four pairs of groups was .82. Thus random groups of 20 subjects performed alike when treated alike. Each subject saw the syllable 32 times and, on the average, spelled them as a correct response from 16 to 18 times during familiarization training.

Paired-associate test lists. Learning curves which depict the test-list performance of the various groups in the present experiment are plotted in Fig. 16. A distinction between the stimulus and response subgroups was made by adding the letters S and R, respectively, to the abbreviations devised in Experiment 3 for summarizing each group's treatment [e.g., Group RSN received relevant (R) stimulus (S) familiarization with a noun (N) familiarization list]. The curve labelled *control* represents the combined performance of the groups for which irrelevant familiarization preceded test-list learning, for, when considered separately, the performance of these four groups was virtually identical. The mean total number of correct responses during test-list learning was 51.15, 49.70, 49.20 and 49.65 for Groups ISN, IRN, ISF, and IRF, respectively ($F < 1$, obviously). The performance of these groups, aside from providing a baseline against which to compare the effects of the relevant treatments, is also important because it shows that the two versions of the test list were of equal difficulty. That is, the only difference in treatment for Groups ISN versus IRN and ISF versus IRF was the position of the syllables and paralogs on the test list. Therefore, the stimulus- versus response-familiarization groups under conditions of relevant familiarization can be compared directly without resorting to comparison via the interaction terms as discussed in connection with the design of Experiment 2 (cf., pp. 130–131).

A consideration of the other curves in Fig. 16 reveals the following facts:

1. Performance in conditions where the response units of the test list had been familiarized was vastly superior to performance in conditions which involved familiarized stimulus terms.

2. Response familiarization facilitated test-list performance. Furthermore, the amount of facilitation was about the same regardless of whether familiarization training had taken place with noun lists or with form lists.

3. Performance was not facilitated by stimulus familiarization which, in fact, with noun lists appears to have inhibited test-list performance somewhat.

The above observations are, with one exception, supported by an over-all three-factor analysis of variance with total number of correct responses during test-list learning as the score for each individual. The exception was the inability to consider the inhibition of performance in Group RSN reliable by statistical standards. The other effects of the treatment noted in Fig. 16 are significant at well beyond the .1 per cent level. The mean total number of correct responses over all learning trials was 40.65, 69.15, 48.85, and 70.50 for Groups RSN, RRN, RSF, and RRF, respectively.

An analysis of variance failed to reveal any reliable sources of variation among the total number of overt errors made during test list learning under the various conditions of the present experiment. The trends indicated that slightly more overt errors were made by the response-familiarization groups than by the stimulus-familiarization groups. However, since this trend was present with both relevant and irrelevant familiarization, it was probably due to the difference in test lists for these groups. A second trend indicated that, except in one group, slightly fewer errors were made following relevant familiarization than after irrelevant familiarization.

Discussion

The present experiment leaves no doubt that the learning of a paired-associate list in which the response units have been familiarized by serving as response units during the learning of two prior paired-associate lists is dramatically facilitated. Contrariwise, but with equal lack of ambiguity, was the failure to find any benefit from familiarization of the stimulus units. Thus, the results of the present experiment agree with the results of Experiment 1. The facilitating effects of response familiarization are again most readily interpreted as having resulted from the response integration which took place during familiarization training; the spew hypothesis is further supported. As can be seen from Table 20, where overt errors in the response familiarization con-

TABLE 20. Experiment 4. Frequency (f) and Percentage of Overt Errors by Types During Test-List Learning Following Response Familiarization for Four Different Groups

					Groups			
	RRN		RRF		IRN		IRF	
Type of Error	f	%	f	%	f	%	f	%
Misplaced Response	225	76.3	129	71.3	154	60.6	95	47.5
Mixed	70	23.7	52	28.7	100	39.4	105	52.5
Total	295	100.0	181	100.0	254	100.0	200	100.0

ditions have been classified as to type, the percentage of misplaced response errors is consistently higher with relevant than with irrelevant familiarization. In contrast, the percentage of mixed errors is higher with irrelevant familiarization than with relevant familiarization for both kinds of material.

The reader may have wondered from time to time why the high percentage of mixed errors with irrelevant familiarization should not be interpreted as reflecting interference from the irrelevant syllables rather than lack of integration. The following facts argue compellingly against such an interpretation.

1. For the 140 subjects serving under irrelevant-familiarization conditions in Experiments 3 and 4, only *one* "full-fledged" intrusion (TOV) from irrelevant familiarization occurred during the learning of the test lists.

2. The test-list syllables have no first letters in common with the first letters of the irrelevant syllables. Similarly, the last letters are completely different in the two sets of syllables. Of the first letters in mixed errors for Experiments 3 and 4, 15.1 per cent could have come from the irrelevant syllables. Of the 91 letters which make up this percentage, 34 of them came from the mixed error *ZON*, a common "misperception" of *XON*, because it also occurs with high frequency with relevant familiarization. Furthermore, the identification, as to source, for the letters C, J, L, V, X, and Z is not without some ambiguity, because these letters occur in both sets of syllables, although not in the same position. When the 10 letters which occur *only* in the irrelevant syllables are considered, regardless of position, they appear a total of only 51 times (4.2 per cent of the total letters) as a part of a mixed error in Experiments 3 and 4.

3. If irrelevant familiarization were a potent source of interference, it should have interfered more with the test-list performance of Groups IRN and IRF than with the performance in Groups ISN and ISF, because for the former groups the response members of the test list were syllables, whereas for the latter groups they were paralogs. Yet, performance was identical in all four irrelevant-familiarization groups.

One final point regarding response familiarization warrants brief consideration. It will be remembered that in Experiment 3 familiarization training with nouns as stimulus units in the familiarization list was not as effective as familiarization with forms as stimulus units. In contrast, form lists and noun lists were found to be equally effective in producing facilitation via response familiarization in the present experiment. The test list of the present experiment was a paired-associate list which did not require the familiarized syllables to serve as both stimulus and response as was the case with the serial list of Experiment 3. Hence, it would appear that the results of this experiment give indirect support to the notion that interference from R-S learning produced the decrement in performance on the serial list when familiarization had taken place with the noun lists.

When the effects of stimulus familiarization in the present experiment are considered, it is apparent we have completed a cycle. In Experiment 1 we found some suggestions of inhibition in performance following stimulus familiarization and after failing to replicate this finding in Experiment 2, we concluded that this phenomenon lacked generality. Here we are back to finding inhibition, although if we wanted to ignore it, statistically we would be justified in doing so.

However, the fact that this finding has been obtained quite often in the present series of experiments, as well as by other investigators, argues against considering it a chance phenomenon. It is perhaps not surprising that we have failed to find facilitation with stimulus familiarization since the effects of stimulus M are far from potent themselves. That is, it may be unrealistic to expect to build up sufficient frequency in the short space of a laboratory session to reproduce the small effect which accompanies even the widest variations in stimulus M. Yet, to find an effect and have it be inhibitory is still another matter.

The similarity between the present results and those of Experiment 1 are quite startling if one ignores the curve for Group ISF in Fig. 16 and compares it with Fig. 14 of Experiment 1. If the similarity of these results is more than coincidence, it would suggest that an explanation for the inhibition in both experiments with stimulus familiarization is not likely to be found in the method of familiarization training since the method was quite different in the two experiments. On the other hand, the failure to find this inhibition in Group RSF suggests, at least for the present experiment, that the familiarization training with nouns was the culprit. The mechanism by which the nouns would produce inhibition in the present experiment could have been R-S learning just as in Experiment 3. Thus, during test-list learning, *XON* tended to elicit its associates *heart* and *eagle*, and these response tendencies interfered with the recall of the correct response, the paralog *BYSSUS*. Since the differences in error frequency among conditions were small, another way of viewing the difference in the performance of Group ISN and Group RSN, aside from the fact that the former made more correct responses, is to look at the failure of the subjects in the latter condition to respond as often as those in the former. Since competition among alternative responses is often accompanied by failure to respond because of the conflict this competition creates, such an interpretation would support the notion that R-S learning interfered with learning in Group RSN. To continue in a speculative vein, it is interesting to note that the mean difference in correct responses between Group RN and RF of Experiment 3 is 10.43, while the difference in mean correct responses for Group ISN and RSN of the present experiment is 10.50. Although this may again be pure coincidence, it does suggest that the decrement resulting from familiarization with the noun lists is about the same in the two experiments.

How is the above interpretation to be applied to Experiment 1? Frankly, we simply do not know. One thing is certainly clear from the present experiment and its predecessors: they have raised more issues than they have settled regarding the effects of stimulus familiarization.

Finally, in a recent experiment which appeared after the present study was in progress, Bailey and Jeffrey (1958) have, among other things, a set of conditions which correspond roughly to those of the present experiment. They asked subjects to learn three successive lists of paired nonsense syllables (Glaze, 87 per cent) in which the stimulus term was different in each list but the response term remained the same. Then the response terms were paired with a new syllable in a test list. Under one condition the familiarized syllables were in the response position; in another they were in the stimulus position on the test list. The test-list learning of these pairs under either condition did not differ from learning under control conditions. While the results of this study agree with the present one regarding stimulus familiarization, they do not agree concerning the effect of response familiarization. The explanation for this disagreement is most probably to be found in the fact that these investigators used syllables with very high association value. Since these syllables are already well integrated and available, one would not expect much benefit to derive from familiarization with them. However, there are so many additional differences in material, procedure, and design between our study and theirs that no firm conclusion can really be reached concerning the difference in results.

SUMMARY

In this chapter we have attempted to show how frequency exerts its influence on the verbal learning process.

1. We began by formulating the *spew hypothesis* which states that the frequency with which verbal units have been experienced directly determines their availability as responses in new associative connections.

2. The evidence leading to a spew notion was reviewed. Here it was found that the frequency with which the subject uses verbal units in various free-association situations is highly correlated with the frequency with which these units occur in language usage. This high correlation exists in spite of the fact that the subject responds to specific stimuli in these situations. Furthermore, and most importantly, other evidence showed that the order in which verbal responses were emitted in these and related types of situations was also predictable from a knowledge of the subjects' prior frequency of experience with the units being emitted.

3. The application of the notion of spew to the verbal-learning process required the making of a distinction between the two stages of verbal learning: namely, a *response-learning* or *response-recall* stage which precedes the second *associative* or *hook-up* stage. The spew hypothesis was shown to apply *only* to the response-recall stage in that the frequency with which units had been experienced determines their priority of occurrence during this stage of learning.

4. Up to this point the argument that frequency was the fundamental variable underlying M had been derived mainly from theoretical considerations and correlational evidence. The more definitive step of manipulating frequency experimentally was then taken. The question was, can the effects of M on verbal learning be reproduced by manipulating frequency? They can, in part. When we combine the results of the four experiments reported in this chapter with the results from previous investigations the following facts emerged: (1) Serial learning has been facilitated by giving familiarization training of several different types. The amount of facilitation was related to the amount of familiarization. (2) Response familiarization in paired-associate learning facilitated learning. This facilitation was greater with some methods of familiarization than with others. (3) Stimulus familiarization has not facilitated paired-associate learning in any of the present or past studies. In fact, more often than not, there have been indications that stimulus familiarization has inhibitory effects. (4) To produce clear effects in either serial or paired-associate learning the amount of familiarization training must be relatively large.

REFERENCES

Bailey, J. H., & Jeffrey, W. E. Response strength and association value in stimulus predifferentiation. *Psychol. Rep.*, 1958, 4, 715–721.

Bousfield, W. A., & Barclay, W. D. The relationship between order and frequency of occurrence of restricted associated responses. *J. exp. Psychol.*, 1950, 40, 643–647.

Bousfield, W. A., & Cohen, B. H. Masculinity-femininity in the free recall of a categorized stimulus word list. *Percept. mot. Skills*, 1956, 6, 159–166.

Brown, W. Incidental memory in a group of persons. *Psychol. Rev.*, 1915, 22, 81–85.

Cohen, B. H., Bousfield, W. A., & Whitmarsh, G. A. *Cultural norms of verbal items in 43 categories.* Technical Report No. 22, ONR Contract Nonr-631 (00), Univer. of Conn., 1957.

Cromwell, R. L. Factors in the serial recall of names of acquaintances. *J. abnorm. soc. Psychol.*, 1956, 53, 63–67.

Feldman, S. M., & Underwood, B. J. Stimulus recall following paired-associate learning. *J. exp. Psychol.*, 1957, 53, 11–15.

Foley, J. P., Jr., & MacMillan, Z. L. Mediated generalization and the interpretation of verbal behavior: V. 'Free association' as related to differences in professional training. *J. exp. Psychol.*, 1943, 33, 299–310.

Goldiamond, I., & Hawkins, W. F. Vexierversuch: The log relationship between word-frequency and recognition obtained in the absence of stimulus words. *J. exp. Psychol.*, 1958, 56, 457–463.

Havron, M. D., & Cofer, C. N. On the learning of material congruent and incongruent with attitudes. *J. soc. Psychol.*, 1957, 46, 91–98.

Hovland, C. I., & Kurtz, K. H. Experimental studies in rote-learning theory: X. Pre-learning syllable familiarization and the length-difficulty relationship. *J. exp. Psychol.*, 1952, 44, 31–39.

Howes, D. On the relationship between the probability of a word as an association and in general linguistic usage. *J. abnorm. soc. Psychol.*, 1957, 54, 75–85.

Jantz, E. M. & Underwood, B. J. R-S learning as a function of meaningfulness and degree of S-R learning. *J. exp. Psychol.*, 1958, 56, 174–179.

Johnson, D. M. Word-association and word-frequency. *Amer. J. Psychol.*, 1956, 69, 125–126.

Key, C. B. Recall as a function of perceived relations. *Arch. Psychol.*, N. Y., 1926, 13, No. 83.

Mandler, G. Response factors in human learning. *Psychol. Rev.*, 1954, 61, 235–244.

Morikawa, Y. Functions of stimulus and response in paired-associate verbal learning. *Psychologia*, 1959, 2, 41–56.

Noble, C. E. The familiarity-frequency relationship. *J. exp. Psychol.*, 1954, 47, 13–16.

Noble, C. E. The effect of familiarization upon serial verbal learning. *J. exp. Psychol.*, 1955, 49, 333–338.

Noble, C. E., & McNeely, D. A. The role of meaningfulness (*m*) in paired-associate verbal learning. *J. exp. Psychol.*, 1957, 53, 16–22.

Noble, C. E., Stockwell, F. E., & Pryer, M. W. Meaningfulness (*m'*) and association value (*a*) in paired-associate syllable learning. *Psychol. Rep.*, 1957, 3, 441–452.

Riley, D. A., & Phillips, L. W. The effects of syllable familiarization on rote learning, association value, and reminiscence. *J. exp. Psychol.*, 1959, 57, 372–379.

Robinson, E. S. *Association theory today*. New York: Century, 1932.

Rosenzweig, M. R., & Postman, L. Frequency of usage and the perception of words. *Science*, 1958, 127, 263–266.

Sheffield, F. D. The role of meaningfulness of stimulus and response in verbal learning. Ph.D. dissertation, Yale Univer., 1946.

Thorndike, E. L. *The fundamentals of learning.* Teachers College, Columbia Univer., 1932.

Underwood, B. J., Runquist, W. R., & Schulz, R. W. Response learning in paired-associate lists as a function of intralist similarity. *J. exp. Psychol.,* 1959, 58, 70–78.

Underwood, B. J., & Schulz, R. W. Response dominance and rate of learning paired associates. *J. gen. Psychol.,* 1960, 62, 153–158.

Waters, R. H. The law of acquaintance. *J. exp. Psychol.,* 1939, 24, 180–191.

Weiss, R. L. Role of association value and experimentally produced familiarity in paired associate learning. Ph.D. dissertation, Univer. of Buffalo, 1958.

Chapter 7

Initial Experiments on Response Frequency

The results of Experiments 1 through 4, taken in conjunction with the work of other investigators, were interpreted as giving substantial support to the frequency hypothesis. They made it clear that it is possible to manipulate frequency *in the laboratory* and thereby produce an effect that is quite in accordance with theoretical expectations. Having demonstrated that the effects of manipulated frequency are consistent with the theory, we may proceed to examine the results of experiments in which differences in frequency of verbal units are inferred from correlated attributes (e.g., association value).

Four experiments are reported in this chapter. They are not closely interrelated (as compared with those of later chapters), but each has relevance to the frequency hypothesis. Some of the results found in the four experiments gave us our first serious theoretical jolts and, as most experiments do, somewhat changed the direction of our research.

EXPERIMENT 5

In two senses we may conceive of Experiment 5 as a reference experiment. First, it uses "standard" learning materials; that is, it uses materials which have been scaled by other investigators and used in other experiments. Second, it is an attempt to examine the effect on learning of variation along the complete range of response M.

Method

Lists. The four lists used were homogeneous paired-associate lists which differed with respect to response M. They were homogeneous or unmixed in that all items within each list had about the same M value. Each list had eight responses as follows: List 1, Witmer consonant syllables, 0 to 21 per cent; List 2, Witmer consonant syllables, 67 to 79 per cent; List 3, Glaze nonsense syllables, 47 to 53 per cent; List 4, common three-letter words. It was believed that List 1 and List 4 represented almost as extreme instances of M as it is possible to obtain with three-letter units. The responses for each list, with association values, are shown in Table 21. Thorndike-Lorge ratings are given for the responses of List 4.

TABLE 21. Experiment 5. Responses, M Values, and Mean Number Correct Anticipations in 20 Trials

	List 1			List 2	
Response	Witmer M	Mean Correct	Response	Witmer M	Mean Correct
ZKQ	21	1.22	GLN	75	13.17
GCZ	13	3.94	RFL	71	11.28
CJX	8	3.61	QTD	67	9.67
FPN	21	9.33	MPZ	67	8.22
HKM	13	7.39	HSK	79	9.94
XBD	17	6.33	XPR	71	7.78
QJF	0	1.50	NSC	71	10.17
SBH	17	12.89	DTH	79	11.22
	Mean	5.78		Mean	10.18

	List 3			List 4	
Response	Glaze M	Mean Correct	Response	T-L Value	Mean Correct
FEC	47	11.83	NOW	AA	14.61
LAH	47	11.00	ROT	8	13.83
NUR	53	14.89	WIN	AA	15.78
CAZ	53	13.94	HIS	AA	15.17
HEB	47	13.78	CAP	A	16.06
RIK	53	11.78	SUM	A	14.39
QUD	47	12.28	BAR	A	15.56
TIQ	53	11.28	LUG	2	15.78
	Mean	12.60		Mean	15.15

Choice of stimuli for this experiment, as well as for later paired-associate experiments, provided a difficult problem. Those who have worked with paired-associate lists are aware of the interaction which may occur between stimuli and responses when both consist of items from the same class of material. Indeed, evidence was presented on this problem in Experiments 1 and 2. Since the intent of Experiment 5 (as well as later experiments) was to get as pure an effect of response M as possible, it seemed necessary to use stimulus items of a class quite different from the responses. Our decision was to use numbers as stimuli, and in the present study they were single-digit numbers, 2 to 9 inclusive, always written as numerals.

In constructing unmixed or homogeneous lists, we believe that the necessity of maintaining intralist similarity constant among lists is of considerable importance. It is known that the lower the M, the greater are the effects of formal intralist similarity (Underwood & Richardson, 1956). However, even if it were possible to adjust accurately for this (by making intralist similarity lower for lists of low M than for those of high M), it does not seem desirable to do so. In the conceptual framework in which we are working, the fact that intralist similarity *does* have greater effect at low levels of M is essentially an effect of M on response integration. Therefore, intralist similarity, in terms of letter duplication, has been held relatively constant across lists. There is no duplication either among first letters or among third letters for a given list. All told, there are 9, 8, 8, and 8 letters duplicated in Lists 1 through 4, respectively.

Presentation of lists. The lists were presented on a memory drum at a 2:2-second rate. That is, the stimulus was presented alone for 2 sec., and the stimulus and response together, for 2 sec. The intertrial interval was 4 sec. The first trial was always a study trial with the subject being instructed to anticipate as many responses as possible on the second trial and on every trial thereafter. The responses were spelled. All lists were presented to all subjects for 20 anticipation trials.

In order to minimize the possibility that a particular stimulus and particular response may, when paired, form a "useful" association and thus bias the learning of that response, we used three different random pairings of the stimuli and responses for each list. Four orders of presentation were used. Furthermore, each order was used approximately equally often as the first order which a subject saw on the first trial. The use of different start orders avoids the same pair always being seen first on the first trial for all subjects.

Subjects and assignment to lists. All subjects were Northwestern University students enrolled in the elementary psychology course. Most of the subjects were not naive to verbal learning experiments, having served in one or more prior to the present one. A separate group of 18 subjects was assigned to learn each list. Subgroups of six subjects each were given different stimulus-response pairings. A randomized order of 72 entries was made up, subject to the restriction that each list be represented 18 times in the listing. Then the subjects were assigned successively in order of their appearance at the laboratory.

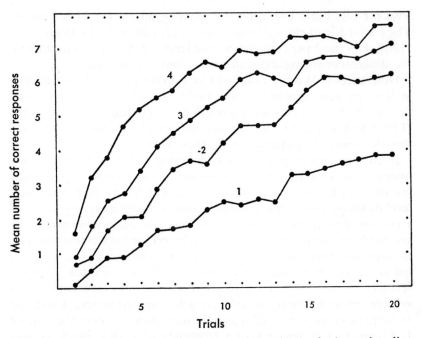

Figure 17. Experiment 5. Acquisition curves for four paired-associate lists varying in M of responses from low (1) to high (4).

Results

Over-all. As expected, and as may be seen in Table 21, large differences in the mean number of correct anticipations over 20 trials for the different lists were found. The items of List 1 were anticipated correctly on the average only 5.78 times, those of List 4, 15.15 times. The acquisition curves (Fig. 17) show absolutely no overlap on any trial. The number of subjects achieving one perfect trial within the 20 anticipation trials was 0, 8, 13, and 16 for Lists 1 through 4, respectively. Thus, it is quite clear that response M, as defined by these lists, produces wide differences in learning. The analysis now proceeds to a more detailed consideration of certain aspects of the learning.

Differences within lists. As noted earlier, items within lists were fairly homogeneous although the necessity of equating intralist similarity among lists produced more heterogeneity than desirable. An inspection of Table 21 shows considerable variation in learning among items within List 1. Analyses of variance for item differences within each list show the F to be significant beyond the 1 per cent significance level for List 1 and List 2, but far from significant for Lists 3 and 4. The F's for Lists 1 through 4 are 16.67, 3.23, 1.29, and 1.16. With 7 and 119 df, F at the 1 per cent significance level is 2.79. Some evaluation of the differences among items in Lists 1 and 2 is needed.

Differences in Witmer values of List 1 do not predict the differences in learning very accurately (see Table 21). The item learned most slowly (ZKQ) has an association value higher than all but one item (FPN) in the list. Are there other indices which might better predict differences in learning among these items?

In the previous chapter, when considering the spew hypothesis, we placed some emphasis on letter frequency per se when a response was not integrated. List 1 consists of syllables which have nearly as low a level of integration as it is possible to obtain. Integration may occur as a consequence of an item being pronounceable, as a consequence of associative strength between successive letters, or by a combination of these factors. Pronunciation ratings are not available for these syllables, but an inspection indicates they would be very low if rated. Some inferences of the associative strength between successive letters in a syllable might be made by evaluating bigram frequency. There are 16 bigrams in the list, 13 of which do not appear in either the T-L or U Count, two of which have a frequency of 1 (PN and BD), and one, a frequency of 21 (SB). (The fact that the syllable SBH is learned so rapidly probably reflects this high bigram frequency. However, it may also be noted that a well-known bookstore near Northwestern University, called the Student Book Exchange, is commonly known as SBX, so the "true" frequency of SB for these subjects is probably much higher than indicated by the tables.) In the aggregate, then, the syllables of List 1 consist of letters which have very little associative strength connecting them. Under these circumstances, letter frequency as such should be of importance as a determinant (or at least as a predictor) of learning.

To assess the relevance of letter frequency to the learning of List 1, we used the following procedure. The frequency of occurrence of each letter in the language was expressed as a proportion of the most frequent letter (E) given by the U Count (see Table 6, Chapter 5). For present purposes, the decimal was ignored and the converted value expressed as a whole number. The value for each letter in each syllable in List 1 was determined and then summed to get a single value for each syllable. The values for each letter and the sums for each syllable are shown in Table 22.

While a certain amount of good fortune may have attended these computations, the fact is that the summed letter values for the eight syllables when ranked from highest to lowest correspond perfectly with the learning scores when they are ranked from highest to lowest. In short, summed letter scores predict learning perfectly for this list of consonant syllables.

The evaluation of List 2 is less clear. Here, 14 of the 16 bigrams appear in the language count. In addition, an inspection of the list indicates some clear differences in pronunciability, with GLN, HSK, and DTH being most clearly pronounceable. But intralist similarity factors do not fall equally on the various letters in these syllables. Further-

TABLE 22. Experiment 5. List-1 Syllables
Converted into Individual Letter Values

(See text for complete explanation.)

	First Letter	Second Letter	Third Letter	Sum
ZKQ	1	6	1	8
GCZ	17	22	1	40
CJX	22	1	2	25
FPN	18	15	56	89
HKM	42	6	21	69
XBD	2	12	32	46
QJF	1	1	18	20
SBH	54	12	42	108

more, the differences in learning, while significant statistically for all items considered, are small relative to the differences in List 1. Nevertheless, at the gross level, simple summed letter values do predict to a certain extent. The four most rapidly learned syllables have summed values of 105, 99, 144, 132, whereas the four syllables learned most slowly have values of 103, 37, 82, 66. Certain other differences among items in List 2 will be pointed out in subsequent analyses.

The foregoing analysis leads to the conclusion that when very low associative connection exists between letters in a syllable, learning can be predicted fairly accurately by simple summed letter frequency. As the associative connection between letters increases, and as pronunciability differences begin to appear, the summed-letter predictor will clearly break down. The mean summed-letter values for the four lists are 51, 96, 118, and 124 for Lists 1 through 4. This progression merely confirms the fact, presented by correlational techniques in a previous chapter, that the higher the M of a verbal unit, the more closely the letters approximate the frequency of letter occurrence in words.

It should be apparent, also, that with an increase in letter frequency, there must also be an increase in bigram frequency. For the present four lists, the median bigram frequency is 0, 137, 571, and 735 for Lists 1 through 4.

Overt errors. Over the 20 anticipation trials the mean number of total overt errors was 20.33, 20.39, 12.67, and 9.33 for Lists 1 through 4. The interpretation of these differences is severely hampered by the fact that the amount learned during the 20 trials was widely different for the four lists. However, since amount learned is inversely related to number of errors for these lists, it is quite clear that if learning had been taken to the same criterion, the number of overt errors would decrease from low to high M.

A certain understanding of the processes producing these error differences can be obtained by looking at the different types of errors that are made. In Table 23 the total errors are broken into three types,

TABLE 23. Experiment 5. Types and Frequencies (f) of Overt Errors

	List 1		List 2		List 3		List 4	
Error Type	*f*	%	*f*	%	*f*	%	*f*	%
Misplaced	26	7.1	92	25.0	92	40.4	124	73.8
Mixed	156	42.6	121	33.0	62	27.2	4	2.4
Partial	184	50.3	154	42.0	74	32.4	40	23.8
Totals	366	100.0	367	100.0	228	100.0	168	100.0

each type then being expressed as a percentage of the total for the list. The types are the same as distinguished in Experiment 1, namely: (1) misplaced response: response unit given to the wrong stimulus; (2) mixed error: any three-letter response which is not a three-letter unit in the list; (3) partial error: only one or two letters given.

First, it may be observed that in learning List 4, subjects gave very few mixed errors. This would be expected in view of the fact that the words in List 4 are integrated three-letter units at the outset of learning. On the other hand, List 1, which is assumed to have responses consisting of non-integrated letters, produced a large number of mixed errors. As will be shown later, these responses consisted of letters from the list but were merely "put together" wrong. Of course, had the learning of List 1 been carried to the same level as List 4, the number of these mixed errors would have been still greater for List 1.

The argument that the responses of List 4 were integrated at the start of learning might seem to be self-evident. However, it might also seem to be contradicted by the fact that 40 partial responses were given in learning this list. A more likely interpretation of these partial responses, however, is that the subject started to spell a response and then recognized it was the wrong response for that stimulus. Of the 40 errors, 36 could be so interpreted in that the one or two letters given were the first (or first two) letters of a word in the list which was not paired with the stimulus to which the error occurred. Only four of the partial responses were the initial letters of the appropriate word for that stimulus. Thus, nearly all of the partial errors of List 4 can be interpreted as misplaced responses.

A point of method should be made about partial errors. In the learning procedure, the subject is allowed a 2-sec. anticipation interval. If the three letters are not given before the end of the interval, the experimenter records only those letters which were given before the shutter on the memory drum rises indicating the end of the 2-sec. interval. It is known (Waters, 1939) that the lower the M of three-letter verbal units, the longer is the time required to spell those units. Thus, if we assume that the anticipation latency of the first letter of a word and of a consonant syllable were the same, the number of partial responses would be expected to be greater for the consonant syllable than for the word. In none of the experiments reported here has any correction been made for this; as a consequence the number of partial responses is artifactually somewhat greater the lower the M. Probably no critical bias is involved; that is, had some adjustment been made, the relative differences would have remained the same although the magnitude would have been reduced somewhat.

Table 23 suggests that as M decreases, there is a corresponding decrease in the tendency to give misplaced responses, i.e., to give three-letter responses which are correct for another stimulus in the list. However, it must be remembered that the subjects learning List 1 had acquired many fewer responses which could be misplaced than had the subjects learning List 4. Many of the responses in List 1 were never given correctly at any time during the 20 learning trials. A resolution of the problem can be obtained by another measure. The question may be asked: "When a response was given, in what proportion of the times was it paired with its stimulus?" In learning List 1, the subjects gave 832 correctly-paired responses and 26 misplaced responses; the subjects learning List 4 gave 2181 correct responses and 124 misplaced responses. Thus, misplaced responses occurred about 3 per cent and 5 per cent, respectively, of the times the response was given. Hence, it may be concluded that when a subject gives a correct three-letter sequence, he is very likely to give it to the correct stimulus, and this does not vary greatly as a function of M.

As noted several times, List 1 is considered to be made up of items with very low response integration. The three letters making up the syllables are virtually impossible to integrate by applying even loose rules of pronunciation. And, as noted earlier, the associative connections between the letters within a syllable are presumed to be very low at the start of learning. As seen in Table 23, many mixed errors occurred, and many two-letter sequences (partials) were incorrect in that they did not occur among the responses in the list. What is the nature of these errors?

Of considerable importance is the fact that the subject only *rarely* gives a letter which is not in the list—he does not import letters. In all the overt wrong responses there were 789 letters given in learning List 1, only 20 of which were not in the list. This was true in spite of the fact that at least several of the 11 letters of the alphabet not in the list would, in general, have high associative connection with the consonants in the list. More particularly, vowels rarely occurred. There was continual misplacement of letters from within the list, primarily among the second and third letters. For example, the subject would say ZBD instead of ZKL or XBD. So, it isn't that the subject doesn't get "mixed up"; rather, it is that the "mix-up" occurs almost exclusively among letters within the list.

An analysis of two- and three-letter errors in terms of bigram frequency shows that, on the average, these errors have higher frequency in the language than do the correct bigrams. However, since the correct bigram frequency is essentially zero, the bigram frequency of the errors almost *has* to be greater than zero.

A more precise analysis of the particular letter errors will not be made since the differential similarity among items within a list hinders clear interpretation. There are two essential facts that have been made with regard to overt errors: first, the nature of these errors varies as a function of M, and, second, letters are rarely imported in learning even the most difficult combinations of letters.

Stage analyses. It is believed that the major difference in learning as a function of response M is to be attributed to differences in Stage 1, the response-learning stage. Looking at the extremes, we see that the responses of List 4 are integrated, have high spew strength and would, therefore, be quickly available for Stage 2 (the development of associative strength with the stimuli). List 1, on the other hand, consists of responses which are not integrated in any manner, thus requiring a long Stage-1 learning phase. Indeed, in examining the raw data sheets of List 1, one is impressed by the gradualness with which

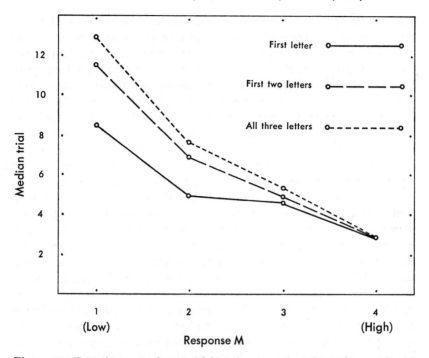

Figure 18. Experiment 5. Stages of learning as a function of response M (see text for complete explanation).

the letters making up the responses become associated. In essence, there are two sub-second phases involved within the broadly conceived Stage 1. The second letter must be associated with the first, and the third with the second. An attempt has been made to plot the response learning phase for the different lists. The end product is shown in Fig. 18. Considerable explanation is required to show how each of the curves was derived.

First, it may be noted that the four lists are given along the X axis, with equal distances between them. This is conceived of as a dimension of M, with the equal distances between lists used merely for convenience.

In the learning records, the first indication that any response learning had occurred would be the giving of a first letter of a response. This would not have to be paired with an appropriate stimulus, although it may have been; that the subject had given the first letter in the first position, was the essential requirement. It may have been a single-letter response, the first of two letters, or the first of three.

When this occurred, the trial on which it occurred was noted. If the first letter first occurred in the second or third position of a two- or three-letter response, it was ignored for the present analysis. (It may be noted, however, that the first letter of a syllable is infrequently given as a second or third letter. But because of intralist similarity factors, the present lists are not good ones to make a precise determination of the frequency with which a letter is misplaced in position, particularly misplacements between the first and third positions).

The above tally results in a distribution of trials on which the first letter of the units was first given for each list. Next, the median trial on which this occurred was determined. The median was used in preference to the mean, since the distributions for Lists 1 and 4 were badly skewed (in opposite directions) and since many of the first letters were never given within the 20 anticipation trials for List 1. A value of 21 was assigned arbitrarily to these items. The median values are plotted for each list as the lower curve in Fig. 18, the legend being: "First Letter." As M increases, the trial on which the first letter was first given decreases.

The second determination involved the first *two* letters. That is, the trial was noted on which the first two letters of each syllable in the list were first given, with the requirement that the two letters must be in proper sequence. The result is the middle curve of Fig. 18.

Finally, a determination was made of the trial on which the three letters of each syllable were first given (in correct sequence), and these median values form the upper line in Fig. 18. This curve represents the point in learning at which the response *might* be said to be integrated, and, clearly, this varies greatly as a function of M.

It may be seen that for List 4, the three points cannot be distinguished for plotting purposes. This means that when the subject first attempted to give a three-letter word, he gave all three letters.

For List 1, the first letter of a response was first given, on the average, after 8.5 trials had elapsed. Is it to be concluded that these 8.5 trials were required to learn the first letter? Very likely not. There are wide individual differences in the propensities of subjects to respond with incorrect or partial responses. For example, total overt errors for List 1 varied from 1 to 59 among the 18 subjects. Some subjects will rarely respond until they can give the complete three-letter sequence in its proper order; others seem to respond with each additional letter they learn. Thus, the separation between the three curves for List 1 is minimal; in actual fact, they are probably much more widely separated, but the learning records do not provide an index of the "true" separation. In any event, the curves of Fig. 18 fully warrant the conclusion that there is an inverse relationship between M and the amount of time spent on the response-learning phase.

The next question concerns the associative phase—the association of the response with the numerical stimulus. Once a response is integrated, does the associative phase take place at the same rate for the different lists or does response M further influence the rate at which this stage occurs? While no definitive answer can be given to these questions, the evidence suggests a conclusion that response M *does* influence the associative stage. More particularly, the lower the M of the response, the slower is the associative stage, but the effect of M for this stage is considerably less than its effect on the first stage. Why this conclusion cannot be asserted more convincingly will become apparent as the problems of analysis are presented.

In Fig. 18 the end of the response-learning phase was assumed to be at that point where the response was first given correctly, whether paired with its appropriate stimulus or not. But it seems unlikely that a response in List 1 would be as well integrated at this point as would a three-letter word in List 4. If integration is not complete, a portion of the nominal second phase must be given over to further integration.

On the other hand, the responses of List 1, at least the first letters of those responses, might develop associative strength with their respective stimuli during the long first phase. If this did occur, once the response *was* integrated, the second phase might appear to take place very rapidly and perhaps even as rapidly as for the three-letter words in List 4. It was previously shown that the number of misplaced correct responses was about 3 per cent for List 1 and 5 per cent for List 4. This suggests a small effect; that is, it suggests that some association of the stimuli and at least the first letter of the responses in List 1 did occur during Stage 1 learning. Further evidence bearing on the issue can be obtained by asking a somewhat different question, namely: "When a response is *first* given as a correct three-letter sequence, in what proportion of the cases is it given to the correct stimulus?" For Lists 1 through 4, the values are 93 per cent, 83 per cent, 88 per cent, and 83 per cent. While there is no progression as a function of M, the extremes indicate again that the subjects in learning List 1 are a little less likely to misplace responses, thus suggesting again that some associative connection between the stimulus and the response has occurred during Stage 1.

Another way to view the problem is to ask about the development of associative strength between the stimulus and the response *after* it is first correctly anticipated, i.e., the correct response being given to its correct stimulus. Growth curves (not shown here) of associative strength have been plotted as a function of number of correct anticipations for each list. They leave no doubt that the rate of growth is directly related to M; the curves of Lists 1 and 4 do not overlap at any point. In fact, these differences are underestimated, since the most difficult items of List 1 often did not enter into the calculations because they were never anticipated correctly. But these data suffer the same ambiguity of interpretation. Is the growth of associative strength slower for List 1 than for List 4 because response M influences this growth in the second-stage sense or because the response was not completely integrated at the time it was first given correctly? A definitive answer is not possible from the present data, although it could be gotten by pre-training on the items of List 1 (somewhat as was done in Experiment 1) until they were obviously very well integrated. However, another analysis has been made which is suggestive.

For this analysis, only Lists 1 and 4 were used. All items which were used had been given correctly once before trial 13. For each of these items a tabulation was made of "what happened" on the next eight trials. For example, if an item were first given correctly and paired correctly on trial 3, what happened on trials 4 through 11 was recorded. Thus, for each item used, eight trials of history subsequent to the first correct anticipation were available.

For List 1 only 73 responses met the criterion, while for List 4, 139 responses were available. Since there were eight trials involved, for List 1 there was a total of 584 opportunities to respond; for List 4, 1,112 opportunities. Of these, 81 per cent turned out to be correct responses for List 4; only 62 per cent for List 1. For List 4 only 14 per cent were blanks; for List 1, 26 per cent. Other responses intruded in 5 per cent of the cases for List 4; 1 per cent for List 1. The critical datum is whether or not the subjects learning List 1 gave responses indicative of incomplete integration. Of the total possible responses, 10 per cent were errors which could be interpreted as indicating lack of integration. This would be indicated in the responses having the three letters out of order, or those with only the first or first two letters given. Errors were not classified here if it was clear that a misplaced response was involved. Certain ones, amounting to 2 per cent of the total possible, could not be so classified. Not a single response indicating lack of integration was found in the records for List 4.

Now, while these data do not completely resolve the issue, they certainly suggest that Stage 1 was not complete for List 1 at the time a response was first correctly anticipated. Even if we allow for latency differences, which may have produced some of the partial responses, the fact still would seem to hold.

Can lack of integration of response account for all of the apparent difference in development of associative strength between the stimulus and response as a function of M? This seems unlikely. Therefore, it is concluded that response M does influence development of associative strength between the stimulus and response over and above its effect on Stage 1. However, relative to its effect on the first stage, its effect on the second stage is small. Indeed, it is our belief that the effect of M on the second stage is of the same order of magnitude as the effect of a corresponding range of stimulus M on learning. Later experiments will give more definitive evidence on this matter.

Further Implications

The major results of Experiment 5 have been presented in the context of a frequency theory and, at this point, require no further elaboration. However, there is one issue which has not been discussed and which should be considered at this time.

At the start of learning, the associative connection between the letters of a given consonant syllable in List 1 was, to say the least, weak. But the associative connection between the letters and letters *not* in the list (especially vowels) would be relatively high. Yet, the results have shown that it is a very rare occurrence for these "foreign" letters to appear overtly. This fact is simply another manifestation of what has been termed the interference paradox (cf., Chapter 4).

The interference paradox comes about because behavior doesn't correspond to logical expectations. The paradox is this: If there is a strong associative connection between A and B, and if the subject is asked to learn C to A, between which there is little associative connection, why doesn't the response B continually appear as an intrusion during the learning of A-C?

Without attempting to answer the question "why," the evidence is overwhelming that a selective response mechanism exists. Just as few letters were imported in the present learning, so also: (1) in the negative transfer paradigm, A-B, A-C, few B responses intrude during the learning of A-C; (2) subjects rarely give words as responses when learning nonsense syllables; (3) when learning words, subjects infrequently give words from outside the list even though there are strong associative connections with these other words, and so on. In short, if one accepts the facts at face value, it seems apparent that one should likewise accept the existence of a response selector mechanism. The subject responds only with items or letters from which he has received recent stimulation. The mechanism in the present situation is "set off" by the responses acting as stimuli, the result being that only the recall strength of those responses (letters) is activated. Items or letters not in the list are not activated.

The selector mechanism, itself unexplained, is assumed here as a fundamental behavioral law. It serves as a modifier to the general frequency hypothesis when that hypothesis is applied to a particular learning situation. The spew hypothesis had its origin in the order of emission of responses in a relatively free situation. The order of emission is directly related to frequency of experience. In the verbal-learning situation, the selector mechanism restricts the spew to those response units within the list. Within this restricted group of responses, the spew hypothesis is said to hold; the order of availability is directly related to frequency.

Even if we assume the selector mechanism as a way of "getting around" the interference paradox, it can be seen that the paradox is only partially resolved, for the question can be raised as to whether or not covert interference occurs. For example, in List 1 an item was HKM. K has very weak associative strength connecting it to H, whereas vowels have strong associative connection to H. Is the difficulty in learning HK due to covert interference from these other strong associations? Or is the difficulty merely due to the fact that the associative connection between H and K must essentially be built up from "scratch"? This is a part of the age-old question of whether or not the subject knows what is wrong but doesn't know what is right. However, does the knowing of what is wrong interfere with the learning of a new association?

The question remains unanswered. The assertion has been only that a selector mechanism operates to prevent the *overt* occurrence of strongly associated responses which are not within the list being learned.

EXPERIMENT 6

Experiment 6 continues the study of the effect of variation in response M on learning. Rather than use traditional learning materials, however, we have used trigrams as responses. These units had also been subjected to pronunciation ratings, and it was the results of the present experiment that first called our attention to the importance of pronunciability as an integrating habit.

Method

In most details the procedure is the same as for Experiment 5. Four lists were constructed, but unlike Experiment 5, these lists were heterogeneous or mixed lists. That is, items with widely different trigram frequencies occurred in each list. The four sets of responses are shown in Table 24. Several characteristics of these lists need to be pointed out and discussed.

TABLE 24. Experiment 6. Lists Used, Trigram Frequencies (f), Pronunciation Ratings (PR), and Mean Number of Correct Anticipations in 20 Trials

List 1				List 2			
Response	f	PR	Mean Correct	Response	f	PR	Mean Correct
RCH	156	7.27	14.73	XPE	141	8.05	11.87
ZON	10	3.15	15.87	VIZ	3	3.03	16.60
WAS	486	2.19	18.40	CYR	8	5.44	14.40
XPE	141	8.05	11.27	GHT	534	7.63	14.27
BUT	270	1.91	16.87	STI	660	2.49	15.67
IFO	55	4.34	15.47	JOK	34	4.89	18.33
TLY	295	5.75	14.73	MAN	395	1.66	18.80
DGM	10	8.42	14.07	ULD	297	5.00	15.27
Means	178	5.14	15.18	Means	259	4.77	15.65

List 3				List 4			
Response	f	PR	Mean Correct	Response	f	PR	Mean Correct
EIG	229	5.86	14.20	ART	449	1.97	18.47
CKB	7	8.39	8.00	QUE	255	4.23	13.47
MPT	53	7.56	11.53	CHA	271	2.95	15.47
NDF	7	8.31	7.67	ING	1673	2.36	18.00
SOU	184	4.15	16.27	XPO	56	7.81	11.93
VER	545	2.60	16.20	STY	92	3.19	13.60
WHO	316	2.29	17.87	MBK	1	8.18	10.93
YAL	85	3.67	15.47	DFL	1	7.66	11.47
Means	178	5.35	13.40	Means	350	4.79	14.17

1. The lists were constructed at the time when only the T-L Count was available. Two items which had approximately the same frequency were used in each list; thus, four different frequency levels were represented. In Table 24, however, the frequency values are from the total column in Appendix D; they represent the summation of all three counts of trigrams. It can be seen that the use of these values results in

some fairly large differences in the mean frequency for the different lists. However, this is largely attributable to one or two items and, as pointed out previously, even large differences among already highly frequent units are probably of little consequence.

2. The PR column in Table 24 represents the mean pronunciability ratings. The details of the procedure for obtaining these ratings were presented in Chapter 2.

3. It should be noted that the structure of the trigrams is varied. That is, vowels or consonants may occur at any position in the sequence of three letters. Three consonants may occur, two vowels and a consonant, two consonants and a vowel, and so on.

4. Intralist similarity is relatively low. Only two letters are repeated in each list.

5. One trigram (XPE) is used twice, occurring in both Lists 1 and 2.

In terms of the spew hypothesis, each list constitutes an independent test. The higher the frequency of an item within the list, the sooner it should be available for entering into an associative connection with the stimulus with which it is paired.

As indicated above, details of the procedure are much the same as for Experiment 5: numbers 2 through 9 were used as stimuli; there were four different orders of presentation; there were four groups of subjects, and so on. The only deviation from Experiment 5 was in the use of 15 instead of 18 subjects for each list. For one pairing for each list, only three subjects were used, with six being assigned to each of the other two pairings.

Results

There are two general approaches which may be used when handling results from several mixed lists. First, each list may itself be considered a test of the frequency hypothesis; therefore, in the present study there would be four independent tests of the hypothesis. The second approach is to allow each list to lose its identity and "throw" all items together as a single test of the hypothesized relationship between learning and response frequency. This might be done by correlation procedures over all 32 items, or it might be done by grouping items according to frequency so that, say, four new lists are made up consisting of items which are relatively homogeneous with regard to frequency. Then comparisons could be made between the four lists which will differ in mean frequency. Some representation of all these procedures will be used in presenting the results.

Only a single response measure will be used—mean number of correct anticipations over 20 trials. This value for each item is given in Table 24. A second measure was based on the trial on which a response was first given, whether paired with its proper stimulus or not. However, the rank-order correlation between this measure and the mean number correct over 20 trials for the 32 items was −.98; hence, little is to be gained by working with both response measures.

Over-all evaluation. Without presenting any of the statistical details, we may report that the differences in learning among lists were not significant statistically, whereas the differences among items within each list were highly significant statistically. Implied in the first fact is the justification for throwing all items together without regard to lists, and in the second fact that frequency, or some other variable, is producing a difference in learning among items within lists.

Within-list relationships: frequency. For each item within each list there is not only a learning score based on the mean performance of 15 subjects, but also a frequency measure. Correlations between these two arrays have been determined as a test of the frequency-learning hypothesis. The product-moment correlations for Lists 1 through 4 are .53, .00, .72, and .73, respectively. The corresponding rank-order correlations are .42, −.07, .83, and .95. These data indicate that for Lists 3 and 4 the relationship between frequency and learning is striking, but that for List 1 the relationship is only moderate and for List 2 breaks down completely. If all 32 items are thrown together, the rank correlation is .56, the product-moment correlation, .46. Statistically speaking these are significantly different from zero. Nevertheless, the relationship is not of the magnitude we expected. As we puzzled over these results, especially the results for List 2, the importance of the role of pronunciability first became apparent.

Within-list relationships: pronunciability. The product-moment correlations between pronunciability and learning for Lists 1 through 4 are .86, .76, .90, and .95. The corresponding rank-order correlations are .95, .90, .90, and .98. (Since the pronunciability scale has low values for easy pronunciation and high values for difficult pronunciation, the above correlations are actually negative. The sign is ignored here as it will be in reporting the results of subsequent experiments.)

For List 4 we determined rank-order correlations between pronunciability and learning for *each subject*. These ranged from .16 to .95, with a mean of .59. Clearly, an astonishingly large proportion of the variance is accounted for by the pronunciability dimension.

An examination of the relationships within the four lists indicates

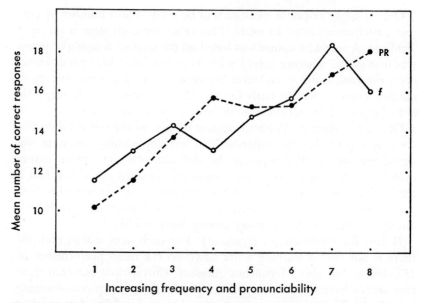

Figure 19. Experiment 6. Mean number of correct responses in 20 trials as a function of frequency (*f*) and pronunciability (PR).

that in nearly every instance where pronunciability runs counter to frequency, the learning scores covary with pronunciability rather than with frequency. Rank-order correlations between frequency and pronunciability for Lists 1 through 4 are .45, .17, .87, and .91. It is clear that whenever the correlation between learning and frequency is low, the correlation between frequency and pronunciability is also low.

Turning again to the relationship between pronunciability and learning, we find the product-moment correlation for all 32 items to be .85, the rank-order correlation, .88. A partial correlation between pronunciability and learning with frequency constant is estimated at .82.

The relationship between learning and frequency and between learning and pronunciability is shown graphically in Fig. 19. Each point represents the mean number of correct anticipations for four items. The 32 items were rank ordered on frequency (and on pronunciability), and successive groups of four items each were plotted.

Discussion

In Chapter 2 a study was reported in which subjects rated how fast they thought they could learn certain verbal units relative to other units. These ratings correlated very highly with other dimensions used to define M. One of the criteria which subjects reported they used in making their ratings was the degree of ease (or difficulty) they found in pronouncing the unit. The results of the present experiment, in which pronunciability ratings and learning are highly related, suggest that these reports were valid. The fact that the subjects were required to spell the responses in learning the present lists is probably of little consequence; spelling is merely the instrumental response required by the instructions. The unit of recall is, when possible, a pronounceable, hence an integrated unit.

The central question which the data of Experiment 6 raises is: "What happens to the frequency hypothesis?" The data have clearly shown that frequency breaks down as a predictor when it runs counter to pronunciability. Obviously, the frequency hypothesis has to be abandoned, modified, or expanded. As a preliminary to refining the frequency hypothesis (there is no intention to abandon it as yet), the frequency theory as developed thus far will be summarized.

The theoretical development started with the empirical observation that when a subject is allowed to respond with verbal units in a relatively free situation, the order of emission is directly related to the frequency with which these units have been experienced. This is the spew hypothesis. The second step was the application of the hypothesis to the response units of a list the subject is asked to learn. A selector mechanism limits the responses to those response items in the list, and the order in which these items become available for entering into associations with the stimuli is determined by frequency. When elements (letters) of the response units are not integrated, that part of response learning leading to integration follows the frequency principle. Once the response is integrated, the frequency principle applies to it.

It becomes apparent from Experiment 6 that if a relatively infrequent combination of letters is pronounceable by virtue of well-developed habits which the subject brings to the situation, the response integration phase is accomplished via this pronunciation. The frequency principle may be said to apply to pronunciability in the sense that the units with which the subject has had most frequent experience are at least of syllabic size. In speaking or listening this is clear. In reading, the units may be larger. Only in writing might there be the possibility that the letter is the unit of experience, and this is by no means clear. Thus, in learning three-letter units, the subject applies the habit most frequently used with such units. Only when this habit breaks down or is inappropriate, does the subject revert to smaller units (letters). The frequency principle applies to whatever unit the subject "uses" in the situation. When a syllabic unit can be used, it is used, since this conforms to the most frequent experience.

The data have shown that relatively high-frequency units which are rated as difficult to pronounce are learned more slowly than those which are less frequent but rated easy to pronounce. Units of the former variety are made up of letters which cut across syllables (e.g., XPE, DGM) and have relatively low frequency in terms of the manner in which a subject usually deals with verbal units.

For a nonintegrated three-letter unit, a unit which is not pronounceable and in which the associative connection between letters is low, the frequency principle holds for letters. If three syllables, all easily pronounced, were put together in an order not to form a word and so that the associative connection between syllables is low, the frequency principle should apply in integrating the three syllables. So, too, if three, three-syllable words had to be learned in sequence, and the order of these words was such that little or no associative connection existed between them, the frequency principle should also apply in the integration of the three words. Variation in word sequence to provide different approximations to normal word sequence essentially deals with this situation (e.g., Miller & Selfridge, 1950).

Once again it should be repeated that the theory as developed thus far states nothing about how the associative connection between units develops; it states only that frequency determines the priority with which associations will be developed since frequency determines availability.

Therefore, while Experiment 6 has shown the importance of pronunciability as an integrating habit, the fundamental principle may still be frequency. One critical test would be the learning of items equally pronounceable but differing in frequency. Another would be the learning of items differing widely in pronunciability but equivalent in integration of letters. Later experiments will give some evidence on such tests.

Two final comments should be made. It must be remembered that the frequency values being used are for the printed language. This in turn raises two questions which have been raised earlier but should be repeated. First, how does frequency input as a function of hearing, speaking, and writing correspond with printed frequency (reading frequency)? This is unknown. Undoubtedly there are wide divergencies. For example, the syllable JOK occurs with relatively low frequency in the language samples used to determine trigram frequency.

It does not seem improbable that it may occur with relatively high frequency in emitted language. The second question concerns the relative frequency effects produced by, say, emitted frequency by speaking, as compared with the effects of frequency of reading. As we noted in a previous chapter, the more important role has been assigned emitted frequency by other writers, but there are no data bearing on the question.

The second general comment concerns the pronunciation ratings as such. These ratings have been shown to relate very highly to learning, and they form a quite finely graded continuum on which even small separations are related to learning. Yet, it is a little perplexing to examine some of the differences in pronunciability for some items. For example, STY is rated as appreciably more difficult to pronounce than STI, and both more difficult than MAN or ART. When a subject makes ratings of such units, where differences in pronunciability may be "really" slight or nonexistent, is it possible that he may "slide over" into the use of other characteristics of the material, such as familiarity? A test of this could be made by having subjects rate simultaneously on pronunciability and familiarity with careful instructions concerning the fact that these need not covary.

The problem facing a subject when he is requested to rate verbal units on a particular characteristic is a difficult one, especially when other attributes of the material are dominant. It seems possible that the subject may, under such circumstances, "slip over" into rating on the more dominant characteristic, especially when differences in the to-be-rated attribute are small. An illustration which suggests that this *may* happen is available. Noble (1958) reported a correlation of .57 between M of his 96 dissyllables and affectivity ratings of these same syllables. Since it has been very difficult to show any consistent relationship between affectivity and learning, and very easy to show a relationship between M and learning, it seemed possible that when Noble's subjects rated affectivity, they may have instead been unduly influenced by familiarity differences among the dissyllables. Indeed, as Noble pointed out (personal communication), the dissyllables were deliberately chosen *not* to have high affective connotations.

In view of these considerations, it might be expected that if subjects were asked to rate these dissyllables along with other words which obviously had high affective tone, they would be less inclined to make judgments on familiarity. As a test of this, 27 of Noble's dissyllables were chosen to represent the full scale of M. Combined with these were 34 additional words which had more obvious affective characteristics (e.g., *kiss, love, vomit, death*). The 61 words were randomized, and subjects were requested to rate them along a nine-point scale of affectivity.

For the 27 dissyllables, the correlation between M and affectivity as scaled by Noble was .51. (Dr. Noble kindly supplied the data necessary for this calculation.) For these same 27 items, the ratings between M and affectivity as scaled in the context of the more affective words was −.003. Seventeen of the 27 items did not deviate more than .5 from the neutral point on the scale. Actually, this is not a very good test of the proposition since all 96 dissyllables were not used and since Noble used weighted scale values from a four-category scale. Nevertheless, the data are suggestive, and it seems likely that caution is in order when dealing with ratings of attributes of verbal units when those units differ with respect to more dominant characteristics. In fact, the evidence was suggestive enough to push us into further evaluation of pronunciability ratings.

Further Evaluation of Pronunciability Ratings

Is it possible that when subjects were asked to rate pronunciability, they may have "slipped over" into making ratings on familiarity in certain portions of the scale where pronunciability differences are small but familiarity differences rather large? The above results on affectivity ratings suggest that this could possibly happen. Therefore, when the results for experiments to be reported in the next chapter continued to show a depressingly low relationship between trigram frequency and learning but a continued high relationship between pronunciability and learning, we felt this possibility should be explored. Since the results were essentially negative, they will be reported briefly.

A total of 95 trigrams were rated. For 35 subjects "standard" instructions for rating pronunciability were given (as reported in Chap. 2). For 35 comparable subjects special instructions were given to avoid rating on the basis of frequency and familiarity. These instructions were long and need not be quoted here. It is sufficient to say that they rather forcefully warned the subject against rating on the basis of familiarity. Extreme illustrations were given. That is, examples were given of high-frequency trigrams which were both easy and difficult to pronounce and low-frequency trigrams which were also both easy and difficult to pronounce. We feel confident that the subject understood what was expected of him, i.e., he was not to let familiarity or frequency influence his ratings of pronunciability.

The rank-order correlation for the mean scale values resulting from the two sets of instructions was .96. For medians, the value was .95. Clearly, the magnitude of the effect on the ratings produced by the instructions was not great enough to "make sense" of a frequency theory for the learning data of Experiment 6 as well as the results of experiments to be reported later. We must conclude that *if* familiarity responses were contaminating the pronunciability ratings, our instructions did not eliminate these responses.

One fact concerning the reliability of pronunciation ratings is worth reporting. Our original ratings were obtained in 1957 from 181 subjects. The above ratings were carried out in 1959 with 35 subjects (standard instructions). Thirty-one of the items which appeared in the list rated in 1957 also appeared in the list used in 1959. The product-moment correlation between the mean ratings for these 31 items was .98.

We have obtained pronunciability ratings on 239 three-letter units, and these are given in Appendix E. Insofar as these 239 units can be considered representative of all three-letter units, it can be reported that the ratings are bimodally distributed. Subjects find very few items that they place in the middle of the scale; it is almost as if a unit can or cannot be pronounced. The expert on correlation will see immediately that this bimodality would not only be a serious violation of an assumption underlying the use of a product-moment correlation, but would also tend to inflate the magnitude of the coefficient if some relationship is present with another variable. We will deal with these problems in a later chapter.

EXPERIMENT 7

Thus far we have drawn no fundamental distinction between words and nonwords. It has been suggested that the range of frequency differences represented in the Thorndike-Lorge list is too small to expect any large differences in learning. But as far as any scaling operations are concerned and as far as the basic relationship between learning and frequency is concerned, we have not sought to dichotomize words and nonwords. Nevertheless, it is quite a reasonable question to ask if there will be a difference in learning words and nonwords when these two classes of items are equated for frequency. Is there something about "wordiness" per se which will facilitate learning?

If one examines the results for Experiment 6, he will see that when words and nonwords are in the same list, words tend to be learned more rapidly. This fact is not entirely unambiguous either in Experiment 6 or in several later experiments. However, none of these experiments is completely satisfactory as a test of the issue. Is it conceivable that one or two words in a list in which there are six or seven nonwords may be facilitated by an isolation effect (see Kimble & Dufort, 1955)? We believe that isolation effects can be derived from principles relating intralist similarity and learning. Without amplifying this position, we will state that the question can be given an unambiguous answer only by having an equal number of words and nonwords in a list. To make such a test is the purpose of Experiment 7.

Method

Two paired-associate lists were used, each being considered an independent test of the question under investigation. The response items in these two lists are shown in Table 25. Four of the items in each list are trigrams and four are three-letter words. The lists were constructed originally to have equal frequencies for the words and nonwords as determined by the T-L Count. However, the frequencies given in Table 25 are based on the total count.

TABLE 25. Experiment 7. Lists Used, Trigram Frequencies (f) and Mean Number Correct Anticipations in 20 Trials

List 1			List 2		
	f	Mean Correct		f	Mean Correct
CLO	281	14.73	SPE	284	12.13
GEN	251	13.07	SHO	369	13.20
ONG	306	13.87	ITY	358	16.47
GHT	534	15.47	EAD	307	15.67
EAT	367	18.53	THE	2512	16.27
FOR	773	17.20	ROW	248	15.80
SON	341	17.80	HAS	309	13.87
ACE	277	18.07	LOT	284	17.20

The procedure was exactly the same as for Experiment 6. Indeed, these two lists were run simultaneously with the four lists of Experiment 6. Single-digit numbers were used as stimuli, and all 15 subjects learning each list were given 20 anticipation trials.

Results

The mean number of times each response was correctly anticipated in 20 trials is given in Table 25. The over-all learning for the two lists

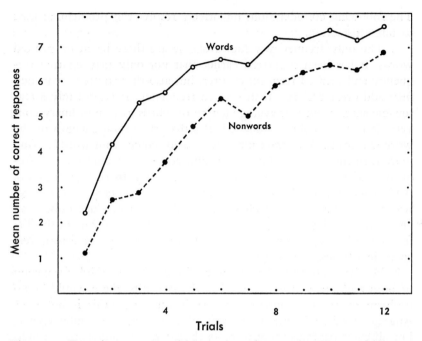

Figure 20. Experiment 7. Acquisition curves for words and nonwords.

does not differ significantly ($t = 1.14$). For each list the average number of correct anticipations for the words is greater than for the trigrams. For List 1, the t is 4.36, for List 2, 2.89. When we combine the eight words for one curve and the eight trigrams for another, the acquisition over the first 12 trials shows no overlap (Fig. 20). If all 16 units are rank ordered, it can be seen that the five most rapidly learned items are words. Only the word HAS falls well down in trigram "territory." Clearly, the results show that, in general, words will be learned more rapidly than will trigrams of approximately the same frequency.

The data of Table 25 suggest that the four words of List 1 are learned more rapidly than those in List 2. This difference is significant statistically, the t being 2.98. The difference in learning the two sets of trigrams does not attain statistical significance.

Discussion

Considered in the context of the frequency hypothesis as developed thus far, the results of Experiment 7 obviously pose a problem: equal frequency of words and nonwords does not produce equal learning.

The following considerations tentatively resolve this problem, at least to our satisfaction.

1. The only frequency values available are those based on printed words. It has been suggested earlier that not only may emitted frequency and printed frequency differ, but also that emitted frequency may add greater effects than printed frequency. It is probably a reasonable assumption that average length of words used in ordinary conversation of the college student is less than the average length of the words he reads. A trigram must necessarily come from words having more than three letters. Therefore, emitted speech should increase frequency of three-letter words disproportionately to that of trigrams. And, while we have consistently argued that frequency differences within the range with which we are dealing will produce only small effects on learning, it is worth pointing out that a small part of the difference in learning words and nonwords may be attributed to differences in emitted frequency.

2. We had supposed that because of the relatively high frequency of both trigrams and words used in the two lists, there would be no problem of response integration. As it turns out, this is not true. Among certain trigrams there was clear evidence for interference. For all eight trigrams there were 44 three-letter responses which indicated interference. Confusion between SHO and SPE accounted for 23 of them, the subjects giving SHE instead of SHO, and SPO instead of SPE. Both of these three-letter errors have high trigram frequency. Only one error indicating lack of integration occurred in learning the words (one subject twice gave RAW instead of ROW). It must be concluded that part of the over-all difference in learning between words and nonwords is due to greater interference among nonwords than among words. This difference in interference among words and among nonwords may in turn be due to differences in pronunciability. We do not have pronunciability ratings on these items, but it seems quite likely that if they were rated, the trigrams would, as a group, be rated more difficult to pronounce than the words as a group.

3. The evidence points not only to a difference in Stage-2 learning between trigrams and words but also to differences among words. An indication of differences in difficulty in this associative stage is given by the number of times a response was given correctly but was not paired with its appropriate stimulus (misplaced response). For the trigrams there were 103 such errors, and for the words, 59. The data indicated that the four words of List 2 were learned more slowly than those of List 1. Since there is no reason to believe (and no evidence in

the records) that these words would differ in availability (response-recall phase), the difference must occur in the associative phase. During the learning of List 2 there were 42 cases of a word response being paired with the wrong stimulus, but in List 1 there were only 17 such cases. Such evidence points again to differences in the associative phase. Since we have not yet considered possible mechanisms accounting for differences in the associative stage, these findings will not be pursued further at this point.

The results thus suggest three possible points of difference in learning words and nonwords. First, words may be more available than nonwords in a response-recall sense because of greater emitted frequency. Secondly, the particular trigrams used here interfered more with each other than did the words. Finally, there may be a difference in the rate with which the associative phase occurs.

EXPERIMENT 8

Experiment 6 determined the relationship between response frequency and learning for paired-associate lists. In the present experiment, frequency of trigrams is manipulated among *serial* lists.

For analytical purposes, serial learning is much inferior to paired-associate learning. There are two reasons for this. First, in serial learning the stimulus and response functions are completely confounded since each item is both a stimulus and a response. Secondly, the powerful effect of serial position imposes an order on the learning of items which may, even with homogeneous lists, dampen the effects of frequency. Nevertheless, in the interests of determining the generality of the relationship between frequency and learning, we report the following experiment.

Method

Lists. Homogeneous lists of 13 trigrams each were made up. One had low trigram frequency, one medium, and one high. These lists, as originally constructed, had no overlap in frequency based on the U Count. However, as can be seen in Table 26, when total frequency values are used, there is some overlap, although the mean frequencies remain widely separated.

Two sets of lists were used so that there are two independent tests of the relationship between learning and frequency. The first group of three lists is called Set I, the second, Set II. Within each set the same

TABLE 26. Experiment 8. Serial Lists Used with Frequency (*f*) of Each Item

Set I						Set II					
List 1	*f*	List 2	*f*	List 3	*f*	List 4	*f*	List 5	*f*	List 6	*f*
BAF	4	BER	110	BLE	382	ANF	1	ADI	40	AVE	418
CAI	9	CEN	225	COM	301	FAU	2	FER	146	FRO	117
DLA	1	DRE	368	DER	438	HOV	2	HOS	118	HAN	238
GUR	15	GER	104	GHT	534	ISK	2	IRL	24	ITH	269
HTM	1	HAR	236	HIN	293	LTO	2	LIG	115	LIN	309
NUF	64	NTR	91	NCE	661	NUD	1	NTA	80	NTE	611
PUZ	1	POS	243	PER	479	OWT	3	OPL	38	OTH	354
RLO	29	REL	116	REA	733	PEL	1	PEC	194	PLE	197
SAU	49	SIO	212	STR	448	RUP	25	RIS	192	ROU	260
TYR	6	TAI	150	TIO	1025	SFE	2	SED	53	STR	448
VOR	7	VED	52	VER	545	TAF	2	TIV	201	THI	298
WAU	1	WHA	61	WHE	225	USK	9	UTI	70	URS	239
ESN	1	EOP	39	ERS	295	WAU	1	WOU	57	WHI	258
Mean *f*	14.5		154.4		489.2		4.1		102.2		308.9

first letters were used for each list, and the intralist similarity considered over-all is roughly comparable. For example, in Set I there were 8, 7, and 8 different middle letters for Lists 1, 2, and 3, respectively, and 9, 10, and 8 different third letters. Although we do not have pronunciation ratings on these trigrams, we are unable to discern any large bias among lists on this attribute.

Procedure. The lists were presented on a memory drum at a 2-sec. rate, and the intertrial interval was 2 sec. Three horizontally-printed asterisks were used as the anticipatory cue for the first trigram in the list.

A different group of 18 subjects was assigned to each set. However, the 18 subjects learned all three lists in a set, the order of learning the lists being completely counterbalanced among subgroups of six subjects. Three different random orders of each list were made, each order being learned by a different subgroup of six subjects. A list was presented for 20 anticipation trials and every subject was presented his three lists during a single 50-min. session.

Results

The mean total correct responses for 20 trials for each list in both sets is shown in Fig. 21. As mean trigram frequency increases, amount learned in 20 trials increases. Both sets of lists show much the same relationship, and although those of Set I appear to be more difficult than the ones of Set II, the differences are far from being statistically

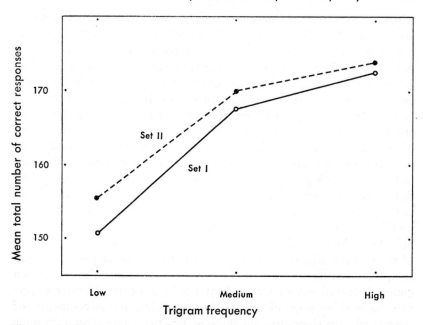

Figure 21. Experiment 8. Learning of two sets of serial lists as a function of trigram frequency.

significant. Nevertheless, it is worth noting that the lists of Set I have somewhat higher frequency values than those of Set II, and the fact that the difference in learning is in the opposite direction would not be anticipated. The sets may differ a small amount on some other characteristic (e.g., pronunciability), but this is not known. Since subjects were assigned to one or the other set at random, there is no reason to believe that the groups of subjects differed in learning ability.

Fig. 21 has shown an increase in amount learned as trigram frequency increases, but the differences do not attain a high level of statistical significance. For Set I the F is 5.75. With 2 and 34 df, an F of 5.29 is needed for the 1 per cent significance level. For Set II, however, the F of 2.44 is short of the 5 per cent significance level. Combining both sets (e.g., Lists 1 and 4, 2 and 5, 3 and 6) gives an F that is significant beyond the 1 per cent level. Comparable analyses on performance on the first six trials show essentially the same results. Learning curves plotted over 20 trials demonstrate that the low-frequency lists are consistently lower than the medium- and high-frequency lists throughout the course of learning, and there is considerable overlapping between the medium- and high-frequency lists in the later trials. Thus, while trigram frequency of items in homogeneous serial lists and rate of learning are directly related, the effect is of relatively small magnitude.

Our use of a counterbalanced design for presenting these lists assumed that while there may be transfer effects from list to list, they would not be differential for the different frequency levels. A breakdown in terms of stage of practice shows this expectation was not borne out. The results for both sets were combined to give 12 subjects at each of the nine points, e.g., three frequency levels and three stages of practice. A plot shows that for the low- and medium-frequency lists, performance first increases and then decreases from Stage 1 to Stage 2 to Stage 3. The high-frequency lists, on the other hand, produce about the same performance for Stages 1 and 2, but give a sharp increase between Stages 2 and 3. The effect of this differential transfer is such that on Stages 1 and 3 the lists are properly ordered (low, medium, high), but not on Stage 2 where the order is low, high, medium. The causes of these differential transfer effects are not an issue for present discussion; these effects are pointed out here to indicate that the choice of a counterbalanced design was unfortunate. Differential transfer effects may be masking some differences in "pure" learning as a function of frequency. But since the first stage of practice alone shows the same general result as do all stages combined, it is quite unlikely that differential transfer effects can be responsible for the relationship between learning and frequency.

Discussion

This experiment has shown a direct relationship between serial learning and the trigram frequency. The effect of frequency—*be* it an effect of frequency—was not large but was consistent for both experiments. It now appears that a reasonable question to ask is whether or not the differences obtained could be due to pronunciability differences. Since Experiment 6 showed (by partial correlation) that the relationship between pronunciability and learning was high even with frequency held constant, perhaps the same law is working in the present experiment. As noted earlier, we have not obtained pronunciability ratings on the items in the serial lists. However, tangential evidence suggests strongly that the so-called frequency effect for these serial lists may well be a consequence of differences in pronunciability. Two sets of evidence suggest this.

1. Although it is quite possible to choose trigrams in which there is a negative correlation between ease of pronouncing and frequency,

our experience has been that if one chooses items for frequency differences alone, there is likely to be a positive correlation. One example comes from ratings. In the rating procedures reported earlier in the chapter, 95 items were employed. The rank-order correlation between mean pronunciability ratings on these items and frequency (U Count) was .38. As a second example, consider the lists in Experiment 6, where in three of the four lists a positive correlation existed between pronunciability and frequency. Generally speaking, then, there seems to be a positive relationship between frequency and pronunciability. It seems very likely, therefore, that this correlation held for the items in the serial lists of Experiment 8 and that the critical factor involved in the differences in learning is pronunciability rather than frequency.

2. In an experiment reported elsewhere (Underwood & Postman, 1960), serial lists were constructed having different mean frequency values but, according to the rough judgments of the investigators, were not clearly different on pronunciability. However, when the items were actually rated for pronunciability, the relationship between frequency and pronunciability was positive, and the pronunciation ratings predicted the differences in learning that occurred. Even small differences in mean pronunciation ratings can produce a rather astonishingly large difference in learning.

In view of this sort of evidence, we find it necessary to conclude that the differences in learning observed for the serial lists of Experiment 8 are probably due to differences in pronunciability or are, at least, a function of the joint effect of pronunciability and frequency. It is apparent that we have arrived at this conclusion reluctantly, but the evidence from Experiment 6, and from the experiments to be reported in the next chapter, has left us little alternative.

SUMMARY

Four experiments have been reported, all of which, in one way or another, were tests of the frequency hypothesis. The more critical results, which should be kept in mind in evaluating the experiments in the next chapter are:

1. When responses in paired-associate lists are constructed of letter sequences which rarely occur in printed words, the differences in learning rate of such responses can be predicted by simple summation of letter frequency for each response. The more frequently the letters of a given response occur in the language, the faster is the learning.

2. Trigram frequency, as determined from printed text, does not

appear to be very highly related to rate of learning, and what predictive power it has may stem from a correlation between frequency and pronunciability. This finding does not conform to expectations based on a frequency theory, but further tests are needed to untangle frequency and pronunciability.

REFERENCES

Kimble, G. A., & Dufort, R. H. Meaningfulness and isolation as factors in verbal learning. *J. exp. Psychol.*, 1955, 50, 361–368.

Miller, G. A., & Selfridge, J. A. Verbal context and the recall of meaningful material. *Amer. J. Psychol.*, 1950, 63, 176–185.

Noble, C. E. Emotionality (*e*) and meaningfulness (*m*). *Psychol. Rep.*, 1958, 4, 16.

Underwood, B. J., & Postman, L. Extraexperimental sources of interference in forgetting. *Psychol. Rev.*, 1960, 67, 73–95.

Underwood, B. J., & Richardson, J. The influence of meaningfulness, intralist similarity, and serial position on retention. *J. exp. Psychol.*, 1956, 52, 119–126.

Waters, R. H. The law of acquaintance. *J. exp. Psychol.*, 1939, 24, 180–191.

Chapter 8

Further Experiments on
Response Frequency

All experiments to be reported in this chapter are concerned with the effect of frequency of response units in paired-associate learning. More particularly, since they are concerned with the role of individual letters in learning and the relationships among pronunciability, frequency and learning, they represent a further examination of the facts suggested by Experiments 5 and 6.

The several experiments to be evaluated studied the influence of potential interacting variables on the frequency-learning relationship as this relationship was originally conceived. The rationale for investigating the effects of the particular interacting variables will be most meaningfully presented in the light of the results of each successive experiment.

EXPERIMENT 9

This experiment used single letters as responses. In an analytical sense, the use of single letters has the advantage of eliminating response integration as a factor in the learning process. Experiment 7 showed that some problem of response integration in learning still remained even with trigrams of high frequency. Viewed abstractly, single-letter responses should provide a very pure test of that part of the frequency hypothesis which says that the order in which the responses start entering into associations is directly related to the frequency with which those responses have been experienced. But a theoretical notion which one loves and cherishes in the abstract might not return that love if the experimental conditions put undue stress on it. It seemed to us that this estrangement might indeed happen if the frequency theory were tested by the use of single letters as responses. The major reason for our skepticism was the fact that letters, even infrequently used letters, have such an enormous absolute frequency that little difference in acquiring these as responses in a paired-associate list should occur. Yet we felt that such a test should be made if for no other reason than to set the limits on the scope of the phenomena which we might reasonably incorporate under the theory.

Certain reflections led us to increase the number of responses over the number used in our previous paired-associate studies. We felt that the task should be difficult enough to allow a clear possibility for the occurrence of an ordering effect among the responses. For example, if six single-letter responses were used, the subject might, after a single presentation, remember all responses, so that any differences which occurred (if they did) would be in the associative stage. If this is true, the length of the list should be such that the subject cannot hold all responses in mind in a memory-span sense. Our decision was to use lists of 12 paired associates.

Method

Lists. In keeping with our previous practice, we have constructed two lists with single-letter responses. Each may be considered an independent test of the relationship between single-letter frequency and learning. Each list represents the near complete range of frequency as determined by the U Count. The responses in each list, their frequency, and the mean total correct responses are shown in Table 27.

Procedure. Two-digit numbers were used as stimuli: 16, 29, 31, 38, 47, 52, 64, 67, 73, 85, 91, and 94. A different group of 18 subjects learned each list. Within each group there were three subgroups of six subjects each, and each of them had a different set of stimulus-response pairings. The list was presented for 15 anticipation trials at the 2:2-sec. rate, with a 4-sec. intertrial interval.

Results

The first question we ask is whether or not there are differences in learning within each list. For List 1 the F is 2.70, with 2.37 needed for the 1 per cent significance level. For List 2 the F is 1.95, with 1.85 needed for the 5 per cent significance level; we conclude that there

TABLE 27. Experiment 9. Single-Letter Responses Used in Each List, Letter Frequency (f), and Mean Number of Correct Anticipations in 15 Trials

	List 1			List 2	
Response	*f*	Mean Correct	Response	*f*	Mean Correct
C	1893	9.17	P	1308	8.61
N	4820	8.67	Z	67	7.61
Y	1331	6.83	L	2761	7.67
V	688	6.89	F	1494	6.56
D	2697	8.06	U	2085	7.39
A	5417	11.44	X	132	7.44
K	493	7.56	W	1378	7.44
R	4217	8.78	B	1049	9.00
H	3596	6.67	O	4982	11.17
S	4578	9.22	T	5983	8.06
J	119	8.50	E	8532	9.50
M	1751	7.83	Q	61	7.61

are reliable differences in learning among the letters within each list. It may also be observed that the two lists as such are quite comparable in difficulty, the mean total correct responses for List 1 being 99.61, and for List 2, 98.06.

The next question is whether or not the differences in learning within the lists are associated with differences in frequency. The answer is clearly an affirmative one. The product-moment correlation between mean number of correct anticipations for a letter and its frequency is .59 for List 1, and .56 for List 2. Corresponding rank-order correlations are .58 and .37. If all 24 items are pooled (which is justified in view of the fact that over-all learning was fairly equivalent for the two lists) the product-moment correlation is .68, and the rank order, .50.

In Fig. 22 four groups of six responses each have been formed so that each successive grouping represents increasing frequency of occurrence of the letters in the language. The plot shows that as frequency increases, the mean numbers of times the responses in that group were correctly anticipated increases.

An evaluation of certain of the larger discrepancies between the rank orders for learning and the rank orders for frequency suggests certain additional facts. For example, the letter J is learned much more rapidly than its frequency would predict. When the subjects' records whose first or last names began with this letter were removed, the mean learning score decreased. There were four such subjects, and they had learning scores of 12, 14, 15, and 15 for this response. It is reasonable to suppose that J was a much more frequent letter for these subjects

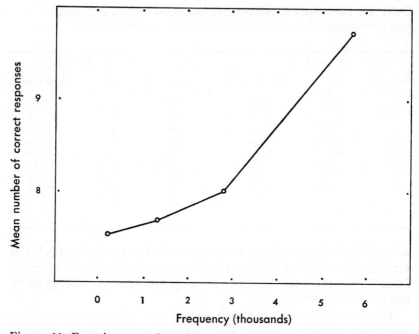

Figure 22. Experiment 9. Learning of single-letter responses in paired-associate lists as a function of frequency.

than is indicated in the language count. This is given as an illustration, but it is quite possible that if all records were removed for subjects whose names began with a letter which was a response in the list, the relationship between learning and frequency would have been higher. This removal cannot be accomplished systematically in the present experiment since the number of subjects involved is too small.

Another large discrepancy between learning and frequency occurs with the letter H. It has high frequency in the language but is learned slowly. In actual fact, the high frequency for H comes about as a result of high frequency in a few words (e.g., THE), and, as will be seen in a later chapter, it is very low in the subjects' repertoire of consonants.

Many overt errors were evident in the learning records. For List 1 there was a total of 427 such errors, and for List 2, 540. Evidence to be presented in later experiments strongly indicates that the two-digit stimuli used in the present experiment function as if they possess high interstimulus similarity. However, the issue of why so many errors occurred was not the major purpose in counting these errors. The major point to be made is that subjects gave very few letters which were not in the list—the subject did not import letters. For List 1, only 3 per cent of the total errors were not letters in the list; in List 2 the value was 4 per cent.

In evaluating the results of Experiment 5, we called attention to the fact that importation of letters in learning difficult consonant syllables was a rare occurrence. At that time we suggested that we must accept the existence of a selector mechanism which limits the range of responses to those letters within the list. The present results strongly support the operation of such a mechanism. It would appear that via recency in stimulation the selector mechanism almost completely limits response attempts to those letters which have produced this stimulation.

Discussion

The results of this experiment clearly conform to the frequency hypothesis. The letters which the subject has most frequently experienced are learned most rapidly. We interpret this to mean that frequency establishes a priority of order in which associations will be formed. A number of years ago the senior author had a Master's candidate who performed a study on concept formation in which consonants were used as responses. For some reason, which is now forgotten, the student had calculated the relationship between speed of learning the concepts and the frequency of the letters used as responses. His rank-order correlation was unity for the nine letters used. It is quite apparent now that his advisor should not have dismissed this finding so lightly by asserting that such correlations will occur by chance once in a great while.

The rather happy results of the present experiment will be replaced by progressively more gloomy ones as we move to experiments in which two-letter and three-letter responses have been used.

EXPERIMENT 10

Experiment 9 used single-letter responses. In the present one, two-letter responses (bigrams) have been used. The empirical problem is to determine the relationship between learning and bigram frequency.

Method

Except for the nature of the responses, Experiment 10 was designed exactly as was Experiment 9. The two lists used as responses are shown

TABLE 28. Experiment 10. Bigram Responses, Frequency (f), and Mean Number of Correct Anticipations in 15 Trials

	List 1			List 2	
Response	f	Mean Correct	Response	f	Mean Correct
SU	598	8.11	QU	430	5.28
XP	237	6.83	KB	7	4.33
CA	1055	5.56	UG	249	7.17
LD	682	6.11	TR	1028	7.61
OW	676	9.78	LY	1100	6.56
BY	68	8.67	GS	64	6.00
UM	288	4.11	IM	441	11.17
DS	95	4.94	HA	1396	9.50
NE	1689	5.78	EV	377	8.78
IT	1334	8.94	NC	795	4.61
ER	4034	10.33	DE	1476	5.44
GF	3	4.94	ON	3107	7.22

in Table 28. The frequency values given are the sums of the T-L and U Count. In both lists four letters are used as both first and last letters, but there is no repetition either among first letters or among last letters.

Results

An analysis of variance on each list showed that differences in learning among items within each list were highly significant, but the difference between lists was not.

For List 1 the product-moment correlation between frequency and learning is .52; for List 2 the value is .11. Corresponding rank-order correlations are .43 and .29. When all 24 items are pooled, the product-moment correlation is .34, and the rank-order correlation, .35. None of these correlations differ significantly from zero. However, in view of previous results, it does not seem unwarranted to conclude that there is a small positive relationship between frequency of these bigrams and the rate at which they are learned as responses in paired-associate lists.

The most severe disturbances in the relationship between frequency and learning occur with bigrams of moderate frequency. This can be seen in Fig. 23 where four frequency groupings of six items each are plotted against mean total correct responses.

The discussion of the results will be delayed until after presenting Experiment 11, for the results of Experiment 11, in which trigram frequency is varied, produce an even more severe strain on the frequency hypothesis than do the present ones. Since we believe that the results of both experiments are a consequence of the same factors, they may be most economically discussed together.

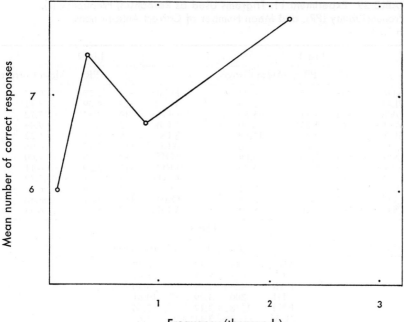

Figure 23. Experiment 10. Learning of bigram responses in paired-associate lists as a function of frequency.

EXPERIMENT 11

Experiments 9, 10, and 11 were run simultaneously, and as the subjects used were drawn from the same common pool and assigned randomly to the experiments, the results of the three experiments may be compared directly. Experiment 11 used trigrams as responses; therefore, a comparison of the results for Experiments 9, 10, and 11 will give evidence on learning as a joint function of frequency and number of letters making up the response. Another purpose for performing Experiment 11 was to make further tests of the role of response frequency in learning. It will be remembered that Experiment 6, in which trigrams were used as responses, gave a substantial relationship between frequency and learning although it appeared that without the correlation between pronunciability and frequency the relationship between frequency and learning would have been slight. It was clear that further tests of the relationship between frequency and learning were needed for three-letter responses.

TABLE 29. Experiment 11. Trigrams Used as Responses, Frequency (*f*),
Pronunciability (PR), and Mean Number of Correct Anticipations
in 15 Trials

	List 1				List 2		
	f	PR	Mean Correct		*f*	PR	Mean Correct
NDE	253	7.63	4.28	HAT	333	1.77	9.17
PLO	44	3.11	5.39	WHE	225	4.09	5.11
OUS	444	3.34	5.50	DGM	10	8.37	7.72
WHA	61	3.23	6.50	CUB	2	1.80	9.44
BOY	23	2.26	11.89	YIN	79	3.17	6.22
VIF	1	3.83	5.50	ALI	115	3.57	6.06
ING	1673	2.46	8.89	SOU	184	3.40	7.00
ATI	799	4.34	4.89	FRO	117	2.40	6.11
URN	56	2.40	8.33	UND	384	3.83	5.39
HER	679	2.06	9.61	ITS	78	2.69	6.72
CQU	3	8.23	2.28	OMP	117	4.11	5.56
EST	742	2.46	8.39	VER	545	2.91	6.33

	List 3		
	f	PR	Mean Correct
MPA	58	7.34	6.17
YLV	3	8.37	6.61
PAR	425	1.74	8.50
CHI	200	3.29	10.61
ENT	1778	3.17	7.06
JUM	3	3.11	5.67
ABL	317	5.57	6.67
NCE	661	7.60	4.61
LED	145	1.91	8.06
TIO	1025	3.94	5.61
ROP	76	3.46	5.28
ISH	258	2.23	9.67

Method

Three lists of 12 pairs each were used. The stimuli were the same
two-digit numbers as used in Experiments 9 and 10. The trigrams used
as responses in each of the lists are shown in Table 29, with the frequency values as obtained from the combined language counts. Pronunciation ratings (PR) are also given for each response, although
these ratings were not available at the time the experiment was run.

Each of the three lists was presented to a different group of 18 subjects for 15 anticipation trials. All procedures were exactly the same as
for Experiments 9 and 10.

Results

The mean total correct responses given in 15 trials were 81.44, 80.83,
and 84.51 for Lists 1 through 3 respectively. Since the *F* is less than 1,

it may be concluded that the learning of the three lists did not differ. Differences among items *within* lists are highly significant statistically for each list. Do these differences relate to trigram frequency?

Frequency and learning. The rank-order correlations between learning and frequency for Lists 1 through 3 are .24, −.40, and .07. Perhaps we should repeat that this correlational procedure ignores subjects; the correlations were obtained between frequency values and mean number of correct responses for each item (as determined by the learning of 18 subjects). Each correlation is based on an N of 12 items. If all 36 items are pooled, the rank-order correlation between learning and frequency is .06.

Product-moment correlations do not change the picture. For each list the values are .27, −.23, −.11, and the over-all relationship for the pooled 36 items is .09. Clearly, we have no alternative but to conclude that for these lists the relationship between frequency and learning is essentially zero.

Pronunciability and learning. For Lists 1 through 3 the rank-order correlations between PR and learning are .93, .56, .59, with a value of .68 for all 36 items pooled. Corresponding product-moment correlations are .81, .21, and .52, with an over-all value of .57. (We should repeat that by the nature of the PR scale these values are negative, since a high scale value represents difficult pronunciability. We will continue to treat the relationship as a positive one between ease of learning and ease of pronunciability.)

The results again show a substantial relationship between PR and learning, but it is not of the magnitude shown in the results of Experiment 6. List 2 is particularly discrepant. Quite out of line in this list is the response, DGM, which is rated as most difficult to pronounce but is third in rank order in terms of number of times given correctly. The relationship between PR and learning in this list might be attenuated further by the fact that differences in learning among items, while significant at the .01 significance level, are not as great as for the other two lists.

For all 36 items the product-moment correlation between PR and frequency is −.03; PR predicts learning for the items; frequency does not. Thus, the evidence indicates that a simple frequency theory of the first-stage of learning is not appropriate when multiple-letter responses are used. On the positive side, the substantial relationship between PR and learning supports the idea that PR may be taken as one measure of degree of integration of the responses, a critical factor in response availability. However, we still have some concern over the relationship

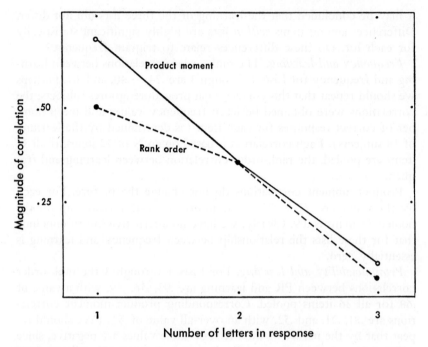

Figure 24. Magnitude of the correlations between frequency and learning as a function of the number of letters in the response.

between PR and learning as shown in these data: the relationship is not as high as found in Experiment 6. We will return to this matter after making some comparisons among the results of Experiments 9, 10, and 11.

Frequency and learning as a function of number of letters in the response. For single-letter responses the correlation between learning and frequency was substantial, but for three-letter responses, it was essentially zero. This change in the relationship between learning and frequency as a function of the number of letters in the response is plotted in Fig. 24. Both rank-order and product-moment correlations are plotted. As the number of letters increases, the correlations decrease. We interpret this function to mean that as the number of letters in the response increases, there is a corresponding increase in the problems of integration, and since degree of integration apparently cannot be predicted from printed language frequency, the relationship between frequency and learning breaks down as the number of letters in the response increases.

Discussion

For the present we will ignore theoretical problems relating frequency and learning and consider another issue which we believe the results of Experiment 11 raise. The product-moment correlation between pronunciability and learning for the 36 items was .57. As noted earlier, the magnitude of this relationship is somewhat less than we would expect from the findings of Experiment 6. This observation, plus certain internal evidence in the learning records, led us to a further experiment to examine the role of intralist stimulus similarity in the PR-learning relationship.

In Experiments 9, 10, and 11, two-digit numbers were used as stimuli. (See method section of Experiment 9). Since there were 12 such stimuli, there is considerable duplication of numbers. This similarity could lead to interference which, if it did not fall equally on all pairs, could reduce the relationship between PR and learning. And, although we used three different pairings of stimuli and responses, we did not in fact know that the result would be equal distribution of interferences over all associations for all items and subjects considered. Furthermore, it is possible that certain pairings could lead to an interaction between stimulus similarity and response similarity. That is, if certain responses with duplicated letters were paired with stimuli with duplicated numbers, the interference might be maximized for these particular pairs. Such considerations led us to believe that differential interference effects, due to relatively high stimulus similarity, were a distinct possibility as a cause for the reduced relationship between PR and learning in this experiment as compared with Experiment 6. Since shortly we will report an experiment to test directly this hypothesis about intralist stimulus similarity, we shall not present the internal analyses of Experiment 11 which tended to support the hypothesis nor our rationalization of the differences in the magnitudes of the correlations between PR and learning for the three lists.

There is another obvious possibility for the reduced correlation between PR and learning for Experiment 11 as compared with Experiment 6. This is length of list—number of pairs. Experiment 6 had eight pairs, and Experiment 11, twelve pairs. It is conceivable not only that a subject attacks the learning of a long list in a different way from the manner in which he attacks a short one, but also that these different attacks could change the PR-learning relationship. However, the results of Experiment 12 do not indicate that length of list is a strong interacting variable in the PR-learning relationship.

EXPERIMENT 12

The purpose of Experiment 12 was to evaluate the role of intralist stimulus similarity in the PR-learning relationship. In Exp. 11, two-digit numbers were used as stimuli. In the present experiment the stimuli were the numbers 1 through 12. We presume that these stimuli have less intralist similarity than the two-digit stimuli used in Experiment 11.

Method

The responses used and the procedure for Experiment 12 were exactly the same as for Experiment 11. Only the stimuli differed. Three random pairings of stimuli and responses were used, with eight subjects assigned to each pairing for each list. Thus, three groups of 24 subjects each were required.

Results

Pronunciability and learning. The mean number of correct anticipations over 15 trials for each response is shown in Table 30. The first question we ask is whether the relationship between PR and learning is higher than was true for Experiment 11. The answer is clearly affirm-

TABLE 30. Experiment 12. Mean Number of Correct Responses for Each Trigram

List 1		List 2		List 3	
NDE	6.62	HAT	10.79	MPA	6.83
PLO	7.29	WHE	6.71	YLV	4.21
OUS	9.58	DGM	6.37	PAR	11.33
WHA	8.12	CUB	11.29	CHI	9.21
BOY	12.67	YIN	9.25	ENT	8.04
VIF	5.46	ALI	9.92	JUM	7.71
ING	10.04	SOU	9.08	ABL	6.87
ATI	7.37	FRO	8.12	NCE	6.62
URN	9.12	UND	7.75	LED	9.29
HER	12.08	ITS	10.67	TIO	9.42
CQU	7.04	OMP	6.67	ROP	7.42
EST	9.04	VER	9.08	ISH	11.37

ative. The rank-order correlations between PR and learning are .82, .83, and .84 for Lists 1 through 3, respectively. The corresponding product-moment correlations are .61, .74, and .84. In Experiment 11 the over-all rank-order correlation was .68; in the present experiment it is .82. The comparison for the product-moment is .57 and .76. In the present experiment, while the relationship between PR and learning drops somewhat for List 1 (as compared with Experiment 11), large increases in the relationship are shown for the other two lists. The magnitude of the relationship between PR and learning for Experiment 12, using 12-item lists, corresponds favorably to that shown in Experiment 6 where eight-item lists were used.

Evidence on intralist similarity. We believe that intralist similarity among 12 two-digit numbers is greater than among the numbers 1 through 12. We believe further that this greater intralist similarity among the stimuli in Experiment 11 resulted in a smaller relationship between PR and learning than was true for Experiment 12. If intralist similarity is the critical factor, certain other facts must follow in the data. First, the number of correct responses in Experiment 11 should have been less over the 15 trials than in Experiment 12. This expectation is supported. The mean number of correct anticipations per item in Experiment 11 was 6.79, 6.74, and 7.04 for Lists 1 through 3, and for Experiment 12, the values were 8.70, 8.81, and 8.19.

Differential intralist stimulus similarity may also show itself in the number of errors produced. For Experiment 11, the mean number of overt errors was 20.89, 26.06, and 21.17 for Lists 1 through 3. For Experiment 12 the means were 14.67, 15.13, and 16.63. For the three lists combined, both the differences in number of correct responses and number of errors between the two experiments are significant statistically. (The *t* for correct responses is 3.80, and for errors, 2.79.)

The question may be raised as to whether or not the error *rate* differed. Since, in Experiment 12, more correct responses were given than were given in Experiment 11, there were fewer possibilities or opportunities for errors to occur. On this matter we take the position that the greater number of errors in Experiment 11 *prevented* as many correct anticipations from being given as were given in Experiment 12. However, even if one corrects for differences in opportunities to give errors, the difference in error frequency still remains. A score was obtained for each subject as follows. There were 180 possible opportunities to respond (15 trials x 12 pairs). The number of correct responses was subtracted from 180 to give the number of opportunities for errors. Then, the number of opportunities was divided by the number of overt errors to get an error-rate score for each subject. For all lists for all subjects in Experiment 11, this mean was .240; for Experiment 12 the value was .189. The *t* for the difference is 2.17, which is significant beyond the .05 level. Thus, no matter how one views the errors, it appears that a greater number occurred in Experiment 11 than in Experiment 12. We attribute this to differences in stimulus similarity.

Experiments 11 and 12 were identical except for the stimuli. If differential interference effects were more potent in Experiment 11 than in Experiment 12, the correlation between the learning scores for the 36 items for the two experiments should be considerably less than unity. Actually, of course, this could also be concluded from an evaluation of the correlations relating PR and learning for the two experiments. Yet, it is comforting to find that the over-all rank-order correlation between the two arrays of 36 scores is only .66.

We conclude from Experiment 12, evaluated in conjunction with Experiment 11, that high intralist stimulus similarity may reduce the relationship between PR and learning. Logically, such a reduction need not inevitably occur; it should occur only when interference effects fall differentially on the items in mixed lists.

Discussion

The importance which we have attached to differences in similarity of the stimuli in Experiments 11 and 12 has further implications for the frequency hypothesis.

The data do not indicate that length of list is a critical variable influencing the PR-learning relationship; therefore, *if* a relationship existed between frequency and learning, we presume length of list would not be a critical factor for such a relationship. In Experiment 12, the over-all relationship between frequency and learning, as given by a product-moment correlation, was .16. So Experiment 12 has not given us hope of restoring a simple frequency theory for multiple-letter responses.

If stimulus similarity distorted the learning-PR relationship for Experiment 11, it is reasonable to presume it may have also done so for Experiments 9 and 10. In both of these experiments the stimuli were the same two-digit numbers as were used in Experiment 11. In Experiment 9, the results showed a rather strong relationship between frequency of single letters and the order of learning these letters. If these results were somewhat distorted by the intralist stimulus similarity, it is quite possible that the relationship between learning and frequency of single-letter responses is appreciably higher than has been shown. And if this is true, the frequency theory as previously outlined remains quite tenable as applied to single-letter responses.

In Experiment 10, two-letter responses (bigrams) were used. We have not obtained pronunciability ratings on these bigrams, but an inspection of the results (Table 28) suggests some clear reversals in the

PR-learning relationship. For example, XP is learned more rapidly than UM. Such distortions were probably due to the stimulus similarity among the two-digit numbers. Therefore, in the learning of the bigrams in Experiment 10, stimulus similarity probably reduced both the frequency-learning relationship and the PR-learning relationship.

Our two general conclusions are:

1. As the number of letters in a response in a paired-associate list increases from 1 through 3, the relationship between learning and frequency decreases. With single-letter responses the relationship between learning and frequency will be high; with three-letter responses the relationship will be low.

2. The relationship between pronunciability and learning remains astonishingly high.

At this point in the series of experiments it seemed that the frequency theory as applied to multiple-letter responses should have been abandoned. Yet, the tenuousness of the relationship between fact and theory was more than matched by the tenaciousness of the investigators. Some further experiments were undertaken.

EXPERIMENT 13

In all the experiments reported thus far variation in response frequency has occurred among responses *within lists*. The use of two or more lists in each experiment has been merely to establish the fact that the relationships found were not a function of the peculiarities of a single list.

In Experiment 13 response frequency is manipulated within lists as we have been doing (mixed lists), and the same responses are also used in unmixed lists, i.e., the frequency of all items within a list is low, or medium, or high. The basic question is, will we continue to find essentially a zero relationship between learning and frequency when unmixed lists are used?

Method

The lists. We have constructed entirely new lists for this experiment, although some of the items previously used appear again. In Experiments 11 and 12, we felt the choice of a few items was an unfortunate one as far as our frequency index was concerned. For students at Northwestern University, the trigrams CUB and CHI probably have a much higher frequency than indicated by our language count. Such trigrams were not used in the present lists. A second decision made was to eliminate all obvious words from the lists.

At the time the lists were constructed we did not have pronunciability ratings on the items. (These were subsequently obtained and will be used in the analyses.) However, by careful examination of the items used in the list, we attempted to make a rough equation for pronunciability. The procedure for doing this follows.

First, three mixed lists were constructed, each consisting of 12 trigrams representing twélve different frequency levels. Of the three trigrams for each trigram frequency, we attempted to select one that was easy to pronounce, one that was difficult, and one that was in-between. At the extremes we were reasonably successful, as judged from the ratings we later obtained. For successive frequency levels, we balanced the judged pronunciability differences among the three lists so that, for all items considered, the average pronunciability of the items in the lists would be about equivalent.

In Table 31 the items in each list are given in order of increasing frequency. The equation for pronunciability turned out to be reasonably successful, and it can be seen that in each list there are items easy and difficult to pronounce at low, medium, and high frequency levels. Thus, we have avoided any clear correlation between frequency and pronunciability. Furthermore, the intralist similarity among the items is almost exactly equivalent in terms of duplicated letters. Therefore, the three mixed lists are roughly equal in similarity, frequency, and pronunciability.

To evolve the three unmixed lists from the mixed lists so that a difference in frequency obtained, sets of four items from each mixed list were put together. That is, to form the low-frequency list, the four lowest frequency items from the three mixed lists were put together; to form a list with moderate frequency, the four moderate frequency items from each list were listed together, and the four remaining items from each list became the high-frequency unmixed list. These lists are shown in the lower section of Table 31.

Table 31 shows that the unmixed lists differ widely in the mean frequency of the items. As it turns out, the mean PR ratings for Lists 2 and 3 are a little lower (easier to pronounce) than those for List 1. Too, the intralist similarity increases somewhat as frequency increases. This is almost an inevitable correlate of increasing frequency since high frequency trigrams are made up of a limited number of letters. Actually, the differences in letter duplication are not large, with 23, 19, and 18 different letters used in Lists 1, 2, and 3, respectively. It should be noted that if these small differences in similarity affect learning, it would work against the hypothesis that increased frequency facilitates learning.

The stimuli for all six lists were the numbers 1 through 12. As in the previous experiments, three different pairings of the stimuli and responses were used for each list. Furthermore, it was possible to pair each trigram in the unmixed lists with the same three numbers with which it was paired in the mixed list. Therefore, any difference in learning the items must be attributed to differences in the nature of the list (mixed vs. unmixed) and not to particular stimulus-response pairings.

Procedure. Twenty-four subjects were assigned to each list. The 144 subjects required for the six lists were assigned in a random man-

TABLE 31. Experiment 13. Mixed and Unmixed Lists, with Frequency (*f*), Pronunciability (PR), and Mean Number Correct Anticipations in 15 Trials

			Mixed Lists				
		List 1				List 2	
	f	PR	Mean Correct		*f*	PR	Mean Correct
KBR	2	8.34	4.83	KIV	1	3.86	8.75
HTF	4	8.40	2.54	WSE	5	7.06	6.54
BON	10	2.11	12.04	DGM	10	8.42	5.87
JEC	19	3.66	5.79	LTY	20	7.03	4.00
DYI	45	6.11	4.92	MPO	35	7.23	5.71
MBE	68	7.80	3.96	SLO	63	2.20	9.87
FET	108	2.49	7.67	COU	106	3.14	8.42
SCI	162	3.60	10.54	NDR	143	8.14	4.50
RCE	197	6.83	4.92	JOR	214	3.51	6.42
LAR	240	2.23	9.67	BLI	257	3.37	6.71
TLY	295	5.75	4.92	RTI	280	7.43	2.33
GHT	534	7.63	5.29	VEN	448	2.66	9.71
Means	140.3	5.41	6.42		131.8	5.34	6.57

	List 3			
		f	PR	Mean Correct
	TJU	1	7.74	4.50
	LIR	5	4.03	5.79
	GOI	11	4.60	7.50
	XPL	15	8.43	6.25
	VIL	46	3.14	8.67
	KNO	56	4.40	6.50
	MPR	101	7.94	4.25
	JUS	136	3.29	8.58
	FAI	215	3.83	6.42
	NDE	253	7.63	4.37
	COM	301	2.31	10.21
	BLE	382	4.23	7.17
	Means	126.8	5.13	6.68

TABLE 31. (continued)

				Unmixed Lists				
	List 1					List 2		
	f	PR	Mean Correct			*f*	PR	Mean Correct
KBR	2	8.34	1.62		DYI	45	6.11	4.96
HTF	4	8.40	2.50		MBE	68	7.80	4.54
BON	10	2.11	11.87		FET	108	2.49	10.46
JEC	19	3.66	7.17		SCI	162	3.60	8.54
KIV	1	3.86	7.21		MPO	35	7.23	5.21
WSE	5	7.06	6.33		SLO	63	2.20	7.96
DGM	10	8.42	4.37		COU	106	3.14	6.54
LTY	20	7.03	2.50		NDR	143	8.14	4.50
TJU	1	7.74	1.79		VIL	46	3.14	9.71
LIR	5	4.03	4.33		KNO	56	4.40	6.58
GOI	11	4.60	7.42		MPR	101	7.94	3.62
XPL	15	8.43	3.92		JUS	136	3.29	9.71
Means	8.6	6.14	5.09			89.1	4.96	6.86

		List 3	
	f	PR	Mean Correct
RCE	197	6.83	3.00
LAR	240	2.23	6.33
TLY	295	5.75	5.21
GHT	534	7.63	7.04
JOR	214	3.51	5.71
BLI	257	3.37	5.96
RTI	280	7.43	1.79
VEN	448	2.66	9.08
FAI	215	3.83	5.54
NDE	253	7.63	4.04
COM	301	2.31	9.83
BLE	382	4.23	7.75
Means	301.3	4.78	5.94

ner. Within each group, eight subjects were given each of the stimulus-response pairings. Fifteen anticipation trials were given.

Results

Over-all learning. As may be seen in Table 31, the mean correct anticipations per item are almost identical for the three mixed lists. The *F* is less than 1. For the unmixed lists, however, small differences occur. The *F* is 3.24, with a value of 3.13 required for the .05 significance level. However, even these small differences do not reflect the effect of frequency, since the subjects learning List 2 gave the greatest number of correct anticipations while List 3 had the highest average frequency. The difference in learning between Lists 1 and 2 may reflect differences in PR. It is also possible that the small differences in re-

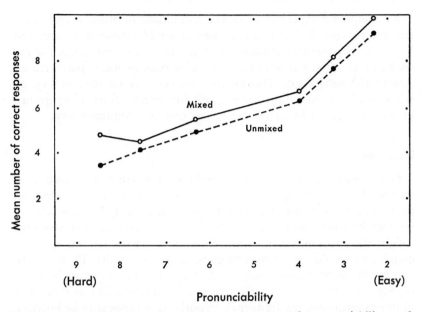

Figure 25. Experiment 13. Learning as a function of pronunciability and mixed versus unmixed lists.

sponse similarity may have had an effect. In any event, we will not be concerned with these small differences and will conclude that differences in trigram frequency across the unmixed lists show no consistent effect on learning.

The means in Table 31 suggest that the over-all performance was somewhat better for the mixed than for the unmixed lists. For the 72 subjects learning the mixed lists the mean total correct anticipations was 78.68; for those learning the unmixed, the value was 71.56. However, these means do not differ significantly, yielding a t of 1.52. We may conclude, therefore, that no sizeable effect may be expected in learning lists which are heterogeneous versus homogeneous with regard to frequency when the over-all mean frequency is equivalent.

Within-lists relationships. Once again we have obtained a substantial relationship between PR and learning. For the mixed lists the product-moment correlations are .84, .81, and .81, for Lists 1, 2, and 3, respectively. Pooling all 36 items the value is .82. For the unmixed lists the values for the three lists are .83, .89, and .67, with an over-all value of .79. Adjusting this latter value because of the small differences in learning among the three groups gives an r of .80.

As would be expected from the magnitude of these correlations, items in the mixed lists "behaved" very much like those in the unmixed lists. The correlation between the two sets of learning scores for the 36 items is .88 when adjusted for differences in mean performance among the subgroups. This correspondence can be seen in Fig. 25 where we have plotted the learning-PR function by forming six groups of six items, each based on increasing ease of pronunciability.

Discussion

Once again the data force the conclusion that trigram frequency, as measured by counting the frequency of three-letter sequences in printed text, does not predict learning when those trigrams are responses in paired-associate lists. In view of the fact that we have sought the relationship in several different experiments, our negative conclusion would appear to have considerable generality. By now, any ego-involvement we originally had in the theory ought to be thoroughly extinguished. But, affective considerations aside, at this point in our experiments, the frequency hypothesis did appear to be horribly deficient for multiple-letter responses. Nevertheless, we felt compelled to make one further test, and it is to the rationale for this new experiment that we now turn.

At a previous point (the discussion of Experiment 6) we noted that adult subjects rarely deal with words letter-by-letter. The units used in speaking, in reading, or in listening, are at least of syllabic size or larger. We ventured to suggest that only in writing does it appear that letter-by-letter handling may occur. We expressed doubt, however, even of this. It is difficult and often quite misleading to project "things" into a subject's mind and then draw conclusions from those projections. Nevertheless, let us suppose that the writing of responses (as opposed to spelling orally) does force the subject into a letter-by-letter form of memory as well as a letter-by-letter form of responding. Under these circumstances, differences in associative strength between letters, as inferred from differences in printed frequency of occurrence, might have a better opportunity to "show" themselves. That is, under such circumstances, pronunciation might be less important as a habit and letter-sequence habits more important. On the other hand, if the unit of recall or the unit of memory is the same, regardless of the way the subject is asked to provide the response, i.e., regardless of the instrumental response, having the subjects write the responses would produce little difference from oral spelling (as has been the case in all previous experiments).

EXPERIMENT 14

Method

In this experiment subjects were given alternate learning and recall trials. The recall trial consisted of giving the subject a sheet of paper on which all the stimuli were listed and instructing him to write the responses after the appropriate stimuli.

The lists were the mixed ones used in Experiment 13. A total of 36 subjects was assigned to the lists in a random manner so that 12 subjects learned each one. Fifteen learning and fifteen recall trials were given.

For the recall trials, five different orders of the stimuli were printed, each subject being given each order three times for his 15 recall trials. The study trials consisted of presenting each pair for 2 sec. After the completion of the first trial, the experimenter stopped the drum and gave the subject a sheet on which the 12 stimuli were listed with a blank after each one. The subject was requested to write the appropriate response after each stimulus and to do this rapidly. However, in no sense was his time limited; he had an opportunity to attempt a response for each stimulus. When the subject had written all the responses he could, he was given another study trial; then a new order of the stimuli was presented on a new sheet of paper, and again the subject wrote all the responses he could. These procedures continued for 15 trials.

Results

The results may be summarized briefly.

1. The 36 items learned here had also been learned by the traditional method in Experiment 13. The product-moment correlation between the learning of these items in Experiment 13 and in Experiment 14 was .89. For the individual lists the values were .91, .84, and .93. These high relationships obviously preclude the possibility of obtaining a changed relationship with predictor variables. This expectation is verified.

2. For Lists 1 through 3, the product-moment correlations were −.06, .08, and .35 between learning and frequency. Corresponding values for pronunciability and learning were .77, .73, and .81. Both sets of values correspond closely to those of Experiment 13.

3. The above correlations were based on mean total correct responses over 15 trials. A second learning measure was derived, namely, the mean trial on which the response was first given (whether paired with the appropriate stimulus or not). However, since this measure correlated −.91 with the other measure (total correct in 15 trials), it

was apparent that relationships would not change by use of this early trial measure.

We conclude that having the subjects write the trigrams, rather than spell them orally, does not change the relationships found in the earlier experiments. Frequency and learning remain unrelated; pronunciability and learning remain highly related.

FURTHER ANALYSES OF FREQUENCY

The experiments have consistently shown that for multiple-letter responses, the frequency with which those responses occur as trigrams in words does not predict the rate of acquisition. We will now report a series of analyses which not only added to the woes of an already moribund frequency theory, but also helped lead us to a possible conclusion with implications that were contrary to well-established beliefs.

Frequency Ratings

Any reader who has carefully examined the trigrams used in the preceding experiments may have been puzzled by the frequency values associated with some of these units. Where (in what words), for example, do RCE, NDR, RTI, and NDE get their relatively high frequency? These trigrams cut across syllables and, apparently as a consequence, are much like "hidden figures." It is difficult to see in what words they may occur.

In a previous chapter, data were given on the accuracy of judging the relative frequency of trigrams. Judged frequency and actual frequency were positively and significantly related, but the relationship was not a sharp one. Assume that one took the position that the frequency theory may be adequate only when differences in frequency are measured phenomenally. Or, to say this another way, it could be assumed that frequency *is* effective in determining rate of learning when the frequency values are assigned by the subjects rather than by an objective criterion. The correlation between objective frequency and judged frequency is low enough so that it would be quite possible to find a strong relationship between judged frequency and learning, whereas no such relationship occurs between objective frequency and learning. To say the least, we did not relish the notion of having to tie a frequency theory to judged frequency, but we felt that we should at least evaluate learning against judged frequency. So again we turned to a rating procedure.

The ratings. The trigrams rated for frequency were those used in Experiments 12 and 13, plus a few additional items, for a total of 80. They were presented to groups of subjects who were given the following instructions:

On the following page is a list of combinations of three letters called trigrams. After each is a blank. Your task is to rate each trigram on how often you have come in contact with it. That is, you will rate it in terms of how often you think you have seen or heard or used the trigram in writing or in speech.

Your ratings will be made along a 9-point rating scale. This scale may be visualized as follows:

Very infrequently			Average					Very often
1	2	3	4	5	6	7	8	9

Please note that trigrams which you think you have experienced most frequently are to be given high numbers, those least frequently experienced, low numbers.

Your judgment of how often you have experienced a trigram is to be made relative to how often you have experienced the other trigrams in the list. To carry out your ratings, proceed as follows: First, look carefully at the first combination of letters in order to get a "feeling" of how often you have experienced it. Then look at the second, then the third, and so on for approximately the first 10 trigrams. Then skip around over the page examining approximately 10 more trigrams. The reason for this is that it will give you an idea of what a trigram is that you have experienced very often, and what a trigram is that you have rarely if ever experienced.

After you are confident that you know how to "anchor" the rating scale, go back to the first item in the list and assign it a number which you think represents its location on the 9-point scale. Use only whole numbers 1 through 9; do not assign fractional or decimal values. If you think the first trigram, relative to the others, has been experienced quite frequently, you might assign it an 8 or a 9. If you think you have rarely seen or heard the trigram, you would give it a 1 or 2. You will probably find trigrams which you will judge to have been experienced with about average frequency relative to the others and you would assign a middle number—4, 5, or 6.

Some of the trigrams actually form words, others do not. In either case your job is the same; you are to judge how often you have experienced it. Do not spend much time on any one trigram; your first reaction is the one we want.

Remember, those trigrams you have experienced very frequently are to be assigned high numbers, those infrequently, low numbers. The scale is reproduced on the next page also so that you can refer to it and thus avoid reversing your scale numbers. After you have completed your ratings, check back to make sure you have not omitted any.

The ratings were carried out by a group of 48 students at the University of California (Berkeley) and, subsequently, by 38 students at Northwestern University. For each item a mean scale value was determined. For the 80 items, the product-moment correlation between mean scale values obtained from the two groups of subjects was .99.

The relationships. Experiment 12 and Experiment 13 (mixed lists) each had 36 trigrams. For each trigram we have a learning measure, an objective frequency measure, a frequency rating, and a pronunciability rating. The interrelationships among these measures are shown in Table 32.

TABLE 32. Experiments 12 and 13. Relationships (Product-Moment Correlations) Among Trigram Frequency (f), Frequency Ratings (FR), Pronunciability Ratings (PR), and Learning (L)

	FR and f	FR and PR	FR and L	PR and L	f and L
Experiment 12	.46	.79	.69	.76	.16
Experiment 13	.51	.73	.68	.82	.08

Table 32 shows first of all that while there is a positive relationship between objective frequency (f) and judged frequency (FR), it is not high; the relationship between pronunciability (PR) and FR is considerably higher. With this latter relationship present, it is not surprising that FR predicts learning with considerable success although not quite as well as does PR.

The relationship between PR and FR should be considered further. It is probably best characterized by the remark of a subject asked to make the frequency ratings. After the instructions had been read, the experimenter asked if there were any questions before the subjects actually started making the ratings. This subject asked, "How can I rate some of these when I can't pronounce them?" In Table 33 the 36 items used in Experiment 13 are listed along with the ranks on each of the four variables. Tied ranks were ignored since it is only the larger discrepancies which are of interest. The following facts are suggested by this table:

1. Some high-frequency trigrams (e.g., GHT, TLY) are rated with considerable accuracy, and, although the subject "knows" that these trigrams have high frequency, they are difficult to learn. The learning of such units corresponds more closely to PR than to FR.

2. Some high-frequency trigrams (e.g., RTI, NDE) are "hidden figures" and are rated low on both PR and FR and are learned very slowly.

3. Low-frequency trigrams which are relatively easy to pronounce are rated as having a higher frequency than they in fact do have (e.g., BON, SLO).

Thus, these data suggest that judged frequency, while predicting

TABLE 33. Experiment 13. Relationships Among 36 Trigrams Ranked on Pronunciability (PR), Frequency Rating (FR), Objective Frequency (f), and Learning (L)

	L	FR	f	PR		L	FR	f	PR
BON	1	8	29	1	XPL	19	33	27	36
SCI	2	2	13	12	DGM	20	34	30	35
COM	3	1	4	4	JEC	21	23	26	13
SLO	4	4	20	2	LIR	22	20	31	16
VEN	5	10	2	6	MPO	23	25	24	25
LAR	6	7	9	3	GHT	24	9	1	27
KIV	7	24	35	15	TLY	25	6	5	20
VIL	8	13	22	7	RCE	26	21	12	22
JUS	9	11	15	9	DYI	27	27	23	21
COU	10	12	17	8	KBR	28	35	34	33
FET	11	15	16	5	NDR	29	32	14	32
GOI	12	19	28	19	TJU	30	36	36	29
BLE	13	5	3	17	NDE	31	22	8	28
BLI	14	17	7	10	MPR	32	26	18	31
WSE	15	29	32	24	LTY	33	14	25	23
KNO	16	3	21	18	MBE	34	30	19	30
JOR	17	18	11	11	HTF	35	31	33	34
FAI	18	16	10	14	RIT	36	28	6	26

learning far better than objective frequency, is not fundamentally related to learning. Subjects can judge correctly that certain trigrams have very high objective frequency; still these are learned slowly. When trigram frequencies are less apparent, ease or difficulty of pronouncing them seems to be the basis on which frequency judgments are made. Multiple correlations, combining FR and PR as predictors, did not raise the accuracy of prediction for learning the 36 items in either experiment. We conclude that the frequency ratings provide a measure of the discrepancy between objective frequency and phenomenal frequency but that they lack fundamental significance for our central problem.

Homogeneous Groupings

In all of the experiments in which trigram frequency was varied, the trigrams within a given list also varied with regard to various vowel and consonant combinations. This may be called *form-class* differences among trigrams. Is it possible that these differences in form-class are masking differences in learning as a function of frequency?

To evaluate this possibility, we have categorized the 72 items of Experiments 12 and 13 by vowel and consonant sequences. Four classes emerged with sufficient frequency in each to give some confidence in the results (no trigrams which included the letter Y were used). Twenty trigrams consisted of consonant-vowel-consonant (CVC) combinations. This form-class makes up nearly one-third of all three-letter sequences in words (cf., Chapter 9) and has the lowest mean PR (are rated easiest to pronounce) of any of the groupings. For these 20 items the product-moment correlation between PR and learning was .86, and between frequency and learning, .51. With PR constant, however, this latter correlation reduces to .16.

Nine trigrams had a VCC structure. For these trigrams the correlation between PR and learning was .81, and between frequency and learning, .03. For 21 items in the CCV class, PR and learning showed a product-moment of .70; that between frequency and learning was −.08. There were eight items having the CCC form. Neither PR nor frequency showed any relationship with learning for these eight items. However, it may be noted that differences in learning among these items were not great, and the PR ratings had a very small range, varying between 7.63 and 8.43.

These analyses allow two conclusions: (1) Frequency and learning remain unrelated even when the potential relationship is examined among items having identical consonant and vowel structure. (2) The relationship between pronunciability and learning remains striking even when trigrams are grouped according to form-class.

A Final Frequency Analysis

The data continue to point unmistakably toward a conclusion that the frequency with which trigrams occur in words is unrelated to rate of learning these trigrams as responses in paired-associate lists. Apparent positive relationships between frequency and learning were attributed to the relationship between pronunciability and frequency, and when pronunciability was held constant through the use of partial correlations, the "relationship" between frequency and learning disappeared. Only in Experiment 13, where we used unmixed lists varying in frequency but equivalent on pronunciability, did we show directly that frequency was of small consequence to learning. Let us look at the data in a new way. Using data from mixed lists, we can match items on pronunciability and let frequency vary, and we can match on frequency and let pronunciability vary. The data from Experiments 6, 12, and 13 (mixed lists) are used for these analyses.

The procedure for matching is simple. Assume that we are going to hold PR constant. First, we rank-order the trigrams with respect to PR for a given experiment and then examine the first *pair* of trigrams, putting the one with the highest frequency into a high-frequency group and the one with the lowest frequency into a low-frequency group. The next pair is treated in the same way, and so on through the pairs, so that two groups of items will emerge, each consisting of one-half of the total number of trigrams used in the experiment. These two groups should be nearly equal on PR, but should differ on frequency. Just how much they differ will depend upon the magnitude of the correlation between PR and frequency; the higher the correlation, the less is the difference in mean frequency between the two groupings. But if the procedure results in a sizeable difference in the mean frequency of the two groups of items, a test can be made of the difference in mean learning performance for the two groups of items.

TABLE 34. Statistical Manipulation of Pronunciability (PR) and Frequency (f)

(See text for complete explanation)

| | | Pronunciability Constant, Frequency Varied | | | | | | |
| | | High Group | | | Low Group | | | |
Exp.	No. Pairs	PR	f	Learn	PR	f	Learn	t
6	15	4.80	362.9	14.79	4.82	132.9	14.81	.03
12	18	3.82	564.9	8.53	3.91	110.6	8.45	.13
13	18	5.37	197.1	6.08	5.21	68.9	7.04	1.28

| | | Frequency Constant, Pronunciability Varied | | | | | | |
| | | High Group | | | Low Group | | | |
Exp.	No. Pairs	PR	f	Learn	PR	f	Learn	t
6	15	3.70	292.4 *	15.90	5.93	203.4	13.70	2.24
12	18	3.63	130.2	8.00	6.95	135.8	5.12	4.80
13	18	2.93	325.4	9.51	4.81	336.6	7.50	3.65

* That this mean is higher than the corresponding mean in the Low Group is due entirely to the very high frequency of one trigram (ING)

We have carried out both types of "crossruffs" for three experiments. The results, summarized in Table 34, are very clear: when PR is held constant and frequency allowed to vary, the differences in learning as a function of frequency are very small and statistically insignificant. But when frequency is held constant and PR allowed to vary, the differences in learning between the resulting two sets of items are rather large, and all would be interpreted as being significant statistically. Of course, if one accepts the validity of the partial-correlation procedure, the results shown in Table 34 were inevitable. The fact is that any way we slice our data we emerge with the same conclusion; frequency of trigrams does not relate to learning, pronunciability ratings for those trigrams do relate to learning.

FURTHER EVALUATION OF PRONUNCIABILITY

It was mentioned earlier that pronunciation ratings for our lists tend to be bimodally distributed. In none of our correlational procedures have we considered the consequence of this bimodality. In view of the fact that pronunciability is evolving into a major predictive attribute of verbal units, some account of this bimodality should be taken. Our accounting consists of a re-evaluation of the PR-learning relationships for three experiments (6, 12, and 13). To do this, we have divided the distributions of PR ratings for the items in each experiment into two groups so that each group has a somewhat more unimodal characteristic. These distributions, along with the subgroupings, are presented in Table 35. The number of items becomes quite small in one distribution (Experiment 12, items with high PR), but otherwise there is a minimum of 11 cases on which to base the correlations. The correlations between learning and PR for these segmented distributions are indicated.

TABLE 35. Correlational Relationships Between Pronunciability (PR) and Learning for Separate Sections of PR Distributions

PR Distribution	Exp. 6 No. Items	r	Exp. 12 No. Items	r	Exp. 13 No. Items	r
1.0–2.0	3		4		0	
2.1–3.0	6		9		6	
3.1–4.0	4	.59	13	.71	9	.69
4.1–5.0	5		3		4	
5.1–6.0	3		1		1	
6.1–7.0	0		0		2	
7.1–8.0	5	.57	3	.38	9	.08
8.1–9.0	6		3		5	

First, it is clear that when PR ratings are in the low range (indicating easy pronunciability), the correlation between PR and learning maintains itself. In view of the results found earlier with form-class groupings, we are inclined to believe that some variance is added by form-class and that the correlations among items easy to pronounce would be a little higher if several form–classes were not represented in the distributions.

Turning to the correlations between learning and PR for items in the difficult-to-pronounce range, we see that the data lack consistency. Probably little attention should be paid the correlation in Experiment 12, since there are only six items involved. For Experiment 6, the relationship is substantial, for Experiment 13, it is essentially zero. This last value has been "checked" by using the results of Experiment 14 (which was the same as Experiment 13 except that the subjects wrote their responses). The value for Experiment 14 was .10. As further evidence we took data from Experiment 15 (to be reported in Chapter 10). This experiment involved 48 items in six eight-pair lists and for present purposes may be considered highly similar to Experiment 6. The correlation between learning and PR for items easy to pronounce was .68; for the items hard to pronounce the value was .42. This latter correlation is considerably attenuated for reasons that are not relevant to the present discussion, and a more reasonable estimate of this relationship would be .75.

We are inclined to believe that the data warrant the idea that for items with relatively high PR values (difficult to pronounce), the correlation between learning and PR is substantial for eight–item lists but is essentially zero for twelve-item lists. This distinction pits Experiments 6 and 15 against Experiments 12, 13, and 14, the former having eight items, the latter, 12. We had earlier concluded that length of list was not a *critical* factor in the PR-learning relationship. However, it is a fact that the correlations between learning and PR have tended to be a few points lower for 12-item lists than for eight–item lists. We attribute this to the lower correlation among the harder-to-pronounce trigrams. Furthermore, we think this is an interpretable conclusion, and we will return to this finding in the final chapter.

A REASSESSMENT AND A NEW CONCLUSION

At every turn in our analysis of the learning of trigrams as responses in paired-associate lists, we have failed to find the expected relationship between frequency of trigrams and rate of learning. Thus, we are forced to reassess the basic evidence which lured us to assert originally that there should be a relationship between frequency and learning.

In Chapter 5 we presented analyses translating M (as defined by several techniques) of consonant and nonsense syllables into frequency values. The results were very clear in showing:

1. The higher the M of consonant and nonsense syllables, the greater is the probability that the syllable occurred as a trigram in words.

2. For trigrams that do occur as nonsense syllables, the frequency of the trigram in words increases as M increases.

3. The bigram frequency of nonsense and consonant syllables (when each syllable is considered two bigrams) increases as M increases.

The results of learning experiments (reviewed in Chapter 3) in which M was varied were consistent in showing a relationship between M and learning, and this relationship was especially marked when the M was varied on the response side of paired-associate lists. Experiment 5 in Chapter 7 showed that learning was directly related to M of consonant syllables. If M and learning are highly related and if trigram frequency and M are highly related, it seemed very probable that trigram frequency and learning would be related. Our experimental facts flatly deny this expected relationship. (We are not, of course, referring to *manipulated* frequency as used in Experiments 1–4, Chap. 6).

For some time we resisted a conclusion implied by the above series of facts, but we now believe it to be the only reasonable conclusion possible. Namely, it must be concluded that M (defined as number of subjects who get an association, or defined by the production method or by rated number of associates) *has nothing to do with the relationship between M and learning which has been observed*. Or, to say this another way, the M of verbal materials does not influence the rate of learning, at least when the materials are used as responses in paired-associate lists. Rather, we believe the apparent causal status of M derives from a certain amount of covariation with pronunciability, and if that covariation is removed, only the relationship between pronunciability and learning will hold up. However, having become, by now, very wary of asserting the relevance of one attribute and the irrelevance of another when the two are correlated, we turn quickly to the examination of our data to see if the conclusion can be given any additional empirical backing.

Rated pronunciability and association value. In an earlier chapter we reported a correlation of .78 between M as scaled by the production method (Noble) and PR for 100 nonsense syllables. While this relationship was somewhat less than those shown among other related characteristics (e.g., PR and rated speed of learning), we did not originally attach any significance to it. Perhaps we should, for, while the correlation does indicate a strong relationship, there is still considerable variance not common to the two attributes. We have tested this relationship again using the Glaze values. From among the items scaled for PR, we found 114 nonsense syllables which also occur in Glaze's list. The product-moment between the two sets of values was only .67. Thus, it would appear that we need not inevitably find high covariation between M and PR. There is "room" for independent variation. But the critical question is whether or not it can be shown that PR (or some other index) is related to learning when M is not. There are some data available.

Experiment 5. In Experiment 5 two paired-associate lists, made up with Witmer consonant syllables as responses, were employed. These were constructed to be relatively homogeneous in M within each list, one having low-M items, the other having items of moderate M on the Witmer scale. For each list, there were significant differences in learning among the items.

In presenting the results of Experiment 5, we noted that the Witmer values did not predict the learning very well, whereas summed individual letter frequency did. Indeed, for the list made up of responses of low M, the rank ordering for summed letter values and for learning were in perfect correspondence. We do not have PR ratings for these items, but we can make comparisons between the predictive power of association value versus summed letter frequency.

For summed letter frequency (LF) the product-moment correlation with learning is .98 and .64 for Lists 1 and 2, respectively. The corresponding values between Witmer values and learning is .45 and .50. If all 16 items are combined into a single distribution, the correlation between LF and learning is .88 and that between learning and Witmer values, .66. However, a partial correlation holding LF constant reduces the Witmer-learning relationship to .30, a value which is far from significant statistically. When the Witmer values are held constant, the relationship between LF and learning is .79. The correlation between Witmer values and LF is .63.

We may conclude that the association value of these particular 16 consonant syllables does not predict learning as well as summed letter frequency. Furthermore, it appears that the association value depends upon the relationship with summed letter frequency for what predictive power it does have.

Experiments 12 and 13. From among the trigrams used in Experiments 12 and 13, we found 14 nonsense syllables which also appear in Glaze's list. For these 14 syllables the correlation between PR and Glaze value was only .19. (We see no reason why this correlation should be so low for these items, but the fact that it is allows a very clear test of the relationship between learning and PR vs. the relationship between association value and learning.) The product-moment correlation between learning and PR was .68 for the 14 items and that between association value and learning, .07. PR and learning are clearly related; association value and learning are not.

Experiment 15. From the lists used in this experiment we found 11 trigrams which also appear in Glaze's list. The product-moment between the learning scores and PR was .87 and that between Glaze and learning, .75. However, for these 11 syllables, PR and Glaze values correlate .84. Therefore, a partial correlation was calculated holding PR constant; as a result the relationship between Glaze values and learning dropped to .07.

The three sets of data we have reviewed manifestly support the position that M (defined as association value) is not a relevant attribute—at least not a directly relevant attribute—for learning. That for many years it has appeared to be so related apparently stems from the fact that it is partially correlated with attributes which *are* fundamental to learning. It should be clear that in making these statements, we are referring only to the response-learning phase; we are not saying that M has no pertinence to the associative phase.

Can we find any evidence from other investigators which would support the position that M is not a critical factor in the response-learning phase? We have not been able to find substantial data of this nature, but some fragmentary evidence is supportive.

Postman & Rau (1957), in a study of retention, had used a serial list of 12 nonsense syllables which had three items from each of four Glaze scale levels (0 per cent, 33 per cent, 66 per cent, 100 per cent). The M values of the different items were balanced against serial position. The results show only a slight (and statistically insignificant) superiority in the learning of the 66 per cent and 100 per cent syllables over the learning of 0 per cent and 33 per cent syllables. Thus, for whatever reason, M and learning were not related.

Dr. Richard Lindley reported an ingenious experiment at the 1959 meetings of the Midwestern Psychological Association, and he was kind enough to make a copy of his paper available to us. He constructed two lists of nonsense syllables to have equal association value (mean Glaze value of approximately 85 per cent for both lists), but differing in familiarity. His high-familiarity list consisted of nonsense syllables which were the first three letters of very high-frequency words (e.g., HOM), whereas his low-familiarity list employed syllables which were *not* the first three letters of any word appearing in the Thorndike-Lorge list. The list of highly familiar items was learned much more rapidly than the list of items of low familiarity. Since the two lists were equal on association value, it is clear that some other factor is responsible for the differences in learning. If our experiments on variation in trigram frequency had shown the frequency to be related to learning, we would gloatingly cite these findings as support for the frequency hypothesis we earlier advanced; by our trigram counts these lists differ widely in frequency.

Lindley interpreted his results in terms of number of associations "used" by the subjects in learning. The subjects learning the highly familiar items reported more associations during learning than did the subjects learning the list of low familiarity. Lindley suggests, therefore, that this difference reflects an associative factor which is probably responsible for the differences in learning. This may be true, but it is also possible that his two lists differed on some other characteristic, such as pronunciability. In any event, the basic fact is clear: items equal on association value were learned at quite different rates, and such a fact supports our contention that association value may have nothing to do with learning directly.

A study by Taylor (1958), while at best tangentially related, may be worth mentioning. She found no relationship between visual recognition thresholds and Glaze M values. It so happened that she chose items so that the same letters were used at each M value and all syllables were said to be easily pronounceable. We will not discuss the complicated matter of whether or not M value should influence visual recognition thresholds; it is a fact, however, that such thresholds are sensitive to task variables and tend to be lower when any factor makes the verbal unit more available. It is possible that by essentially equating syllables on pronunciability, she may have also equated them for availability, in which case the results would support the position we have been discussing.

We suspect that others, who may have reached this point with us in our attempts to eliminate M as a factor in response learning, will conclude that it is high time to perform an experiment specifically designed to test the position we have assumed. We reached the same conclusion, but, in fact, it is a very difficult position to test experimentally. The reason for this lies in the over-all rather high correlation between

M and other attributes. The objective of such an experiment would be to construct two lists differing on M but equal on other attributes. The danger is in the likelihood that (because of the relatively high correlation among the attributes) when items are found which are equal on one attribute but differ appreciably on another, the selection in effect "makes use of" random variation, so that the differences on the attributes are likely to be unreliable. Furthermore, one may include some of those few maverick items—items which have certain peculiarities or uncommon attributes which make their scaling (on the dimensions common to most units) quite unreliable.

We did, in fact, try such an experiment with small groups of subjects and the results were completely negative; it is perhaps more accurate to say they were a mess. Neither pronunciability nor association value showed a respectable correlation with learning. Furthermore, since a few of the items appeared in more than one list, we had some indication of the reliability of the learning. In our previous experiments, when the same items have been used in more than one list or in more than one experiment, we have obtained very high reliability. (See the results for Experiments 12, 13, and 14). This was not the case here for several of the items. In one list they would be learned very rapidly, in another very slowly. There was no apparent reason for this instability as far as procedures were concerned, since they were identical to those we have used in most of our previous work. We concluded that in looking for items that were equal on one attribute but quite different on another, we had picked a few of these maverick items.

We do believe that the above experiment can be done but that it will require many, many lists and many, many pairings of items so that the peculiarities of the extreme cases will not overshadow the effects of small differences on one attribute when matched on another. As a matter of fact, it would probably be wise to avoid large differences and "bank on" small but reliable differences to produce in the long run a consistent result for one attribute when the items are equated on the other. Insofar as the two attributes are not perfectly correlated, the results of many "crossruffs" should give the expected differences.

In spite of the fact that our observations made above lack decisiveness, we will conclude that M (as defined by the Glaze or by the Noble procedure) is not responsible for the relationship between M and response learning. We have identified two other factors which are substantially related to learning, namely, summed letter frequency and pronunciability. We still hold open the possibility that M may be attributed causal status for the associative stage of learning.

THE REMAINING PREDICTORS

Our distillation of the facts concerning response learning of trigrams in paired-associate lists leaves us with two predictors: (1) summed letter frequency, and (2) pronunciability. As such, these two factors must enter into our final accounting. However, a few comments about each is necessary to carry us into the next chapter.

When we initiated our experiments we were "sold" on response integration as a primary factor in the response-learning phase. Our frequency hypothesis was stated to accommodate this integration. One weakness in this early formulation was the failure to consider mechanisms which might telescope the process of letter integration—the process as we had conceived it and had related it to frequency. When our experiments began to show how strongly pronunciability predicted learning, it became obvious that our frequency mechanisms were being given the run-a-round. The gross frequency theory was found quite inadequate for trigram learning. But in every case where we have equated on other attributes, pronunciability has consistently remained as a stable and powerful predictor.

It appears, then, quite unexpectedly and quite without theoretical direction, that we have stumbled upon an attribute of verbal units which has more predictive power by far than any other attribute we have discovered or methodically set about to measure. Having now placed pronunciability on the summit, the critical question remains as to whether or not we should try to impute fundamental causal status to it. To help us arrive at such a decision, we must carefully consider whether or not some other psychological variable may lie behind pronunciability and is in fact responsible for the relationships observed. We think we have reduced the diameter of the cause-effect circle, but it is still a circle. If we do take the step of declaring that pronunciability should have causal status, we must also provide some notion of how it operates to affect learning. Our final three chapters will be pointed in the general direction which should allow us to reach some conclusions on these important issues.

We have shown that summed single-letter frequency has some predictive power for learning. This index predicted better than association value for the consonant syllables used in Experiment 5. However, as responses become more and more integrated—as they become more and more pronounceable—summed letter frequency breaks down; the relationships with over-all learning are usually positive, but low, and most of the positive relationship results from the predictive value for responses with low initial integration of letters. Now, it is quite possible that pronunciability will predict as well as summed letter frequency for items of low initial integration. Our data are not very conclusive on this matter. Actually, when we have compared pronunciability and summed letter frequencies for items of low integration, the two seem to vary together. Pronunciability appears to predict a little bit better than summed letter frequency, but when pronunciability breaks down (as it does in Experiments 12 and 13 for items with low initial integration), so also does summed letter frequency. Such findings suggest that pronunciability and summed letter frequencies will be correlated. In our list of trigrams which have been rated for pronunciability, we found 39 units which had pronunciability values above 7.50. Such items should have very low letter integration (except for alphabetical sequences which were omitted). The product–moment correlation between the pronunciability values and the summed letter frequency values for these 39 units was .54. It seems apparent that there is a certain amount of tangling between these two measures, and they may not be easy to untangle.

One final comment should be made about the summed letter frequencies. Others, more skilled in manipulating numerical values, may find a way to increase the prediction by the individual letters of trigrams by using various weighting techniques, probability techniques, or other devices whether theoretically directed or not. We mention this now, but it will become a more acute problem in handling the data to be presented in Chapter 10.

SUMMARY

The experiments in this chapter represented further tests of the frequency hypothesis. In all experiments the frequency of units in the response position of paired-associate lists was varied. The differential frequency of these units was varied in terms of the frequency with which they occur in printed text. Our critical conclusions are:

1. When single letters are learned as responses in paired-associate lists, the relationship between frequency and rate of learning is substantial, and this fact conforms to expectations of the frequency theory.

2. As the number of letters in a response increases, the relationship between frequency and learning decreases; with three-letter responses the relationship is essentially zero. No manner of slicing the data could avoid this conclusion.

3. The above facts indicate that for multiple-letter responses the frequency theory is inadequate. A reassessment of the facts that led to the theory, viewed in conjunction with the results of the experiments, led to the conclusion that M (defined as association value) is not related to response learning. Some evidence was mustered in support of this contention. (See also a recent study by DiMascio, 1959).

4. The one predictor of learning which held up throughout the several experiments was the pronunciability of the verbal units; more and more pronunciability seems to point to a very fundamental attribute of verbal material.

REFERENCES

DiMascio, A. Learning characteristics of nonsense syllables: A function of letter frequency. *Psychol. Rep.*, 1959, 5, 585–591.

Postman, L., & Rau, L. Retention as a function of the method of measurement. *Univer. Cal. Pub. Psychol.*, 1957, 8, 217–270.

Taylor, J. Meaning, frequency, and visual duration threshold. *J. exp. Psychol.*, 1958, 55, 329–334.

Chapter 9

Letter–Sequence Habits

Our experiments on M and the changes in our thinking about M have been ordered thus far in a manner that is quite faithful to the actual order of events. This historical fidelity is to be broken in Chapters 9 and 10. These researches were initiated early in our program and were viewed at that time as another line of attack on the problem of how M influences learning. Therefore, we must locate the researches in the period of thought which spawned them.

At the time the present studies were undertaken, we knew that the M of consonant and nonsense syllables was related to the frequency with which two- and three-letter sequences occur in words (cf. Chapter 5). Our interpretation of these relationships at that time was straightforward; the more frequently two or three letters occurred in sequence in words, the greater would be the associative connection between these letters. Thus, the relationship between M and learning was thought to be a consequence of differences in degree of integration of the letters in a syllable; the differences in integration, in turn, were produced by the differences in the frequency with which the sequences of letters had been experienced by the subject. From these facts we elaborated the frequency hypothesis presented in Chapter 6.

It is apparent that our ability to "plot" a dimension of associative strength (as inferred from frequency) for two- and three-letter sequences was limited to those sequences which occur in words. For all sequences which did not occur in words, we would have to assign a value of zero. The number of different trigrams which occur in words was known to be small relative to the total number of possible three-letter combinations. Even now, by combining all three counts

(T-L, U, and Pratt), we have approximately only 3,500 different trigrams appearing in words. There are 17,576 possible three-letter combinations from the 26 letters. Roughly speaking, therefore, there would be 14,000 combinations of three letters for which we would have no index of associative strength between letters. It seems absurd to conclude that all such combinations would have zero associative strength. It was apparent that if we wanted to fill this gap, we had to have information from sources other than printed text sources. Two other points in our thinking entered into the decision to try to determine directly the associative strength between all letters.

1. The data that were available relating frequency and learning (cf., Chapter 4) led us to conclude that for trigrams occurring in words, we might not find a very marked relationship between learning and trigram frequency. The frequency of these trigrams should be, in an absolute sense, relatively high in the experiences of our subjects, and, at best, only a small ordering effect in learning might occur. We wanted to get the full range of strength of associative connection between letters—we thought at the time, the full range of M.

2. When we conceive of M as representing habits leading to different degrees of associative strength between letters, and when we infer different associative strengths only from frequency of letter sequences in words, we must be ignoring certain other habits which influence the associative strength between letters. Alphabetical habits are obvious ones which receive little representation in trigrams derived from words. There are probably other habits which affect the degree of association between letters, and these might have at least fairly high spoken frequency. Moreover, there may be second-order habits of certain kinds which we would not "get at" if we merely used trigrams as obtained from printed words.

It was for the above reasons that we set about to determine emitted letter-sequence habits. We believed that with such information we could construct three-letter sequences with varying degrees of composite habit strength (hence, varying degrees of integration) which would represent the complete range of M. The composite habit strength would incorporate not only habit strength induced by experience with printed language, but should also incorporate any other habits built up through other sources of experience with letters.

In the present chapter the procedure and results of the research used to determine letter-sequence habits will be presented. In the following chapter the results of learning experiments, using three-letter sequences of different composite associative strength, will be reported.

METHOD

The method was patterned after the classic word-association experiments. The subject was given single-letter stimuli and asked to write for each stimulus a single additional letter which most naturally followed it. So also were two-letter stimuli presented with instructions to write a third letter which most naturally followed.

Three samples of subjects were involved. The major data were obtained from elementary psychology students at Northwestern University during the 1956–57 school year. Two smaller samples of subjects, working under somewhat different instructions with a selected group of stimuli were obtained at the University of California (Berkeley) in the fall of 1958. These different samples will be referred to as the NU and UC samples.

NU Sample

The subjects in this sample were presented with each of the 26 single-letter stimuli as well as all possible (676) two-letter stimuli. The material was given to the subject in the form of a booklet with the cover sheet consisting of instructions as follows:

1. Number the *following* pages 1 through 7. Make sure you have seven sheets beyond this one. All sheets have four columns on them except one which has only two columns.

2. On these following seven pages are a series of two-letter combinations with a few instances of single letters. After each is a blank. Your task is very simple; we want you to fill in the blanks with a single additional letter. To do this, say the letters (or letter) to yourself and then fill in the blank with the letter which to you seems to follow. Your first reaction is the one we want; don't study them in an effort to decide what is "right" or "wrong" for there are no right or wrong letters.

3. Let us consider an illustration. Suppose the two letters are EN—. Your first reaction might be to fill in the blank with "D," or "T," or "E." Whatever it is that is what we want, so put it down.

4. While we have said there are no right and wrong answers, there are a few things you should do and a few things you should not do.

(a) Do *not* go through the pages filling all the blanks with the same letter or with the alphabetical sequence.

(b) Do *not* fall in a rut of always putting down the next letter in the alphabet. That is, if the letters were "EN"—, don't fill in the blank with "O" simply because that is the letter after "N." In some cases this may be the strongest tendency and if so of course put down that letter. But don't let yourself fall into a set or habit of merely putting down the next letter in the alphabet for all blanks.

(c) Work quickly but look at each letter combination separately; try to ignore what you have put down for previous blanks. In general, let the letter be put down which seems to come quickly and naturally.

(d) Do *not* skip any blanks as you go through the pages but when you finish check back to make sure that you have not inadvertently missed some.

(e) Print all your letters in block type—they are much easier to read and less likely to be confused with other letters.

5. When you finish, fill in your name, class, and time. We will explain to you what to put in the "Time" blank.

The two-letter combinations were listed in a random order, subject to the restriction that the same first letter was not allowed for any two successive stimuli. There were four columns on each page (except for one page on which there were only two columns), each column consisting of 27 stimuli. A single-letter stimulus occurred in each column, its position in the column varying. The seven pages were stapled together in such fashion that each occurred approximately equally often at each position.

The instruction sheet refers to a time measure. This is the time taken by the subject to fill in all the blanks. All subjects started working at the same time. Each minute, on the minute, the experimenter wrote on a blackboard the elapsed time since the subjects started working. When the subject finished he simply recorded on his booklet the elapsed time as seen on the blackboard.

Despite the instructions about not merely filling in the blanks with repeated alphabetical sequences, a monitor noted that one subject was doing this. This subject completed all blanks in 13 min. It was also noted that the subject who required 44 min. to complete the booklet (the longest of any subject) tended to meditate before putting down a response. In view of these two extreme cases, a distribution of the number of subjects completing in successive 1-min. intervals was drawn up. Breaks in the continuity of the distribution at the extremes were then used to eliminate records for subjects who were atypical and who might not have been following the instructions as per the two cases noted. This eliminated three subjects for being "too fast" and six for being "too slow." The final tabulation was based on 127 subjects obtained in one group procedure and 146 in another, for a total of 273.

For these 273 subjects the mean and median times to complete the 702 responses both fell between 26 and 27 min. Thus, on the average, a little over 2 sec. per response was required.

Tabulation. The responses were tabulated so that the frequency of each letter as a response to each of the 702 stimuli is available. As would be expected, all responses could not be read unambiguously. Scorers * tabulated a response only if they were reasonably sure of it; that is, they tabulated it if they were reasonably sure they were reading the response correctly. Otherwise, the item was placed in an "omitted" category. There were also a few bona fide omits. Both sources of omissions average about two per stimulus so that "good" data are available for approximately 271 subjects.

Reliability. No attempt will be made here to give exhaustive data on reliability. However, enough will be presented to demonstrate that there is some stability in the responses to these stimuli.

It will be remembered that there were two subsamples of NU subjects, one consisting of 127 subjects and the other of 146. In the initial tabulation the responses for these two groups were kept separate. A count has been made of the agreement between the two subsamples with respect to the most frequent responses to each stimulus. First, for each of the 702 stimuli, the most frequent responses given by the subjects in one of the subgroups was determined. Then, the rank of this response for the corresponding stimuli for the subjects of the other subgroup was determined.

The following comparisons indicate the extent of the agreement: (In making the comparisons, ties for rank were always resolved in the direction that would give greatest agreement between samples.)

1. For 72 per cent of the 702 stimuli the agreement was perfect on the most frequent response.

2. For 15 per cent of the stimuli the most frequent response in the first subgroup was the second most frequent in the second subgroup.

3. For 7 per cent of the stimuli the most frequent response for the first subgroup was the third most frequent response for the second subgroup.

4. For 2 per cent of the stimuli the most frequent response for the first subgroup was the fourth most frequent for the other.

* This very tedious tabulating job was done by Mrs. Selma Segall and Mrs. Nan Lewis, to whom we are very grateful.

5. Finally, for 3 per cent of the stimuli, the most frequent response for the first subgroup did not occur among the four most frequent responses for the other subgroup.

Somehow in the process of getting the stimuli mimeographed for presentation to the subjects, two two-letter stimuli were printed twice (in place of two others that were omitted). The stimulus UR occurred twice, and US was omitted. Likewise, ZW occurred twice, and ZX was omitted. These errors can be turned to an advantage, for, to each of the two stimuli, each subject has responded twice. The two distributions of responses given to the stimulus UR gave a rank-order correlation of .78; for the stimulus ZW the correlation was .88.

We will conclude that there is evidence for considerable stability among responses to these single- and two-letter stimuli. Furthermore, comparisons between the responses given by the NU subjects and by the UC subjects, which will be detailed at various points in the presentation of the results, provide further evidence on reliability.

UC Samples

The procedure for these two samples of subjects differed from each other only in terms of the instructions. The first sample was given instructions which correspond quite closely to those given the NU Sample, the major difference being that no specific instructions for avoiding alphabetical habits were included. This sample will be labelled UC-R, the R implying "regular" instructions. The instructions in their entirety were as follows:

> On the following page is a series of two-letter combinations with some instances of single letters. After each is a blank. The basic idea is simple; we want you to fill in each blank with a *single* additional letter which to you most naturally follows.
> To carry this out, say the letters (or letter) to yourself and then fill in the blank with the letter which seems to follow. Work quickly, but look at each entry separately; try to ignore what you have put down for previous blanks. Your first reaction is the one we want; don't study a combination in an effort to decide what is "right" or "wrong" for there are no right or wrong letters for these blanks. Let the letter be put down which comes quickly and naturally.
> Print your responses as CAPITAL LETTERS.

The purpose of the instructions for the other sample of subjects was to see if it is possible to "set" subjects so that they would respond in a manner that closely approximates the printed language. If this could be done, discrepancies in the responses for the two groups could be attributed to habits other than those induced by the language. That is, the responses given by the first sample would include all habits, and those of the second (if the instructions could be carried out), only those letter-sequence habits built up by the occurrence of letter combinations with differential frequency in words. This second subgroup will be labelled UC-L, the L indicating language instructions. These instructions were as follows:

> On the following page is a series of two-letter combinations with some instances of single letters. After each is a blank. The basic idea is simple; we want you to fill in each blank with a *single* additional letter which to you most naturally follows. However, to do this we want you to think of each two-letter combination as the first two letters in words, and each single letter as the first letter of words. You are not supposed to think of specific words nor words of any particular length. Indeed, a few of the two-letter combinations are never used as the first two letters of a word. So, you are to "set" yourself merely in a general way to view these letters as the first part of a word and then write down whatever letter most easily comes to mind.
>
> To carry this out, say the letters (or letter) to yourself and then fill in the blank with the letter which seems to follow. Work quickly, but look at each entry separately; try to ignore what you have put down for previous blanks. Your first reaction is the one we want; don't study a combination in an effort to decide what is "right" or "wrong" for there are no right or wrong letters for these blanks. Let the letter be put down which comes quickly and naturally.
>
> Print your responses as CAPITAL LETTERS.

The UC-R sample consisted of 84 elementary psychology students and the UC-L, of 83. The data were collected by a group procedure. No time-to-complete measure was taken.

The stimuli for both samples were identical and consisted of all 26 single-letter stimuli and 119 two-letter stimuli. The latter stimuli were selected so that they constituted a good sampling of the 676 used for the NU sample; that is, there were stimuli with high and low language frequency, various combinations of vowels and consonants, and so on. All stimuli were printed on a single sheet of paper, and two independent random orders of the stimuli were prepared. In the UC-R group the two orders were divided 42–42 among the 84 subjects, and the UC-L group, 42–41.

As indicated earlier, our major reason for carrying out this research was to collect data which would indicate differences in associative strength of letter-sequence habits. Using this information, we could construct verbal units which had different degrees of associative connection, and we could, in turn, use these different degrees of associative connection as an indication of differences in response integration. However, the data obtained from our procedure have some interest in themselves. They have some relevance to the frequency hypothesis, and, of course, they give some understanding of the habits elicited in this situation. Nevertheless, it will be seen that our analyses will not be comprehensive in the sense that all data are analyzed at all possible levels. Essentially, our analyses sample the data.

The complete tables of response frequencies for the NU Sample are given in Appendix F.

SINGLE-LETTER STIMULI
Over-all Response Frequency

The first question we ask concerns the relative frequency with which each letter was given as a response when responses to all single-letter stimuli were combined. The frequency of each letter is expressed as a percentage of the total number of responses given to all stimuli by all subjects (Table 36). If we deal solely in correlational terms, no clear differences exist among the three samples of subjects. The rank-order correlations are as follows: NU versus UC-R, .91; NU versus UC-L, .91; UC-R versus UC-L, .89. Clearly, there is high agreement among the three samples with respect to the relative frequency with which each letter is emitted. For all samples, approximately one in four responses will be O; this vowel occurs with much greater frequency than do other vowels. Among consonants, T is given most frequently.

The fact that the relative frequency of different letters is comparable among the three samples should not obscure the fact that the absolute frequencies differ as a consequence of the special instructions given the UC-L group. The major effect of the instructions to "think of the stimuli as the first letter of words" is, insofar as we can tell, virtually to eliminate responding to a letter stimulus with the next letter in the alphabet when such a response does not conform to letter sequences in words. Thus, low-frequency letters have a lower fre-

TABLE 36. Frequency (Percentage of Total
Responses Given) with Which Each Letter Occurred
as a Response to Single-Letter Stimuli for the Three
Samples of Subjects

Response	NU	UC-R	UC-L
A	8.3	10.5	14.3
B	2.5	1.2	.7
C	1.4	1.1	.7
D	3.2	1.2	1.0
E	5.1	12.1	11.0
F	1.4	1.7	.9
G	.8	.8	.2
H	1.1	.9	1.6
I	7.1	6.2	8.7
J	.6	.1	.1
K	1.4	1.3	.4
L	2.6	2.3	1.1
M	4.0	2.2	1.3
N	3.6	4.5	3.8
O	24.7	25.5	27.7
P	3.5	1.7	2.7
Q	.9	.4	.3
R	3.8	3.5	2.8
S	3.5	2.9	1.8
T	7.8	6.2	6.7
U	5.0	7.0	7.6
V	1.7	.8	.7
W	1.0	.6	.6
X	1.5	1.2	1.2
Y	2.2	2.1	1.5
Z	1.4	1.8	.6

quency for the UC-L group than for the other two groups. This may
be seen in Table 37, where the number of subjects giving an alphabetical-sequence response for each letter is reported. Of course, it must be
remembered that an alphabetical-sequence response and a "true" language response often converge. Nevertheless, there are differences
between the two groups of subjects. For example, to the stimulus Y, 18
subjects in the UC-R group gave Z, but only one in the UC-L group
did so. However, the over-all effect when all responses are summed for
all single-letter stimuli is relatively small, as witness the high correlations reported above.

Correspondence with letter frequency in language. An inspection of
Table 36 will show that frequency of response to the single-letter
stimuli does correspond somewhat with the frequency of appearance
of the letters in the language. The relationships are not simple, however, and will require considerable discussion. First we will need to
indicate the source of our information about letter frequency.

In the U Count the total number of times each letter occurred was

TABLE 37. Frequency of Alphabetical-Sequence Responses to Single-Letter Stimuli for the UC-R and UC-L Samples

Stimulus and Response	UC-R	UC-L
A-B	15	1
B-C	6	1
C-D	6	2
D-E	8	6
E-F	7	2
F-G	11	0
G-H	1	0
H-I	23	27
I-J	2	0
J-K	11	1
K-L	10	5
L-M	4	1
M-N	12	3
N-O	52	59
O-P	10	12
P-Q	3	1
Q-R	9	5
R-S	8	5
S-T	7	8
T-U	4	3
U-V	7	3
V-W	4	0
W-X	9	5
X-Y	21	21
Y-Z	18	1

determined (cf. Table 6). For the present analyses we have used a slightly different index. For reasons which will become apparent in a later section, we wanted to know how frequently each letter *followed* a consonant in a word and how frequently each followed a vowel. To obtain this, the bigrams were analyzed and a frequency obtained for each letter, this frequency indicating how often each letter follows a vowel and how often each follows a consonant; the sum of these indicates the frequency with which each letter occurs in words *excluding* the frequency with which each occurs as a first letter in a word. Insofar as the frequency with which a letter occurs as a first letter is disproportionate to its frequency of occurrence at all other positions, the two measures (total frequency and frequency excluding first letters) will diverge. In actual fact the discrepancy is minor, the rank-order correlation between the two distributions being .97. But it should be clear that when we refer to total single-letter frequency in the present chapter, we are referring to a total which excludes first-letter frequency.

The subjects in the UC-L Sample were given instructions to consider the stimuli as first letters in words. Obviously, if we are to relate the frequency of their responses to letter frequency, the most appropriate measure of the latter would be the frequency of each letter as second letters in words. The information on frequency of second letters was obtained from the original tabulations made for the U Count. A rank-order correlation between frequency of letters as second letters and total letter frequency is .85.

So, we have two measures of individual letter frequency, namely, total letter frequency and frequency as second letters in words. These measures may now be related to total frequency with which each letter was given to all single-letter stimuli. The rank-order correlations for the three samples for each of the two letter-frequency measures are shown in Table 38. First, it is clear from the table that relative fre-

TABLE 38. Rank-Order Correlations between Frequency of Response to All Single-Letter Stimuli for Each Sample and Total and Second-Letter Frequency

	Frequency	
	Total Letters	Second Letters
NU Sample	.76	.71
UC-R Sample	.76	.74
UC-L Sample	.81	.89

quency of emission of letters to single-letter stimuli is substantially related to relative frequency of occurrence of those letters in the language. Second, it can be seen that the responses of the UC-L Sample correspond more closely to true letter frequency than do the responses for the other two samples. This is most apparent when second-letter frequency is involved; that is, when the frequency measure reflects most closely the intent of the instructions given the subjects in the UC-L Sample.

Certain letters occur with very high frequency in the language but follow only a very limited number of different letters. The outstanding example is H, which, as a consequence of a few words (e.g., THE, THAT), occurs with very high frequency as a second letter. Indeed, in the U Count it is the second most frequent second letter (O being first). The letter H also occurs with relatively high frequency as a first letter. The U Count shows, however, that H follows only eight *different* letters in the language. In calculating the rank-order correlations shown in Table 38, it was noted that H consistently showed a rather marked discrepancy between its frequency in printed text and its frequency as a response in the letter-association experiment. This suggested the possibility that a better predictor of emitted frequency might be the number of different letters which each letter follows in words. If the subject is responding only partially to the particular stimulus and partially in accordance with an over-all language probability, correlations between number of different letters which each letter follows and frequency of emission might be expected to be substantial. And in fact this is true. The rank-order correlations are .86, .88, and .82 for the NU, UC-R, and UC-L Samples, respectively.

The above correlations indicate a fairly strong relationship between the frequency with which each letter is elicited as a response and, (1) the frequency with which those letters occur in words, and also (2) the number of different letters which each follows. As might be expected, the distributions of frequencies are badly skewed; many letters are given infrequently, and a few very frequently. Rank-order correlations are usually higher in these letter-frequency data than are product-moment correlations. For example, for the NU Sample, the rank-order correlation between frequency of letters emitted and frequency of these letters in the language was .76. The product-moment correlation is only .52. For the same subjects the rank correlation between number of different letters which a given letter follows and the frequency of emission of that letter is .86. The corresponding product-moment is .54.

These contrasts between the values of the rank-order and product-moment correlations are given as illustrations, but it is probably accurate to say that they are fairly representative of a situation that prevails throughout these data. The statistical reason for the discrepancies is probably quite apparent. Discrepancies in ranks for letters in two distributions may be relatively small, but discrepancies in absolute frequencies may be very large.

However, we are less interested in the statistical than in the behavioral implications of the distributions. For, these distributions indicate that whatever letter is emitted *most* frequently is emitted with higher frequency than would be anticipated if the frequency of the *most* frequent letter in the language is used as a predictor. This principle may be expressed in another manner. We may state the frequency with which each letter occurs as a percentage of total frequency (as was done in Table 36). This may also be done for total letter frequency in the language. When this is done, it will be seen that percentage frequency of the most frequent response to the single-letter

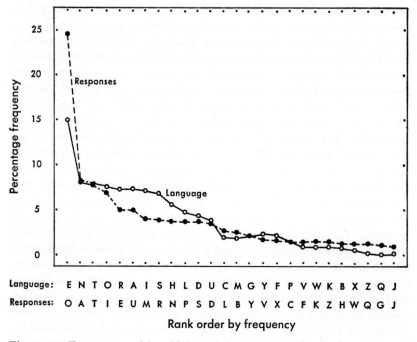

Language: E N T O R A I S H L D U C M G Y F P V W K B X Z Q J

Responses: O A T I E U M R N P S D L B Y V X C F K Z H W Q G J

Rank order by frequency

Figure 26. Frequency with which each letter occurs in the language and frequency with which each letter occurred as a response to single-letter stimuli (see text for complete explanation).

stimuli will be greater than the percentage frequency of the most frequent letter in the language.

The principle is illustrated in Fig. 26. Along the baseline we have rank-ordered the letters with respect to the frequency with which they occur in the language and have made a separate ranking for the frequency with which they occurred as responses to all single-letter stimuli in the letter experiment (NU Sample). While E is the most frequent letter in the language (15 per cent of the total), O is the most frequently emitted response and constitutes nearly 25 per cent of the total responses emitted. Response-frequency to single-letter stimuli falls rather quickly below that of language frequency (for comparably rank-ordered letters) but then crosses over so that with the most infrequent letters, the frequency of letters emitted in the letter experiment is higher than for the frequency in the language. One factor contributing to this relatively high frequency of infrequent letters is the alphabetical sequence response. However, certain idiosyncratic responses (abbreviations, initials, etc.) are also undoubtedly present. The major point we wish to make with Fig. 26 is that responses given in the letter experiment "exaggerate" frequencies for the most frequent and least frequent letters when evaluated against the frequency of these letters in the language. Yet, it is also clear that there is a rather high rank-order correspondence between the two distributions. We do not mean to imply that there are no puzzles remaining. For example, why is O the most frequently emitted letter? E is the most frequent in the language. It is true that O is the most frequent second letter in words, being slightly more frequent than E and H. But one might also speculate that the use of "OH" as an expression of understanding, exclamation, questioning, and so on, gives it a frequency far beyond the frequency of other vowel sounds, and this frequency would not be included in language counts except for counts of texts which are essentially literal reports of conversation.

Equalizing the frequency of stimuli. Thus far we have said nothing about the responses to specific single-letter stimuli. Samplings of such responses will be made shortly. However, there is an issue regarding analysis which pertains to responses to specific stimuli even when responses to specific stimuli are being disregarded (as they have been thus far). In all of the above tabulations the responses to each letter have been given equal weight. It can be seen that this might introduce a bias when comparisons are made with frequency of letters in the language. If subjects are responding to the letter stimuli in a manner that is appropriate only for that letter, then the equal weighting of responses for each letter is inappropriate. For example, J is a very infrequent letter in the language, and E a very frequent one. Yet, in the above analyses the responses to both letters weigh equally in the totals. So, will the results change if responses are assigned weights according to the frequency with which their stimuli occur in the language?

We have tried this weighting in several different samples of responses to single and two-letter stimuli. For the single-letter stimuli we proceeded as follows. Since E is the most frequent letter, the responses to it were weighted 100 per cent. Responses to other stimuli were weighted in proportion to the frequency with which they occur in the language relative to E. For example, the frequency with which N occurs in the language is approximately 55 per cent of the frequency with which E occurs. Therefore, the frequency with which each letter was given to the single-letter stimulus N was multiplied by .55. After this conversion was made for all 26 single-letter stimuli, the total frequency of each letter as a response was determined. Essentially this procedure gives all letters a stimulus value equal to the "stimulus value" they have in the language.

The results of such procedures do not, in fact, alter the relative frequencies appreciably. For example, for the UC-L Sample, the adjusted and unadjusted frequencies show a rank-order correlation of .95. When only the vowels are used as stimuli for the NU Sample, the rank-order correlation between adjusted and unadjusted frequencies was .97. Such facts have led us to conclude that the use of unadjusted frequencies does not introduce a serious distortion. The reason why this is true will become clear as the analysis becomes more and more concentrated on specific stimuli.

The tabulations thus far have been concerned with combined re-

TABLE 39. Percentage of Times That Vowels (V) and Consonants (C) are Given as Responses to Vowels and Consonants, and the Percentage of Times These Sequences Occur in Words

	Stimulus			
	Vowel		Consonant	
	Response		Response	
	V	C	V	C
NU Sample	22	78	62	38
UC-R Sample	18	82	77	23
UC-L Sample	24	76	85	15
Words	15	85	62	38

sponses (by letter) to all single-letter stimuli. Now, we categorize the stimuli as vowels or consonants and treat the responses to each separately. The letters A, E, I, O, U, and Y are considered vowels.

We ask first if responses to the single-letter stimuli differ when the stimuli are vowels and when they are consonants. The rank correlation between the frequency of each letter as a response to vowels and its frequency as a response to consonants for the NU Sample was .54. What is the situation in the language? From the U Count the frequency with which each letter followed vowels and followed consonants was determined. The rank correlation between the two distributions was .43. This latter correlation merely indicates that the probability of a given letter following a vowel differs appreciably from its probability of following a consonant. The former correlation suggests that this is also true in the subjects' responses to single-letter stimuli.

A more complete picture of these differences in probability is given in Table 39. An example will show how the table may be read. In the

NU Sample, when the stimuli were vowels, 78 per cent of the responses were consonants and 22 per cent vowels. When the stimuli were consonants, the percentage of responses which was vowels and consonants was 62 per cent and 38 per cent, respectively. The correspondence between these percentages and the percentages as they exist in the language (words) may be obtained by comparing the emitted percentages with the percentages in the bottom row.

Earlier a correlation of .54 was reported as representing the relationship between the frequency with which each letter was given as a response to vowels and the frequency with which each was given as response to consonants. This correlation, taken in conjunction with the data in Table 39, makes it quite clear that subjects are responding with *some* regard to the particular stimulus. Clearly, when the stimulus is a vowel, the probability of emission of a consonant is much higher than when the stimulus is a consonant, and the relative percentages of emission are in fair correspondence to the percentages existing in the language.

Such evidence might suggest the existence of second-order response habits. That is, one might infer from these data that there are second-order habits of responding to a vowel with a consonant and vice-versa with the subject ignoring the specific stimulus other than to "classify" it as a vowel or as a consonant. But it can be seen that if the subject responded entirely on the basis of the *specific* letter stimuli and responded to them with letters with a frequency that corresponds to the frequency with which these letters follow the specific letter stimulus in the language, the above results would be obtained. So, the data are not definitive on this matter of second-order habits.

It will be noted in Table 39 that the UC-L Sample (instructed to respond as if the stimuli were first letters in words) deviates somewhat from the other two samples, and their percentages are in less correspondence with the language percentages than are the responses of the other two samples. We have no ready explanation for this discrepancy. One obvious possibility is that this sample is indeed responding in the manner instructed. That is, they may be responding in a manner that reflects the proportionality of vowels and consonants as second letters in words following vowels and consonants as first letters. However, we have determined that this is not true. When only second-letter frequency in words is considered, the percentages of these which are vowels and consonants are 10 per cent and 90 per cent, respectively, when the first letter is a vowel, and 69 per cent and 31 per cent when the first letter is a consonant. Thus, even when the most appropriate percentages are used, the correspondence is no higher.

Specific response frequency to vowels and consonants. How does the frequency of emission of each letter correspond to its frequency of appearance in the written language when responses to vowels and responses to consonants are tabulated separately? The data to answer this question are given in Table 40. The left part of the table shows various rank-order correlations for the responses when the stimuli are vowels, and right, the correlations when the stimuli are consonants. Two facts are to be noted. First, the relationships among samples are

TABLE 40. Correlations (Rank Order) for Frequency of Specific Letter Response When the Stimuli Are Vowels and When They Are Consonants

| | Vowels | | | Consonants | | |
	UC-R	UC-L	Words	UC-R	UC-L	Words
NU Sample	.83	.89	.65	.89	.81	.72
UC-R Sample		.87	.58		.81	.76
UC-L Sample			.70			.75

fairly high, but far from indicating perfect reliability. Second, there is a positive relationship between the frequency of specific letters given as responses (to vowels and to consonants) and the frequency with which these letters occur in words following vowels and following consonants. Although the relationships are apparent, there is still a considerable amount of the variance left unaccounted for.

Specific Responses to Specific Stimuli

The final step in analyzing the responses to the single-letter stimuli is to consider response frequency to specific stimuli. For example, when the letter D is presented to the subjects, do the response frequencies of the letters given in response make any sense in terms of the frequency with which they follow D in words? Relevant data will be given for the responses to ten different single-letter stimuli. It is presumed that the relationships found for these letters will be representative of what would have been found had the responses to all 26 letters been analyzed.

For these analyses a multiple-regression technique has been employed. We are much indebted to the personnel of the University of California Computer Center (Berkeley) for making these calculations on the 701 Computer and to Dr. Jack Block of the Department of psychology at Berkeley for planning the runs.

The 10 letters used were A, E, I, O, U, F, H, Q, T, and V. The intent was to try to predict the response frequency to each of the 10 letters. The results for the subjects in the NU Sample were used. Six predictor variables were tried:

1. The frequency with which each of the 26 letters occurred in the U Count. The actual score entries were ranks 1 through 26.

2. The frequency with which each of the 26 letters occurred as *second* letters in words in the U Count. Entries were ranks.

3. The bigram frequency with which each of the 10 stimuli preceded each of the 26 letters in words. The score entries were the actual frequencies as determined in the U Count.

4. The bigram frequency when each of the 10 stimuli were *first* letters in words.

5. The number of different letters which each of the 26 letters follows anywhere in a word.

6. The number of different letters which each of the 26 letters follows as second letters of words.

For each of the 10 stimuli, which of the six predictors will best account for the observed frequency and will some combination of predictors add to the accuracy of the accounting? As might be expected, the nature of some of the distributions of scores involved would be a nightmare to anyone interested in preserving the integrity of the assumptions underlying the correlation statistic. We intend no assault on these assumptions; rather, we ask what sort of predictions can be made in spite of the flagrant violation of assumptions.

Let us first inquire about some of the relationships which emerged from among the predictor variables. Variables 1 and 2 correlate .84; 5 and 6, .89; 1 and 5, .86; 1 and 6, .83; 2 and 5, .83; 2 and 6, .93. All of these correlations, of course, are constant across all stimuli used. The correlation between variables 3 and 4, however, will vary as a function of the stimuli since only values relevant to each of the stimuli were involved. For the letter Q the correlation is unity since only U follows Q in words, and this is true whether Q is the first letter of a word or whether it occurs in the body of a word. For the other nine letters the correlations are as follows: I, .94; T, .93; F, .92; H, .92; A, .89; V, .74; O, .66; U, .55; E, .23. The correlations between variable 3 and variables 1, 2, 5, and 6 vary from .04 to .70, and those between 4 and 1, 2, 5, and 6, from −.05 to .62.

The critical inquiry concerns the prediction of the responses to each stimulus (as given by the subjects in the NU Sample). The evidence is summarized in Table 41. The column labelled "First Variable" in Table 41 is the best single predictor; its correlation with response

TABLE 41. Relationship Between Predictor Variables and Response Frequency of Each Letter to Each of 10 Single-Letter Stimuli

(See text for complete explanation)

Stimulus	First Variable Number	r	Second Variable Number	r	Third Variable Number	r	Fourth Variable Number	r
A	3	.50	4	.56	—	—	—	—
E	1	.63	6	.68	4	.71	5	.73
I	4	.63	1	.63	6	.65	—	—
O	3	.34	—	—	—	—	—	—
U	4	.33	—	—	—	—	—	—
F	4	.88	3	.88	—	—	—	—
H	4	.53	5	.54	3	.57	—	—
Q	4	.52	5	.66	—	—	—	—
T	2	.38	—	—	—	—	—	—
V	4	.66	3	.78	1	.80	—	—

frequency of the letters is given. If additional variables added to the correlation they are indicated in successive columns. For example, for the stimulus A, Variable 3 (frequency with which the stimulus and different following letters occur as bigrams) shows a correlation with frequency of the various letters emitted to A of .50. The addition of Variable 4 increases the prediction to .56, but the addition of none of the other variables increased the magnitude of the correlation. The last correlation for each letter stimulus shows the maximum r which can be obtained with these particular predictors.

From Table 41 it is apparent that, considering all stimuli, the best prediction comes from bigram frequency (Variables 3 and 4), particularly bigram frequency limited to the first two letters of words. One or the other of these two predictors is the best single predictor for 8 of the 10 letters used as stimuli. For the two letters for which neither of these is the best predictor (E and T), the best is either Variable 1 or Variable 2, both of which refer to frequency of letter occurrence in the language.

The data suggest a secondary law with regard to the magnitude of the correlations between Predictor 4 and actual response frequency. This law states that the more frequently a letter occurs in the language, the less well does bigram frequency (where that letter is the first letter of a bigram) predict response frequency. The rank-order correlation between the magnitude of the correlation for Predictor 4 and the frequency with which the stimulus letter occurs in words is −.76. This fact yields no clear general interpretation to the present writers. For certain letters the reason seems fairly apparent. For example, H is by far the most frequent letter which follows T, but only one subject in

273 gave H as the response to T. We believe that counterposed against this specific habit is the more general one of giving vowels to consonants, and O, according to this habit, is by far the most frequent response to T. Both E and I follow T in words more frequently than does O, but, as noted before, O is a favored vowel to nearly all consonants by all three samples of subjects. In short, we have no general accounting of the fact that the more frequently a letter occurs in the language, the less likely will Variable 4 (bigram frequency of the first two letters of words) serve as a substantial predictor.

From the analyses in this section we conclude that specific responses to single-letter stimuli relate to the frequency with which these letters follow the stimuli in words. There are wide variations in the magnitude of the relationship. Other habits, either of a specific nature (e.g., alphabetical habits) or of a general nature (responding to a vowel with a consonant or to a consonant with a vowel) are believed to be involved in these variations, and operate differentially for different stimuli. However, we will mention again that the variation in the magnitude of these correlations will be influenced by the widely different characteristics of the distributions of the predictor variables. Nevertheless, it seems quite justifiable to conclude that when a single-letter stimulus is presented to the subject, more is involved in determining his response than the frequency with which each letter follows that stimulus letter in words. Other habits, by virtue of their high frequency of occurrence in the subject's experiences, interact, converge, or interfere with specific letter-sequence habits.

TWO-LETTER STIMULI

In sampling the results for the two-letter stimuli, we will proceed again from the general to the specific. That is, we will consider in order: (1) the relative frequency of responses elicited without regard to specific stimuli, (2) the responses to various vowel and consonant combinations, and (3) the responses to a few specific stimuli. Throughout the analyses we will make comparisons between the frequencies with which various letters occurred as responses to these stimuli and the frequencies with which these letters occur in words.

Over-all Frequencies

With 676 two-letter stimuli, and approximately 270 subjects in the NU Sample responding to each, there is a total of roughly 183,000 responses. How did these responses distribute themselves among the 26 letters? The most frequently elicited letter was T (12 per cent), and the second most frequent was O (9 per cent). The letters least frequently given were J (.9 per cent) and Q (1.1 per cent). The percentages for all letters are given in Table 42.

TABLE 42. Total Response Frequencies (Per Cent of Total) for Each Letter to Two-Letter Stimuli and Per Cent of Times Each Letter Was the Maximal-Frequency Response for NU Sample

	Per Cent of Total Frequency	Per Cent Times Maximal Frequency
A	7.1	8.7
B	3.2	1.0
C	3.6	1.7
D	4.7	2.0
E	5.9	7.1
F	1.9	.4
G	1.7	.6
H	1.2	.3
I	5.3	5.8
J	.9	.1
K	2.0	1.4
L	4.3	2.5
M	4.1	1.9
N	3.9	1.3
O	9.0	19.4
P	4.2	1.7
Q	1.1	.1
R	5.1	5.8
S	5.3	4.5
T	12.0	28.3
U	3.1	1.2
V	1.9	.3
W	1.6	.6
X	2.0	.3
Y	2.5	1.9
Z	2.2	1.0

Another method of over-all analysis is to consider the distributions of the most frequent letter elicited by each two-letter stimulus. We will speak of this as the maximal-frequency letter. For example, the greatest number of subjects responding with a given letter to a two-letter stimulus was 164; this many subjects responded with T to the stimulus ES. T, therefore, is the maximal-frequency letter to this stimulus. The smallest number of subjects involved in producing the maximal-frequency to any two-letter stimulus was 24. This many subjects responded with D to BJ and with R to TF. The percentage of times that each letter was the maximal-frequency letter is shown in the right column of Table 42. The letters J and Q were maximal-frequency letters only once, J being most frequent to the stimulus JJ, and Q to PD. All other letters were maximal-frequency letters at least twice, with T being the maximal-frequency letter 195 times. (In Table 42, for the maximal-frequency distribution, the base N is 690, since if two letters were tied for maximal frequency, both were included.) The maximal-frequency letter for all stimuli was determined, on the average, by 54.0 subjects, and the standard deviation was 22.58.

The two measures of letter frequency in Table 42 give a rank-order correlation of .95. It will be remembered that letter-response frequency to single-letter stimuli showed a clear positive relationship with the frequency of occurrence of letters in words. The same relationship holds for the responses to the two-letter stimuli. The rank-order correlation between the frequency with which each letter occurs in words and the frequency with which each occurs in response to two-letter stimuli is .77. The correlation between the frequency to the two-letter stimuli and to the single-letter stimuli is .91.

Habits determining responses. Evidence throughout this section will show clearly that responses to the two-letter stimuli reflect to a certain extent the letter sequences occuring in words. We infer from this that experience with words has established habits of responding which are in turn elicited by the two-letter stimuli. Let us accept this correspondence and proceed to an examination of the influence of habits of responding which cannot be attributed to sequences in words.

There are, first of all, *alphabetical-sequence habits*. Given a stimulus with two letters in alphabetical sequence, it is highly probable that the maximal-frequency letter will continue the alphabetical sequence. Thus, given AB as a stimulus, the most frequent response will be C. Out of the 24 possibilities of completing a three-letter alphabetical sequence, the maximal-frequency letter *did* complete the sequence in 17 cases. In conjunction with the discussion of alphabetical habits to single-letter stimuli it was noted that other habits may converge with alphabetical-sequence habits. This convergence is also suggested in the responses to the two-letter stimuli. For example, to the stimulus RS, 160 subjects gave T. Not only is it true that T follows alphabetically, but it is also true that: (1) T has high generalized response strength to nearly any stimulus, (2) RST occurs with some frequency in words, and (3) ST is a very frequent bigram. So, we cannot conclude that alphabetical habits are alone involved in these responses, although, in other examples (e.g., ABC, XYZ), habits other than alphabetical-sequence habits probably play a very minor role.

When the stimulus consists of two identical letters the subject is likely to respond with the same letter. Actually, the frequency of elicitation of these *continuation* habits is not as great as might be expected. For any such stimulus the maximum frequency of response was 127; 127 subjects responded with A to AA, although other habits probably contribute to this frequency. The minimum number of subjects responding to such a stimulus was 50. Since the mean maximal-frequency letter for all stimuli was 54, it is apparent that continuation responses are clearly present. That the maximal frequencies are not greater than they are might be due to the fact that a continuation response runs clearly counter to letter-sequence habits as these habits develop from experience with words.

We will refer to a third class of habits as *initial* habits. As is well known, many government bureaus, corporations, products, people, and so on, are often referred to by initials. If associations develop between these letters making up the initials, some evidence should be present in our data. In Table 43 is a series of such initials listed together with the frequency of subjects responding with the third letter given the first two. For all these illustrations the response is a maximal-frequency letter. None of these three-letter sequences occurs in words, nor does one occur as initials in the printed texts used in any of the three trigram counts included in the appendix. We do not mean to imply, however, that these initials have not been seen in print by the subjects; rather, we suppose that such habits cannot be a consequence of the fact that these three-letter sequences occur in words. Some idea of the strength of these initial habits can be obtained by remembering that the mean maximal-frequency response to all stimuli was 54.

While it seems justifiable to assert that language habits developed from experience with specific letter sequences in words are of minimal importance in these initial responses, it is still quite possible that generalized response habits for letters may be involved. For example, O has strong generalized strength as a vowel. The fact that 61 subjects responded with O to the stimulus RK may not indicate that an initial habit was entirely responsible for the responses because we know that when two consonants occur as a stimulus, a vowel has a high probability of occurring. Furthermore, we have not attempted to get "control" measures. That is, we have not attempted to find illustrations of responses which occur with equally high frequency as given in Table 43, but which do not complete recognizable initials. However, in many of these illustrations given in Table 43, the fact that the subjects were responding with initial habits is self-evident. For example, D as a response occurred with greatest frequency to the stimulus AN (110 subjects responded with D). The second most frequent occurrence was to BV, with the frequency indicated in Table 43. Or, consider IBM. The 103 subjects giving M to IB made up the highest frequency with which M was ever given to any two-letter stimulus. The second most frequent was to the stimulus KL, to which 77 subjects gave M. The fact that M occurs with relatively high frequency to this stimulus may represent the convergence of an alphabetical habit (L to M) and an initial habit (since KLM is a rather widely advertised set of initials).

Further comments about initial habits seem appropriate. The responses to many two-letter stimuli resulted in a rather high frequency

TABLE 43. Response Frequency to Two-Letter Stimuli Completing Initials of Well-Known "Institutions"

(The first two letters are the stimuli, the third the response; NU Sample only)

BVD	99	GBS	42	PDQ	47
CBS	65	GCA	42	PHD	55
CPA	87	GMC	72	RKO	61
DDT	91	HFC	72	TCU	54
FBI	52	IBM	103	TNT	88
FCC	39	IGA	96	TVA	65
FDR	46	NBC	51	VFW	57
FHA	56	NYC	68		

of initials, but many of these three-letter sequences also occur as sequences in words. Some examples, with the number of subjects represented are: HST, 70; IKE, 52; IOU, 67; TWA, 76. Certain other initials did not evolve with high frequency probably because other habits were appreciably stronger. To the stimulus GO, only 20 subjects responded with P. Perhaps with some justification, T and D were both more frequent responses to this stimulus. Different soap manufacturers would find evidence in the data to promote varying degrees of enthusiasm. To the stimulus DU, 28 subjects responded with Z. Only the letter T occurred more frequently (34 subjects), and since Z is a very infrequently used letter (low generalized strength), the result might be viewed favorably by the manufacturer, especially so since our college-student subjects probably do not get heavily involved in detergents. On the other hand, to the stimulus FA, only 21 subjects responded with B, which is not high in view of the strong alphabetical-sequence habit between A and B. To VE, 19 subjects responded with L.

Other responses completed three-letter initials, some with very high frequency, but the initials are relevant only to Northwestern University or the Chicago area. For example, the Student Governing Board at Northwestern is commonly known as SGB, and to the stimulus SG, 117 subjects responded with B. The Chicago Transit Authority is known as CTA; to CT, 88 subjects responded with A. Such examples are pointed out for two reasons. First, they add to the evidence already noted that responses are determined in part by initial habits. Second, if these letter-experiment data are to be used to form materials for use in learning experiments (of the nature reported in the next chapter), certain responses would be expected to be predictive only for Northwestern or for the Chicago area. That is, there is no reason why the students at New York University should respond with B to the stimulus SG.

Concerning initial habits, it should be mentioned finally that undoubtedly many subjects responded with the initials of their last names when the stimuli formed the first two initials. Initials of the names of close associates or relatives may also influence responses. We are inclined to believe that much of the "noise" involved in the responses to each stimulus may result from such idiosyncratic habits. Although we will not systematically examine the evidence on the matter, it is clear that the responses given by the UC-L Sample showed less of this noise than did the other two samples.

Another habit involved in the responses to the two-letter stimuli will be called a *context* habit. This habit appears to evolve from other strong habits. In effect, the subject responds to the two letters of a stimulus as if they were in reverse order; the letter elicited is interpretable if the two letters making up the stimuli were in the reverse order from what they actually were. We shall document this only by illustration. We have seen that IB elicits M for many subjects. So also, when IM is a stimulus, B is a very frequent response (71 subjects) although IMB has very low frequency in words. To MR, S was given by 112 subjects. To MS, R was given by 47 subjects although MSR does not occur as a three-letter sequence in words. To the stimulus XZ, 99 subjects responded with Y. There are many other such illustrations which can be found by examining the tables in the appendix. These context habits appear to operate for all other habits discussed and indicate that the habits we are dealing with are not unidirectional; the subject may respond to two letters as a unit without particular regard for their order.

Finally, we should take note of another mode of response which occurs to many stimuli. We shall call this a *selection* habit. What appears to happen is that the subject ignores one of the letters in the two-letter stimulus and responds to a single letter. This may be the first letter or it may be the second one. The most striking examples occur when Q appears as the first or second letter in a two-letter stimulus. When Q was the first letter in two-letter stimuli, R was the most frequent response in 13 (50 per cent) of the 26 cases. When Q was the second letter, R was the most frequent response in 22 (85 per cent) of the cases. Data from the single-letter stimuli showed that R was the most frequent response to Q. It thus appears that a single letter may determine the response to certain two-letter stimuli. While we have not attempted to evaluate this habit systematically, it appears fairly evident from examining the tables that this response is likely to occur when the two-letter stimulus does not elicit the other habits we have discussed.

A brief summary is in order at this point. In this section we have pointed out habits which seem to be operating when the subject is presented a two-letter stimulus and is asked to respond with a third letter. We accept the fact that one of these habits is built up by sequences of letters in words. But the data have strongly suggested the following other habits which may also determine responses:

1. Alphabetical-sequence habits.

2. Continuation habits, in which the subject responds with a letter that is in the stimulus. This is clearly apparent when the same two letters are the stimulus.

3. Initial habits. These habits complete a three-letter sequence which makes well-known initials of bureaus, businesses, products, people, and so on.

4. Context habits, in which the subject responds in a manner appropriate to the stimulus if the letters of the stimulus are reversed.

5. Selection habits, in which only one of the letters of the two-letter stimulus determines the response.

Responses to Selected Two-Letter Stimuli

In this section we will examine responses to certain selected two-letter stimuli. The stimuli are in four groups, namely, groups consisting of vowel-vowel (VV), vowel-consonant (VC), consonant-vowel (CV), and consonant-consonant (CC). Within each group the responses are examined with an eye toward the correspondence of the over-all response frequency of each letter with its frequency in printed text. We have, therefore, selected stimuli which are followed by several different letters when these stimuli are two-letter sequences in words.

Vowel-vowel. Five stimuli, consisting of two vowels each, were used as sample stimuli. The five were AI, EA, IE, OU, and UI. The responses to these five stimuli were summed by letters, and the sums provide the basic data. From the trigram count, we also determined the frequency with which each letter follows these VV stimuli in words. The trigram count used throughout is the U Count.

Following these five vowel combinations in words, the probabilities of a vowel occurring is .02, and of a consonant, .98. In the three samples of subjects, the responses given to these stimuli split between V and C as follows: NU, 16 per cent and 84 per cent; UC-R, 12 per cent and 88 per cent; UC-L, 12 per cent and 88 per cent. Thus, the subjects tended to give more vowels as responses than would be expected for these particular stimuli when the expectation is based on trigram counts. However, there may be a reasonable explanation for this if it is assumed that subjects are not responding entirely on the basis of the specific stimuli involved. We shall consider this reason after presenting some evidence that will be needed for this analysis as well as for additional analyses to be made later.

From the U Count we have determined the frequency with which a V and a C follow each two-letter combination (VV, VC, CV, CC). That is, we took all VV combinations, summed the frequency of each letter which followed them, and then determined the percentage of those which were vowels and the percentage which were consonants. In one case this was done by considering only the first two letters in words (then determining whether the third letter was a V or C), and in another case, by considering *all* forward two-letter sequences if followed by a third letter in the word (and then determining the percentages of Vs and Cs following). The results of these counts are given in Table 44. An example will show how the table is to be read. When two

TABLE 44. Frequency (Percentage) with Which a Vowel (V) or Consonant (C) Follows the Four Two-Letter Combinations of Vowels and Consonants. For the Left Column, Only the Combinations Represented in First Two Letters of Words Were Counted; For the Right Column, All Two-Letter Combinations Were Counted.

Combination:	First Two-Letters in Words Followed by		All Two-Letter Sequences Followed by	
	V	C	V	C
VV	47	53	10	90
VC	31	69	41	59
CV	17	83	18	82
CC	96	4	81	19

vowels occur at the beginning of a word, the third letter will be a vowel in 47 per cent of the cases and a consonant in 53 per cent. These values differ appreciably from those found when the two vowels are taken anywhere in a word (provided they are followed by a letter). This discrepancy is to a large extent accounted for by remembering that Y was considered a vowel, and that YOU and YOUR occur with considerable frequency. If Y is considered a consonant, the percentages change to 15 per cent and 85 per cent, which is more in line with those proportions in the right-hand column.

The percentages of vowels and consonants elicited by these five stimuli in the three groups of subjects were given earlier. Since the percentages for the three groups do not differ appreciably, it may be concluded, at this level of analysis, that the instructions to the subjects to respond as if the stimuli were the first two letters in a word had little effect.

How did the frequencies of specific letters elicited agree among the three samples of subjects, and how did the frequencies agree with the frequencies of letters which actually follow in words? The essential data are given in terms of a rank-order correlation matrix in Table 45.

TABLE 45. Rank Order Relations of Frequency of Individual Letters Given To Various Vowel and Consonant Combination Stimuli

	Stimuli: VV (AI, EA, IE, OU, UI)		
	UC-R	UC-L	Words
NU	.90	.82	.68
UC-R		.88	.71
UC-L			.83

	Stimuli: VC (AR, EN, IT, OL, UN)		
	UC-R	UC-L	Words
NU	.90	.78	.62
UC-R		.83	.71
UC-L			.70

	Stimuli: CV (BO, DE, LI, NI, RO, TE, WA)		
	UC-R	UC-L	Words
NU	.79	.86	.56
UC-R		.92	.44
UC-L			.58

	Stimuli: CC (CH, FR, MP, PR, SH, TH)		
	UC-R	UC-L	Words
NU	.86	.81	.87
UC-R		.76	.82
UC-L			.77

The relationships for the VV stimuli are in the top section. All correlations are rank-order correlations between frequencies of the 26 letters.

For the VV stimuli, the correlations among the three samples of subjects are fairly high. Furthermore, the correlations between frequency of letters elicited by the stimuli and the frequency with which letters follow the five stimuli in words are quite high. This relationship is, numerically, highest for the group instructed to respond as if the stimuli were the first two letters in words. We have "checked" this rank-order correlation by a product-moment, the result being .67. It is clear that we are dealing with a substantial relationship between responses elicited and letter frequency in words. But, it is also clear that considerable variance remains, and this variance must be attributed to other habits the subjects bring to the situation.

Vowel-consonant. Five vowel-consonant stimuli were chosen, and the responses to them were analyzed. These VC stimuli were AR, EN, IT, OL, and UN. The responses to these stimuli show the following percentages of vowels and consonants: NU, 31 per cent and 69 per cent; UC-R, 39 pre cent and 61 per cent; UC-L, 40 per cent and 60 per cent. In words, the division for letters actually following these VC stimuli is 30 per cent V and 70 per cent C. Again then we see fair correspondence between sequences in words and the responses elicited by the stimuli.

The relationships for specific letter frequency are shown in the second section of Table 45. Unlike the results for the VV stimuli, there is no evidence in the responses to these five VC stimuli that the UC-L responses correspond more highly to letter sequences in words than do the other groups. But as seen in the table, the rank-order correlation between letter frequency in response to the five stimuli and letter frequency actually following the five stimuli in words is .70 for the UC-L subjects. The product-moment correlation is .69. Thus again, we have a relationship between frequency of letters elicited by stimuli and the frequency with which those letters have followed the stimuli in printed text.

Consonant-vowel. The responses to seven CV stimuli were summed to sample the responses to CV stimuli. In this case, as in the previous cases, we have chosen stimuli which, as a two-letter sequence in the language, are followed by a number of different letters. We did not select combinations which have low frequency in the language since it would be very difficult in such cases to get a measure of agreement between the responses to the stimuli and the "responses" which follow those stimuli in the language. The seven CV stimuli used were BO, DE, LI, NI, RO, TE, and WA. The percentages of vowels and consonants given to these stimuli were: NU, 12 per cent and 88 per cent; UC-R, 10 per cent and 90 per cent; UC-L, 13 per cent and 87 per cent. Not only do the three samples of subjects agree well on this index, but they also agree well with the percentage of vowels and consonants (17 per cent and 83 per cent) which actually follow the seven combinations in words.

However, when the analysis is reduced to specific letters, the picture changes, as can be seen in the third section of Table 45. The three samples of subjects still agree fairly well among themselves, but the agreement with letters in words is lower than for the previous two combinations. A product-moment between the frequency of letters given by the UC-L group and the frequency following the "stimuli" in words is only .24. This is compared with a rank-order correlation of .58. An inspection of the distributions reveals that there is a great discrepancy between the frequency with which T follows these stimuli in words and the frequency with which T was elicited by these stimuli. For all three samples of subjects, T was by far the most frequent letter elicited. In sequences in words, nine other letters actually have a higher frequency than T following the seven stimuli. We think, therefore, we are dealing again with the effect of a strong generalized response, since T occurred with very high frequency for all 676 stimuli combined. It should be noted that to all seven stimuli T is an appropriate response in the sense that T does follow all these stimuli in words. But other letters occur with much higher frequency. For example, consider BO. In words, the letters A, D, L, O, R, U, V, and Y follow BO more frequently than does T, but T was the most frequent response given by the subjects. We have suggested the generalized response strength of T as being one possibility for the discrepancies noted, but there probably are somewhat more subtle reasons. Let us consider one of these reasons.

If we refer back to Table 44, it can be seen that given all CV combinations, the chances are about 4 to 1 that a consonant will follow. If we assume that a second-order habit has been built up as a consequence of experience with these probabilities, then it is very likely that the subject *would* respond to a CV stimulus with a consonant. Now, following the particular seven CV stimuli with which we are dealing, vowels occur with fairly high frequency in words (as per the illustration above for the sequence BO). But if we assume that a CV stimulus is likely to produce a consonant as a response due to over-all language structure, then among the consonants T has the strongest generalized strength. We do not, of course, actually know that this is the way "things happened," but, viewed over-all, it seems quite probable.

Consonant-consonant. The responses to six CC stimuli (CH, FR, MP, PR, SH, and TH) were selected. Again, we determined the number of times each letter occurred as a response to these six stimuli. The first summation was in terms of vowels and consonants. The vowel-consonant division was: NU, 59 per cent and 41 per cent; UC-R, 79 per cent and 21 per cent; UC-L, 85 per cent and 15 per cent. The percentages for the UC-L group most nearly approximates those in words (92 per cent and 8 per cent).

The intercorrelations may be seen in the bottom section of Table 45. It seems fair to say that the relative frequency of different letters given to the six stimuli and the relative frequency following the six letter combinations in words is quite high. In fact, the agreement is as high as the correspondence among the three samples. The NU Sample shows a rank-order correlation of .87 with the frequency of the letters in words; the product-moment (.90) does not change the estimate of this relationship.

"Non-language" stimuli. All of the above analyses used stimuli which occur with fairly high frequency in words, and which are followed by a number of different letters in words. The data we sample now involve eight CC stimuli (RJ, VB, WZ, MH, QS, BC, FG, GC) which do not appear as two-letter sequences in the U Count. Again, we obtain the summed frequencies for each letter and then determine the correspondence among the three samples of subjects. By rank-order correlations this correspondence was as follows: NU and UC-R, .89; NU and UC-L, .89; UC-L and UC-R, .92. Clearly, the three samples of subjects behaved in nearly the same way in response to these stimuli.

Responses to Specific Two-Letter Stimuli

As a final level of analysis, we have selected four stimuli, and for each of them we have determined the relationship between the frequency of different letters elicited and the frequency with which different letters follow in words. Out of the necessity of avoiding too many zero frequencies we have chosen stimuli which in words are followed by many different letters.

The four stimuli used were AR, EN, SE, and MA. For each of them there was a distribution of frequencies representing the frequency with which each letter was given as a response by the NU Sample, and there was also a distribution representing the number of times each letter followed in the language (Total Count). A product-moment correlation was calculated for each, with results as follows: AR, .85; EN, .38; SE, .83; MA, .58.

The reasons for variations in the magnitude of these correlations are believed to be related to the matter of habit compositions (divergences and convergences) to which we will turn next. It is sufficient to say, by way of summary, that all the analyses in this section have shown a relationship between the responses elicited by the subject and the frequency with which those responses follow the stimuli in the language. That the relationship is far from perfect leads us to discuss further the matter of other habits involved.

FURTHER EVIDENCE ON HABIT COMPOSITION

In an earlier section of this chapter we identified certain habit tendencies (other than specific sequential letter habits built up by experience with letter sequences in words) which appear to influence the subjects' responses to two-letter stimuli. This section is a continuation of that earlier discussion.

To introduce the problem, we will consider a specific situation. Consider two two-letter stimuli, one of which is never followed in words by an additional letter (e.g., WZ) and one which is followed by many letters, several of which in turn follow very frequently (e.g., AR). To which of these stimuli will the most subjects respond with the same letter? Superficially, at least, it would seem that for the latter stimuli, where several different letters should have strong associative strength to the two-letter stimulus, the maximal frequency should be low. The momentary strength of one letter should be strong for a certain number of subjects, the momentary strength of another, for other subjects, and so on, so that no single letter should be given with high frequency. Thus, it would appear that the responses would be scattered over several letters; none is given with high frequency. Now, in fact, quite the opposite occurs. The law can be stated that the greater the number of different letters which follow a given two-letter sequence in the language, the *more* frequent will be the maximal-frequency letter. A plot of this relationship is shown in Fig. 27. The mean maximum frequency of response when *no* letter follows two-letter sequences in words is about 45, i.e., 45 subjects give the same letter; this is the greatest number giving any one letter. When a large number of different

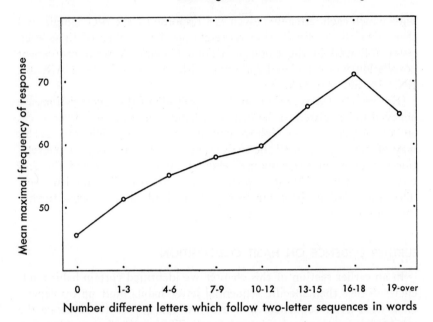

Figure 27. Mean maximal frequency of response to two-letter stimuli as a function of number of different letters which follow two-letter sequences in words.

letters follow a two-letter sequence in words, the mean maximum frequency may be as high as 70, i.e., 70 of the 273 subjects in the NU Sample give the same letter as a response.

The number of different letters which follow a two-letter sequence in words is correlated with (1) total "associates" (the number of times all letters follow a two-letter sequence) and (2) the maximum frequency with which any letter follows a two-letter sequence in words. The correlations are by no means perfect (e.g., number of different associates and maximal-frequency letter correlate .59), but they are high enough so that a plot of either of these other two variables against mean maximum frequency of response to the two-letter stimuli gives a relationship much like that shown in Fig. 27. What implication does this plot in Fig. 27 have for an understanding of the habits involved?

It was suggested earlier that the more frequently a given two-letter stimulus occurs in words (the greater the number of different letters which follow), the smaller would be the maximal-frequency response to it. The expectation was that with several strong letter-sequence responses possible the subjects would "scatter" their responses among the several alternatives. As Fig. 27 has shown, this is patently not the case; the maximal-frequency response increases rather than decreases as the number of alternative sequence responses increases. Yet, the expectation of a "scattering" over the several strong alternative language responses seems reasonable, and our interpretation of the stimulus situation and the habits involved essentially demanded that this scattering be present. It was our belief that when a two-letter stimulus with high frequency in words was presented to the subject, the letter-sequence habit superseded or blocked out all other habits and the responses elicited would be letters which follow the stimulus with appreciable frequency in words. On the other hand, if the subject were presented a stimulus which had zero or low frequency of occurrence in words, habits other than letter-sequence habits would be instigated. Furthermore, we saw no reason why such stimuli should elicit the same habits in all subjects unless the stimulus were an "obvious" one (e.g., XY). Rather it seemed that any of the various habits discussed earlier (and perhaps others we have not identified) might be activated and so "scatter" the responses of the subjects among several different letters. In fact, this seems to be what happened, for we found that the mean maximum frequency of response was lower for such stimuli than for stimuli which occurred frequently as two-letter sequences in words.

However, even with this interpretation, the problem as originally stated remains: "Why isn't there scattering of responses among the several possible letters when the stimuli used are ones which are followed by a number of different letters in words?" Actually the fall in the curve in Fig. 27 at the far right may indicate this scattering. But this is fairly weak evidence. And the correlations between frequency of letters following in words and frequency of letters following as responses to the two-letter stimuli were high enough to indicate that some scattering of responses was occurring. However, we felt that without further evidence we could not firmly maintain the position stated above, namely, that when a stimulus has low frequency of occurrence in the language, several different habits are invoked and when it has high frequency, only letter-sequence habits are invoked.

We must emphasize a rather obvious fact in the frequency-of-response data obtained for the two-letter stimuli. A subject gives only one letter response to each stimulus. If 100 subjects gave the same letter response, there would remain (in the NU Sample) approximately 170 subjects to distribute responses among the other alternatives. On the other hand, if 50 people gave the same response, there would remain 220 subjects to distribute themselves among other responses. We know from Fig. 27 that the greater the frequency of the stimulus in words, the greater the number of subjects who "chose" the most frequent response. This means that fewer subjects remain to distribute themselves among the other responses. This implies, in turn, that if we could show that the *second* most frequently elicited response had higher *absolute* frequency the greater the frequency of the stimulus in words, our interpretation would be doubly strengthened. For, it would show that in spite of the fact that fewer subjects "remained" after the most frequent response was elicited, the number of subjects giving the second most frequent response was greater.

To test this expectation, we took the extreme cases. For the stimuli which are not followed by letters in words, we chose 22 fairly representative stimuli, eliminating any that formed an alphabetical sequence and any that had the same two letters. Each of the 22 stimuli had different first letters. We also chose 17 stimuli which had 19 or more different letters following them in words. For each stimulus in each grouping not only was the maximal-frequency letter recorded, but also the letter occurring with second greatest frequency, and the one occurring with third greatest frequency were recorded. Finally, for each class of stimuli the mean frequency was determined. The results are plotted in Fig. 28. They clearly conform to the expectation. Not only is the mean frequency of the second most frequent response greater for the stimuli which occur in words than for those that do not, but even the third most frequent is slightly larger. This is true in spite of the fact that the number of subjects "remaining" to make the second most frequent, and in turn the third most frequent, is less for the stimuli that have high frequency in words than for those that do not.

It will be noted that the mean maximal-frequency response for stimuli which do not occur in words is less in Fig. 28 than in Fig. 27. This results from the elimination of stimuli which would produce continuation responses (e.g., AA) and stimuli which would produce alphabetical responses (e.g., AB).

We conclude:

1. The more frequently a two-letter stimulus is followed by letters in words, the greater are the probabilities that this stimulus will elicit letter-sequence habits, i.e., habits which reflect the sequence of letters in words.

2. When a two-letter stimulus is one that occurs with low frequency in words, other diverse habits will be invoked, differing for different

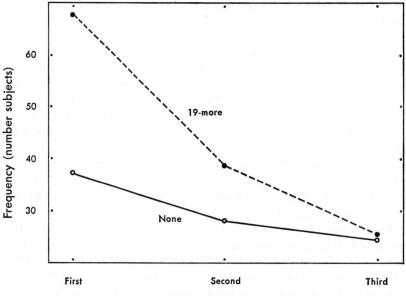

Figure 28. Mean frequency of first, second, and third most frequently given letter when 19 or more letters follow the two-letter sequence in words and when no letters follow the sequence in words.

subjects. These habits were identified earlier as alphabetical sequence habits, continuation habits, initial habits, context habits, and selection habits. There are probably others.

3. At both extremes (stimuli which never occur and stimuli which frequently occur as two-letter sequences in words) there is scattering, but the scattering is less in the second case. Furthermore, in this second case the scattering is primarily *within* letter-sequence habits, i.e., the responses are "reasonable" when evaluated against the sequences of letters in words.

SCALED MEANINGFULNESS AND LETTER HABITS

In the next chapter we will show how trigrams can be generated from the letter-experiment tables. These trigrams differ in terms of the associative connection between letters, and it will be shown that learning varies as a function of these associative connections. The question we ask now, however, is whether or not one can generate "back" syllables of different known M values. The answer, it will be seen, is essentially negative.

Consonant syllables. The procedure for generating a value for a syllable is simple and may be illustrated by the use of a particular syllable. QJF is a Witmer syllable with zero association value. Looking at the tables of frequencies for responses to single-letter stimuli, we see that one subject (out of 273 in the NU Sample) gave J when Q was the stimulus. When QJ was presented as a two-letter stimulus, five subjects responded with F. A simple numerical value for this syllable would be the sum of the number of subjects responding with the second letter when the first was given and the third when the first two were given. Obviously, this sum is six. Will such an index differ as a function of association value? More specifically, will these summed values increase as association value increases?

Every tenth syllable in Witmer's list was given a summed generated value as in the above illustration. Groupings were then formed so that association value increases from low to high with from 24 to 63 syllables in each grouping. There is only a slight progression in the mean summed values as association value increases. The following data sample the association continuum, with the first numbers being the association level and the second, the mean summed generated values: 0 per cent to 13 per cent, 6.5; 25 per cent to 29 per cent, 8.8; 38 per cent, 11.9; 45 per cent, 10.0; 54 per cent, 13.2; 67 per cent to 75 per cent, 13.6; 79 per cent to 100 per cent, 15.8. Thus, the progression is slight.

The reasons why these generated values do not relate sharply to association value are fairly apparent. Witmer's syllables, it will be remembered, do not contain the letters A, E, I, O, U, Y, and V. No alphabetical sequences were allowed in the syllables, and the same letter was not used twice in a given syllable. Now, consider the habits exhibited by the subjects in response to the single-letter stimuli. Vowels were most frequently given to consonants. If a consonant occurred with some frequency as a response to a consonant, it usually was a clear alphabetical-sequence response. Since alphabetical sequences were eliminated from the consonant syllables, this habit had no possibility of producing differential summed values even if this habit should, for some reason, be related differentially to association value. That some initial habits resulted in a consonant's being given to a consonant seems clear (e.g., T to Q), but again there is no reason why such responses should vary as a function of association value. The frequencies which are of necessity used to get the summed values appear to be what we have previously called "noise" frequencies. The total of from 6 to 10 subjects responding with these letters remains roughly constant through-out all association values of the Witmer syllables.

Nonsense syllables. For this analysis all the Glaze syllables at three association-value levels were used, namely, 100 per cent, 53.3 per cent and 0 per cent. For each syllable a summed generated value was obtained in the same manner as for the consonant syllables, and the means determined. For presentation here we have kept the mean frequencies between the first and second letters and between the first two and the third letter separate, as may be seen in Table 46.

It may be noted first that the summed values are much greater than for the consonant syllables. This results primarily from the far greater number of subjects responding "appropriately" with a vowel when a

TABLE 46. Mean Generated Values for All Nonsense Syllables at Three Association Levels

	Mean Number Subjects Responding		
Glaze Values	First to Second	First Two to Third	Sum
0%	23.3	6.1	29.4
53.3%	30.3	10.1	40.4
100%	30.8	11.6	42.4

consonant was given than with a consonant when a consonant was given. Why is the frequency of subjects responding with an appropriate third letter so low, especially when we know that when a CV stimulus is presented to a subject, there is a high probability of his responding with a consonant? This would correspond to the CVC structure of all nonsense syllables.

It will be remembered that at low-association values, consonants which are used have low frequency; in view of what we now know about the letter-response habits of subjects, we would not expect these low-frequency consonants to be emitted with high frequency. At high association values, however, the consonants which appear in the third position have appreciably higher frequency than those consonants in the same position in low-association value syllables. Why, therefore, isn't this more clearly reflected in the number of subjects responding with an "appropriate" consonant? The answer seems to be, in part at least, that the high-frequency consonants given by the subjects complete words for many of the CV stimuli. It may be remembered from the analyses in Chapter 5 that the correlation between frequency of consonants in syllables and frequency of consonants in words was far from perfect for syllables with high association values (.68). In Chap-

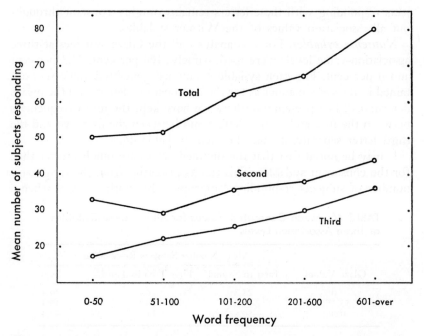

Figure 29. Mean number of subjects responding with the second letter of a three-letter word when the first was the stimulus, and with the third when the first two were the stimulus, and the mean total, as a function of the frequency of the word.

ter 5 we suggested that the reason for this was that high-frequency consonants in written text often complete words, and words are automatically eliminated from the Glaze list.

If the above accounting has validity, then it should follow that if we generate summed values for three-letter words of the CVC structure, these values should be higher than those for nonsense syllables. Furthermore, it is possible that a fairly sharp relationship between the summed values and frequency of occurrence of words may emerge. We will turn now to the results of such a tabulation.

Words. From the Thorndike-Lorge tables we listed all three-letter words having the CVC structure and also tabulated the frequency of each as determined in the Lorge magazine count. The 331 words were divided into five groups having frequencies of 1–50, 51–100, 101–200, 201–600, and 601 and over. The number of words in each grouping was 125, 48, 44, 45, and 69, respectively. For the words in each group we generated values just as was done for the nonsense syllables. The mean number of subjects responding with an appropriate second letter when the first letter was presented was calculated, and the mean number responding with an appropriate third letter when the first two were presented was calculated. The relationship between these means and the frequency groupings are shown in Fig. 29. The mean total frequency is also plotted.

Figure 29 shows that the number of subjects responding with letters that complete these three-letter words increases sharply as the frequency of the words increases. This is seen in the lower curve of Fig. 29. The second-letter frequency also increases as a function of word frequency (it did not increase as greatly as a function of M of nonsense syllables). This indicates that more of the vowels given with high frequency (to single-letter consonant stimuli) eventually "end up" in words having high frequency than in words having low frequency.

SUMMARY

In this letter-association study, we have examined the letters elicited in a "free" situation to all single letters and to all possible two-letter stimuli. The purposes were to investigate the correspondence between emitted-letter frequency (completing two- and three-letter sequences) and frequency of sequences in words, and to identify habits, other than those evolving from letter sequences in words, which may also influence responses. The conclusions which we consider most relevant to the central problem of the book follow:

1. Emitted response frequency of letters shows some correspondence to the frequency of letter sequences in words. The degree of correspondence varies considerably depending upon the nature of the stimulus. The lowest agreement between emitted letter frequency and frequency in words appeared with two-letter stimuli consisting of a consonant-vowel sequence.

2. Habits other than those induced by letter sequences in words are clearly inferred from the data. Several such habits were identified. The more frequently two-letter stimuli occur in words, the less likely are these other habits to be invoked.

3. The M value of learning materials cannot be generated "back" with any degree of precision through the use of the letter-association data. Nonsense syllables generate out to have higher values than consonant syllables, but within each type of material, only small changes in generated values occur as M increases. Differences in the frequency of three-letter words are, however, clearly reflected in the generated val-

ues. Such facts may be taken as evidence for the generalized nature of certain letter responses and as evidence for the "spewing" of such responses. When letter-sequence habits, built up by experience with letter sequences in words, are elicited, the response frequencies of the most frequent responses are much greater than the frequency with which these responses occur in words.

Chapter 10

Letter Association and Learning

The data we have sampled on letter association demonstrate that there is some correspondence between the frequency with which letter sequences occur in words and the strength of letter-associations in the subject's repertoire of habits. Sketchy analyses also demonstrated that habits other than those built up by letter-sequence frequency in words contribute to letter associations. In the experiments reported in the present chapter, we have utilized learning materials constructed from the letter-association data. These materials consist of three-letter units having varying degrees of associative connection between letters. We presume these differences in associative connection represent differences in the composite strength of all habits that subjects have built up from all sources of experience.

In these studies we will engage ourselves with the relationship between stimulus M and learning as well as response M and learning. Our procedures allow a direct comparison between the magnitude of the two effects.

EXPERIMENT 15
Method

Derivation of materials. The three-letter units constructed from the letter-association data will be called *generated trigrams*. A specific illustration will show the basic procedure involved in generating trigrams which appear to have different strengths of associative connection between letters. We will use the letter S as the first letter. From the letter-association tables giving the number of subjects responding with each letter to single-letter stimuli, we choose three letters given with high, medium, and low frequency to the stimulus S. Thus, one might choose O, T, and B, since their frequencies were:

$$\begin{array}{ll} \text{S-O:} & 110 \\ \text{S-T:} & 50 \\ \text{S-B:} & 0 \end{array}$$

We next turn to the tables showing the responses given to two-letter stimuli, and we choose three different frequencies for each stimulus:

SO-T:	50	ST-U:	40	SB-G:	64
SO-B:	33	ST-D:	25	SB-T:	30
SO-Y:	0	ST-P:	0	SB-M:	0

The generated trigram SOT "comes out" with the highest value if we simply sum across (110 plus 50); SOB comes in second. The trigram SBM would be judged to have the lowest associative connection between letters; indeed, it occurs as a consonant syllable in Witmer's list and has an association value of 29 per cent.

If one wishes, of course, the procedure can be carried out in the reverse direction (as we did in the previous chapter for various learning materials). That is, given a three-letter unit, one can determine what associative value it has. For example, let us generate a value for the initials of the American Psychological Association (APA). To the single-letter stimulus A, eight subjects gave P; to the two-letter stimulus AP, 19 subjects gave A, resulting in a summed value of 27. Clearly, this trigram does not have very high interletter associative strength in the sophomore's letter-sequence habits.

When the final tabulations from the letter-association procedures were received and some trial runs in generating trigrams were first made, we were convinced immediately that the generated trigrams had face validity in the sense that they could be constructed so as to show graded difficulty for learning. The present experiment resulted from this belief.

The major problem we faced, and it is one which we still have not handled to our own satisfaction, was the assignment of a numerical value to the generated trigram as a whole. Whether or not we should include some value for the first letter became the first issue. We knew at the time that single-letter frequency could be used as a predictive measure for materials differing in M; that is, we knew that, in general, nonsense and consonant syllables of low-association value were made up of letters occurring infrequently in words and that syllables of high association value were generally made up of letters occurring frequently in words. Thus, it seemed to us that if one generated trigram began with K and another with T, the difference in the frequency of these first two letters should be reflected in our numerical value for the trigram as a whole. But should the first letter be given the same weight as the other two? Our decision was to weight all letters equally and then make post hoc adjustments if the learning data warranted it.

The value of the first letter in the trigram was based on a 100-point scale. A score of 100 was assigned to the letter which occurred most frequently as the *first* letter in words as determined by the T-L Count, as this was the only count we had made at the time the trigrams were generated. Our choice of first-letter frequency as the appropriate frequency to use resulted from a feeling—and nothing else—that this might be most realistic for the actual learning situation. In the T-L Count, S is the most frequent first letter, so it was given a value of 100 and all other letters were given values in proportion to the frequency with which they occur relative to the frequency of S. (This is the same procedure used in deriving single-letter values for consonant syllables in Experiment 5.)

Values for the second letter in the trigrams—more precisely values for the associative connection between the first and second letters of the trigrams—were also based on a 100-point scale. The greatest number of subjects responding with the same letter to any single-letter stimulus in the letter-association procedure was 170; this is the number of subjects who responded to N with O. Therefore, this frequency of response was assigned a value of 100, and all other frequencies were assigned values in proportion. Thus, if 50 subjects responded with a given second letter to a single-letter stimulus, this letter would receive a value of 29. Our reason for using 170 as a base was very simple. We assumed that this must represent the strongest letter-association habit; therefore, all other associations should be assigned values in proportion if we were to have a graded series of associative strength.

The numerical value for the third letter of the trigram was based on a 100-point scale determined in the same manner as for the second letter. The maximum frequency of response to any two-letter stimulus was 164 (164 subjects responded with T to the stimulus ES); therefore, this received a value of 100 and all others were assigned in proportion.

To obtain a single numerical value for each trigram we summed the values for each letter. Undoubtedly there is a much more elegant way to handle this than simple addition, but we had no strong theoretical predilection for doing it any other way. It will be seen that we have yet to find another measure which predicts learning any better than the measure we used originally in constructing the trigrams.

Table 47 shows the 48 generated trigrams used in Experiment 15. For each trigram we have given the converted value for each letter and the sums of these values. These summed values will be spoken of as generated values and will be abbreviated as GV.

There are six lists of eight items each. Roughly, we tried to get four

TABLE 47. Experiment 15. Lists of Generated Trigrams

(See text for complete explanation)

	List 1					List 2			
	1st Ltr	2nd Ltr	3rd Ltr	Sum		1st Ltr	2nd Ltr	3rd Ltr	Sum
LZR	4	0	2	6	KBV	4	2	1	7
ING	26	18	1	45	JAD	7	25	9	41
HOB	34	25	21	80	ITE	26	38	21	85
RAT	27	22	58	107	SUL	100	6	4	110
VXK	8	2	2	12	RZQ	27	0	1	28
FTQ	37	9	2	48	HFG	34	0	9	43
PUS	53	12	5	70	WXY	26	8	34	68
CED	50	5	20	75	MOP	32	41	20	93
	List 3					List 4			
JPV	7	12	0	19	GVS	18	0	8	26
WFI	26	1	17	44	NUW	23	8	13	44
CRS	50	5	13	68	FIB	37	19	20	76
BOT	36	42	42	120	CAT	50	19	85	154
YQG	2	1	1	4	QZP	3	3	6	12
EKL	29	5	23	57	XYH	0	30	0	30
HUM	34	1	22	57	MEL	32	20	9	61
AND	42	11	67	120	DOK	30	77	0	107
	List 5					List 6			
XFH	0	0	0	0	VGJ	8	0	0	8
BUG	36	11	6	53	CFL	50	0	12	62
TRC	35	4	7	46	KIT	4	18	54	76
NOP	23	100	26	149	SOM	100	65	7	172
ZJM	0	0	6	6	UNH	6	8	2	16
IDW	26	9	0	35	EQR	29	0	20	49
ELK	29	11	6	46	BAD	36	28	23	87
SAY	100	7	7	114	XYZ	0	30	86	116

GV levels for each list with two items for each level. However, as a consequence of equalizing the lists for intralist similarity, we found it possible only to approximate this objective. Nevertheless, it is clear that within each list there are trigrams with widely different GV. The use of six lists merely continues our policy of getting a good sampling of items.

The employment of generated trigrams for learning materials has a very great virtue: intralist similarity can be kept at zero (as indexed by duplicated letters) if no more than eight trigrams are used in a list. In the present lists 24 different letters were used in each list so that intralist similarity is zero. There is one exception; somewhere between the time the lists were constructed and the time they were printed on the memory-drum tape, FJQ in List 1 got changed to FTQ; as a result, T was used twice in the list.

The generated trigrams, paired with numbers 2 through 9, were used in paired-associate lists. Two parallel sets of conditions were run. In one set the six lists of trigrams were used as responses, and the numbers as stimuli; in another set, the trigrams were used as stimuli, and the numbers as responses.

TABLE 48. Experiment 15. Basic Results

(GV is the generated value; PR, pronunciation rating; R, mean number of correct anticipations in 20 trials when the trigram was in the response position, and S, when in the stimulus position)

	List 1 GV	PR	R	S		List 2 GV	PR	R	S
LZW	6	8.53	8.22	16.16	KBV	7	8.51	8.22	16.39
ING	45	2.36	16.83	18.44	JAD	41	3.35	14.33	17.72
HOB	80	2.29	15.11	17.72	ITE	85	3.41	17.17	19.22
RAT	107	1.81	18.17	18.89	SUL	110	3.03	15.83	17.50
VXK	12	8.64	6.44	15.83	RZQ	28	8.59	7.00	16.72
FTQ	48	8.00#	10.67	16.22	HFG	43	8.40	6.17	15.67
PUS	70	2.82	16.06	18.06	WXY	68	8.59	12.83	18.89
CED	75	3.07	15.61	17.56	MOP	93	2.04	17.39	18.89
Mean	55.4	4.69	13.39	17.36		59.4	5.74	12.37	17.63

	List 3 GV	PR	R	S		List 4 GV	PR	R	S
JPV	19	8.47	9.56	17.33	GVS	26	8.04	12.33	18.33
WFI	44	7.93	10.94	17.33	NUW	44	5.56	14.28	17.94
CRS	68	7.42	14.61	18.28	FIB	76	1.92	16.67	19.39
BOT	120	2.64	17.50	18.61	CAT	154	1.60	18.28	19.11
YQG	4	8.77	7.61	17.39	QZP	12	8.28	9.67	17.11
EKL	57	6.59	12.17	17.39	XYH	30	8.51	10.56	17.83
HUM	57	1.80	17.67	18.78	MEL	61	1.99	17.17	18.72
AND	120	2.15	19.06	19.78	DOK	107	3.54	17.06	17.33
Mean	61.1	5.72	13.64	18.11		63.8	4.93	14.50	18.22

	List 5 GV	PR	R	S		List 6 GV	PR	R	S
XFH	0	8.72	7.56	14.67	VGJ	8	8.73	9.22	16.83
BUG	53	1.87	19.06	17.67	CFL	62	7.38	15.78	17.67
TRC	46	6.49	12.56	15.39	KIT	76	2.15	16.56	18.56
NOP	149	2.63	15.83	15.94	SOM	172	2.36	16.50	17.89
ZJM	6	8.34	7.83	14.78	UNH	16	7.10	13.44	17.22
IDW	35	7.92	13.89	16.33	EQR	49	7.80	12.56	17.89
ELK	46	2.81	17.11	18.67	BAD	87	1.50	18.50	19.50
SAY	114	1.82	18.28	18.17	XYZ	116	8.75	17.56	18.67
Mean	56.1	5.08	14.02	16.45		73.3	5.72	15.02	18.03

Arbitrarily assigned

Procedure. Since a given subject learned a single list, twelve groups of subjects were required. For six of the groups the trigrams were stimuli; for the other six they were responses. There were 18 subjects in each group, the particular list to which a subject was assigned being determined randomly. As in our previous experiments, we had three different stimulus-response pairings for each list and four orders of presentation. Each list was presented for 20 anticipation trials. All other details of the procedure were the same as in our other experiments.

The basic learning data (mean number of correct anticipations in 20 trials) and the two predictor variables for each trigram are given in Table 48. The pronunciation ratings were obtained in our original scaling (cf., Chap. 2) and are based on the mean ratings of 171 subjects.

Results: Response Variation

When the trigrams were responses, AND and BUG were correctly anticipated the greatest number of times. Their mean, 19.06, indicates that, on the average, they were omitted or incorrectly anticipated less than once in 20 trials. At the other extreme is HFG, which was correctly anticipated only 6.17 times out of the 20 possible times. Thus, the range of differences is on the order of 3 to 1, or from approximately 30 per cent to 95 per cent of the total possible.

It is, perhaps, needless to say that statistically speaking the variations in learning among items within each list are highly significant. Differences in performance of the groups assigned different lists were not significant, the mean number of correct responses per item per list ranging from 12.37 to 15.02.

Basic correlational data. We are interpreting both pronunciability (PR) and the generated values (GV) to be measures of response integration. Both, in a manner of speaking, should indicate how easily the letters of the trigrams go together. The basic correlational data for PR, GV, and learning the trigrams as responses are shown in Table 49. Product-moment correlations are given for each list as well as for all 48 trigrams combined.

Table 49 shows that GV predicts learning quite well. The lowest correlation for any list (List 5) is .67 and the over-all correlation is .76. But it is also apparent that PR predicts learning noticeably better than does GV. For only one list does GV predict better than PR (List 6), and this is a special case to which we will return momentarily. The over-all correlation of .87 between PR and learning is nearly as high as we would expect for the reliability in learning scores. Our previous experiments have shown a strong relationship between PR and learning, and we have grown accustomed to the high sensitivity of PR; in spite of this, we found the present correlations between learning and PR somewhat astonishing. It is our belief that we probably have evolved the most favorable conditions possible for demonstrating the relationship between PR and learning. The favorable conditions obtain as a consequence of the fact that all formal similarity is removed so that

TABLE 49. Experiment 15. Product-Moment Correlations When Generated Trigrams Are Learned as Responses

(L indicates learning score; GV the generated values, and PR, pronunciability ratings)

	L & GV	L & PR	GV & PR
List 1	.87	.97	.84
List 2	.81	.89	.71
List 3	.89	.93	.79
List 4	.85	.96	.80
List 5	.67	.93	.76
List 6	.72	.61	.52
Over-all	.76	.87	.72

minor disturbances (interference) resulting from duplicated letters are completely removed in these lists.

As observed earlier, the product-moment correlation between PR and learning breaks down—to .61—in List 6. An examination of specific trigram scores for this list in Table 48 makes the reason for this breakdown apparent. The trigram XYZ is rated very difficult to pronounce, but it is learned quite rapidly. Another three-letter alphabetical sequence (WXY) is included in List 2, but its GV is appreciably less than the GV for XYZ, and the discrepancy between its PR and learning score is also considerably less. Nevertheless, it is worth noting that this list shows the second weakest relationship. If the relationships are expressed by rank-order correlations, they are found to be only .74 and .48 for Lists 2 and 6, respectively, whereas the lowest rank correlation among the other four lists is .86.

Another alphabetical sequence, NOP, occurs in List 5. However, in this case PR and GV are in agreement; in fact, based on these two indices, this trigram is learned more slowly than it should be.

In view of the unsettling effect on the PR-learning relationship produced by alphabetical sequences, we have calculated the relationship again after removing all trigrams in which alphabetical sequences occur. There are nine trigrams in which two or three letters occur in alphabetical sequence. When these are removed, the product-moment

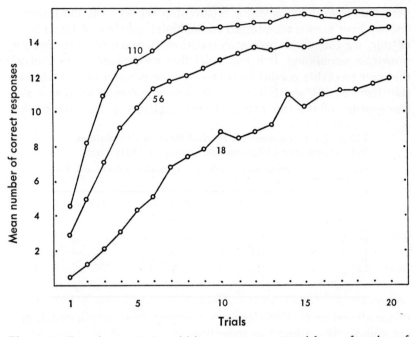

Figure 30. Experiment 15. Acquisition curves over 20 trials as a function of generated values (18, 56, 110) when generated trigrams are responses in paired-associate lists.

correlation between PR and learning for the remaining 39 items is .91. For the same trigrams, the GV-learning correlation is .78.

As further tests of the PR-learning and the GV-learning relationships, we have determined rank-order correlations with learning for each of the 18 subjects assigned to List 4. For GV and learning these correlations ranged from .40 to .95, with a mean of .72; for PR and learning, the range was from .17 to .93, with a mean of .71.

Acquisition curves over 20 trials are shown in Fig. 30, with the plotting variable being GV. The 48 trigrams were rank-ordered according to GV and the learning scores for each successive group of 16 items averaged to obtain the three curves. The wide differences in learning, suggested by the correlations we have been examining, are quite apparent. The higher the GV the greater is the number of correct responses, and this holds true for each trial.

GV versus PR. The product-moment correlation between GV and PR for all 48 items combined is .72. When we remove all trigrams having alphabetical sequences, the value is .78. These relationships indicate that when we generate trigrams so that the number of subjects responding to the single and double-letter stimuli varies, we are also varying the degree of pronunciability. Generally speaking, favored letter sequences are easily pronounceable sequences. But, the data also indicate that when the subject rates the trigrams for pronunciability, the rating is likely to correspond somewhat more closely with learning than will pronunciability values that we might *infer* from the correlation between PR and GV.

The former comments suggest that there may be a certain joint action of PR and GV; that is, the two measures together might predict better than either alone. If this is so, we have been unable to obtain evidence for it. A multiple correlation does not improve the prediction. If we hold GV constant by means of a partial-correlation procedure, the PR-learning relationship (all 48 items) drops to .72; holding PR constant, the correlation between GV and learning falls to .39. In order to look at the relationships among learning, PR, and GV from another angle, we have used the crossruff system explained in the previous chapter. We formed two groups of 24 trigrams each, one relatively high on GV, and one relatively low, but both equal on PR. The difference between the mean learning scores associated with the two groups of trigrams was 1.10; the *t* was only .96. When GV was held constant and PR allowed to vary, the difference between the two means was 2.49, and the *t* was 2.31; this *t* would be interpreted as significant statistically. The PR prediction breakdown only in the case of certain trigrams where alphabetical habits prevail.

It may therefore be concluded that, except for trigrams in which alphabetical-sequence habits are operating, PR dominates GV in learning. When a GV value "goes against" PR, PR will predict the learning more accurately than will GV.

The GV measure. The GV measure is a very simple-minded numerical index used to reflect differences in degree of integration of responses. It is a simple summation of values assigned to each letter, with each letter receiving equal weight. We have been unable to find any index which predicts the learning better than the original generated values; by the same token we have found that other measures predict learning almost as well as our GV. We will mention some of our attempts to derive a better index and report the rank-order correlation between learning and the index for all 48 items. Their degree of adequacy can be gauged roughly by bearing in mind that the rank-order correlation between GV and learning is .80.

If the first letter is given no weight—if the value for the trigram is merely a summation of the values for the second and third letter—the correlation between learning and the summed values is .71. Apparently, the first letter should be given some weight.

Our GV values are based on the maximum number of subjects responding to any stimulus. That is, the maximum frequency responding to any single-letter stimulus was 170, and the value assigned second letters in trigrams was always calculated as a proportion of 170. It is possible that such an absolute base is not appropriate; perhaps a relative one would be better. Let us consider the trigram RZQ. To give Z a relative value, we could determine what proportion the number of subjects responding to R with Z is of the number of subjects determining the maximal-frequency response to R. Thus Z would be assigned a value relative only to response frequencies to R. The third letter would be handled similarly; its value would be based on the ratio between the number of subjects responding with Q to the stimulus RZ and the number determining the maximal-frequency response to RZ. Without any weight given to the first letter, the summed values based on the above procedure correlated .65 with learning.

Another way to view the situation is for us to ask how many letters are likely to interfere with the letters the subject must learn in sequence. The number of potential interfering letters could be taken as the number of letters given more frequently to a particular stimulus than the letter the subject is asked to learn in sequence. For example, to the single-letter stimulus R, perhaps 12 letters were given with greater frequency than was Z; 12 might be taken as an index of the amount of interference to be expected in learning Z to R. A similar value could be determined for the third letter. Finally, to assign a value for the first letter we could use the number of letters which occur with greater frequency. If we add the three values, the resultant might be interpreted as the sum of all interference tendencies likely to occur in integrating the response. Or, one might conceive of the interference pyramiding across letters, in which case perhaps a multiplicative function would give a better index. We have tried both methods. The additive-interference index correlated .78 with learning, the multiplicative, .72. Thus, the additive-interference index is as good as our GV index and might actually be preferable because of the theoretical rationale on which it is based.

Several other derived measures were tried, but, as we said earlier, none predicted better than GV, yet all had some predictive value. Even simple summed letter frequency correlated .53 with learning. In short, we hold no brief for the GV measure we have used in most of

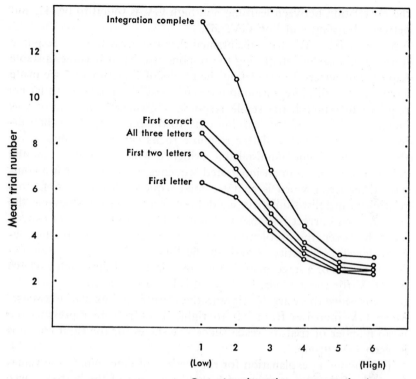

Figure 31. Experiment 15. Stages of learning with trigrams as responses as a function of generated values (see text for complete explanation).

our analyses; we have not found a better one, but probably others, more skilled than we in such matters, could find a better one.

Further sub-correlations. The distribution of pronunciability ratings for the 48 trigrams are, as in our previous experiments, bi-modally distributed. In fact, there is a piling up at both extremes so that splitting the total distribution in half results in two sub-distributions which are badly skewed. For the 24 trigrams rated easiest to pronounce, we find a correlation with learning of .68; for 24 trigrams on the hard-to-pronounce end of the scale, the value is .42. However, using 17 items with PR ratings of 5.56 and above, and which do not have alphabetical sequences, we find the correlation with learning to be .78. Thus, even with a very restricted range of PR values, the relationship between PR and learning remains striking.

When we divide the 48 items 24–24 on the basis of their GV values, the correlation between learning and high GV is found to be .42, and between learning and low GV, .67.

Stage analysis. We have maintained that the great bulk of response learning consists of integrating the response so that it becomes a stable sequence of letters. In evaluating the results of Experiment 5 we made an analysis of this integration in terms of successive hook-ups of letters required to establish the stable response. However, that analysis was incomplete; it traced the learning only to the point at which the subject first gave the three-letter response to its correct stimulus. After this point we found unmistakable evidence which indicated that the response was far from an integrated sequence in the sense that a common three-letter word is an integrated sequence. Because of factors relating to intralist similarity, we did not feel that analysis beyond the stage of first correct response was very "clean." In the present experiment, however, the problems of integration can be traced further because intralist similarity is zero in the lists.

The results of a stage analysis are shown in Fig. 31, in which we have used GV for the abscissa. Each point is based on the analysis of eight trigrams; since there are 48 trigrams there are six points on the abscissa. Mean GV increases from left to right. The ordinate represents the mean number of trials to reach successive stages for the eight trigrams in each GV group.

The following explanation for the method of determining the values for each of the curves starts with the description of the bottom curve and works up.

1. *First letter.* Mean trial on which the first letter of the trigram was given in the first position, although not necessarily paired with the correct stimulus.

2. *First two letters.* Mean trial on which the first two letters of the trigram were given in proper order, although not necessarily paired with the correct stimulus.

3. *All three letters.* Mean trial on which all three letters were given in proper sequence, although not necessarily paired with the correct stimulus.

4. *First correct.* The trial on which the trigram was first given correctly to its appropriate stimulus.

5. *Integration complete.* This curve represents the major addition to the stage analysis as given for Experiment 5. To derive this curve we asked ourselves the following question for each item: "What was the number of the trial after which no evidence of integrative difficulty was found, given that a correct response had occurred on that trial?" Our criteria for integrative difficulty were as follows:

(a) Single letter given as response, but this was the second or third letter in the trigram.

(b) Two or three letters of the trigram given, but in wrong order.

(c) One or two letters from other trigrams given along with one "correct" letter. The particular stimulus to which such a response was given was used to note which trigram was not integrated.

(d) First two letters from a correct response, paired with the correct stimulus. Such a partial response might or might not mean incomplete integration. It could mean long latency, but this also might indicate incomplete integration. In any event, this type of response formed only a very small proportion of the total evidence used for evidence on lack of integration.

The following were *not* used as evidences of incomplete integration:

(a) Response given correctly, but paired with wrong stimulus.

(b) No response.

(c) The appearance of only the correct first letter of a trigram, given either to an appropriate or an inappropriate stimulus.

All of the above determinations were made for each trigram for each subject and the mean values determined for the eight trigrams in each grouping.

The wide separation between the fourth and fifth curves—between the trial on which the response was first given correctly and the trial after which no further evidences of lack of integration occurred—indicates that even after a three–letter sequence is first given correctly, a great deal more learning must occur before trigrams of initially poor integration can be said to be well integrated. For items with poor initial integration, the learning period extended over a total of 13 trials—four trials beyond the point at which the item was first given correctly to its stimulus.

Results: Stimulus Variation

It will be recalled that the lists for studying the effects in variation of GV among stimuli were exactly the same lists used for the study of response variation except that they were "turned over"; the generated trigrams were stimuli with the single–digit numbers as responses.

Over-all learning. Differences in learning when the trigrams were stimuli and when they were responses are apparent even from a casual inspection of Table 48. When the trigrams were stimuli we see that the range of scores is from 14.67 (XFH) to 19.78 (AND) correct anticipations. This is to be compared with the range from 6.17 to 19.06 when the trigrams were responses. However, specific and more detailed comparisons of learning when trigrams were stimuli and when they were responses will be made in a later section; for the present, our interest is in the learning as a function of stimulus variation only.

Differences among items in learning within each list are relatively small. In spite of this, they are highly reliable; the F test shows significant differences among items within each list. Unfortunately, the F for differences among lists is statistically significant, and the significance is largely due to the deviance of the learning scores of List 5. We do not have an explanation for this deviation. The *list* was not aberrant

TABLE 50. Experiment 15. Product-Moment Correlations for Learning When Generated Trigrams Are Stimuli

(L indicates learning score; GV the generated values, and PR, pronunciability ratings)

	L & GV	L & PR	GV & PR
List 1	.82	.99	.84
List 2	.69	.63	.71
List 3	.78	.83	.79
List 4	.47	.67	.80
List 5	.39	.82	.76
List 6	.54	.62	.52
Over-all	.55	.73	.72

when the trigrams were responses; if the cause of the deviation were in the list per se, we would expect this to show up most clearly when the trigrams were responses. The other alternative is to consider the possibility that the group of subjects assigned to this list were slower learners as a group than the other five groups.

If our addition is correct, we have drawn random groups of subjects 55 times in Experiments 1 through 14. We suppose that the laws of probability are going to catch up with us sooner or later and that we will draw by chance a group of subjects that will allow us to make an entry at one extreme or the other of the normal probability curve. We tend to believe that we should make this entry for the group of subjects assigned to List 5. Actually, the fact that the group is deviant does not introduce any serious complications into the analyses.

Correlational data. Correlations, comparable to those given for response variation, are shown in Table 50. The over-all correlations are adjusted to take into account the deviation of the group learning List 5. The picture the correlations sketch is quite clear: (1) both PR and GV predict learning; (2) PR predicts better than GV; (3) the correlations are of lower magnitude than found when trigrams were used as responses; (4) PR breaks down as a predictor when trigrams are an alphabetical sequence (Lists 2 and 6). In short, the results provide a mirror image of those found for response variation except that the correlations are of reduced magnitude. This mirroring is marred by only one fact, namely, the relatively low correlation found for List 4 between PR and learning.

Comparisons of Trigrams as Responses and Trigrams as Stimuli

Correlational. The 48 trigrams have been used as stimuli (with numbers as responses) and as responses (with numbers as stimuli). How is the learning related in the two situations? For Lists 1 through 6 the product-moment correlations are: .99, .91, .89, .64, .86, and .84. For all 48 items the correlation is .85. We do not know why List 4 should be inconsistent with the relationships shown by the other five lists.

Graphical comparisons. We have formed six groups of eight items; in one case these groupings were based on PR, and in the other they were based on GV. The six successive groups represent increasing GV and PR. These groups were formed simply by rank ordering the 48 items on a given variable and then using the first eight items for the first group, the second eight for the second, and so on. Associated with each group is a mean learning score for the eight items.

The successive groupings based on PR and GV are placed equidistant from one another along the abscissa. The mean PR and GV values for each group could be used, but the baseline gets a little messy. When actual PR values of the groupings are used along the baseline, three of the points occur close together on the left and three close together on the right; this results from the bimodality of the distribution.

When the trigrams were stimuli, List 5 was deviant. We attributed this to a chance selection of slow learners. To remove this deviation for plotting purposes we have added a value of 1 to the mean score for each item. Obviously, this increases the mean for the list as a whole by one, and it makes this mean almost identical with the lowest mean performance shown by any of the other five groups who had trigrams as stimuli.

The correlational data which we have already discussed would lead us to expect the clear relationship between learning and the GT and PR values. What Fig. 32 shows clearly that is not given in the correlational data is the fact that the amount of change in learning associated

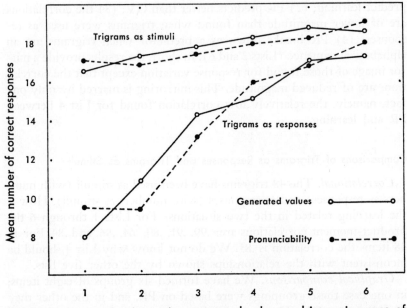

Groupings representing increasing generated values and increasing ease of pronunciability

Figure 32. Experiment 15. Learning as a function of pronunciability and generated values when trigrams are used as stimuli and when they are used as responses.

with PR and GV is much, much greater when the trigrams are responses than when they are stimuli. Insofar as GV and PR are related to the "old" M dimensions, the results are quite in harmony with those found by most other investigators (cf., Chap. 3).

It will be observed that the curve relating PR and learning shows an inversion between the first and second groupings. This results from the two alphabetical-sequence items (XYZ, WXY) appearing in the first group; they are rated very difficult to pronounce but are learned very rapidly.

Discussion

Pronunciation ratings. Once again we have shown that when three-letter trigrams, differing widely in initial integration, are used as responses in paired-associate lists, pronunciability ratings give an extraordinarily fine ordering of the learning of the trigrams. Although the improvement in prediction in the present experiment (as compared with earlier experiments) is not large in terms of the numerical increase in the magnitude of the correlation coefficient, it is substantial in terms of the difficulties usually encountered in increasing correlations when they are already of high magnitude. The increase in the accuracy of the prediction is to be attributed to the increase in accuracy among items which are difficult to pronounce. We attribute this increase, in turn, to the use of zero intralist response similarity. When trigrams are made up of "strange" combinations of letters, a long learning period is required to integrate them (as shown by the stage analysis in Fig. 31). We do not know precisely the basis on which pronunciability ratings are made for such items, but it seems very likely that interference due to duplicated letters can distort the PR-learning relationship for them. This was suggested by the results of Experiments 12 and 13 where the PR-learning correlation was low for the difficult-to-pronounce items in the 12-unit lists. Inevitably, as length of list increases, intralist similarity must increase, and this, we believe, produces differential disturbances in learning among the poorly integrated items, thus reducing the PR-learning relationship.

If it is clear that pronunciability is a remarkably fine predictor of learning, we may observe that it is equally clear it loses its magic for certain kinds of trigrams. More specifically, when alphabetical sequences are involved, pronunciability may give exactly the wrong prediction. Most assuredly there is nothing unique to alphabetical sequences which produce this breakdown. Any habits which run counter to letter-sequence habits built up as a consequence of experience with words, and which result in a unit that is difficult to pronounce (by conventional standards) but which has high associative connection between letters, will undoubtedly produce the same result as have some of the three-letter alphabetical sequences in the present experiment. For example, we believe many initial habits (see previous chapter) will produce such units. If IBM and BVD were response units in a list, we are confident that they would be learned very rapidly but that they would be rated difficult to pronounce.

Learning of trigrams as responses will be best predicted by an index that includes all habits which lend their strength to the associative connection between letters so that the response to the unit is an immediate and stable one. It so happens that pronunciability ratings will provide an extremely precise index of such integration for "standard letter sequences"—sequences of a syllabic nature that occur in words. However, the fact that pronunciability will break down only emphasizes the more critical and more general principle involved, namely, the level of integration of the letters.

Generated values. If the above is true, a reasonable question to ask is: "If the generated values are presumed to reflect all habits, whereas the pronunciability ratings do not, why do generated values predict learning less well than pronunciation ratings?" We have no completely satisfactory answer to this question, but some comments may be relevant to the ultimate answer.

First of all it should be realized that lists of trigrams could be constructed in which the generated values would predict better than pronunciability ratings. This could be done by generating trigrams which are difficult to pronounce but which have high associative connection between letters. Thus, if we capitalize on alphabetical-sequence habits, initial habits, and so on, which often result in trigrams difficult to pronounce, we could quite easily reverse the relative predictive capacity shown for the two measures in the present experiment.

As a second point, we must mention again that there may be other ways to derive numerical values for the trigrams—ways that we have not tried—which will predict as well or better than the pronunciation ratings for the 48 items used in this experiment. At the same time, we have reasons to believe that it might *not* be possible to derive a better index—a better generated value—with letter-association data available. Our reasons are tied to the nature of the responses elicited in the letter experiment. It will be recalled that we pointed out in the previous chapter that a few letters have very high generalized response strength. More particularly, the vowel O and the consonant T were most conspicuous in this regard. Relative to other vowels and consonants, they occurred with very high frequency. Thus, if a consonant was an appropriate response to a two-letter stimulus, the response T was given with greater frequency than its frequency of occurrence in the language would indicate. This does not mean that habits leading to other letters never superseded the T and O habit. But it does mean that unless the two-letter stimulus was highly specific to a given third letter, T or O was likely to occur with much greater frequency than their frequency in words would predict.

There is a consequence of these generalized habits of responding: other letters, which would form near-equally integrated or near-equally pronounceable units if given as a response, received very low frequencies, hence very low generated values. For example, to the stimulus IN only one subject gave G as a response. By our generated values, therefore, the trigram ING has a relatively low sum. Yet, there can be little doubt that ING elicits a very stable integrated response. In short, when a two-letter stimulus can be followed by several letters, all of which would form trigrams of fairly high degrees of integrativeness, some of these letters are bound to receive the short end of the deal. Those which are shorted are the letters with relatively low generalized habit strength.

The above comments imply that the frequencies of response obtained in an association procedure may not reflect accurately the associative strength for alternative responses. If, in a word-association experiment, 95 per cent of the subjects responded to the stimulus *black* with the response *white*, and 5 per cent with *blue*, it might be implied that in a paired-associate learning task the pair black-white would be learned much more rapidly than black-blue. There are data which suggest (Cofer, 1958) that successive responses from the same subject do not differ markedly, proportion-wise, from the proportion of responses obtained when many subjects give one response each. But this is not the issue with which we are dealing. The issue is how to translate the differences in the proportions into differences in associative strength.

It is concluded that on theoretical grounds the generated values should give the best over-all predictions of learning—they will incorporate all letter-sequence habits—but that by the nature of the data obtained in a letter-association experiment, the appropriate values cannot be derived. Of course, we should remember that the generated values we used were not "bad" predictors; pronunciability was simply better.

Trigrams as stimuli. The lists for which trigrams were stimuli (and numbers were responses) showed clear relationships between learning and the two predictor variables. Let us be sure we understand what this means. The responses were single-digit numbers; in our manner of speaking no response integration is required for the numbers, nor is there much of a problem of differential availability. Let us state this in another manner; the first stage of learning was essentially nonexistent when the numbers were responses. Therefore, differences in learning must be attributed to the second, or associative stage. Since pronunciability and generated values were related to learning in this situation, it is reasonable to conclude that the attributes implied by these measures must have something to do with the associative stage. The over-all range of differences in learning numbers when trigrams were stimuli was not great, but the differences among the items were highly reliable. Furthermore, these small differences correspond very closely to the differences which occur when responses are trigrams. If, as we have argued, the major component in response learning is response integration, and if pronunciability and the generated values are indices of degree of integration at the beginning of learning, then it is reasonable to suppose that degree of integration or a highly correlated attribute must be responsible for the differences observed in learning when the stimuli were trigrams.

We originally felt that the relatively low correlation between pronunciability and learning of the trigram-number lists was due to the restricted range of learning differences found with these lists. However, the high correlation (.85) reported between the learning when the trigrams were stimuli and when they were responses suggests that this restriction in range may not be entirely responsible for lower correlation between pronunciability and learning when trigrams are stimuli. When we use separate groupings for the two extremes of pronunciability, the correlations with learning are much lower when the trigrams are stimuli than when responses. Thus, it remains possible that some other attribute, quite highly correlated with pronunciability, may enter into the learning when trigrams are stimuli. Something over and above degree of integration of the stimulus could be involved. This is a matter we will return to at a later point.

Figure 32 has shown that the learning of the generated trigrams with high values was nearly perfect; several trigrams were given correctly over 19 times out of a total of 20 possible. We are referring here to the trigram-number lists. This fact has two implications for us, one of which is relevant to an issue raised earlier, and the other of which is relevant to the problem of the interaction between stimulus and response M.

Among the reasons for rejecting an associative-probability theory for the explanation of the effect of M on learning was the implication from the theory that the greater the number of associations "tied" to a verbal unit, the faster was the learning. We suggested the alternative possibility that the greater the number of associations, the greater were the probabilities of interference from old associations in attaching a new response to the stimulus. If this interference interpretation is valid, we would expect that with high generated values and easy pronunciability (both measures which will subsequently be shown to be related to number of associates tied to them), learning would be slower than with, say, somewhat lower generated values. Our data indicate that this does not happen. In the trigram-number lists, several items are anticipated almost perfectly from the beginning of learning. If there is interference resulting from the many associates they are presumed to have, we can find no evidence for it in the learning records.

In the present experiment the effect of response M on learning was much greater than the corresponding range of stimulus M on learning. Differences as a function of stimulus M were small but highly reliable. The question may be raised as to whether or not this function relating stimulus M and learning is attenuated by the very rapid learning which occurred as a consequence of using the single-digit numbers as responses. Perhaps a "ceiling effect" is operating, in view of the fact that several items were correctly anticipated on nearly every trial. Perhaps if the responses were more difficult to learn, stimulus M would produce the same range of effect as response M.

We noted in Chapter 3 that the facts concerning the interaction between stimulus M and response M were ambiguous. However, by our two-stage conception of learning, we would never expect the effect of stimulus M on learning to be as great as the effect of response M unless all units were perfectly integrated, in which case the variable is essentially eliminated. Therefore, it becomes of some importance to the validity of our two-stage conception to demonstrate that the effect of stimulus M on learning will never be as great as the effect of response M. Experiment 16 was designed for this purpose.

EXPERIMENT 16

The purpose of Experiment 16 was to determine if the magnitude of the effect of stimulus M on learning approached the magnitude of the effect of response M when trigrams are paired with items which make the list as a whole more difficult to learn than the lists of Experiment 15.

Method

Lists. Two lists of trigrams were used, namely, Lists 1 and 4 from Experiment 15. However, instead of pairing these trigrams with numbers, they were paired with paralogs from Noble's list (Appendix C). We chose eight paralogs which had the lowest M possible and yet, in our judgment, could be pronounced rather easily. The M value of the eight paralogs varied from 1.04 to 1.39. The eight units were: *neglan, balap, tarop, latuk, quipson, gokem, zumap,* and *bodkin.* We presume that these paralogs have lower M than the single-digit numbers used in Experiment 15, but we do not in fact know this, nor do we know whether the similarity among the paralogs would be considered higher or lower than the similarity among single-digit numbers. In any event, lists with paralogs proved much more difficult to learn than lists with the numbers. Like numbers, paralogs allow us to retain a fairly clear distinction between the trigrams and the units with which they are paired.

For each of the two lists the paralogs were used as stimuli in one instance and as responses in another, so that there was trigram-paralog and paralog-trigram learning for each list. The learning under these conditions may be compared with trigram-number and number-trigram learning as exhibited for the two lists in Experiment 15.

Procedure. Four groups of 18 subjects each were used, each group learning a single list. Except for the use of paralogs rather than numbers, all procedures were exactly the same as those used in Experiment 15.

Results

The essential results will be given in graphical form. The learning scores for Lists 1 and 4 of Experiment 15 are used for comparison purposes. By combining the results for both lists there are 16 different trigrams and four different kinds of pairings for the trigrams, namely, number-trigram, trigram-number, paralog-trigram, and trigram-paralog. The 16 trigrams were formed into four groups of four items each so that successive groupings represented increasing ease of pronunciability (PR) or increasing generated values (GV). Thus, the procedure is basically the same as that used to plot Fig. 32 for the results of Experiment 15. In Fig. 33 the learning associated with GV groupings and learning associated with PR groupings are essentially indistinguishable.

The upper two sets of curves show the mean number of correct responses given in 20 trials when trigram-number and number-trigram pairings are used, and the lower two sets show the same learning scores when paralog-trigram and trigram-paralog pairings are involved. The two lower curves clearly indicate that the lists were made sufficiently more difficult through the use of paralogs that there is no possibility of a "ceiling effect." Because there are several ways to look at the findings, we will list the comparisons we think are most important.

1. The results "behave" as if the paralogs *do* have lower M than single-digit numbers. The difference in learning trigram-paralog versus trigram-number pairings is very great; the difference in learning number-trigram versus paralog-trigram pairings is much less. These results are exactly those that should be found if paralogs have lower M than numbers, for the effects of stimulus M are less than the effects of re-

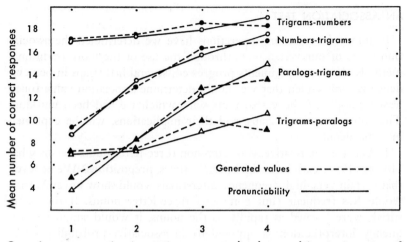

Groupings representing increasing generated values and increasing ease of pronunciability

Figure 33. Experiment 16. Learning as a function of pronunciability and generated values of trigrams when paired with numbers and with paralogs.

sponse M. It is quite unlikely that the differences attributable to numbers and paralogs are a consequence of differences in intralist similarity among numbers and paralogs. This conclusion follows from the fact that the effect of intralist stimulus similarity on learning is greater than the effect of intralist response similarity (e.g., Underwood, 1953)—effects just opposite from those shown in Fig. 33.

2. There is no decided increase in the slope of the functions relating stimulus PR (or GV) and learning as the lists become more difficult to learn. To state this in another manner: if we consider the paralogs to have lower M than numbers, the changes in learning associated with stimulus M do not seem to depend much on the M of the response.

3. There is no decided change in the slope of the functions relating response M and learning as the lists become more difficult to learn. Again, if paralogs are assumed to have lower M than numbers, we conclude that the effect of response M on learning is neither dependent upon nor interacts with stimulus M.

We conclude from this experiment that the effects on learning of a given range of response M (as represented by PR and GV) are much greater than the corresponding range of stimulus M on learning. Furthermore, we see no evidence to indicate an interaction of any magnitude between the response M and stimulus M.

AN ASSOCIATION TEST

In none of our scaling operations have we determined the association value of our verbal units through the use of the more traditional methods. As our experiments progressed, several little gaps in our evidence recommended that we should determine association value for at least a sample of the verbal units with which we had been working. The above mentioned gaps, and their implications, will be explained in some detail.

1. What is the relative M of common three-letter nouns versus what Howes (1957) calls interstitials, e.g., articles, prepositions? We believed that certain very high-frequency interstitials would show lower M than would less frequent (but common) three-letter nouns. If the interstitials were learned as rapidly as the nouns, it would support a frequency interpretation as opposed to an associative-probability interpretation as far as response learning was concerned.

2. We wanted to obtain association norms on three-letter alphabetical sequences. Experiment 15 has shown these to be learned very rapidly, and we know they have low pronunciability ratings. If, furthermore, these units could be shown to have low M in the traditional sense, it would support the notion of integration—however it may come about—as being a fundamental factor in the response learning stage.

3. We wanted a direct comparison of the predictive power of association value and pronunciability.

4. Finally, we were looking forward toward trying to attain some understanding of the second or associative stage of rote learning. Our position on the mechanisms involved in the associative stage had never become firmly set, but our predilection had always pointed in the direction of an associative-probability theory. Our enthusiasm for such a theory, meager in the beginning, was never given any considerable push by the results of our experiments. The association test, we hoped, would help us catalyze our thoughts on the associative stage and on an associative-probability theory.

Method

Materials. Association data were obtained on 42 three-letter units. Twenty-two of these units were used in Experiment 15 and represent the complete range of pronunciability and of generated values of the 48 items in that experiment. In addition, we added some common three-letter nouns, some interstitials, and some three-letter alphabetical sequences. The complete list of the 42 items on which association data were collected is given in Table 51.

Procedure. The association value was determined by the production method as outlined by Noble (1952a). His instructions were used verbatim, except for minor changes required to accommodate differences in the material to be scaled. The method he devised to minimize chain associations was also used. Each verbal unit appeared on a separate page and was repeated on each line. The subjects were instructed to write only one association on a given line and to look at the stimulus unit heading each line before writing a new association. No subject filled all lines on any sheet in the time allowed. The order in which the words appeared on successive pages in the booklet was essentially random.

The production period was 40 sec., with 10 sec. between each stimulus unit, and a 1-min. rest was inserted after the 15th and after the 30th units. Two practice items were used to establish the routine of the procedure and to clarify any questions about the instructions.

A total of 58 subjects completed the group test, but the records of four were discarded because their native language was not English. "Good" data are available, therefore, on 54 subjects, although as a consequence of subjects' skipping pages, the results of two items are based on 53 subjects and one on 52. All others are based on 54. The subjects consisted of 42 undergraduate and 12 graduate students at the University of California (Berkeley).*

Results

The response measure was the mean number of associates elicited in 40 sec. The only editing we did was to remove duplications, i.e., if the subject gave the same response twice to the same stimulus, one of them was subtracted from his production score. We could find no unambiguous way to separate chain associations from those elicited by the stimulus as such; consequently, the mean values are based on the total number of associates given with only duplicates removed. The results are shown in Table 51, where the 42 items are rank-ordered in terms of the mean number of associates produced. The standard deviations are also given. The range of number of associates elicited extended from a high of 10.28 (CAT) to a low of 5.91 (JPV). This latter value is much higher than Noble gives for his lowest value for paralogs;

* We are indebted to Prof. Leo Postman for making these subjects available to us.

this is true in spite of the fact that his subjects were allowed 60 sec. to produce associates versus the 40 sec. in the present procedure. There are obvious differences in the two studies which may account for the discrepancy, e.g., different populations, different units, our failure to remove chain associations.

If we understand Howes' (1957) meaning of interstitial words, we would include 10 items from Table 51 as being of this type: FOR,

TABLE 51. Mean Number of Associations Elicited and Standard Deviations (SD) for Each of 42 Three-Letter Units

	M	SD		M	SD
CAT	10.28	4.02	WAS	8.56	2.85
BAR	9.80	2.59	BUT	8.50	2.47
WIN	9.67	2.80	BOT	8.48	2.38
RAT	9.65	2.63	HAD	8.44	2.72
MOP	9.61	2.14	ING	8.25	2.11
CAP	9.48	2.45	FIB	8.11	2.58
LUG	9.43	2.51	ABC	8.06	2.35
BAD	9.39	2.72	ITS	8.04	2.88
ELK	9.37	2.84	MEL	7.78	2.28
FOR	9.33	2.28	NUW	7.56	2.66
THE	9.20	3.03	LMN	7.39	2.39
BUG	9.00	2.59	XYZ	7.24	2.33
AND	8.87	2.79	TRC	7.11	2.25
SHE	8.85	2.53	LZW	6.69	2.50
WHO	8.81	2.34	QRS	6.50	2.69
SUM	8.67	2.43	WFI	6.41	2.27
HIS	8.67	2.78	RZQ	6.39	2.18
HOW	8.67	2.83	CFL	6.35	2.36
HUM	8.65	2.37	UNH	6.24	2.41
NOW	8.63	3.92	HFG	5.94	2.21
ROT	8.57	2.32	JPV	5.91	2.41

THE, AND, SHE, WHO, HIS, WAS, ITS, HAD, BUT. None of these words occurs among the first nine ranked in order of mean number of associates produced. Omitting HOW and NOW from consideration (are they interstitials?), we note that the mean score for the remaining 14 concrete-like words is 9.26, and that for the above 10 interstitials, 8.73. Small differences on this scale seem to be reliable. Only SUM, HUM, ROT, and FIB have lower mean scores than the 10 interstitials. We conclude that interstitials do elicit fewer associates than common three-letter nouns and adjectives. Although we will not present systematic data, we may note that interstitials elicited a greater number of different associations than did the nouns. For example, to the stimulus CAT, 26 subjects responded with *dog*, and 27 with *mouse*. The most frequently given response to THE was the word *theater*, but this was given by only 11 subjects.

The second fact apparent from the inspection of Table 51 is the relatively low number of associates elicited by alphabetical sequences.

Association Value versus Pronunciability as Predictors

How does association value (AV) compare with pronunciability (PR) as a predictor of learning? In Table 52 we have listed the 22 trigrams which appeared in Experiment 15 and were included on the association test. The trigrams are listed in order of their rank in learning (L) when they were responses (with numbers as stimuli). In successive

TABLE 52. Predictions of Learning (L) by
Pronunciability (PR) and Association Value (AV)
When Trigrams Are Responses

Trigram	Ranks		
	L	PR	AV
AND	1	9	7
BUG	2	5	6
BAD	3	1	4
CAT	4	2	1
RAT	5	4	2
HUM	6	3	8
XYZ	7	22	14
BOT	8	11	9
MOP	9	8	3
MEL	10	7	12
ELK	11	12	5
ING	12	10	10
FIB	13	6	11
CFL	14	16	19
NUW	15	13	13
UNH	16	15	20
TRC	17	14	15
WFI	18	17	17
JPV	19	19	22
LZW	20	20	16
RZQ	21	21	18
HFG	22	18	21

columns we have also ranked PR and AV, with tied ranks ignored for this exhibit. The "breakdowns" in predicting learning can be spotted quite easily. Both AV and PR "miss" on AND. However, it is barely possible that the learning scores for this item are excessively high as a consequence of the fact that numbers were stimuli, and numbers and AND have gone together very frequently, starting at the moment the subjects were introduced to simple addition. The next clear discrepancy in the list is associated with XYZ; PR misses very badly (as discussed earlier in the chapter) and AV misses by a sizeable amount. Continuing down the list, we see that AV misses on MOP and ELK, whereas PR does not, and PR misses on FIB but AV does not. Discrepancies on down the list are smaller, but average discrepancy is greater for AV than for PR.

Table 52 suggests a picture of PR and AV correlating highly for these 22 items; this is valid, for the product-moment between the two sets of values is .92. The product-moment between the learning scores for the trigrams as responses and PR is .81, and between learning and AV, .80. If the one item, XYZ, is removed from the calculations, the PR-learning relationship jumps to .91, and the AV-learning relationship to .84. A partial correlation, with PR constant reduces the latter AV-learning relationship to .04. The 22 trigrams were also used as stimuli in lists in which numbers were responses. The AV-learning relationship is .79, and the PR-learning correspondence, .86. Again, a partial correlation with PR constant reduces the AV-learning relationship to essentially zero.

Among the four lists used in Experiment 5 was a list of eight common three-letter words. These words were learned as responses in a paired-associate list in which single-digit numbers were stimuli. These eight words were also included among the 42 items scaled for association value. In examining the results of the association test we noted that the mean number of associations elicited by the eight words ranged from 9.80 for BAR to 8.57 for ROT. An analysis of variance on differences in learning among the eight items had given an F of slightly over one, leading to the conclusion that differences in learning among items was far from significant by this statistical test. The obvious next step, therefore, was to conclude that either the differences among the eight items on the association test were not reliable or that association value doesn't have much predictive power. However, being accustomed to some of the rather strong relationships mediated by predictors (especially PR) when differences among items are very small, we proceeded to calculate a product-moment correlation between the association values and the learning scores for these eight items. It was .85. Furthermore, rank-order correlations between learning and association value for each of the eighteen subjects showed that thirteen were positive and five, negative. If the eight items were divided into two groups of four each of high and low association value, we observed that there was not a single misplacement of the learning scores for the two groupings. We conclude that the very small differences in learning among the items are reliable and that they are "picked up" by association-value scores. Unfortunately, we do not have pronunciation ratings on these eight items so we cannot tell if association value would do as well or better than pronunciability.

The results of the association test show that we can reproduce the results of others (e.g., Noble, 1952b) who have shown a clear relationship between learning and number of associates elicited by an item. We have been led to conclude in a previous chapter that this is not a critical attribute in response learning; some of our present results support this position, others do not. We will retain the possibility of making association value a fundamental component in the rote-learning process.

SUMMARY

We assumed that the level of integration of a three-letter verbal unit could be indexed by the strength of the habits leading from the first letter to the second, and from the first two to the third. Therefore, we generated trigrams varying in integration by using the letter-association tables. Each generated trigram was assigned a numerical value based on the summed-habit value for each letter. These trigrams were used in learning experiments in which they occurred not only as trigram-number pairs but also as number-trigram pairs in paired-associate lists. The following conclusions were reached:

1. The values assigned the generated trigrams correlated highly with learning but not as high as did pronunciation ratings.

2. The effect of response M (generated values or pronunciability) on learning is much greater than is stimulus M. However, relatively speaking, there was a very high correspondence in learning specific trigram-number and number-trigram pairs.

3. When trigrams were stimuli, pronunciability and generated values did not predict learning as well as when the trigrams were responses. This fact, plus the relatively low correlations found at the extremes when trigrams were stimuli, suggested that some other attribute may be involved in the associative stage of learning.

4. There is very little interaction between stimulus and response M; that is, the degree of relationship between response M and learning is independent of the degree of stimulus M; the reverse statement also holds.

Forty-two items were submitted to a production test to determine association value. For twenty-two of these items the correlation between association value and pronunciability was .92, but pronunciability tended to predict learning better than association value.

REFERENCES

Cofer, C. N. Comparison of word associations obtained by the methods of discrete single word and continued association. *Psychol. Rep.*, 1958, 4, 507–510.

Howes, D. On the relation between the probability of a word as an association and in general linguistic usage. *J. abnorm. soc. Psychol.*, 1957, 54, 75–85.

Noble, C. E. An analysis of meaning. *Psychol. Rev.*, 1952, 59, 421–430. (a)

Noble, C. E. The role of stimulus meaning (*m*) in serial verbal learning. *J. exp. Psychol.*, 1952, 43, 437–446. (b)

Underwood, B. J. Studies of distributed practice: VIII. Learning and retention of paired nonsense syllables as a function of intralist similarity. *J. exp. Psychol.*, 1953, 45, 133–142.

Chapter 11

A Final Appraisal

The major experiments have been reported, and the distillation of their facts is nearly complete. The task remaining is to summarize the facts and give a final appraisal of the theoretical conception involved.

The central question to which our experiments were addressed was: "How does M produce its strong effect on the rate at which verbal units are learned?" "Why is it that a verbal unit such as BAL will be learned so much more rapidly than HQZ?" We viewed rote verbal learning as consisting of two stages. The first stage is the response-learning or response-recall phase during which the responses are learned as responses and, in a recall sense, become readily available. The second stage consists of the associative or hook-up phase; during this phase the response is associated with the specific stimulus with which it is paired or which it follows.

The research we have reported was directed primarily toward attaining an understanding of the first stage. This resulted partly from the fact that we had a theory about the learning in this stage and partly from the fact that M produces its greatest effect when varied on the response side—as contrasted to the stimulus side—of a paired-associate list. So, then, let us proceed with our summing up by evaluating the evidence and theory for the first stage and later turning to some speculations we have about the second stage.

RESPONSE-LEARNING STAGE

The M of verbal units is defined by certain rating or scaling procedures. It was first observed that most of these scaling procedures yielded about the same rank-ordering of verbal units. Thus, the following operations were judged to be tapping the same "thing": (1) proportion of subjects who got an association to a verbal stimulus within a limited period of time; (2) number of associates produced in a given period of time; (3) rated number of associates; (4) rated pronunciability; (5) rated familiarity, and (6) rated speed at which a unit would be learned. In an effort to avoid becoming enmeshed in this tangle of intercorrelations, we asked if there weren't some single variable which lay behind and was fundamental to the intercorrelations. It is possible that the many alternative theoretical approaches suggested directly by the scaling operations produced such severe conflict that we eventually regressed and found ourselves looking favorably upon a frequency hypothesis. This hypothesis, in its most general form, stated that the common variable, unveiled by the results of all of the scaling operations, was differential frequency with which the units had been experienced.

Our confidence and enthusiasm for the frequency notion grew as we demonstrated that various scaled verbal units could be translated successfully into frequency terms. Furthermore, there was evidence from certain investigators showing that learning was directly related to frequency.

How, we asked ourselves, does frequency mediate its effect on learning? We noted evidence from several diverse sources which showed that in a relatively free responding situation the *order* of emission of verbal units is directly related to the frequency with which those units have been experienced. If this law—the spew law—is applied to a verbal-learning situation, and if a selector mechanism is assumed which limits response attempts to items from the list, the order in which the items become available for entering into associations with stimuli is directly related to frequency. The spew hypothesis was further elaborated to account for the sequential integration of letters in units having very low initial frequency.

Our first order of experimental business was to establish the fact that it is possible to manipulate frequency in the laboratory and produce an outcome as predicted by the frequency theory. Experiments 1–4, taken in conjunction with the work of others, assured us that this could be done. The error data demonstrated convincingly that one of the consequences of manipulated frequency was enhancement of response integration; manipulated frequency strengthened the associative connection between letters of verbal units which at the start of the procedures were weakly tied together.

The frequency theory returned our affection in other experiments.

It predicted quite well the order in which single-letter responses would be learned (Experiment 9) and the order in which responses of initially very low integration would be acquired (Experiment 5). But, for other experiments, the theory responded with a coldness that led only to insignificant differences. When trigrams, differing widely in frequency, were used as responses in paired-associate lists, the theory appeared quite inadequate. We could accommodate within the theory the fact that if two trigrams were of equal frequency but differed on pronunciability, that which was judged easiest to pronounce would be learned most rapidly, but, when we equated trigrams for pronunciability, we could still not get an effect on learning from wide differences in frequency. The theory was in serious trouble.

In rendering a final accounting, we will look at certain assumptions of the theory and at the sensitive points in our data. Throughout, it must be remembered that we are concerned only with the first stage of learning, the stage that deals fundamentally with the problem of response availability.

The Spew Hypothesis: Responses Looking for Stimuli

The data which led to the spew hypothesis are clear; in a relatively free responding situation the order in which items are emitted is directly related to frequency. Is it reasonable to apply this fact to the learning of responses in a paired-associate list, or is this a critical point in the apparent breakdown of the theory? We believed the transfer of the spew notion to the verbal-learning situation was reasonable, and we still so believe. In an effort to obtain some further evidence on this matter, we have tried to evolve an experimental situation which combines features of a free-responding situation with those of the more restricted paired-associate learning situation. This work, which will be observed to be of a preliminary nature, was carried out by Mr. Arthur Mattocks at the University of California (Berkeley) under the direction of the senior author.

Procedure. The subject was presented stimuli as in any standard paired-associate situation, but instead of being given the responses to be attached to the stimuli, he had to supply his *own responses*. The first and basic question we were interested in was whether or not these responses would conform to expectations from the spew hypothesis. Would the responses "chosen" or "used" by the subjects be high-frequency units?

First, all subjects were given standard paired-associate learning instructions. Then, they learned a five-pair list to two successive perfect trials, in order to acquaint them with paired-associate learning. The stimuli for this practice list were paralogs, and the responses, three-digit numbers. Finally, the subject was told that he was to learn a list in which the stimuli would be supplied but that he had to provide his own responses. The instructions placed certain restrictions on the nature of the responses:

1. All had to be three-letter words, but no numbers (e.g., six) could be used.

2. The response paired with a given stimulus could not have an initial letter that appeared in the stimulus.

For stimuli, we used eight three-letter generated trigrams, all having very low associative connection between letters: CFY, IGW, KHQ, DSU, XBN, OVJ, TPM, and RZL. They were presented in four different orders on successive trials. Each was presented for 4 sec., but, just as in standard paired-associate learning, the response had to be "anticipated" before the shutter lifted, which was at the end of 2 sec. of the 4-sec. interval. In short, the presentation procedures were exactly the same as those for standard paired-associate learning except that no responses were printed on the tape.

The subject was informed, of course, that he had to use a different three-letter word for each stimulus. Further points in the instructions were as follows: (1) responses were to be spelled; (2) he was to try to give a response to every stimulus on every trial after the first; (3) if he gave a response but later forgot it, that was quite all right; (4) learning would be said to be complete when he had paired a response consistently with each stimulus on two successive trials. Twenty subjects completed the learning.

Results. The task proved to be a fairly difficult one. On the average, 27.05 trials were required to learn, the range extending from 11 to 48 trials. Later we had 13 subjects learn lists (in standard fashion) using the same stimuli with three-letter words for responses. The mean number of trials to learn was 15.38. Since there is no reason to believe that the two groups of subjects differed appreciably in learning ability, we believe that requiring the subject to supply his own responses makes the task much more difficult than if the responses are given him.

The experimenter recorded every response the subject gave, and these responses provide our essential data. On the average, each subject gave 14.6 different three-letter words. This means that 6.6 words were given which were not among the eight he used eventually to achieve his two successive perfect trials. What appears to have happened is that the subject thought of three-letter words, gave them as responses to stimuli, but these responses didn't "stick" to the stimuli to which they were originally given. Fifty-eight per cent of these responses were given only once by the subject, but 42 per cent were given two or more times (to the same or different stimuli) before dropping out. These responses first appeared about 22 per cent of the way through the total learning period and were last heard from about 33 per cent of the way through learning. The values may be contrasted with those for responses we will call correct in the sense that they were the ones given on the last two trials of learning. These correct responses first appeared, on the average, about 36 per cent of the way through learning and were first paired with the stimuli they "ended up with" about 46 per cent of the way through learning. Yet, even after the correct responses were first paired with the stimuli they were to end up with, there was an average of 3.11 misses (not given, or given to wrong stimuli) before the criterion was achieved. For many of the correct and incorrect responses, we believe it clear that the subject was recalling responses without having an association between the response and the stimulus. Literally, they were responses looking for stimuli to which to become attached; some made it and some didn't.

There were 155 different three-letter words given by the 20 subjects. On the average, each of these was given (as correct or incorrect response) by 1.9 subjects. The most frequently used words, CAT and RAT, were given by 10 subjects. Of the 155 words, 97 were given by only one subject, and 58, by two or more subjects. If the spew hypothesis holds in this situation, we would expect that the frequency of the responses given would *not* be representative of the frequency of all three-letter words; rather, we would expect the words to be coming out of the high end of the frequency distribution. Furthermore, those words given by two or more subjects should be of higher frequency than those given by only one. Both of these expectations are supported in the data of Table 53. The data require some explanation.

We went through the list of 20,000 most frequently used words as compiled by Thorndike & Lorge and placed all three-letter words (excluding abbreviations) into one of three categories: AA (most frequent), A (moderately frequent), and 1–50 (least frequent). This distribution, and percentages in each category, are shown in the left part of Table 53. Comparable distributions were then constructed for the three-letter words given by only one subject and for the ones given by two or more subjects. A comparison of the distributions shows that the subjects did indeed tend to give words from the high end of the frequency distribution. For words that are given by two or more subjects 65 per cent are AA words. This may be compared with 24 per cent AA words for all three-letter words. Only 26 per cent have frequencies of from 1 to 50, as compared with 67 per cent for all words. For responses given by only one subject, the differences are less clear. There is evidence that some subjects imposed additional restrictions upon themselves and thereby changed the conditions for spew. The purest measure of spew should be on the early trials where the subject is under instructions to respond to every stimulus and where it is less likely that he has yet imposed additional restrictions upon his responses.

TABLE 53. Frequency and Percentage of AA, A, and 1–50 Words Among Those Given by Only One Subject and by Two or More, to Be Compared with the Values for All Three-Letter Words in the Columns to the Left

Frequency Class	Thorndike-Lorge		Given Once		More Than Once	
	f	%	*f*	%	*f*	%
AA	119	23.7	19	19.6	38	65.5
A	46	9.1	17	17.5	3	5.2
1–50	338	67.2	51	52.6	15	25.9
Not Listed	. . .	. . .	10	10.3	2	3.4
Totals	503	100.0	97	100.0	58	100.0

Therefore, we checked frequencies for words given by the subject on the first trial that he *did* respond; in spite of the instructions, many subjects did not emit a response on the first trial, and many blanks occurred on later trials. Of the 66 responses examined, 56 per cent were AA, 12 per cent were A, and 32 per cent were 1–50. We conclude that the responses tend to come from the upper levels of the distribution of frequencies, and insofar as they do, support is given to the application of the spew hypothesis.

Perhaps a word of explanation is required about the 12 units in Table 53 which were given as responses but which do not appear in the Thorndike-Lorge list. It is a somewhat difficult situation for the experimenter if he thinks a response given by the subject is not a word but obviously the subject does think so. Thus, if the subject gives KAW, the experimenter can hardly stop the drum and argue the matter out with the subject. Arbitrary decisions by the experimenter relayed immediately to the subject may cause disturbance in the subject's learning. Therefore, we were lenient in accepting almost anything the subject gave as responses. The two units given by two or more subjects, and which do not appear in the Thorndike-Lorge list, were TAT (given by five subjects) and WAT (given by two subjects). The 10 given only once were: EGO, GAT, KAW, MOM, MIT, NIT, REB, SIB, TAD, and ZIP. In certain circles, many of these would be considered high-frequency words.

We should not leave the impression that the stimuli had nothing to do with the particular responses used. Some subjects reported that they took, say, the first letter in a stimulus, thought what letter followed, and then tried to think of a three-letter word which began with that letter. For example, several subjects reported that for the stimulus CFY they went from C to D to DOG. That they said DOG instead of DAW, however, is quite in line with the spew principle. Another common way of "getting" responses was to use an associate of a response that was already being given. If the subject was using DOG as a response to one stimulus, he often also gave CAT as a response to another and reported to us that as DOG made him think of CAT, he looked for a stimulus to associate with CAT. The most extreme instance of getting responses through inter-response associations was shown by a subject who managed to give eight three-letter words as correct responses, all of which had AT as the last two letters (HAT, GAT, BAT, CAT, WAT, MAT, SAT, PAT). He was not a fast learner, requiring 38 trials.

We are impressed by the number of responses used which end in T. Of the 58 words given by two or more subjects, 22 of these ended in T. In view of such results, perhaps we should not be surprised at the high generalized response strength which we found T to have in the letter-association data reported in Chapter 9.

We believe Mattocks' study makes it reasonable to presume that an ordering effect as a function of frequency could occur in the learning of responses of different frequencies in a paired-associate list. We see no reason to believe that the breakdown in the frequency theory occurred at this point; the spew hypothesis, relating order of recall to frequency, appears valid.

In passing, we may mention that the technique used by Mattocks shows considerable potential for studying a number of problems. Suppose we required the subject to respond with three-letter units which are *not* words (perhaps adding restrictions that a letter may occur only once in a unit, and that no alphabetical sequences may be used). From everything else we have learned in our experiments, we could certainly predict that the responses would be not only easily pronounceable units but probably also high-frequency units. If one asks further how the nature of the responses may change as a function of stimulus M, or as a function of interstimulus similarity, a great many other studies immediately open up which will offer checks on a number of predictions.

Frequency and Well-Integrated Units

We continue with the summary and with our search for the critical points in the failure of the frequency theory. The frequency hypothesis was supported by the results of Experiment 9 in which single letters were used as responses. In our manner of speaking, single letters would be said to be well-integrated responses; indeed, they would probably be said to be so in any manner of speaking. When we used three-letter units the frequency theory was not supported. However, we have not evaluated thoroughly the extreme case of very well integrated three-letter units which differ in frequency. This extreme case would be relatively common three-letter words for which sizeable differences in frequency still obtained.

Some of the evidence which suggested the spew hypothesis involved common words, and that evidence showed that in a relatively free responding situation, high-frequency words were emitted first. Our application of this principle to learning presumed that if responses in a paired-associate list varied in frequency, the most frequent response would be available first for entering into an association with its stimulus. We have not made a specific test under conditions appropriate for this case. That is, we have not had subjects learn a paired-associate list in which common (well-integrated) three-letter words, differing appreciably in frequency, were the response units. We have, of course, used words in some of our lists, but for a number of reasons (which we will not detail) these cannot be used satisfactorily in a post hoc manner to test the frequency theory. As a matter of fact, if one wishes to make a completely satisfactory test of the frequency notion for this extreme case, a very rigid set of conditions must be met.

1. The list should be fairly long (12 to 14 pairs) so that we are well beyond the memory span of the subject.

2. The stimuli should be constituted of a class of materials other than words, and several different stimulus-response pairings should be used.

3. Ideally the number of associates elicited by the words of different frequency should be fairly equal. This will not be an easy condition to meet since there is a clear correlation between word frequency and number of associates elicited. However, with the use of a number of

different lists and with rough equations on number of associates, the test can probably be made. The reason why frequency and number of associates should not be allowed to covary rests partly on the need to untangle the two factors and partly on the need to keep the two stages of learning from being too intertwined. Absolute differences in response-learning stage as a function of frequency may be expected to be small, and (as it will later be argued) if the associative stage of learning *is* related to number of associates, the response-learning phase could be contaminated by the associative phase.

4. There is a final factor which remains somewhat of an unknown in the above situation; this factor is the associative connections *among* words. The fact that associative connections do exist among common words raises two complicating issues. First, these associative connections may facilitate the recall of some items and not others. Very likely, a greater number of associative connections will exist among high frequency words than among low frequency words, and if these associative connections facilitate response recall, the results will be biased toward the frequency hypothesis. However, the associative connections may also exert a contrary effect, namely, interference during the associative stage. Clearly, if the net effect of these two factors does not fall equally on all items, the procedures would not be a satisfactory test of the frequency notion. We are not sure that word-association norms which are available will allow one to equate on associative connection among items and still have frequency varied appreciably.

Frequency and Poorly-Integrated Units

We will now look to the other extreme in our summary of how the frequency theory fared. The extreme case of poorly-integrated responses is given by a consonant syllable of low-association value or by a generated trigram with a low value. For these types of items, summed letter frequency has been a fairly successful predictor of learning. In Experiment 5 it predicted the learning of consonant syllables much better than did association value. It was also shown to be a substantial predictor of initially poorly-integrated items in other experiments when intralist response similarity was low (Experiments 6 and 15). For example, in Experiment 15, using 17 items which were rated difficult to pronounce and which did not include alphabetical sequences, we found summed letter frequency and learning to correlate .73.

We make a point of the relationship between summed letter frequency and learning because if integration cannot be telescoped by pronouncing the unit, the frequency theory predicts that summed letter frequency (or some other formula whereby the frequency of each letter enters into the total value) should predict rate of learning. The mechanisms involved were detailed in Chapter 6.

Unfortunately, the pronunciation ratings have given us almost the same prediction as has summed letter frequency for these poorly integrated items. When pronunciability failed with such items (due to intralist similarity, we believe), as in Experiments 12 and 13, so also did summed letter frequency. We have not been able to untangle these two measures; indeed, there is some reason to believe that they are not independent basically. How do subjects make judgments of pronunciability for units that are poorly integrated? For items which have a pronunciability rating over 7.5 (difficult to pronounce) those with a vowel are likely to be given a lower rating than those with three consonants. Our summed-letter measure gives heavy weight to vowels because they are frequent letters. There is also the possibility that subjects, in making the pronunciability ratings, essentially sum the letters phenomenally. We reported a study in which ratings of pronunciability were made under instructions to avoid being influenced by frequency of the unit *as a whole;* these instructions had no effect. Yet, in spite of the fact that the special instructions failed to produce any critical difference, it is still possible that the frequency of one or more letters in the unit may influence pronunciability ratings. If this is the case, pronunciability differences result from frequency differences, and frequency retains a fundamental status for these extreme cases of low integration. Thus, while the evidence for poorly integrated items is far from definitive, we see no basis for rejecting the frequency theory for these types of items.

Frequency, Associative Connection, and Association Value

The breakdown. The review, as carried thus far, indicates that there are no firm grounds for rejecting the frequency hypothesis in the learning of single letters as responses, highly integrated multiple-letter responses, and very poorly-integrated responses; indeed, the evidence we have can be interpreted as favorable to the frequency theory. The rather complete breakdown in the theory occurs with multiple-letter units in the broad range between the extremes of well-integrated and poorly-integrated units. Ironically, within this range falls the scale of M for nonsense syllables, and our frequency theory essentially had its beginning as a consequence of our analysis of nonsense syllables in terms of their frequency of occurrence as parts of words.

Let us review the background facts involved and our conclusions from them. It was shown that as M increases, the number of nonsense syllables which occur as three-letter units in words increases. It was also demonstrated that the frequency of those syllables which do occur in words increases as M increases. After a study of these facts we concluded that since M and learning were directly related, and since M and frequency were also related, frequency and learning should be related. With considerable confidence we proceeded to elaborate our frequency theory. The theory assumed that different trigram frequencies would represent differences in strength of associative connections between letters. The greater the initial strength of such connections, the faster is the learning of the unit as a response in a paired-associate list. By such reasoning we were led into a series of experiments in which trigram frequency was varied. The data from these experiments soon caused theoretical pause; trigrams of widely different frequencies were not learned at different rates. We were, therefore, obliged to backtrack in an effort to understand where the failure occurred in the reasoning or in the theory.

Since the conflict between fact and frequency theory is most apparent for nonsense syllables, we will spend some time in reviewing and analyzing the facts as we see them for nonsense syllables. Figure 34 schematizes the relationships among three attributes of nonsense syllables as our data show they exist. We have used the schematic form in order to portray the facts most starkly. The baseline of Fig. 34 is M of nonsense syllables. The ordinate represents increasing trigram frequency and increasing ease of pronouncing the syllables, although no numerical values are given.

The curve representing trigram frequency is essentially a replot of Fig. 9 in Chapter 5 in which trigram frequency was shown to increase as a function of M. The relationship between trigram frequency and M is not linear; while the horizontal portion is probably not in fact exactly parallel to the abscissa, no serious violence is done the facts by so plotting it.

The pronunciability curve is based on data we have not reported previously. It will be recalled that we found a correlation of .67 between rated ease of pronouncing a unit and its Glaze value; the correlation was based on 114 syllables. As may be seen in Fig. 34, this relationship is also not linear. The actual mean pronunciability values on which this schematic curve is based are: 0–7 per cent, 6.3; 13–20 per

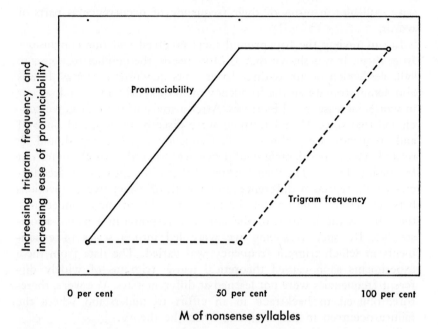

Figure 34. Schematic representation of the relationship among M of nonsense syllables, pronunciability, and trigram frequency.

cent, 4.5; 27–33 per cent, 4.7; 40–47 per cent, 3.9; 53–60 per cent, 3.4; 67–73 per cent, 3.0; 80–87 per cent, 3.1; 93–100 per cent, 3.0. Thus, ease of pronouncing the syllables increases from 0 per cent M to approximately 50 per cent M, with no appreciable change thereafter.

Our data have consistently shown that trigram frequency does not relate to rate of acquisition in the response-learning stage. Figure 34 indicates that within the range of M of nonsense syllables, trigram frequency increases only between 50 and 100 per cent M. Between these two points, however, pronunciability does not increase, and pronunciability is the dominant attribute as far as learning is concerned. Thus, pronunciability is not related to printed frequency of CVC units. Figure 34 also indicates why M should not relate to learning (in the response-learning stage) in the high range of M. In the low range of M, pronunciability and M covary; therefore a relationship between M and learning would be expected. Certain other implications of Fig. 34 will be pointed out, after which we will return to the central question posed by the lack of relationship between trigram frequency and learning.

1. We had suggested in an earlier chapter that the curve relating M and learning for the entire range of M should be sigmoid in shape. Our basis for this suggestion came from the positively accelerated trigram frequency curve as schematized in Fig. 34. In none of our experiments have we found the sigmoid curve. The only suggestion of such a function came from Experiment 1 where familiarization of responses appeared to produce a positively accelerated curve as a function of number of familiarization trials. Fig. 34 indicates that the response-learning stage of nonsense syllables as a function of M should show a negatively accelerated curve to correspond with the pronunciability function. McGeoch's study (1930), reviewed in Chapter 3, clearly showed this negative acceleration although other results (e.g., Sarason, 1957) showed quite the opposite. We believe that if several samples of syllables from each of several M levels are used as responses in paired-associate lists, the negatively accelerated function will obtain. Some distortion may be produced by differences in learning during the second or associative stage, but it should not be great enough to change a basic picture of negative acceleration.

2. If the pronunciability curve of Fig. 34 is extrapolated downward —toward lower M than indicated by 0 per cent association value— learning of such units should be slower and slower the further the extrapolation. The syllables of 0–7 per cent M have a mean pronunciability rating of 6.3; we know that many items are rated more difficult to pronounce and are learned more slowly than 0 per cent nonsense syllables. More specifically, consonant syllables will, on the average, be rated as more difficult to pronounce than nonsense syllables and probably will show some increase in difficulty of pronouncing as association value decreases. However, we do not know where the M scale for consonant syllables and the M scale for nonsense syllables join (identifying items equally difficult to learn).

3. For the 114 nonsense syllables on which we have pronunciability ratings, the mean pronunciability is essentially the same for all items above 50 per cent M. However, if all nonsense syllables were rated for pronunciability, we would probably find some small increase in mean value from 50 per cent to 100 per cent. For the syllables of Fig. 34 the mean pronunciability for items with highest M is 3.0; we know that other units used in our experiments have received higher values than this, although a mean rating of 1.5 is about as high as the scale extends. In other words, we will expect a small change in learning rate between nonsense syllables of 50 per cent M and units, such as common words, rated as being most easy to pronounce. Nevertheless, one implication

of the pronunciability curve in Fig. 34 is that fairly common three-letter words will probably not be learned much more rapidly than nonsense syllables of from 50 per cent to 100 per cent M. We do know in fact (from Experiment 5) that the change in rate of learning between nonsense syllables of 50 per cent M and common words is much less than the change between consonant syllables of low M and nonsense syllables of 50 per cent M.

One conclusion we reached was that M (defined as number of associates elicited, or number of subjects getting an association within a limited period of time) was not a relevant attribute for the response-learning phase of verbal units. This conclusion caused us no alarm; indeed, it helped clear away certain puzzles. But a second conclusion which the data seem to be forcing on us is the conclusion that the frequency with which letters occur in sequence in words does not influence the associative strength of the habits connecting one letter to another. Are we to accept this conclusion? Our frequency theory per se aside, we must note that to accept such a conclusion has general theoretical implications. Almost any theory of learning would predict that frequency and associative connection would be related, although the theories might differ on the mechanisms which are postulated to go along with frequency, to produce the relationship between frequency and learning. In short, it appears that we must be very careful concerning the precise conclusion we reach about the irrelevance of frequency. Our data show only that printed frequency of letter sequences is not related to speed of learning, and this must not be generalized to include all forms or ways in which frequency differences may occur. We will return to this matter shortly, but first we must make a final estimate of the validity of our conclusion that printed trigram frequency and rate of acquisition in the response-learning phase are not related.

Experimental validity. Are there any procedural factors in our experiments which did not allow the frequency-learning relationship "opportunity" to show itself? One may question the accuracy of our trigram counts, and we certainly hold no brief for the reliability of small differences in frequency among the trigrams. Yet, the correlations among the samples were high enough to indicate some stability, and when rather enormous differences in frequencies of trigrams are involved, one would expect some relationship between frequency and learning to emerge—if such a relationship exists.

Most of our experiments in which trigram frequency has been varied have used the mixed-list design. That is, several different kinds of form-classes (CVC, CCV, CVV, etc.) of trigrams were included within a single list. We know that large differences in rate of learning as a function of form-class exist. As a matter of fact, for our samples of the various form-classes, the learning supports a generalized frequency theory perfectly. That is to say, the more frequently a given form-class appears as part of a word, the more rapid is the learning of members of that form-class. For example, CCC sequences make up about 4 per cent of all three-letter sequences in words, and these sequences are by far the most difficult ones to learn. On the other hand, CVC combinations, making up the largest percentage (32 per cent) are, on the average, learned most rapidly; other form-classes fall in between. For two reasons, however, we cannot use such facts to support a frequency theory. First, we have no idea as to the representativeness of the items we have in each form-class; it is possible that they represent a biased sample when all possible items in each form-class are considered the population. Second, pronunciability ratings are perfectly correlated with form-class. That is, CCC combinations are, on the average, rated most difficult to pronounce, and CVC combinations, the easiest to pronounce.

We reported analyses of the relationship between learning and frequency for items of the same form-class, but the results gave no support to the frequency theory. Yet, it is barely possible that if all items in a list had the same form-class, differences in learning as a consequence of frequency might emerge. The mixed-list procedure might mask the influence of frequency. We doubt the likelihood of this, however. In Experiment 5 we had a list of nonsense syllables as responses, all with about the same M value. Although some of these occurred as trigrams, some did not, and while the differences in absolute frequencies were not great, we could find no evidence that learning corresponded to the differences that did exist. The ideal test would be to use different lists of nonsense syllables of differing frequencies which are equal on pronunciability and which fall at the same M level. Such a test might show small differences in learning as a function of frequency, but we wouldn't bet on it.

We had, at an earlier point in the book, raised the possibility that in an absolute sense the frequency of trigrams which occur in words could be very high. We even made some rough estimates of what this absolute frequency might be. If all trigrams which *do* appear in words have a high absolute frequency, it might be argued that no differences in learning would be expected. This position is quite untenable in view of the fact that enormous differences in learning of such items *did* occur, but, alas, the differences in learning were not related to frequency differences.

It is to be realized, of course, that we cannot rule out the possibility that something about the procedures we have used may have prevented the expected relationship between frequency and learning from exhibiting itself. Some attribute of these materials which we have not discovered may be floating around throughout our experiments and leading us to a false conclusion. Obviously, we do not think this is likely since we, above all, would have preferred to support the frequency theory at the level at which it was conceived, i.e., a relationship between learning and frequency of letter sequences in printed texts.

A Reluctance to Reject Frequency

The frequency with which trigrams occur in printed texts does not seem to be related to the associative connection between letters of the trigrams. As noted above, we would insist that this is puzzling; it should be puzzling also to one whose theoretical predilections lead him to assign no importance to frequency as such but who thinks of it merely as a vehicle through which other processes produce a strengthening of associative connection. We find it difficult to reject a frequency hypothesis. We will list and discuss each of the several factors which we recognize as being responsible for this stubbornness, and, it will be seen, the discussion will point to a reconsideration of the *unit* of frequency.

Partial success of frequency. Earlier in the chapter we reviewed the frequency hypothesis as applied to single-letter responses and to multiple-letter units which are either highly integrated or very poorly integrated. We concluded that the spew facet of the frequency theory is substantially supported by our results. Frequency determines the order in which units start entering into the second or associative stage of learning. For poorly-integrated items it determines the order in which the units will become integrated so that they are available for the second stage of learning. Since this aspect of the theory has proven reasonably useful, we are reluctant to dismiss that aspect which states that associative connection between letters can be predicted by the frequency with which those letters have been experienced in sequence in the past.

Familiarization studies. Experiments 1, 3, and 4 (as well as the work of other investigators) have shown beyond doubt that the laboratory manipulation of frequency produces results which are in complete correspondence with expectations from the frequency theory for the response-learning stage. The manipulation of frequency leads to associative connection between letters and, hence, a more integrated unit than was true at the start of the familiarization training. That integration is the basic consequence of this frequency is fully supported by the error data. On the assumption that frequency of sequences in printed texts reflects differences in the frequency with which subjects have experienced the units, why do we not find differences in integration as a consequence of printed frequency? There is, obviously, a difference in the two situations. In experimental familiarization the subject is forced to emit the units as units; in reading, at least silently, the subject (at the adult level) may deal with word or phrase units, not three-letter sequences within larger units. Thus, "true" experienced frequency is not reflected in printed frequency for such short sequences. There is also a difference in the emission aspects of behavior in reading silently and in the familiarization studies, namely, relatively covert versus overt responding. Overt responding may, as Noble (1955) has suggested, produce a motor patterning which enhances the availability of the unit. In any event, we have, in the familiarization studies, a form of frequency which *does* result in the development of associative connection between letters.

Special cases. We have shown that certain letter sequences, which do not appear in our trigram counts, are very highly integrated. Thus, alphabetical sequences are learned very rapidly as responses in paired-associate lists. We presume this occurs because they are highly integrated sequences. We do not see how they became integrated except through some form of repetition—through frequency, and we presume that this is largely emitted frequency, although, undoubtedly, such sequences do occur in printed texts. Although we did not use initials as responses in any of our studies, we suspect that had we done so we would have found them behaving very much like alphabetical sequences. We cannot conceive of a magic process by which such items become integrated; we think it must be a consequence of frequency and, in most cases, emitted frequency.

Letter-association data. To say that printed frequency has no counterpart in the letter-sequence habits of subjects is to deny the findings of the letter-association study (cf., Chap. 9). We never failed to find a positive relationship between the responses of subjects to single- and two-letter stimuli and the frequency with which the letters occur in sequences in words. The magnitude of the relationship varied a great deal depending upon the particular stimuli involved in the analysis, but there was always a relationship present. However, we must minimize the significance of these relationships for letter sequences in general; for the analysis of two-letter stimuli we deliberately chose stimuli which occur with very high frequency in sequences in words. Only with such stimuli could we obtain a correlational estimate of the relationships. With stimuli which do not occur frequently in the language, we do not know what the relationship would be. However, other analyses suggested the following facts which are relevant to the issue we are discussing.

1. With high-frequency stimuli, letter sequence habits are almost entirely responsible for the responses; other habits are of minimal importance. However, as the frequency of the stimulus becomes less and less, the greater is the likelihood that other habits (many of which we identified) will determine the responses. These habits would have very little representation in the frequency counts of trigrams. In other words, letter sequence habits are induced by many sources other than printed text; hence, printed text gives a very poor representation of differences in associative connection between letters when all habits are considered. Since there is no reason to believe that these other habits are not a consequence of frequency, our trigram frequency measures should represent only a very small proportion of habits induced by frequency for stimuli which do not occur frequently in words.

2. The letter-association data showed clear evidence of generalized habits of response. These occur on at least two levels. First, there is the tendency to give high frequency letters at the "expense" of low frequency letters which might actually be more appropriate for the stimulus (appropriate in the sense that they would complete a letter sequence appearing in words whereas the generalized response might not). Of course, since the generalized habit is presumed to evolve because the letter is very frequently used in words, the generalized response will often complete a three-letter sequence which does appear in words.

The second level of generalized responding noted in the letter-association data concerns form-class. Our analyses in terms of vowels and consonants following various combinations of vowels and consonants show that the responses of the subject do correspond quite closely to the vowel-consonant structure existing in words. Thus, when two consonants appear together in a word, it is highly probable that they will be followed by a vowel. The subjects' responses to two-letter stimuli consisting of two consonants followed the pattern of letter-sequences in words—a vowel was usually given. Thus, we see that many habits which were operating in the letter-association procedure must reflect differential frequency of experience.

Generated trigrams. From the letter-association data we generated trigrams which differed in the associative connection existing between the letters. This associative connection represented a composite of all habits discussed above—not just letter-sequence habits induced from printed text. If these habits are a product of frequency, the generated trigrams represent differences in associative connection produced by frequency differences. Acquisition rates for these generated trigrams in the response-learning stage are a function of the degree of integration of the units at the start of learning.

What else is there? The evidence seems overwhelming that frequency lies behind habits which determine the degree of associative connection between letters. We can see no alternative but to conclude that frequency is directly or indirectly responsible for differences in letter-sequence habits. It should be noted that our frequency hypothesis did not give frequency a fundamental causal role in the development of associative connection. We have never committed ourselves on this issue. We *did* assign frequency a fundamental causal role in the spew aspect of the frequency theory, and we have found nothing in our data which denies the usefulness of this conception. The frequency theory went astray in assuming that frequency of printed letter sequences would be indicative of the associative connection existing between letters and would, therefore, be a good predictor of degree of initial integration of a multi-letter unit. In our opinion the results of our experiments make this position quite untenable, but it does not immediately follow, therefore, that frequency, conceived of more broadly, is irrelevant to the development of associative connection. To conceive of frequency more broadly means either or both of two conceptions:

1. Many habits other than those induced by printed-letter sequences enter into the determination of associative connection between letters. These habits are a product of frequency.

2. The frequency most responsible for the development of letter-sequence integration may be emitted frequency in a vocal sense—the subject actually speaking. Letter-by-letter integration may be circumvented by well developed pronunciation habits.

We are inclined to believe that differential emitted frequency is the key to the development of differential associative connection between verbal units, no matter how big these units are and no matter what the habits are. So, we turn to some speculations about the nature of this emitted frequency.

Pronunciability and Frequency

We are left with two substantial predictors of the response-learning phase of verbal learning for multi-letter units—pronunciability and generated values. The easier the unit is to pronounce and the higher the generated values, the greater is the degree of initial integration of the letters, hence, the less the proportion of the formal learning process which must be devoted to integration of the letters.

Pronunciability has been an extraordinarily accurate predictor of the response-learning phase. Correlations between pronunciability and learning for various experiments ranged from .76 to .87, and it should be remembered that predictive accuracy for individual subjects was quite high. The generated values have greater generality than do the pronunciation ratings because they include certain integrative habits which pronunciation does not. Indeed, we believe that if our generated values could be given the "proper" numerical index, they would predict as well as pronunciability for sequences of letters which occur in words and, in addition, would predict for those special cases (e.g., alphabetical sequences) for which pronunciability breaks down.

It is a fact that generated values and pronunciation ratings are quite highly correlated. In Experiment 15 the product-moment correlation was .72. We determined the generated values for the 114 syllables involved in the pronunciability curve of Fig. 34, and when these values were plotted in a manner comparable to that for the plot for pronunciability, the curves had the same shape. This relationship suggests that the most frequent responses to single- and two-letter stimuli in the letter association study will tend to make the resulting three-letter unit an easily pronounceable one. The exceptions, as already noted, are based on special habits. The letter-association data could be interpreted as representing the emitting habits of the subjects. That is, they are responding in a way that corresponds to their most frequently emitted responses in the past. Since these habits by and large tend to make pronounceable units, we might suspect that the most critical frequency for the development of associative connections is emitted frequency.

We have no data on emitted frequency of words as such so our comments must be very speculative. However, if in the future, someone decides to make a frequency count of emitted verbal behavior, we suspect that the unit of analysis should not be letters as such, nor letter sequences as such, but, rather, frequency of specifiable sounds and sound sequences. We are inclined to believe that pronunciation ratings in the range "easy to pronounce" (say, 4.0 or less) may accurately reflect differences in emitted sound frequency. It has been suggested to us that differences in pronunciability within this range might represent singularity of pronouncing a unit. That is, if a given unit is commonly pronounced in one and only one way in all words in all contexts, it may be rated as easier to pronounce than one that is pronounced in two ways, the specific way depending upon the word context. However, as can be seen, this (if true) may be an effect of frequency; a common syllable pronounced in two different ways will have less frequency for each form of pronunciation than will an equally common syllable having only one way of being pronounced.

Our suggestion that sound frequencies should be the unit of analysis stems not only from a belief that emitted spoken frequency is the critical variable, but also from certain trends in the letter-association data. For example, an inspection of the response frequencies, letter by letter, occurring to CA and KA (as well as responses to other C-vowel and K-vowel stimuli) reveals a high degree of correspondence in the frequencies for each letter. In fact, we believe that such correspondence allows us to add another class of habits to those indicated in Chapter 9 as being response determinants. That is to say, the sound associated with a single-letter stimulus, or a two-letter stimulus, is more important as the determinant of the letter elicited than is the visual perception of such stimuli.

These notions, which, we repeat, are quite beyond any data we have, do point to a number of potential research problems. For example, the manipulation of intralist similarity in terms of sound identities and similarities rather than in terms of letter duplications is an obvious problem to attack. Our understanding of the role of different sensory avenues of emitted (vocal and writing) and received (heard and read) frequencies would be enhanced by studies of the blind, the deaf, and the deaf and mute. We might also note that the very positive effect produced in experiments in which active recitation was superior to passive reading (e.g., Gates, 1917) only confirms our belief that emitted frequency is of fundamental importance in the integration of response elements.

Response-Learning Stage: Conclusion

Our data have shown that the frequency with which letters occur in sequences in words cannot be used as an index of the degree of associative connection between letters. Since we have been unable to conceive of how letters can become associated without repetition—frequency— we have suggested that eventually it may be shown that emitted frequency is the critical avenue for the development of verbal habits. We have concluded that the spew facet of our frequency hypothesis remains tenable.

In the long run, of course, whether our notions are supported or not is of minor importance. A number of empirical problems have been solved, and other investigators, with better theories than ours, ought to find the data useful.

THE ASSOCIATIVE STAGE

We have presented no hypothesis relating M and learning in the associative stage. We have presented no theory to account for the associative phase occurring as a subphase of response integration. The spew hypothesis accounts for the order in which responses become available for entering into associative connections, but it has no relevance to the actual process of the connection being established. Of course, we took the position that frequency lay back of the M effects, and it was reasonable, therefore, that some consequence of frequency could be used to account for the associative stage.

How does the stimulus and the response in a paired-associate list get hooked up? This is almost the simplest way to ask about the mechanisms involved in the associative stage. In trying to answer this question we must look to the characteristics or attributes resulting from frequency, and we must look at these from the point of view of a response trying to find its appropriate stimulus and of a stimulus trying to find its appropriate response. We must not overlook the fact that characteristics of the response may be important for the associative stage and that this importance will be over and above the importance of frequency in the first stage. However, by the very nature of the situation it is difficult to separate the effects of characteristics of the response on the two stages. Therefore, we must look primarily to the stimulus for our theoretical cues, for the stimulus is not involved in response learning as we have conceptualized it. But, having obtained some theoretical direction from an analysis of stimulus action, we may be able to generalize it to the response item.

The Basic Facts

The facts relating stimulus M and learning, facts which we believe to be firmly established, may be summarized.

1. For a given range of M, the effect on learning is less when M is varied on the stimulus side of a paired-associate list than when it is varied on the response side. The data of Experiments 15 and 16 confirm those of most other investigators on this matter. Experiments 15 and 16 used almost as complete a range of M as it is possible to obtain with three-letter units. Within this range the magnitude of the effect of response M versus stimulus M was, conservatively speaking, three to one.

2. Experiments 1, 2, and 4, viewed in conjunction with the work in other laboratories, led to the conclusion that the manipulation of stimulus frequency (stimulus familiarization) does not produce a positive effect on learning. The interpretation of the results suffered from some ambiguity, however, in that weak signs of an inhibitory factor were observed. It is conceivable that this inhibitory factor counteracted a positive effect of familiarization.

3. The relationship between the learning of units as responses and the learning when the same units are stimuli is, within a broad range of M, very high; for Experiment 15 the correlation was .85. This strong relationship might suggest that the mechanisms for the associative stage of learning must be the same as those for the response-learning stage. However, this need not necessarily be the case, since we are dealing with a dimension with several specifiably different but highly correlated attributes. One could, therefore, use one attribute for one aspect of learning, and another attribute, for a different aspect. Therefore, the high correlation noted above need not bind one to a single explanatory mechanism for both stages of learning.

With the above facts in mind, let us evaluate some possible mechanisms for the associative stage of learning.

Stimulus Integration

We have declared frequency to be the fundamental characteristic lying behind all attributes of the M dimension. We used frequency as our theoretical mechanism for the response-learning phase—we did not use any of the "old" attributes (e.g., number of associates) which result from frequency. Degree of integration is one of the consequences of frequency, and we used pronunciability or our generated values as an index of integration. Can we use integration as a factor to account for the effect of M of the stimulus?

We might assert that a highly integrated stimulus elicits an immediate and stable response which occurs consistently and with little variation from trial to trial. On the other hand, a nonintegrated stimulus elicits an unstable response, varying from trial to trial. Surely, a stable response elicited by a stimulus would facilitate the association of that stimulus to another unit (or response to another unit). It is, of course, absurd to speak of connecting the stimulus and response as they appear on a memory drum; the response to the stimulus in the paired-associate list must become attached to the response in the paired-associate list. Theorists for years have pointed this out and have used such terms as "stimulus properties of the response," "cue-producing responses," and so on. We accept such conceptions as being logically necessary. Therefore, in the present situation we are asking whether or not a stable response to the stimulus would enter into associations more rapidly than would a variable response. Empirical evidence (e.g., the constancy of conditions facilitating conditioning) would support such a position. Such a notion might also be coordinated in a general way with theories dealing with stimulus sampling (e.g., Estes, 1950), for in effect, a very stable response to a stimulus implies the consistent occurrence of the same stimulus elements.

We were attracted to this position, but certain facts which deny us the position gave us an alternative one, namely, a conception based on associate probability stemming directly from the number of associates elicited by the unit. We will, therefore, look at these facts as evidence for an associative-probability theory and as evidence against a position which assumes integration of the stimulus to be fundamental.

Number of Associates and the Hook-Up Stage

1. Familiarization training for units that become stimuli in paired-associate lists does not facilitate learning. We have interpreted familiarization training to produce an increase in integration of the unit, this interpretation being fully supported by the nature of the errors made when the familiarized units became responses. Since familiarization training did not facilitate learning when the units became stimuli, de-

gree of integration of the stimulus does not seem to be a critical attribute. We are prevented from making this a very strong conclusion by the fact that, as noted earlier, there may be some inhibitory factor involved.

2. Familiarization training does *not* increase the number of associates elicited by an item (Riley & Phillips, 1959). This finding does not work against the notion of integration, but it may be taken as a positive fact for a notion that number of associates is important. Familiarization training does not increase the number of associates, and familiarization training does not produce facilitation when the units become stimuli; therefore, number of associates may be important when the unit is a stimulus. This is only one of several possible conclusions from the premises.

3. In Experiment 5 common three-letter words were used as responses in a paired-associate list. Although the differences in learning among these items were very small, the number of associates predicted learning very well. Since these items were all very well integrated, the response learning phase is a minor factor in these results. We interpret the results to mean that number of associates may facilitate the associative stage. Just how the number of associates of the response unit may produce this facilitation is a matter to be considered later.

4. In Experiment 7 we compared the learning of words and nonwords. Words were learned more rapidly. We suggested several reasons for this at the time we presented the data, but one that we didn't suggest was the obvious one: words elicit more associations than nonwords. The data showed that nonwords produced more misplaced responses—responses given to the wrong stimulus—than did the words. This fact suggests differences in the associative stage between words and nonwords, and we feel quite sure that a production test would show a difference in number of associates elicited by the items we used. This does not mean words will always elicit more associates than nonwords; this need not be true in a general sense, but we suspect it would be true for the particular words and nonwords we used.

5. Finally, too many subjects report that they *do* "use" associates in connecting stimuli and responses for us to ignore this possibility. We have collected some data on this, and among other facts shown is the fact that the degree of integration of the stimulus may be irrelevant because the subject often doesn't "use" the entire stimulus in making his associates. We will turn to these data after sketching roughly how an associative-probability theory might work.

Associative probability. The idea of associative probability is simple: the greater the number of associates elicited by a stimulus, the greater is the probability that one of these will link up with another item. Thus, an already established association, albeit weak, perhaps, can be used as the basic association for new learning. Our use of the word stimulus above is general; we see no reason why the number of associates elicited both by the nominal stimulus and the response in a list should not enter into these probabilities of associative linkage. Both the stimulus and the response may, in a manner of speaking, "throw out" associates in an effort to find one that is common to both.

The notion of associative probability could be treated as an obvious mathematical certainty; that is, the prediction of learning as a function of number of associates *is* a statement of probability that transfer of old learning will occur. One would need go no further than this except, if so inclined, to work out the curve for second-stage learning as a function of the number of associates of the stimulus, of the response, and of both combined. In actual fact, however, associative probability implies mediation, and the moment one places second-stage learning into a mediational framework, certain restrictions are placed on the conception. The major restriction is, we think, that mediation must be simple or relatively direct. As we noted in an earlier chapter, the evidence does not warrant an elaborate conception of mediation, i.e., mediation through several stimulus-response chains. Indeed, the evidence is not very convincing for the operation of mediation chains one step removed. Therefore, the associative-probability theory must not be allowed to get out of hand; there seems to be very little purpose in compounding probabilities across successive chains, since typically learning doesn't appear to occur in such a manner. Also, before the discussion gets out of hand, we should look at some data.

HOW SUBJECTS SAY THEY HOOK UP ITEMS

In Chapter 2 we reported that when subjects are asked to rate the relative speed with which they will learn verbal units, the ratings correlated very highly with other dimensions, e.g., pronunciability. We were impressed by this and also by the attributes of the material the subjects said they used in making their ratings (pronunciability, familiarity, number of associates). In fact, if we were interested only in *predicting* relative rates of learning verbal units, the best single predictor would probably be subjects' ratings of how fast they would learn each item relative to others. It was, perhaps, because of these findings that we felt much less hesitancy than we formerly had felt about asking subjects how they went about learning, more particularly, how they managed to get stimuli and responses tied together in a paired-associate list. We venture to present some of their replies here because they make sense in light of the learning data we have presented. The work was carried out by Mr. Arthur Mattocks following the study reported earlier in the chapter.

The stimuli for the lists were eight generated trigrams used in the earlier study, all having very low generated values. The responses were common three-letter words. Two sets of responses and three sets of stimulus-response pairings of each set were used, but the number of subjects given each pairing differed rather widely. However, we need not be concerned about the lack of niceties in the design since our interest centers in matters for which the design is of little consequence. Rather, it is critical to note that the stimuli had very low M and the responses very high M. This latter fact means that the major portion of the learning period was concerned with the associative or hook-up phase. The 35 subjects, with whose reports we will deal, required 19.6 trials on the average to learn the lists to two successive perfect trials.

Since there were 35 subjects and eight pairs, there is a total of 280 pairings. For 75 of these (27 per cent) the subjects reported that they had not used an association to hook up the response with the stimulus. Do such reports have any validity in the sense that differences in learning occur between pairs for which an association *is* reported and those for which associations are not reported? To answer this question we compared for each subject the learning of items for which he reported an association and those for which he had not. Obviously, subjects who reported associations for all items were not used. In addition, we eliminated all subjects whose reports were split 7 to 1 (seven pairs with associations, one without) on the grounds that the learning of a single item may be unreliable. We were left with 21 subjects. We determined the mean number of times items for which associations were reported were correctly anticipated, and the mean for those for which no associations were reported. A mean for each type of item was determined for each subject and then the mean for all subjects. The mean for items for which associates were reported was 14.88; the mean for those for which associations were not reported was 11.16. A *t* based on correlated measures yielded a value of 4.83, indicating a highly significant difference between the two sets of items. Only two of the 21 subjects showed a reversal in that they gave more correct anticipations for pairs for which no associations were reported.

It is possible, of course, that subjects reported that they had no associations for particular items because it served as a rationalization for their slowness in learning these items. We have no evidence on this possibility. However, it is worth noting that Mattocks believed some subjects sometimes reported no associations because they had forgotten what associations they had used. Very likely, if such forgetting did take place, it would be for items that had been given correctly many times, in which case, the difference in the means reported above is very conservatively estimated. There is some evidence that mediators may drop out (Barnes & Underwood, 1959); that is, a mediator or an association may be used initially to tie the stimulus and response together, but, as learning proceeds, the mediators drop out (are forgotten?) and the association becomes direct. Thus, posed against the possibility of rationalization is the possibility that associations were not reported for some items which in fact had had them. We will conclude that some pairs are learned without a reportable mediating association and that very likely these items are among the last to be learned.

An association was reported for 205 pairs. One of the very clear facts which emerged was the fact that the association used often involved only a *single letter* of the stimulus. In fact, for 62 per cent of the 205 reported associations, a single letter was said to mediate the association; in 38 per cent two or three letters were used. It thus becomes apparent why it is somewhat absurd to talk about the degree of integration of all the letters of the present stimuli as being a critical attribute in the hook-up stage. It appears that if the three-letter stimulus is not integrated—or does not suggest an immediate association—the subject merely selects a particular part of the stimulus on which to base his association. Indeed, one might defend the position that the function relating stimulus M and learning (Fig. 32, Chapter 10) represents the time required by this selection procedure. As the stimulus elicits fewer and fewer immediate associates, the subject must work harder at the task of finding some component of the stimulus which elicits an associate and which might mediate the response.

We have attempted to classify the 205 associations. Although there may be some interpretation involved in classifying particular kinds of associations, one fact is manifestly clear as a consequence of the classification attempts; the greatest proportion of the associations are simple, one-step mediated associations. Out of the 205 there were only 29 (14 per cent) that were classified as involving mediation of two or more steps; we tried to be very liberal in this tally in that if there was any question about whether it was simple or complex, we placed it in the complex group.

We will not present data based on the categorization of the kinds of associations in terms of sound cues, letter identities, meaningful associates, and so on. However, we will give a sample of the associations reported, and included among them will be various types. Our major purpose is to contrast the simple, one-step associations with the more complex ones.

Single-step associates. For each association we will give the pair of items learned by the subject, and his reported association.

CFY-KID:	C and K similar in sound.
XBN-GAT:	GAT is odd word, X is odd letter.
DSU-CAT:	D to Dog to CAT.
CFY-DOG:	C to Cat to DOG.
XBN-RAT:	X suggested poison—poison RAT.
TPM-AND:	T associated with symbol (&) for AND.
RZL-SAT:	R to Rump to SAT.
RZL-SAT:	R and S in alphabetical order.
DSU-BAN:	U-BAN (brand of coffee).
RZL-KID:	RZL suggested Russell; Russell is a KID.
CFY-THE:	Remembered because first one in list.
KHQ-FAN:	KHQ to radio to radio FAN.
IGW-MAN:	W inverted looks like M, hence MAN.
IGW-MAN:	IG to IGnorant to IGnorant MAN.
RZL-BOY:	RZL looks like lazy; hence, lazy boy.
RZL-CAT:	Z is hissing sound of CAT.

In some cases, a mediator would be used, but the subject could not report how he got from the "mediator" to the response. It is possible that these should be classed as "no association." Some illustrations follow:

IGW-AND:	IGW elicited International Geophysical Year; don't know how this suggests AND.
RZL-BAT:	Made Right out of R; just associated Right with BAT.
TPM-PIG:	Tympany to PIG.
OVJ-BAT:	OVJ became JOV and just tied BAT to it.
DSU-HAT:	DU means fraternity house; associated this with HAT.

Multiple-step mediation

RZL-BAT: Someone she knows on baseball team with initials R. Z.
DSU-HAT: D is last letter in heaD; HAT GOES ON HEAD.
DSU-HAT: Desilu Productions—to theater—to theatrical HAT.
DSU-HAT: Desilu; Lucy wears HAT.
OVJ-MAN: OVJ to OVa to woman to MAN.
TPM-AND: TPM signifies time; AND is pause in time.
TPM-AND: TPM to WPM—words per minute on typewriter; AND is word commonly written on typewriter.
IGW-FAN: IGW to igloo to cold to FAN.

We believe the reports establish beyond doubt that the subjects do make use of existent associations for learning at least some of the items in paired-associate lists. Perhaps there was no doubt about this in the first place. These associations, which may be weak or strong initially, are strengthened as trials continue. By what process they are strengthened, we are not prepared to say. It also seems likely that very few of the associations are elaborate in the sense that they require multi-step mediation. Such a finding seemed almost a "must" to us in view of the fact it is very difficult to get a positive effect in learning across mediators more than one step removed when they are set up for the subject by appropriate construction of successive lists.

Another fact, which we have not tried to express numerically, appears quite universally in the subjects' reports. This is the fact that a subject will use several types of mediators in learning the list. One association may be based on letter identity, one on sound similarity, another on meaning. It is possible that the subject tried to use a consistent type of mediation and failed; all we know is that at the end of learning the associations are quite varied in type.

Further Observations and Implications

There are a number of other comments we wish to make about associations and the associative stage of learning, but since these are varied in nature, they may be best presented as a series of points.

1. In the study just reported, the stimuli had low M, and the responses, high M. We observed relatively few multi-step associations. Would the number of such associations increase if both stimuli and responses had high M? We doubt it, but of course the question would be better handled by research than by doubts. However, there are two

reasons for our doubts. First, it seems to us that the use of complex mediation chains is an inefficient form of learning unless the associates between successive steps are very strong. It would be, so to speak, easier to start from scratch. We have no evidence that the learning which takes place without reportable associations is *markedly* slower than the learning which occurs with reportable associations. Further, it seems to us, elaborate but initially weak associations among several pairs of items could result in a great deal of interference.

Our second reason as to why more elaborate associations would not occur with high stimulus and response M is based on the fact that with a greater number of associates involved, the probabilities of a direct or one-step associate making the link between stimulus and response are increased. High-frequency words are already tied together by relatively direct associations. This reasoning might suggest, therefore, that with very low stimulus and response M, where the number of associates is minimal, one would be more likely to find the use of the most elaborate associative schemes. This may in fact be the case, but in view of the first point made above, we would not expect the associates to be much more elaborate than reported by the subjects in the present study.

2. What role does the number of associates elicited by the response play in the associative stage? Our data do not give us direct information on this. What we have obtained from the subjects' reports is the nature of the associations as they were in final form; we are not able to differentiate between links made by associates stemming from the stimulus and those stemming from the response. When a subject reported that D made him think of Dog, and Dog of CAT (the correct response), we do not know but that the original chain was established by going from CAT to Dog to D. Since bi-directional functioning of associations is an established fact, the initial elaboration of response associates is a very real possibility in spite of the fact that the recall direction is opposite.

It may be remembered that we found a high relationship between number of associates elicited and rate of learning for a list of common words used as responses (List 4, Experiment 5). This suggests to us that the number of associates elicited by the response is a contributor to the associative stage. However, we would venture to suggest that when the number of associates elicited by the stimulus and the response is equivalent, more "use" will be made of the stimulus associates than of the response associates. This could result from the fact that in the usual paired-associate learning situation the stimulus is presented twice as long as the response, but it could also be a consequence of a generalized habit of establishing associations when possible in the direction necessary for recall.

3. In the list learned by our subjects, intralist stimulus similarity was zero—no letters were duplicated. Many of the reported associations involved only a single letter. If intralist stimulus similarity were increased, the likelihood of an associate to a single letter being a differentiating cue is reduced. Would increasing intralist stimulus similarity change the magnitude of the relationship between learning and stimulus M? That is, if we held M differences among stimuli constant among several lists, but varied intralist stimulus similarity, would the slope of the function relating stimulus M to learning increase as similarity increased? It seems inevitable that it would. For, as intralist stimulus similarity increases, there will be a corresponding increase in the need to use more and more letters of the stimuli to establish differentiating cues. In a certain sense, more integration of the letters of the stimuli is required. However, this degree of integration need not be as great as is necessary for the same items as responses; in a manner of speaking, the stimuli must elicit differentiating *recognition* responses, and the nominal responses must elicit differentiating *recall* responses. Therefore, under no circumstances would we expect that increments in intralist stimulus similarity would produce increased steepness in the slope of the stimulus M-learning function comparable to the steepness exhibited by the response M-learning function when intralist response similarity was increased in a corresponding manner.

4. Nearly every subject reports that for at least one pair of items no old association mediated the learning. Assuming that such reports are reliable, we are faced with the question of how such learning occurs. Again, if the reports are reliable, we know that such pairs are learned more slowly than those for which associations are reported. In many cases the subjects in effect said they had no association but simply attached the first letter of the stimulus to the response, e.g., X-DOG. Our data give us no new information on the mechanisms involved in such "raw" learning. We would like to think that it is a matter of contiguity of the stimulus and the response, but we also recognize that when responses are readily available—as they were in these lists—the subject can give the correct response to a stimulus as a consequence of response elimination. That is, having given six responses to their appropriate stimuli via simple mediated associations, and having the two other responses readily available, the chances are 1 in 2 that a guess will produce a correct response. It is possible that the process of giving the

response correctly serves as reinforcement to provide initial associative strength between the stimulus and response.

Although we do not pretend to understand the processes involved in learning when no associates are reported, we must point out that an understanding of them is important not only for the associative stage of learning as we are discussing it here, but also for the associative stages which occur as components of the response-learning stage when a response has low integration at the start of learning. We doubt very much that in integrating the response QZP many associations are used. The frequency theory as applied to this case, it will be remembered, determines the order of availability of successive letters; it does not specify how the association is formed between successive letters. We strongly suspect that the associations are established in the same manner as those for which subjects report no associations. However, we have not questioned subjects on this matter, and it is possible that letters will elicit associations that are "useful" in process of integrating the response.

5. The associative-probability theory states that the greater the number of associates elicited by members of a pair, the greater is the probability that an already established association will mediate the learning. In Chapter 4 we reviewed evidence concerning the number of associates given to verbal units by different subjects and the rate at which those units are learned by the subjects. Will a subject who produces a lot of associates learn more rapidly than one who produces few? One study (Mandler & Huttenlocher, 1956) gave evidence of a slight relationship; the other reported essentially no relationship (Scheible, 1954). Such findings were cited as providing a problem for an associative probability theory; they still do, although the contradiction is less acute than when we were considering the associative probability theory as a mechanism for both the response-learning and hook-up stages.

Our present conception of the response-learning stage utilizes frequency as the fundamental variable; association via mediated links may enter into the response integration aspect of response learning, but, as we argued above, we do not think this is very likely. Number of associates elicited by an item is held to be important only for the second stage of learning. If responses in a paired-associate list require a great deal of integration, the second or associative stage constitutes a relatively small proportion of the total learning time. Therefore, to test adequately the relationship between number of associates emitted by different subjects and their rate of learning, the learning measure must primarily reflect the second or associate stage. An adequate procedure could be to use very common responses so that integration and availability produce relatively small differences in learning. Within the learning processes of a given subject, the correlation between first-stage learning and second-stage learning may be far from perfect. If this is true, when we lump both stages together the lack of relationship between number of associates emitted in a pretest by a subject and his rate of learning is understandable. We *would* expect a positive relationship between number of associates emitted in a pretest and rate of learning lists similar to those used in the experiment reported earlier. They are lists with low stimulus M and very high response M. However, failure to find the expected relationship with a list of this kind would not constitute definitive evidence against an associative-probability theory. Our data indicate that for a given subject items for which associates are reported are learned faster than those for which no associates are reported. But, these data should not be interpreted to mean that a subject who reports eight associates (one for each item) learned more rapidly than one who reports only one. The no-associate pairs for one subject may be learned more rapidly than those for which another subject reports associations. If this situation obtains and if the number of associates used in learning reflects number of associates to be expected on a pretest of emitted number of associates, then, clearly, no relationship between number of associates emitted in a pretest and rate of learning would be expected across subjects. Thus, it is quite possible that the associative probability notion is useful in predicting the differences in learning of items for a given subject, but is not useful in predicting differences in learning among subjects.

The Associative Stage: Conclusion

We conclude that an associative-probability theory is a reasonable one with which to account for the effect of M on the associative phase of rote learning. However, as a theory, it provides problems in obtaining definitive data, and we have presented very little which bears directly on the theory. The fact that subjects report that they do use associations doesn't mean that these associations are fundamental to the M-learning relationship in the associative stage. However, we have made a number of points which seem to us to make the associative-probability theory a tenable one. We have also indicated a number of lines of research which could be pursued, the results of which would have relevance for the conception. Nevertheless, we remain a little uneasy; it is not inconceivable that those items for which associates are reported would be learned more rapidly than those for which no associations are reported even if associates had not been used. How does one attack such a problem experimentally?

A FINAL COMMENT

This book has dealt with the effects on verbal learning of a single variable. In spite of a rather rigid discipline we placed on ourselves to prevent straying from the central topic, the report has turned out to be a long one. Nevertheless, the constraints are not quite strong enough to prevent a brief discussion at a more general level.

We have noted evidence pointing toward the existence of what we have called a selector mechanism. The overt response attempts of a subject are limited to items, or elements of items within the list; neither individual letters nor larger units which do not appear in the list are given with a frequency that is much greater than could be expected because of faulty reading or faulty perception. Obviously, this selector mechanism must have greater generality than indicated by our experiments; that is, it must operate in all verbal learning and, perhaps, in other types of learning as well. We noted that the critical variable which throws this mechanism into operation is recency of stimulation, and, in this sense, recency might again be thought of as a variable of great importance for learning. Thus, we find ourselves in the position of defending and promoting the use of two of the classical associationistic variables, *frequency* and *recency*. We believe the responsibility for these recidivistic tendencies rests squarely on the data with which we have had to deal.

We must note that recency is only a term to describe one point on the time dimension. The maximum effect of the selector mechanism will occur when measurement is made immediately after stimulation —recency. With the passage of time following stimulation we presume that the comprehensiveness of the effect of the selector mechanism will be reduced. In any event, by such an assumption certain other facts fall into line. For example, we could interpret the fact that intrusions increase in number as a function of time between learning two lists and the recall of either as representing a deterioration with time of the selector mechanism. Undoubtedly, the mechanism would be classed under the catch-all heading, *set*. However that may be, the incisiveness and completeness with which the mechanism worked in our experiments make it, in our opinion, a very fundamental fact of human learning. As such, it becomes of utmost importance to reach an experimental understanding of it, for, via it, other puzzles will surely be solved.

REFERENCES

Barnes, J. M., & Underwood, B. J. "Fate" of first-list associations in transfer theory. *J. exp. Psychol.*, 1959, 58, 97–105.

Estes, W. K. Toward a statistical theory of learning. *Psychol. Rev.*, 1950, 57, 94–107.

Gates, A. I. Recitation as a factor in memorizing. *Arch. Psychol.*, N. Y., 1917, 6, No. 40.

Mandler, G., & Huttenlocher, J. The relationship between associative frequency, associative ability and paired-associate learning. *Amer. J. Psychol.*, 1956, 69, 424–428.

McGeoch, J. A. The influence of associative value upon the difficulty of non-sense-syllable lists. *J. genet. Psychol.*, 1930, 37, 421–426.

Noble, C. E. The effect of familiarization upon serial verbal learning. *J. exp. Psychol.*, 1955, 49, 333–338.

Riley, D. A., & Phillips, L. W. The effects of syllable familiarization on rote learning, association value, and reminiscence. *J. exp. Psychol.*, 1959, 57, 372–379.

Sarason, I. G. The effect of associative value and differential motivating instructions on serial learning. *Amer. J. Psychol.*, 1957, 70, 620–623.

Scheible, H. Individual meaningfulness ratings and speed of learning with observations on retroactive and proactive inhibition. Ph.D. dissertation, Northwestern Univer., 1954.

Appendices

Syllables were excluded from the present list if they occurred twice in either the Glaze or Krueger list, or if they did not have both a Glaze and Krueger value. The values have been rounded to the nearest whole percentage.

The meaningfulness value for each syllable as determined by Glaze is given in the columns headed G. (Glaze, J. A. The association value of non-sense syllables. *J. genet. Psychol.*, 1928, 35, 255–269. Courtesy, The Journal Press.)

The meaningfulness value as determined by Krueger is given in the columns headed K. (Krueger, W. C. F. The relative difficulty of non-sense syllables. *J. exp. Psychol.*, 1934, 17, 145–153. Courtesy, The American Psychological Association, Inc.)

Syll	G	K	Syll	G	K	Syll	G	K	Syll	G	K
BAF	73	89	BUQ	20	71	CIP	67	74	DAR	100	95
BAJ	53	73	BUR	100	92	CIQ	33	77	DAS	60	86
BAL	100	97	BUV	40	55	CIR	93	86	DAT	73	94
BAP	67	72	BUW	47	67	CIV	67	87	DAV	67	91
BAS	100	97	BUX	87	93	CIW	20	57	DAW	80	89
BAV	73	68	BUZ	93	96	CIX	60	67	DAX	0	48
BAW	60	95	BYC	73	85	CIY	60	64	DEB	87	99
BAX	67	90	BYF	33	84	CIZ	33	66	DEC	100	94
BAZ	40	71	BYG	60	83	COF	93	98	DEF	93	91
BEC	100	92	BYH	33	67	COH	27	82	DEG	67	71
BEF	73	82	BYJ	13	54	COJ	27	51	DEH	27	71
BEH	20	63	BYK	67	73	COK	73	93	DEJ	20	36
BEJ	20	57	BYL	7	85	COL	100	97	DEK	93	90
BEK	47	94	BYN	67	86	COQ	47	77	DEL	80	97
BEL	100	97	BYP	33	43	COR	87	96	DEM	73	98
BEM	60	65	BYQ	27	64	COS	93	94	DEP	100	95
BEP	13	64	BYR	47	87	COV	93	95	DEQ	40	77
BEQ	67	68	BYS	53	73	COZ	93	96	DER	87	91
BER	100	92	BYT	53	82	CUF	93	97	DES	60	90
BES	93	96	BYV	13	62	CUG	40	61	DET	93	97
BEV	100	90	BYX	40	59	CUH	13	68	DEV	80	92
BEW	47	64	BYZ	73	79	CUJ	20	57	DEX	73	89
BEZ	60	77				CUK	60	78	DEY	87	88
BIC	87	83	CAG	73	85	CUL	87	96	DEZ	67	67
BIF	80	80	CAJ	40	72	CUM	93	94	DIB	40	77
BIH	47	47	CAK	87	89	CUN	60	78	DIC	100	91
BIJ	53	58	CAQ	40	59	CUQ	40	63	DIF	100	97
BIK	67	90	CAS	67	97	CUS	100	98	DIH	33	73
BIL	93	93	CAV	80	96	CUV	73	79	DIJ	40	64
BIP	20	57	CAX	40	73	CUW	40	61	DIK	80	95
BIQ	40	76	CAY	67	85	CUX	13	59	DIL	80	94
BIR	87	91	CAZ	53	64	CUY	53	71	DIQ	27	80
BIS	93	81	CEB	27	75	CUZ	73	91	DIS	100	97
BIV	40	60	CED	60	83	CYB	40	60	DIT	80	85
BIW	33	50	CEF	0	64	CYD	53	88	DIV	93	95
BIX	27	58	CEG	53	69	CYF	33	60	DIW	20	72
BIY	33	77	CEH	13	45	CYJ	20	42	DIY	60	79
BIZ	100	95	CEJ	7	38	CYK	33	76	DIZ	80	97
BOC	87	82	CEK	40	66	CYM	60	75	DOB	100	82
BOD	80	93	CEL	80	95	CYN	87	97	DOF	73	77
BOF	7	52	CEM	60	81	CYP	53	76	DOJ	53	73
BOH	60	78	CEN	100	91	CYQ	27	49	DOK	73	96
BOJ	27	70	CEQ	33	51	CYR	53	81	DOM	93	99
BOK	87	89	CER	87	86	CYS	33	89	DOP	93	97
BOL	100	96	CES	47	78	CYT	80	92	DOQ	33	87
BOM	80	98	CEV	33	73	CYV	47	64	DOR	87	98
BOP	53	69	CEW	60	79	CYW	27	50	DOS	93	89
BOQ	53	70	CEX	13	69	CYX	27	63	DOV	100	98
BOR	93	94	CEY	40	78	CYZ	47	70	DOW	80	94
BOT	87	91	CEZ	47	81				DOX	73	85
BOV	73	75	CIB	27	64	DAC	40	89	DOY	80	77
BOZ	53	77	CID	80	87	DAF	53	96	DOZ	100	94
BUC	80	93	CIF	67	69	DAG	67	90	DUC	100	96
BUF	73	91	CIG	87	96	DAH	33	74	DUF	47	90
BUH	27	66	CIH	40	38	DAJ	33	44	DUH	27	60
BUJ	27	82	CIJ	0	44	DAK	47	72	DUJ	33	74
BUK	80	89	CIK	33	84	DAL	80	93	DUK	87	98
BUL	100	97	CIM	73	82	DAP	80	89	DUL	100	98
BUP	47	61	CIN	100	96	DAQ	7	54	DUP	53	85

Syll	G	K	Syll	G	K	Syll	G	K	Syll	G	K
DUQ	67	85	FIJ	80	74	GAH	0	62	GUD	40	89
DUR	87	92	FIK	40	65	GAJ	33	83	GUF	27	79
DUS	93	98	FIL	80	94	GAK	27	65	GUH	20	57
DUT	80	86	FIM	73	62	GAN	80	80	GUK	7	50
DUV	67	86	FIP	53	75	GAV	67	87	GUL	100	95
DUW	40	77	FIQ	47	76	GAW	27	67	GUP	67	70
DUX	60	89	FIS	80	87	GAX	0	55	GUQ	0	41
DUY	53	75	FIV	93	92	GEB	20	64	GUR	73	78
DUZ	47	80	FIW	27	64	GEC	7	42	GUW	20	53
DYF	47	78	FIY	67	67	GED	13	64	GUX	27	43
DYG	73	82	FOC	73	73	GEF	13	71	GUZ	80	88
DYH	27	41	FOD	80	89	GEJ	20	40	GYB	27	79
DYJ	40	51	FOH	33	56	GEK	27	40	GYF	27	68
DYK	87	92	FOJ	20	62	GEL	80	97	GYH	20	33
DYL	53	88	FOK	80	83	GEN	87	98	GYK	7	42
DYM	73	95	FOL	93	95	GEP	33	63	GYL	60	89
DYQ	13	68	FOM	80	75	GEQ	40	41	GYM	100	97
DYR	73	86	FON	93	92	GER	87	92	GYN	87	83
DYS	67	76	FOQ	13	64	GES	87	89	GYQ	0	34
DYT	47	78	FOS	80	96	GEV	53	75	GYR	60	84
DYV	67	88	FOT	80	86	GEW	40	73	GYS	73	68
DYW	13	68	FOV	53	77	GEX	0	38	GYT	40	75
DYX	33	82	FOW	80	85	GEY	47	85	GYV	33	74
DYZ	60	88	FOY	33	77	GEZ	47	71	GYW	7	67
			FOZ	60	74	GIB	87	90	GYX	27	52
FAB	93	92	FUB	13	50	GIC	13	44	GYZ	20	52
FAC	87	92	FUD	80	87	GIF	67	86			
FAH	47	70	FUG	67	89	GIH	20	41	HAB	67	94
FAJ	33	55	FUH	7	76	GIJ	47	54	HAC	73	89
FAK	93	94	FUJ	40	85	GIK	13	46	HAF	73	89
FAL	93	97	FUL	80	97	GIL	87	94	HAJ	40	64
FAM	100	99	FUM	80	90	GIM	67	96	HAK	67	93
FAP	53	60	FUP	20	38	GIP	60	95	HAN	87	97
FAQ	33	77	FUQ	27	81	GIR	87	87	HAQ	47	86
FAS	100	93	FUS	93	97	GIS	67	83	HAR	73	93
FAV	93	92	FUT	93	86	GIV	100	99	HAV	100	97
FAW	67	76	FUV	33	49	GIW	0	67	HAW	80	98
FAX	53	91	FUW	47	75	GIX	7	47	HAX	47	89
FAZ	47	82	FUX	33	87	GIY	20	63	HAZ	100	95
FEB	73	81	FUY	33	71	GIZ	47	67	HEB	47	80
FEC	47	70	FUZ	93	96	GOB	93	97	HED	67	92
FEG	47	69	FYB	60	92	GOC	33	62	HEF	47	87
FEH	0	55	FYD	33	78	GOF	67	83	HEG	20	81
FEJ	47	66	FYG	67	84	GOH	47	74	HEJ	27	76
FEK	60	64	FYH	47	50	GOJ	27	58	HEQ	27	78
FEL	100	99	FYL	67	87	GOK	20	72	HES	27	87
FEM	93	97	FYN	80	92	GOL	87	93	HET	80	92
FEN	73	95	FYP	20	53	GOM	67	87	HEV	73	88
FEP	20	45	FYR	93	96	GON	93	97	HEX	53	86
FEQ	27	46	FYS	53	78	GOP	53	95	HEZ	33	71
FER	80	93	FYT	73	90	GOQ	0	54	HIB	73	77
FES	100	86	FYV	7	74	GOR	80	93	HIF	20	61
FET	60	94	FYW	20	51	GOS	80	88	HIG	87	73
FEV	93	88	FYX	60	83	GOV	93	95	HIK	87	97
FEX	47	81	FYZ	60	81	GOW	47	80	HIL	100	99
FEY	60	70				GOX	27	40	HIN	93	87
FIC	87	91	GAB	93	100	GOZ	60	72	HIR	93	91
FID	73	94	GAC	53	72	GUB	27	69	HIX	40	92
FIH	40	70	GAF	27	78	GUC	13	46	HIY	60	79

Syll	G	K	Syll	G	K	Syll	G	K	Syll	G	K
HIZ	60	84	JEH	13	61	JUZ	20	75	KIL	93	99
HOB	100	87	JEK	40	79	JYB	27	65	KIM	60	89
HOD	87	93	JEL	100	98	JYC	0	42	KIP	80	91
HOF	87	86	JEM	80	94	JYF	40	76	KIQ	53	82
HOK	73	91	JEN	87	93	JYG	47	77	KIR	73	78
HOL	100	98	JEP	47	77	JYH	7	45	KIS	87	99
HOM	100	99	JEQ	7	48	JYK	13	54	KIW	33	48
HON	100	98	JER	93	93	JYL	47	91	KIX	47	80
HOR	87	95	JES	93	95	JYM	87	96	KIY	27	56
HOS	93	90	JEV	47	56	JYN	87	95	KIZ	20	78
HOV	87	90	JEX	0	58	JYP	67	94	KOB	53	83
HOX	73	91	JEY	33	65	JYQ	0	41	KOC	47	73
HOZ	33	83	JEZ	20	82	JYR	33	74	KOF	80	89
HUC	7	80	JIB	60	84	JYS	7	69	KOG	40	74
HUD	87	93	JIC	0	51	JYT	27	77	KOH	40	68
HUF	87	93	JID	0	64	JYV	0	46	KOJ	7	50
HUJ	53	72	JIF	67	96	JYW	7	51	KOL	80	91
HUK	60	81	JIH	20	44	JYZ	0	49	KOM	80	89
HUL	80	98	JIK	13	45				KON	53	86
HUP	80	97	JIL	87	98	KAB	47	87	KOP	67	98
HUQ	20	73	JIN	100	99	KAC	73	67	KOQ	33	55
HUR	100	99	JIQ	7	60	KAD	73	94	KOR	47	89
HUS	73	97	JIR	53	65	KAF	93	87	KOT	73	97
HUV	80	79	JIS	47	74	KAG	27	71	KOV	60	71
HUW	13	69	JIT	67	84	KAH	33	70	KOW	60	96
HUX	60	88	JIV	27	54	KAJ	13	59	KOY	33	89
HUY	40	70	JIW	13	73	KAL	33	93	KOZ	80	82
HUZ	47	92	JIY	27	74	KAM	47	92	KUB	53	79
HYB	47	71	JIZ	27	68	KAN	87	96	KUC	87	65
HYG	67	77	JOC	73	96	KAQ	13	57	KUD	53	82
HYJ	13	61	JOD	33	73	KAR	53	95	KUF	53	87
HYK	60	86	JOF	33	72	KAS	87	83	KUG	40	57
HYL	60	84	JOH	60	80	KAV	73	80	KUH	20	64
HYP	87	99	JOK	93	96	KAW	53	86	KUJ	33	48
HYQ	7	77	JOL	93	93	KAX	27	62	KUP	67	90
HYR	47	81	JOM	33	65	KAY	60	97	KUQ	13	63
HYS	60	88	JON	93	96	KAZ	20	67	KUR	67	93
HYV	47	64	JOP	67	80	KEB	7	62	KUS	60	94
HYW	20	51	JOQ	27	88	KEC	33	59	KUT	60	92
HYX	27	66	JOR	80	80	KED	47	92	KUV	40	76
HYZ	13	75	JOS	80	86	KEF	20	57	KUW	40	57
			JOV	67	93	KEH	20	62	KUX	33	72
JAC	87	98	JOW	73	85	KEJ	20	55	KUY	13	58
JAD	73	85	JOZ	33	72	KEL	87	88	KYB	20	57
JAG	67	97	JUB	67	77	KEM	47	80	KYC	40	66
JAK	73	96	JUC	13	69	KEN	100	99	KYD	73	93
JAL	53	85	JUF	20	43	KEP	87	88	KYF	7	46
JAN	100	99	JUH	7	71	KER	53	89	KYG	7	56
JAQ	67	87	JUK	60	76	KES	60	83	KYH	0	51
JAS	93	96	JUM	87	90	KET	87	93	KYJ	7	38
JAT	20	61	JUN	80	97	KEV	20	46	KYL	40	93
JAV	87	91	JUP	73	74	KEW	73	81	KYM	27	70
JAX	47	87	JUQ	7	64	KEX	13	57	KYN	60	85
JAZ	93	97	JUR	87	92	KEZ	7	51	KYP	33	81
JEB	33	59	JUS	100	97	KIB	53	79	KYQ	27	49
JEC	13	68	JUV	73	74	KIC	60	91	KYR	33	73
JED	53	72	JUW	47	81	KIF	27	47	KYS	60	88
JEF	73	94	JUX	27	63	KIG	20	65	KYT	80	91
JEG	20	66	JUY	47	83	KIH	13	63			

Syll	G	K	Syll	G	K	Syll	G	K	Syll	G	K
KYV	0	42	LOX	80	87	MEP	47	61	MYJ	7	56
KYW	13	52	LOY	93	87	MEQ	0	63	MYL	67	87
			LOZ	53	79	MER	87	91	MYN	60	89
LAF	87	100	LUB	47	88	MES	60	97	MYP	13	47
LAH	47	77	LUD	40	85	MEV	27	39	MYQ	27	72
LAJ	0	70	LUF	67	94	MEX	100	96	MYR	80	92
LAK	93	99	LUH	40	72	MEZ	20	84	MYS	93	94
LAM	87	99	LUJ	47	59	MIB	7	58	MYT	67	95
LAN	93	97	LUK	93	95	MIC	53	95	MYV	0	43
LAQ	73	97	LUM	80	84	MID	87	99	MYW	7	59
LAR	93	88	LUN	93	93	MIF	7	60	MYX	53	86
LAS	87	99	LUQ	53	87	MIG	33	77	MYZ	13	77
LAT	80	93	LUR	80	96	MIH	47	70			
LAV	80	92	LUS	87	93	MIJ	47	69	NAC	47	90
LAZ	93	97	LUT	67	89	MIK	80	95	NAD	60	70
LEB	20	62	LUV	73	96	MIL	93	96	NAF	33	62
LEC	93	79	LUW	47	73	MIP	33	58	NAH	13	85
LEF	87	95	LUY	20	72	MIQ	53	74	NAJ	53	56
LEH	47	77	LUZ	60	77	MIR	93	94	NAL	40	73
LEJ	27	75	LYB	53	86	MIS	80	99	NAM	87	85
LEK	87	84	LYC	80	89	MIV	13	51	NAQ	27	64
LEM	80	86	LYD	93	92	MIW	40	56	NAR	100	84
LEN	87	92	LYF	80	93	MIY	33	78	NAS	80	91
LEP	87	96	LYG	40	78	MOC	87	95	NAV	100	91
LEQ	20	64	LYH	33	67	MOD	100	96	NAW	47	91
LER	53	86	LYJ	27	49	MOF	40	83	NAX	13	71
LES	87	97	LYK	60	97	MOG	40	84	NAZ	80	80
LEV	93	94	LYM	67	89	MOH	40	84	NEB	80	86
LEY	67	91	LYN	87	94	MOJ	33	60	NEC	93	98
LEZ	33	84	LYP	80	95	MOK	67	87	NEF	47	72
LIB	93	91	LYR	60	94	MOL	93	95	NEG	87	90
LIC	93	97	LYS	53	92	MON	100	98	NEH	27	83
LIF	100	98	LYT	73	91	MOQ	40	91	NEJ	20	55
LIG	73	89	LYV	60	87	MOS	87	95	NEK	93	96
LIH	27	71	LYX	73	91	MOT	80	95	NEL	80	95
LIJ	27	53	LYZ	60	87	MOV	87	93	NEM	60	85
LIK	100	96				MOX	20	76	NEP	73	86
LIM	100	98	MAB	80	81	MUB	47	62	NEQ	40	81
LIN	87	95	MAC	80	100	MUC	80	91	NER	73	93
LIQ	100	95	MAF	27	57	MUF	93	97	NES	80	95
LIR	60	92	MAG	87	96	MUH	33	70	NEV	87	95
LIS	100	95	MAH	73	93	MUJ	33	78	NEX	73	87
LIV	100	98	MAJ	80	89	MUK	60	91	NEY	53	91
LIW	20	69	MAK	100	97	MUL	73	86	NEZ	67	71
LIY	73	87	MAL	93	98	MUN	47	94	NID	33	60
LIZ	80	94	MAQ	47	85	MUP	40	75	NIF	60	88
LOB	93	97	MAS	93	99	MUQ	33	77	NIG	93	97
LOC	93	100	MAV	60	74	MUR	93	92	NIH	33	73
LOD	80	94	MAX	80	98	MUS	93	99	NIJ	20	55
LOF	87	98	MAZ	80	97	MUV	60	80	NIK	60	97
LOH	67	80	MEB	40	72	MUW	13	77	NIL	87	97
LOJ	27	74	MEC	7	85	MUX	27	73	NIQ	27	79
LOK	80	97	MED	93	98	MUY	40	70	NIR	47	79
LOM	73	81	MEF	0	44	MUZ	73	87	NIS	60	60
LON	100	98	MEG	67	90	MYB	20	45	NIT	93	99
LOQ	53	92	MEH	40	63	MYC	33	72	NIV	33	74
LOR	80	93	MEJ	13	63	MYF	7	57	NIW	47	61
LOS	100	97	MEK	67	88	MYG	67	66	NIY	40	59
LOV	100	100	MEL	67	95	MYH	40	68	NIZ	27	63

Syll	G	K	Syll	G	K	Syll	G	K	Syll	G	K
NOF	40	70	PAZ	60	74	PYF	60	79	QIR	67	85
NOG	67	83	PEB	87	89	PYG	80	92	QIT	87	96
NOH	53	73	PEC	73	96	PYH	33	55	QIV	67	71
NOJ	13	63	PED	100	92	PYK	53	83	QIW	7	44
NOL	47	83	PEF	40	40	PYL	87	94	QIX	53	74
NOM	93	90	PEH	27	59	PYM	47	74	QIY	13	41
NOP	60	88	PEJ	33	49	PYN	60	93	QOB	0	43
NOQ	47	76	PEK	87	97	PYR	80	87	QOC	0	46
NOS	93	98	PEL	80	86	PYT	73	90	QOD	13	75
NOV	100	88	PEM	33	68	PYV	7	63	QOF	40	66
NOX	67	81	PEQ	47	78	PYX	47	88	QOG	60	50
NOY	47	79	PES	100	93	PYZ	27	64	QOH	20	57
NOZ	80	94	PEX	40	75				QOJ	7	29
NUB	13	73	PEY	87	92	QAB	40	60	QOK	27	72
NUD	67	73	PEZ	33	67	QAC	73	90	QOM	13	60
NUF	93	93	PIB	33	43	QAF	47	70	QON	20	54
NUG	93	91	PIC	93	96	QAH	27	33	QOP	27	43
NUH	53	68	PID	33	65	QAJ	27	37	QOR	47	67
NUJ	27	80	PIF	73	92	QAK	73	96	QOS	7	50
NUK	20	74	PIJ	47	73	QAL	73	79	QOT	53	82
NUL	93	89	PIK	80	98	QAM	20	69	QOV	0	30
NUM	67	90	PIL	100	99	QAN	67	77	QOW	7	49
NUP	73	73	PIM	60	75	QAP	0	57	QOX	20	43
NUR	53	86	PIQ	73	89	QAR	47	89	QOY	13	71
NUS	60	77	PIR	80	91	QAS	7	56	QOZ	53	71
NUV	53	68	PIV	53	75	QAT	53	76	QUB	7	48
NUW	27	89	PIW	7	73	QAV	40	68	QUC	47	68
NUX	7	79	PIX	67	88	QAW	60	64	QUD	47	62
NUY	47	63	PIY	13	66	QAX	27	78	QUG	0	38
NUZ	53	68	POB	47	55	QAY	40	85	QUJ	0	22
NYB	20	78	POF	67	58	QEB	13	48	QUK	20	54
NYF	47	67	POH	20	75	QED	20	72	QUL	27	73
NYG	60	72	POK	93	95	QEF	13	33	QUP	20	58
NYH	33	74	POL	93	99	QEG	27	54	QUR	40	67
NYJ	7	58	POM	80	92	QEH	40	39	QUS	20	69
NYK	53	80	PON	87	94	QEJ	33	24	QUT	40	81
NYL	73	90	POQ	33	72	QEK	40	66	QUV	27	52
NYM	67	70	POS	93	94	QEL	60	78	QUW	7	48
NYP	40	87	POV	53	73	QEM	7	52	QUX	33	43
NYQ	13	65	POW	60	95	QEN	27	55	QUY	33	52
NYR	33	77	POY	53	79	QEP	20	65	QUZ	20	77
NYS	33	71	POZ	47	81	QES	87	85	QYB	13	50
NYT	80	93	PUB	93	85	QET	47	72	QYC	73	79
NYV	27	62	PUD	93	95	QEW	7	67	QYD	27	73
NYW	27	63	PUF	100	100	QEX	13	55	QYF	0	43
NYX	40	86	PUH	40	72	QEY	20	70	QYG	20	32
NYZ	53	48	PUJ	47	73	QEZ	40	75	QYJ	0	18
			PUK	47	83	QIB	47	64	QYK	40	88
PAB	60	60	PUL	93	100	QIC	73	83	QYL	27	79
PAC	100	97	PUM	73	89	QID	20	78	QYP	40	66
PAF	13	41	PUQ	40	83	QIF	0	44	QYR	27	74
PAH	40	85	PUR	93	96	QIG	47	55	QYT	47	82
PAJ	53	65	PUV	40	61	QIH	0	40	QYV	7	59
PAK	87	98	PUW	33	72	QIJ	0	40	QYW	20	39
PAM	80	90	PUX	40	68	QIK	67	91	QYZ	33	68
PAQ	27	88	PUY	40	65	QIL	100	89			
PAS	100	99	PUZ	93	79	QIM	7	58	RAB	93	93
PAV	93	86	PYB	7	33	QIN	33	75	RAC	100	95
PAX	80	83	PYD	20	53	QIP	60	76	RAD	100	95

Syll	G	K	Syll	G	K	Syll	G	K	Syll	G	K
RAF	80	96	RUK	47	76	SIC	93	93	TAC	100	98
RAH	60	100	RUL	93	83	SID	87	97	TAF	67	97
RAJ	87	90	RUP	67	84	SIF	40	90	TAH	20	62
RAK	87	98	RUQ	13	57	SIG	87	94	TAJ	47	70
RAL	100	80	RUS	100	96	SIH	20	78	TAK	100	99
RAQ	73	91	RUV	47	50	SIJ	0	53	TAL	100	93
RAS	93	95	RUW	20	72	SIK	80	96	TAM	100	100
RAV	100	96	RUX	33	65	SIL	93	95	TAQ	67	91
RAX	67	90	RUY	20	56	SIM	67	95	TAS	80	87
RAZ	87	99	RUZ	27	61	SIQ	53	89	TAV	60	71
REB	60	91	RYB	67	82	SIV	73	87	TAW	40	76
REC	80	91	RYC	67	63	SIW	20	71	TAY	60	89
REF	93	93	RYD	53	92	SIY	60	79	TAZ	67	60
REG	100	94	RYF	67	80	SIZ	73	95	TEB	53	68
REH	40	73	RYG	53	86	SOC	100	98	TEC	80	86
REK	87	90	RYH	33	77	SOF	100	96	TEF	20	52
REL	73	95	RYJ	13	74	SOG	73	86	TEG	27	74
REM	93	100	RYK	27	70	SOH	53	87	TEH	33	70
REN	80	86	RYL	60	82	SOJ	33	75	TEJ	40	52
REQ	67	86	RYM	93	93	SOK	73	99	TEK	40	88
RES	87	94	RYN	80	87	SOL	93	100	TEL	93	99
RET	87	95	RYP	80	97	SOM	80	99	TEM	73	89
REV	100	96	RYQ	20	58	SOQ	47	86	TEP	87	86
REW	73	74	RYS	53	85	SOV	93	89	TER	100	95
REY	80	95	RYT	80	91	SOY	80	87	TES	100	98
REZ	33	77	RYV	40	80	SOZ	47	69	TEV	13	43
RIC	93	88	RYW	47	58	SUB	100	91	TEW	27	80
RIF	87	94	RYX	13	57	SUC	73	98	TEX	100	97
RIH	27	57	RYZ	40	85	SUD	93	96	TEY	33	81
RIJ	27	70				SUG	87	89	TEZ	47	65
RIK	53	83	SAB	87	90	SUH	40	87	TIB	73	78
RIL	80	83	SAF	87	86	SUJ	53	61	TIC	100	98
RIN	87	88	SAH	60	81	SUK	60	95	TIF	80	89
RIS	87	85	SAJ	20	72	SUL	87	95	TIG	100	82
RIV	87	95	SAK	93	98	SUQ	27	87	TIH	40	69
RIW	40	51	SAN	80	98	SUR	100	98	TIJ	40	52
RIX	13	63	SAQ	60	89	SUT	100	92	TIK	80	97
RIY	27	72	SAR	100	90	SUW	67	73	TIL	80	100
RIZ	73	85	SAV	93	98	SUX	40	86	TIQ	53	87
ROC	87	97	SAZ	60	84	SUY	33	69	TIR	93	89
ROF	53	85	SEB	13	51	SUZ	67	65	TIS	47	88
ROG	87	94	SEC	93	93	SYC	73	80	TIV	20	51
ROH	67	82	SED	87	99	SYD	60	96	TIW	27	65
ROJ	27	73	SEF	60	66	SYF	40	83	TIX	73	89
ROK	73	94	SEG	67	88	SYG	60	68	TIY	60	86
ROL	67	98	SEH	33	73	SYH	27	66	TIZ	47	68
ROM	100	95	SEJ	33	72	SYJ	13	46	TOB	73	87
RON	80	85	SEK	80	87	SYK	67	91	TOC	53	88
ROP	100	96	SEL	100	88	SYL	87	96	TOF	53	89
ROQ	87	91	SEM	100	90	SYM	73	94	TOG	73	97
ROS	93	95	SEN	80	97	SYN	100	97	TOH	33	74
ROV	100	94	SEP	100	99	SYP	100	90	TOJ	40	53
ROX	73	95	SEQ	67	86	SYQ	20	63	TOK	87	95
ROZ	67	89	SER	100	96	SYR	73	96	TOL	80	98
RUC	33	65	SEV	93	93	SYT	60	90	TOQ	53	68
RUD	100	98	SEY	67	92	SYW	47	56	TOR	87	94
RUF	100	99	SEZ	67	95	SYX	67	80	TOS	93	95
RUH	47	86	SIB	60	74	SYZ	33	75	TOV	0	62
RUJ	93	78							TOX	87	93

Syll	G	K	Syll	G	K	Syll	G	K	Syll	G	K
TOZ	40	69	VEJ	13	57	VUP	33	44	WID	80	90
TUC	80	98	VEK	40	61	VUQ	0	25	WIF	73	93
TUD	47	68	VEL	87	92	VUR	33	61	WIH	47	59
TUF	87	93	VEM	67	81	VUS	40	58	WIJ	40	61
TUH	20	75	VEN	67	93	VUT	47	60	WIK	40	90
TUJ	33	62	VEP	20	65	VUW	27	52	WIL	100	96
TUK	87	95	VEQ	13	57	VUX	7	54	WIM	87	91
TUL	87	82	VER	87	94	VUY	27	60	WIP	87	95
TUM	73	97	VES	100	90	VUZ	20	68	WIQ	47	76
TUN	73	98	VET	93	99	VYB	7	53	WIR	87	87
TUP	67	76	VEW	80	81	VYC	0	82	WIS	100	94
TUQ	33	76	VEY	73	70	VYD	87	59	WIV	73	81
TUR	93	87	VEZ	60	63	VYF	0	64	WIX	27	87
TUS	80	84	VIB	13	63	VYG	27	65	WIY	27	76
TUV	13	68	VIC	100	97	VYH	40	29	WIZ	87	94
TUW	27	75	VID	40	57	VYJ	0	24	WOB	53	71
TUX	80	96	VIF	100	61	VYK	67	71	WOD	87	89
TUY	47	78	VIG	27	84	VYL	73	68	WOF	73	76
TUZ	33	68	VIH	20	69	VYM	47	89	WOG	7	67
TYB	53	66	VIJ	40	43	VYN	40	83	WOH	40	83
TYD	60	83	VIK	100	95	VYP	27	65	WOJ	7	45
TYF	20	79	VIL	93	88	VYQ	0	46	WOK	67	86
TYH	27	77	VIN	100	93	VYR	47	60	WOL	87	90
TYJ	33	44	VIP	53	77	VYS	47	65	WOM	100	92
TYK	40	92	VIR	93	89	VYT	20	65	WOQ	33	60
TYL	80	94	VIS	100	91	VYW	7	47	WOR	87	93
TYM	67	96	VIT	67	88	VYX	7	76	WOS	20	74
TYN	67	94	VIW	47	75	VYZ	20	54	WOV	73	84
TYP	93	97	VIX	40	93				WOY	33	65
TYQ	20	67	VOB	27	48				WOZ	27	74
TYR	73	92	VOC	27	78	WAB	67	77	WUB	0	54
TYS	40	69	VOD	47	68	WAC	67	89	WUC	20	42
TYV	33	43	VOF	27	30	WAF	73	90	WUD	80	80
TYW	13	53	VOG	40	85	WAH	47	83	WUF	60	86
TYX	33	84	VOH	13	39	WAJ	20	57	WUG	13	51
TYZ	13	71	VOJ	20	58	WAK	100	88	WUH	0	57
			VOK	53	73	WAM	67	90	WUJ	7	39
VAB	47	46	VOL	93	97	WAP	33	91	WUK	33	73
VAC	100	97	VOM	53	86	WAQ	60	79	WUL	80	77
VAD	27	76	VON	47	79	WAT	100	95	WUM	60	84
VAF	0	57	VOP	27	69	WAV	87	94	WUN	60	96
VAG	73	94	VOQ	33	58	WAZ	47	77	WUP	13	72
VAH	40	64	VOR	33	62	WEC	60	61	WUQ	0	44
VAJ	40	53	VOS	67	76	WEF	20	67	WUR	67	82
VAK	20	84	VOT	67	93	WEG	40	86	WUS	47	80
VAM	73	71	VOX	60	81	WEH	47	76	WUT	20	70
VAP	53	89	VOY	73	88	WEJ	40	80	WUV	33	53
VAQ	53	76	VOZ	47	69	WEK	60	72	WUY	47	75
VAR	93	85	VUB	60	43	WEM	53	69	WYB	20	58
VAS	93	96	VUC	33	58	WEN	80	94	WYC	60	79
VAW	47	51	VUD	27	47	WEP	53	80	WYD	53	85
VAX	80	83	VUF	7	39	WEQ	20	53	WYF	40	88
VAY	53	75	VUG	73	64	WER	73	92	WYG	27	83
VAZ	33	84	VUH	7	38	WES	80	91	WYH	20	67
VEB	47	58	VUJ	27	49	WEV	100	78	WYJ	27	62
VEC	0	67	VUK	0	44	WEX	53	86	WYK	53	75
VED	33	50	VUL	60	93	WEY	73	89	WYM	60	78
VEF	27	45	VUM	20	66	WEZ	7	72	WYP	53	81
VEG	87	84	VUN	33	72	WIB	33	58	WYQ	33	75
						WIC	80	96			

Syll	G	K	Syll	G	K	Syll	G	K	Syll	G	K
WYR	60	78	XIZ	27	30	YAN	40	64	YUD	0	39
WYS	53	76	XOB	13	38	YAP	40	89	YUF	0	49
WYT	53	87	XOC	20	45	YAS	60	99	YUG	47	59
WYV	7	66	XOD	40	50	YAT	47	79	YUH	27	75
WYX	20	63	XOF	20	29	YAV	7	49	YUJ	7	37
WYZ	53	90	XOG	27	39	YAX	53	62	YUK	40	59
			XOH	20	40	YAZ	7	79	YUL	53	86
XAB	7	45	XOJ	7	14	YEB	27	30	YUM	33	89
XAD	0	42	XOK	20	43	YEC	27	51	YUN	20	67
XAF	20	31	XOL	27	47	YED	27	59	YUP	27	62
XAH	7	27	XOM	33	41	YEF	27	47	YUQ	7	29
XAJ	7	42	XON	13	55	YEG	80	86	YUR	53	86
XAK	40	49	XOP	27	45	YEH	80	85	YUS	20	85
XAL	7	53	XOQ	20	53	YEJ	27	54	YUT	93	58
XAM	87	88	XOR	27	59	YEK	7	41	YUV	0	37
XAN	53	54	XOT	27	74	YEL	93	99	YUW	20	63
XAP	20	45	XOV	13	36	YEM	0	64	YUX	20	44
XAQ	7	31	XOW	47	46	YEP	80	93	YUZ	0	73
XAR	13	49	XOY	27	47	YEQ	33	35			
XAS	60	57	XUB	7	43	YER	67	84	ZAB	33	53
XAT	0	49	XUC	0	31	YEX	33	60	ZAC	27	77
XAV	7	72	XUD	7	51	YEZ	53	95	ZAD	47	72
XAW	13	57	XUF	13	23	YIB	13	39	ZAF	27	48
XAY	20	59	XUG	20	42	YIC	20	42	ZAG	60	72
XAZ	13	39	XUH	0	24	YID	40	84	ZAH	40	39
XEB	7	22	XUJ	13	22	YIF	7	56	ZAJ	7	51
XEC	33	40	XUK	0	35	YIH	13	31	ZAK	53	77
XED	33	53	XUL	7	51	YIJ	13	24	ZAL	27	65
XEF	0	23	XUM	0	60	YIL	0	57	ZAM	53	71
XEG	13	34	XUN	53	51	YIM	0	50	ZAN	40	65
XEH	0	23	XUQ	7	19	YIQ	13	37	ZAP	33	81
XEJ	0	18	XUR	0	45	YIR	40	66	ZAQ	27	69
XEL	53	73	XUS	20	50	YIS	60	79	ZAR	67	79
XEM	60	66	XUT	20	55	YIT	47	71	ZAS	13	55
XEN	33	65	XUV	0	26	YIW	7	38	ZAT	13	83
XEP	40	56	XUW	0	32	YIX	7	34	ZAV	33	68
XEQ	0	42	XUY	0	29	YIZ	27	61	ZAW	13	79
XER	60	55	XYB	0	36	YOB	47	62	ZAX	13	60
XET	27	61	XYC	20	32	YOC	27	62	ZAY	33	70
XEV	27	28	XYD	7	37	YOD	33	63	ZEB	53	73
XEW	20	48	XYF	0	22	YOF	0	23	ZEC	20	51
XEY	13	35	XYG	7	28	YOG	40	55	ZED	27	72
XEZ	7	36	XYH	0	19	YOH	13	63	ZEF	20	65
XIB	33	36	XYJ	0	21	YOJ	20	23	ZEG	7	38
XIC	40	42	XYK	0	34	YOK	93	85	ZEH	13	46
XID	13	50	XYL	13	55	YOL	27	63	ZEJ	0	42
XIF	7	41	XYN	47	40	YOM	7	63	ZEK	73	60
XIG	13	53	XYQ	7	23	YON	80	91	ZEL	33	74
XIH	0	30	XYT	7	53	YOP	0	56	ZEM	53	61
XIJ	7	29	XYV	0	30	YOQ	7	41	ZEN	47	58
XIK	33	55	XYW	7	30	YOR	47	91	ZEP	53	91
XIM	27	41	XYZ	47	79	YOS	40	73	ZEQ	0	35
XIN	27	50				YOT	13	66	ZER	20	62
XIQ	7	39	YAB	13	50	YOV	0	39	ZES	40	71
XIR	53	44	YAC	93	67	YOW	20	85	ZET	53	54
XIS	40	38	YAD	47	43	YOX	7	49	ZEV	20	56
XIV	0	42	YAG	27	53	YOZ	7	51	ZEW	40	67
XIW	0	16	YAH	27	88	YUB	13	46	ZEX	0	63
XIY	7	19	YAL	67	85	YUC	27	53	ZEY	20	66

Syll	G	K	Syll	G	K	Syll	G	K	Syll	G	K
ZIB	20	57	ZIY	13	42	ZOW	7	83	ZUY	7	36
ZIC	20	58	ZOB	13	43	ZOX	27	68	ZYB	7	46
ZID	20	64	ZOC	27	59	ZUB	7	60	ZYC	13	56
ZIF	0	60	ZOD	33	64	ZUC	27	61	ZYD	0	53
ZIG	60	82	ZOF	7	55	ZUD	27	58	ZYF	13	49
ZIH	7	55	ZOG	13	65	ZUF	7	54	ZYG	0	57
ZIJ	27	46	ZOH	7	60	ZUH	7	43	ZYH	13	33
ZIK	7	61	ZOJ	0	41	ZUJ	13	30	ZYK	13	45
ZIL	0	71	ZOK	13	70	ZUK	0	63	ZYL	13	69
ZIM	47	64	ZOL	27	72	ZUL	53	59	ZYP	33	90
ZIN	13	69	ZOM	13	67	ZUM	0	74	ZYQ	0	42
ZIQ	0	34	ZON	33	74	ZUN	40	77	ZYR	13	55
ZIR	13	64	ZOP	20	70	ZUP	7	82	ZYS	0	70
ZIS	13	76	ZOQ	27	44	ZUR	20	66	ZYT	0	65
ZIT	33	79	ZOR	20	74	ZUS	20	55	ZYV	0	43
ZIV	7	60	ZOS	7	43	ZUT	13	58	ZYW	0	31
ZIW	0	31	ZOT	7	64	ZUW	20	27	ZYX	20	56
ZIX	20	69	ZOV	13	54	ZUX	20	41			

ASSOCIATION OR MEANINGFULNESS VALUES
FOR 4,524 CONSONANT SYLLABLES

The values were determined by Witmer. Five duplicate syllables have been removed from the list as given by Witmer. (Witmer, L. R. The association value of three-place consonant syllables. *J. genet. Psychol.*, 1935, 47, 337–360. Courtesy, The Journal Press.)

0%	4%	8%		13%			17%
QJF	BQJ	BHJ	XGQ	BPJ	QXF	ZQC	BFM
QJH	CXJ	BJH	XHF	BQF	QXH	ZQG	BJQ
XFQ	DJX	CJQ	XHJ	CFJ	QXL	ZQH	BMF
XJQ	FHJ	CJX	XHM	CFQ	QZB	ZQS	BQZ
XZF	GCJ	CQH	XJH	CGJ	QZH	ZTF	BWF
ZGJ	GJQ	CXQ	XQG	CGP	QZJ	ZTJ	CJZ
ZJF	GJX	DHJ	XZD	CGQ	QZM	ZTX	CQZ
ZJQ	GQC	DJB	XZJ	CJH	SBQ	ZWJ	CSF
ZQJ	GQJ	DJQ	ZCJ	CQJ	SBZ	ZXG	CWH
ZXJ	GXK	FCJ	ZCX	CXK	SJF		CXF
ZXQ	GXM	FJH	ZFK	DJW	SZJ		CXH
	HFC	FJQ	ZGW	DJZ	TFJ		CXZ
	JFH	FQH	ZHW	DXJ	TFQ		CZJ
	KHX	FQW	ZJC	FHC	TJW		DJH
	KQF	FXQ	ZJT	FPC	TZF		DJS
	KQX	GCQ	ZJX	FPW	TZQ		DQH
	KXB	GJC	ZQX	FQC	WBF		DWB
	MHZ	GQB	ZSJ	FQJ	WCF		FCQ
	MZJ	GXC	ZSQ	GCX	WCQ		FJC
	QGJ	GXQ	ZTK	GCZ	WQH		FJS
	QHJ	HBJ	ZWQ	GKX	WZQ		FJW
	QXB	HFK	ZXC	GQK	XBF		FPJ
	QXJ	HJC	ZXH	GXJ	XBN		FQK
	QXN	JFQ	ZXK	HCJ	XCJ		FWJ
	XBQ	JQF	ZXR	HJX	XDJ		FWQ
	XFJ	JXF		HKM	XFK		GKQ
	XJB	JXQ		HXF	XFP		GKZ
	XJF	KFQ		JCF	XFZ		GXZ
	XKH	KQB		JFC	XGK		GZB
	XMJ	KQH		JFN	XGP		GZK
	XQF	KQZ		JQZ	XGZ		GZQ
	XQH	KXC		JXB	XJC		HBM
	XQJ	KXD		JZH	XKB		HCZ
	XQL	KXH		KBF	XKQ		HFJ
	XTJ	MHJ		KFZ	XNZ		HFM
	XZQ	MHW		KMF	XMZ		HJF
	ZBJ	MJF		KXQ	XQB		HWC
	ZFJ	MWB		KXZ	XQD		HXB
	ZFQ	MZB		KZF	XSZ		HXJ
	ZGX	QCF		KZG	XTG		HXQ
	ZHJ	QDX		KZH	XZC		HZW
	ZJH	QFC		KZS	XZK		JBP
	ZQB	QFH		LCF	XZL		JDF
	ZQF	QGW		LHJ	ZBF		JDH
	ZQW	QGX		MCF	ZBG		JDW
	ZXB	QHN		MFH	ZBH		JFM
	ZXF	QJC		MHB	ZBQ		JHC
		QLJ		MQJ	ZCQ		JHF
		QSJ		MWJ	ZDH		JHW
		TZH		QBJ	ZDW		JQH
		WBH		QCZ	ZFC		JQW
		WBJ		QDJ	ZFW		JSB
		WBQ		QFX	ZHK		JTQ
		WFC		QFZ	ZHX		JXH
		XBJ		QGC	ZKG		JZF
		XDH		QHF	ZKH		KBH
		XFH		QJS	ZLC		KBP
		XFS		QMH	ZMC		KFX
		XGC		QWJ	ZMX		KHB

17% (cont.)			21%				25%
KHF	WBN	ZRJ	BFJ	HWZ	PXJ	WJQ	ZSB	BFP
KHQ	WCJ	ZSF	BFQ	HZC	PXZ	WLJ	ZSG	BFX
KQM	WCZ	ZTW	BFZ	HZF	PZB	WPJ	ZTD	BGQ
KQW	WGP	ZWC	BJS	HZQ	QBF	WQC	ZTQ	BJG
KWQ	WJH	ZWF	BQD	JBW	QBN	WQF	ZXS	BJW
KXN	WQB	ZXD	BQH	JCM	QDH	WQJ		BJX
KXR	WZC	ZXL	BTP	JCW	QDM	WQL		BMJ
KZX	XBD		BWJ	JFS	QFM	WSF		BPX
LJF	XBH		BWQ	JFX	QFN	WSZ		BXF
LJX	XBM		BXP	JFZ	QFW	WZG		BXH
MBH	XBZ		BZJ	JGC	QGD	WZH		BXJ
MBW	XCZ		BZQ	JGP	QGK	XBK		BXZ
MBX	XDF		CFP	JHX	QGZ	XCF		BZP
MGQ	XDL		CFX	JLC	QHD	XCG		BZW
MHF	XFC		CJF	JQC	QHL	XDZ		BZX
MQB	XFM		CJS	JQD	QHW	XHZ		CFZ
MWF	XGJ		CJW	JQS	QJZ	XJM		CGW
MWZ	XHC		CSJ	JWF	QKB	XMC		CGZ
MZQ	XHQ		CXP	JXL	QKH	XMG		CJG
NCF	XJL		DBJ	KBQ	QKX	XNB		CKM
NFB	XJP		DHX	KBW	QLX	XNF		CMJ
NPB	XJS		DJF	KFH	QMK	XQC		CPJ
NQF	XJZ		DJL	KFS	QWG	XQK		CWF
NQS	XKF		DLZ	KHC	QXM	XRH		CWJ
NQX	XKG		DXK	KMH	QXS	XRJ		CWQ
NZK	XKR		FBJ	KMQ	QZF	XSJ		CXS
PJF	XKZ		FBM	KQC	QZW	XTF		CZG
PJZ	XLJ		FBX	KXF	QZX	XZB		CZQ
PXB	XLZ		FCM	KZB	RCJ	XZH		CZT
PXH	XNJ		FHW	KZQ	RJW	XZN		DBX
PZW	XNQ		FJP	LCP	RKH	XZS		DFZ
QCJ	XQM		FPH	LCZ	RLJ	ZBX		DHL
QCM	XQN		FPN	LJB	RWH	ZCF		DHW
QFJ	XSB		FQS	LJH	RWJ	ZCP		DKQ
QFK	XSG		FQZ	LJQ	RXF	ZCW		DLF
QFS	XTD		FSJ	LJS	RZJ	ZDF		DLX
QHX	XZG		FXB	LJW	SFJ	ZDG		DQL
QJB	XZM		FZJ	LNP	SFM	ZFB		DZF
QJM	ZDJ		FZK	LSF	SJZ	ZFN		FHK
QJW	ZDL		FZP	LZQ	SZK	ZFP		FHQ
QJX	ZFH		FZQ	MBJ	TCF	ZFS		FHX
QLB	ZFM		GJW	MBQ	TCJ	ZGC		FJM
QLN	ZFX		GKN	MCJ	TFM	ZGK		FJZ
QWB	ZGB		GQN	MFB	TFW	ZHC		FKP
QXG	ZGQ		GQW	MFP	TFZ	ZHF		FKQ
QXZ	ZJB		GSQ	MFX	TJB	ZHL		FKZ
QZK	ZJL		GSZ	MJW	TJH	ZJD		FNX
RBM	ZJN		GWZ	MWQ	TJZ	ZJP		FPB
RJX	ZJW		GZN	MZC	TLF	ZJS		FPX
SBH	ZKB		GZW	NFQ	TLN	ZKM		FXJ
SGJ	ZKX		HBF	NLQ	TQF	ZKN		FXK
SJH	ZLJ		HBX	NQJ	TZJ	ZKQ		FXZ
SXH	ZLQ		HJL	NQK	WBK	ZLG		FZB
TCZ	ZMF		HJQ	NKQ	WBM	ZLR		FZH
TGJ	ZMJ		HJW	NZX	WDB	ZLW		FZM
TJF	ZMW		HKB	PBJ	WFB	ZMQ		FZW
TJQ	ZNW		HWB	PCJ	WFQ	ZPF		GBQ
TZW	ZPB		HWF	PJX	WGC	ZQD		GCM
TZX	ZQL		HWQ	PXF	WGJ	ZQK		GCS

25% (cont.)				29%				
GDQ	KFC	QDG	WTK	BDF	FMJ	JSF	MFC	RHF
GJS	KFM	QDK	WZM	BHW	FMQ	JSG	MFW	RHJ
GJZ	KFN	QDL	WZP	BHX	FMX	JSQ	MGJ	RJB
GKB	KGX	QDN	XBP	BHZ	FMZ	JTF	MHC	RJM
GKD	KHZ	QGL	XCQ	BJF	FPM	JTH	MJZ	RLB
GKM	KSF	QHC	XCS	BJP	FPZ	JWC	MKF	RLW
GKW	KSX	QJG	XDB	BMW	FQD	JWH	MZP	RMC
GMJ	KSZ	QJN	XDM	BPN	FQM	JXD	MZX	RWC
GMK	KTB	QKZ	XFB	BPW	FSQ	JXG	NCP	RWZ
GNB	KWF	QLH	XHK	BPZ	FWB	JXR	NDB	RXB
GNC	KXP	QMF	XHN	BWP	FWP	JXZ	NDW	RXC
GPJ	KZC	QMJ	XJG	BXK	FXH	JZC	NFP	RXT
GQZ	LDH	QMX	XJT	BXM	FXM	JZQ	NKB	RXZ
GWB	LFJ	QSF	XKD	BZF	GBJ	JZS	NKF	RZC
GWQ	LJC	QSL	XLC	CFH	GCK	JZW	NKZ	RZX
GXT	LJD	QSW	XLG	CFM	GCN	KBX	NLC	SBM
GZJ	LQJ	QSX	XLH	CGK	GCW	KCM	NLP	SBP
HCF	LRP	QWF	XLR	CKH	GJB	KCQ	NPC	SDB
HCX	LXJ	QZL	XMB	CKN	GJL	KDF	NQH	SGB
HFP	LZJ	RGW	XMF	CKQ	GPN	KFW	NQW	SGQ
HFQ	MBF	RHK	XMH	CNQ	GPW	KGC	NQZ	SJB
HFZ	MFJ	RJF	XMQ	CPX	GQL	KMC	NXF	SJG
HJB	MKR	RJL	XNP	CQF	GQS	KPW	NXJ	SZC
HJN	MQD	RJP	XQS	CQW	GSJ	KQD	NXL	SZF
HJS	MQF	RMF	XSF	CSZ	GSM	KQN	NXR	SZG
HJT	MQZ	RMJ	XTQ	CTJ	GSW	KQS	PBZ	SZM
HKQ	MWC	RWF	XZP	CWZ	GXB	KSB	PFH	SZX
HKW	MZF	SBG	XZR	CXG	GZC	KTQ	PFJ	TDH
HKZ	MZW	SBX	XZT	CXM	HBN	KWB	PFZ	TFC
HMC	NCQ	SDH	ZBP	CZF	HCQ	KWZ	PGW	TJC
HNQ	NCW	SFH	ZBW	CZH	HFS	KXG	PJC	TKF
HXL	NDJ	SFP	ZCG	CZL	HJZ	KXS	PJL	TLJ
HXZ	NFC	SGC	ZCS	CZX	HKP	KZD	PJW	TQB
HZB	NFJ	SGW	ZDB	DFJ	HKX	KZM	PSX	TQZ
JBG	NFL	SGZ	ZDT	DJG	HNF	KZN	PXC	TWB
JBH	NFX	SHJ	ZDX	DJM	HNP	KZW	PZC	TZB
JBN	NKR	SJQ	ZFL	DLH	HNX	LBJ	PZX	WBG
JBQ	NLX	SJW	ZGP	DLJ	HQX	LBW	QBM	WCM
JBX	NQG	SZB	ZHB	DLQ	HTJ	LCJ	QBZ	WCP
JCN	NWL	SZH	ZHQ	DQF	HWJ	LDB	QCG	WCS
JCQ	NXQ	SZQ	ZJG	DQK	HXC	LDF	QDB	WDQ
JCZ	NZG	TFH	ZJM	DXG	HXK	LFP	QFD	WFM
JDT	NZR	TFP	ZKF	DXP	HXN	LGP	QGB	WFZ
JFW	PBF	TFX	ZLB	DZH	HXR	LHB	QGT	WGB
JGQ	PJH	TJL	ZLS	FBH	HZK	LHN	QHB	WGQ
JHB	PMW	TJX	ZLX	FBP	JFP	LHX	QHK	WHB
JQX	PWJ	TKZ	ZMK	FBZ	JHL	LJG	QJL	WHJ
JSW	PWZ	TQJ	ZNB	FCK	JHQ	LRH	QKF	WJC
JTB	PZF	TQM	ZNQ	FCZ	JLH	LSJ	QKM	WJG
JTW	PZH	TZG	ZPG	FDB	JLQ	LWG	QLG	WJP
JWB	PZJ	TZK	ZPX	FDK	JLX	LWH	QLW	WLQ
JWP	PZK	WBP	ZWB	FJB	JLZ	LXP	QMB	WQG
JWQ	QBW	WBT	ZXM	FKB	JMC	LZC	QMG	WSG
JZN	QBX	WDK	ZXP	FKC	JMF	LZH	QMH	WSJ
JZP	QCH	WFH	ZXT	FKH	JMH	MBT	QNF	WZB
KCF	QCN	WJF		FKM	JNF	MBZ	QNW	WZL
KDB	QCS	WJL		FKW	JPF	MCG	QSB	WZN
KDH	QCW	WJM		FKX	JQB	MCQ	QZG	WZS
KDQ	QDF	WQZ		FMH	JQN	MCW	RGJ	XCM

29% (cont.) 33%								38%
XCP	BDH	DXH	JBT	LHD	NXZ	SJX	XDN	BDJ
XDP	BFH	DXL	JBZ	LHF	NZB	SKQ	XDS	BDK
XPQ	BFN	DZJ	JCG	LHW	NZJ	SMF	XGB	BGZ
XGD	BFW	DZQ	JCH	LJP	NZP	SQZ	XGL	BHL
XHB	BGP	FBQ	JCR	LJT	NZQ	SXZ	XHD	BHQ
XJD	BHF	FCH	JDL	LJZ	PBW	SZP	XLP	BJD
XJN	BJM	FCW	JFB	LNF	PCZ	SZW	XNL	BNP
XKM	BMG	FDQ	JFD	LPB	PGB	TDF	XPB	BNW
XKN	BMH	FHZ	JGB	LPF	PJB	TDJ	XPH	BPM
XLN	BMX	FJX	JGT	LRB	PMF	TDQ	XRL	BQG
XLQ	BMZ	FKS	JGW	LRJ	PNB	TFB	XRP	BQN
XPJ	BPF	FMK	JLB	LSZ	PWH	TFK	XSD	BQW
XQZ	BQL	FMW	JLF	LXB	PXL	TGB	XTZ	BSF
XTL	BWZ	FNQ	JNB	LXH	PZT	TGP	ZBK	BSJ
XTN	BZG	FQL	JNW	LZX	QDW	TGZ	ZBT	BSX
ZCM	BZH	FQN	JPC	MBD	QDZ	TJD	ZHD	BTQ
ZCN	CFL	FSZ	JQG	MBG	QFB	TJG	ZKP	BWH
ZDP	CFS	FWC	JQL	MBK	QGN	TJP	ZKT	BZK
ZDQ	CFW	FWH	JQM	MFQ	QGS	TKD	ZMB	BZS
ZGS	CGX	FWZ	JRL	MFZ	QJD	TLH	ZNL	CFK
ZHM	CJM	FXP	JRP	MGB	QKC	TLQ	ZRP	CGM
ZKC	CJN	FZC	JSC	MJB	QLC	TLZ	ZRW	CHJ
ZKD	CKF	GBM	JTL	MJH	QLF	TMF	ZRX	CJT
ZKS	CMH	GDW	JWZ	MJT	QLZ	TNB	ZSD	CKZ
ZLH	CMZ	GKP	JXN	MJX	QMZ	TNW	ZSL	CMQ
ZMG	CNP	GKR	JZM	MQC	QNL	TQH	ZWG	CNX
ZMH	CPF	GKT	JZT	MQG	QSG	TQW	ZWK	CPW
ZNF	CPG	GMX	JZX	MQH	QSM	TWH		CQG
ZPC	CPM	GNP	KBG	MQK	QWS	TXJ		CQK
ZPJ	CPZ	GNQ	KBM	MQW	QXC	TZC		CQL
ZPW	CQN	GNX	KCG	MQX	QXD	TZD		CQS
ZQM	CSQ	GPZ	KCX	MWP	QZC	TZL		CRJ
ZQN	CSW	GQM	KDT	MXB	RBH	WBD		CSM
ZRF	CSX	GTD	KDW	NCH	RBW	WBS		CZM
ZSW	CXL	GWC	KFP	NDP	RBZ	WCL		CZS
ZTB	CXR	GXN	KGP	NDQ	RCG	WCN		DBP
ZTC	CZP	HBP	KGQ	NDT	RCZ	WFJ		DBZ
ZTG	CZW	HBZ	KHD	NFK	RHC	WFN		DFH
ZTL	DBF	HCW	KHM	NFS	RHX	WGZ		DFS
ZTM	DBG	HDM	KMT	NGK	RHZ	WHC		DHB
ZWH	DBQ	HFB	KMW	NJH	RJC	WJD		DHF
ZWP	DBW	HFW	KMX	NJW	RKB	WJS		DJP
ZWS	DFQ	HJD	KMZ	NKC	RLC	WKF		DLN
ZXN	DFW	HJM	KRH	NLF	RMW	WKH		DPG
	DFX	HJP	KSN	NLJ	RPB	WLC		DPK
	DHK	HKF	KSQ	NLR	RPJ	WNB		DPX
	DHQ	HKR	KTM	NPF	RPW	WNJ		DSF
	DHZ	HLC	KTW	NQB	RXJ	WNQ		DSQ
	DJN	HLJ	KWC	NQC	RXK	WPZ		DSZ
	DKH	HLQ	KWG	NQD	RZF	WQK		DTJ
	DLB	HMJ	KXM	NQL	RZH	WQS		DWL
	DMX	HSZ	KZP	NRB	RZL	WSQ		DXQ
	DQJ	HWN	LBF	NRF	SBJ	WTJ		DZB
	DQS	HXP	LBZ	NRL	SBK	WTP		FBT
	DQW	HZJ	LCS	NRX	SBW	WZK		FBW
	DSW	HZP	LDJ	NSX	SDZ	WZT		FCP
	DWJ	HZT	LDP	NTP	SGP	XBL		FDH
	DXB	HZX	LDX	NWB	SHB	XCK		FDP
	DXF	JBF	LHC	NWD	SJM	XCN		FDX

38% (cont.)						42%		
FHD	JCS	LGB	PJT	SZL	XPF	BDP	DTQ	HKT
FHM	JCX	LGW	PMG	TCX	XPZ	BFK	DWM	HMK
FHP	JDQ	LGZ	PMZ	TDK	XRB	BGK	DWZ	HNL
FJT	JGX	LHP	PNX	TGL	XRF	BGW	DXS	HPB
FMC	JGZ	LHZ	PWB	TGM	XSN	BHD	DXZ	HQJ
FNP	JHD	LNW	PWG	TGW	XTC	BHK	DZK	HQN
FPR	JHM	LQB	PWM	THL	XTK	BHP	DZM	HQW
FSB	JHP	LQG	PXT	TJM	XTP	BJL	DZP	HRC
FSP	JHZ	LQH	PZG	TKH	ZBD	BJR	DZW	HRJ
FSW	JMG	LQZ	PZM	TNF	ZBL	BMK	FBD	HSJ
FWM	JMX	LSG	PZR	TNL	ZBN	BPH	FBN	HWD
GBP	JNL	LSW	PZS	TQC	ZDN	BQK	FCS	HWM
GJD	JNQ	LTB	QBG	TQD	ZDS	BQS	FDM	HXS
GJM	JNZ	LWB	QBH	TQK	ZFR	BSD	FHL	HZR
GKC	JPH	LWC	QBK	TQL	ZGD	BSG	FJD	HZS
GKS	JPM	LWJ	QCX	TWF	ZGL	BSZ	FJL	JBD
GMZ	JPW	LXF	QDS	TWJ	ZGM	BTG	FJN	JDB
GPX	JPX	LXQ	QFL	TWZ	ZKR	BTW	FMB	JDM
GQD	JRF	LZG	QGM	TZM	ZLD	BXL	FNW	JDP
GSN	JSD	LZS	QKD	TZP	ZLF	BZM	FNZ	JDS
GSX	JSX	MCZ	QSD	WCG	ZLN	CFN	FPD	JDX
GTK	JTM	MFK	QSN	WDM	ZLP	CFR	FPK	JFT
GTM	JTP	MGP	QTX	WDP	ZNJ	CGL	FPL	JGN
GTW	JTX	MGW	QWD	WFK	ZNR	CGT	FQB	JLD
GWJ	JWD	MHX	QWZ	WFP	ZPK	CJP	FRB	JLN
GWP	JWR	MJQ	QXK	WJB	ZPM	CKP	FSC	JLW
GXD	JXC	MPB	QZD	WJT	ZPN	CKX	FSM	JMQ
GXR	JXM	MPF	RBF	WLB	ZRB	CMW	FSX	JPG
GXS	JZB	MWH	RBJ	WLG	ZRH	CNF	FWK	JSL
GZP	JZG	MXJ	RBX	WLR	ZSC	CNS	FXC	JSN
HBK	KBD	MXZ	RCW	WLZ	ZSH	CSN	FZL	JTZ
HCS	KBN	MZG	RFH	WMB	ZSM	CWP	FZN	JWN
HDJ	KBS	MZK	RFK	WMC	ZSN	CWM	FZS	JZR
HDP	KCW	NBH	RGP	WNL	ZSX	CWR	FZX	KBZ
HFL	KCZ	NBP	RGX	WPF	ZTN	CZK	GBN	KDP
HFN	KDZ	NDF	RGZ	WPH	ZWD	DBH	GDJ	KDR
HKC	KGB	NGB	RHW	WRB		DBN	GDM	KFB
HLB	KHP	NGJ	RLP	WRF		DFB	GJP	KFD
HLF	KHR	NKW	RTF	WSM		DFK	GJR	KGD
HLW	KHS	NLB	RWB	WZF		DFN	GJT	KGM
HLX	KHW	NPJ	RXH	WZR		DGZ	GLJ	KGW
HMF	KNZ	NPW	RXL	XBG		DHM	GMQ	KGZ
HMW	KQG	NPZ	RXN	XBT		DJR	GSB	KMB
HNB	KPB	NRZ	RZM	XDG		DKM	GSC	KMG
HNJ	KQT	NSF	SBF	XDK		DLG	GSK	KMR
HNW	KRZ	NSQ	SCZ	XFL		DMH	GTB	KNQ
HQL	KSW	NWC	SDQ	XFN		DMJ	GTX	KNR
HQZ	KTF	NWQ	SFC	XFR		DMQ	GTZ	KNS
HSF	KTP	NWZ	SFL	XGS		DNL	GZM	KRF
HSN	KTX	NXD	SFQ	XHR		DNQ	GZR	KSG
HTB	KWR	NXG	SHZ	XHL		DPF	GZX	KTG
HWP	KXT	NXS	SMB	XHS		DPJ	HBD	KWS
HWR	KZT	NZT	SNJ	XKC		DPZ	HBQ	KZR
HXD	LBP	PBS	SWQ	XKS		DQZ	HCM	LBH
HXT	LBQ	PFW	SXB	XKT		DSB	HCT	LCW
HZN	LBT	PFX	SXG	XLB		DSJ	HDF	LDT
JBL	LBX	PHF	SXK	XLF		DSX	HDK	LFQ
JCL	LFB	PJD	SXL	XMK		DTG	HFX	LFX
JCP	LFC	PJM	SXQ	XNR		DTK	HKD	LGQ

42% (cont.)				45%				
LGX	PBG	SDK	XNK	BDQ	FNJ	KDX	NTC	RGB
LHQ	PBH	SDP	XNS	BDT	FRH	KGN	NWF	RGK
LHR	PBN	SDW	XPC	BDX	FRP	KGT	NWG	RGM
LHS	PGX	SFZ	XPG	BGX	FSD	KPD	NWJ	RHL
LJN	PGZ	SGK	XPM	BJZ	FZG	KPH	NWP	RHP
LPJ	PJS	SHX	XRC	BKM	FZR	KPM	NXH	RKM
LPN	PKH	SJC	XRG	BMQ	FZT	KPN	NZC	RLG
LQF	PLF	SJL	XRN	BMR	GBW	KPZ	NZF	RLH
LQN	PMC	SJP	XRZ	BNF	GCR	KRC	NZL	RLN
LQX	PNR	SMZ	XSL	BNJ	GDX	KRP	PBD	RMB
LRC	PSJ	SXC	XSM	BNL	GDZ	KRW	PBR	RMZ
LRF	PWF	SXF	XSQ	BPG	GJN	KSH	PBT	RNC
LRX	PWK	SXJ	XTM	BPT	GLQ	KTR	PBX	RPF
LSX	PXK	SZD	ZDK	BTD	GMW	KWD	PCF	RPH
LWZ	PXM	TCG	ZFT	BTX	GNL	KWM	PCM	RPK
LZP	PXN	TCP	ZGT	BWG	GPC	LCN	PDB	RTK
LZW	PZN	TCQ	ZKW	BXQ	GPK	LGJ	PFB	RTP
MBP	QBD	TCW	ZNP	BZL	GPL	LNJ	PFC	RTW
MBS	QBL	TDM	ZNX	CJL	GTJ	LNQ	PFK	RWK
MCP	QCL	TDZ	ZQT	CMF	GTL	LPW	PFM	RWL
MFS	QHM	TFD	ZRD	CNJ	GTP	LPX	PFN	RWM
MHD	QHZ	TGN	ZRL	CNZ	GTQ	LRZ	PGJ	RXM
MHK	QJT	TGQ	ZTP	CPN	GWM	LSB	PGT	RXP
MJD	QKG	TJN	ZWL	CSG	GWS	LSC	PHJ	RZG
MKP	QKN	TKM	ZWN	CTF	GXL	LSQ	PHK	RZN
MKW	QKT	TKP	ZWR	CTK	HDT	LTC	PJN	RZW
MXH	QKW	TKQ		CTW	HDW	LWF	PMH	SBN
MXQ	QNG	TLB		CXT	HDZ	LWP	PMK	SCJ
NBG	QNJ	TLC		DGB	HKN	LWQ	PNJ	SCQ
NBX	QNX	TMC		DGJ	HMX	LXG	PNW	SDJ
NCJ	QSZ	TMJ		DGK	HPF	LZB	PRJ	SDX
NCS	QTF	TMZ		DGW	HPW	LZF	PSB	SFB
NDZ	QTM	TPB		DHS	HPX	MGZ	PSK	SFW
NFH	QWC	TQX		DKB	HQK	MHR	PTC	SGX
NFW	QWM	TXH		DKF	HSD	MJP	PTL	SJN
NGQ	RCP	TZN		DKG	HSQ	MKC	PTM	SKB
NGW	RFB	WBL		DKP	HSW	MKH	PWC	SLJ
NHL	RFJ	WBZ		DKT	HTF	MKQ	PXG	SMJ
NJF	RGC	WCR		DKW	HTK	MKZ	PZL	SNX
NJQ	RJD	WDH		DLW	HXM	MPW	QBS	SQG
NJS	RJG	WDJ		DMF	JDN	MWD	QBT	SQJ
NJT	RJH	WDZ		DMW	JDZ	MXS	QDT	SQK
NJX	RJN	WGK		DNZ	JFL	MZD	QMS	SXP
NKP	RKP	WJN		DPB	JHR	MZT	QND	TBD
NLD	RKZ	WKB		DPM	JHT	NBT	QNZ	TCM
NLH	RMH	WKP		DQX	JMD	NCG	QTG	TCR
NPX	RMK	WKQ		DTW	JMZ	NDK	QTJ	TDB
NRH	RNB	WMJ		DWQ	JNH	NFZ	QTK	TDG
NRP	RNF	WMQ		DXM	JPB	NGZ	QTW	TDP
NSK	RNP	WNF		DXT	JPL	NJB	QWH	TGC
NSL	RPX	WPM		DZX	JQT	NKH	QZN	TGK
NSZ	RPZ	XBS		FCN	JSZ	NLG	QZS	THJ
NTQ	RWP	XGM		FCX	JTR	NLW	RBK	TKB
NWK	RXG	XGN		FDT	JWG	NLZ	RBP	TKW
NXB	RZK	XGT		FDW	JXP	NPR	RCF	TLG
NXK	RZP	XHP		FHN	JZL	NRG	RCX	TLW
NZD	RZT	XKP		FKN	KCP	NRJ	RDJ	TLX
NZS	SDF	XLS		FKT	KCR	NSD	RDW	TMH
	SDG	XNC		FMR	KDM	NTB	RFW	TMQ

45% (cont.)	50%						54%	
TMW	BDN	FDZ	JPZ	NDH	RPN	XMT	BDW	FNB
TMX	BDZ	FHB	JRG	NDL	RTB	XND	BHR	FNR
TNJ	BFS	FHR	JRH	NDX	RWG	XNH	BHS	FQT
TPC	BFT	FHS	JTN	NFD	RZB	XSC	BLJ	FRX
TPX	BGJ	FJR	JXT	NGX	SBD	XTB	BPR	FTL
TQN	BHN	FLJ	JZD	NKT	SFD	ZCH	BPS	FTM
TWC	BJN	FPS	KBR	NKX	SFK	ZHT	BRJ	FTP
TWM	BJT	FQX	KCS	NJD	SFN	ZLT	BSW	FTQ
TXF	BKP	FTJ	KDG	NJL	SFX	ZNH	BTK	FWR
TXK	BKQ	FTK	KHT	NJP	SGD	ZRG	BTM	FXL
TXZ	BKT	FWS	KMD	NJR	SHQ	ZRM	BTZ	FXN
TZR	BKX	FXT	KMS	NPL	SJD	ZRN	BWS	FXS
WDF	BKZ	FZD	KPF	NRK	SKC		BWT	GBL
WFS	BLP	GBD	KPG	NRW	SLH		BXG	GBT
WKC	BNR	GBK	KPR	NTW	SLZ		BXS	GCP
WKZ	BPK	GBX	KPX	NZW	SNQ		BZT	GDK
WLH	BQM	GBZ	KSC	PBK	SPB		CJR	GDT
WLN	BSP	GDP	KTC	PCN	SQC		CKG	GMT
WMF	BTF	GLC	KTD	PCR	SQF		CKR	GNZ
WMT	BTJ	GLX	LBD	PCX	SQN		CMK	GPS
WNC	BWM	GMB	LCG	PDF	SWC		CNH	GRJ
WPB	BXN	GNJ	LCH	PDH	SWJ		CNW	GRX
WPC	CKW	GPD	LDZ	PDR	SXD		CPL	GWL
WPK	CLJ	GPM	LFH	PDZ	SXM		CQT	GZD
WQD	CLZ	GTC	LFN	PHT	TBH		CRF	HCN
WRJ	CMG	GTN	LFR	PLJ	TBJ		CRZ	HDQ
WSL	CMX	GWT	LFS	PLX	TBM		CTP	HLZ
WTF	CNR	GXP	LJR	PMX	TBX		CTZ	HPL
XDT	CPH	GZT	LNR	PNF	TDN		CXN	HQB
XFD	CPK	HBL	LQW	PNZ	TDR		DGQ	HQF
XFT	CQM	HBS	LSD	PSC	TGX		DHN	HMD
XNG	CSL	HBT	LTJ	PTW	TKR		DHP	HMQ
XPK	CTG	HBW	LTQ	PXR	TPJ		DJT	HMR
XQT	CTL	HCP	LXC	QHS	TQG		DKR	HNZ
XRM	CTQ	HCR	LXS	QLS	TXM		DLP	HSL
XSH	CTX	HDX	MCS	QMC	WDL		DLS	HTP
ZBS	CWG	HFR	MCT	QNB	WDT		DMK	HTR
ZCL	CWK	HJR	MDJ	QNC	WFD		DMZ	HTW
ZCR	CWS	HLR	MDQ	QNH	WGD		DNB	HTX
ZCT	DBK	HMB	MGD	QSC	WGM		DNJ	HWS
ZDR	DBM	HMZ	MGX	QSK	WHD		DQG	JGM
ZFD	DFL	HNC	MHP	QWK	WHQ		DQN	JLG
ZGN	DFM	HNS	MHT	QXT	WMD		DQT	JLR
ZGR	DFP	HPK	MKB	QZT	WMK		DSG	JLS
ZHR	DGP	HPZ	MKS	RCL	WMZ		DSN	JMT
ZMS	DMG	HQC	MPJ	RCM	WNP		DTB	JND
ZND	DNF	HQD	MPX	RDK	WQM		DTM	JRB
ZPH	DNX	HRF	MQT	RDP	WQT		DTP	JRC
ZRC	DQB	HTC	MSJ	RFN	WSB		DTX	JRX
ZSK	DQM	HZD	MTF	RFP	WSN		DTZ	JSM
ZSP	DTF	HZM	MTW	RHB	WTB		DZG	JTC
ZWM	DTL	JBM	MWG	RKD	WTD		DZS	JWS
ZWT	DWK	JBR	MWK	RKG	WTL		FBK	JXS
	DWP	JGR	MXF	RKN	WTQ		FBL	KBT
	DXR	JGS	MXK	RKX	WZJ		FDN	KHN
	DZL	JHS	NBD	RMX	XCH		FKR	KNC
	DZR	JMR	NBJ	RNJ	XCL		FLQ	KPC
	FCR	JPR	NCX	RNW	XDR		FMD	KRM
	FDS	JPS	NCZ	RNZ	XJR		FMT	KSD

54% (cont.)			58%[1]					63%
KSM	NXP	WBR	BDM	HDB	MRC	RCN	XNT	BFR
KWP	NZH	WHK	BFD	HFD	MSF	RDB	XPS	BGD
LBG	PBM	WJR	BFL	HLN	MSG	RDF	XPT	BGL
LCQ	PDJ	WKT	BGM	HPC	MSZ	RDL	XRD	BGT
LCX	PDM	WLP	BHM	HPD	MWT	RFM	XTH	BLG
LDW	PDX	WNH	BHT	HPJ	MXG	RFX	ZMD	BLQ
LFW	PFR	WNZ	BKF	HPT	MZR	RFZ	ZNT	BLR
LFZ	PFS	WPL	BKH	HQM	NBF	RHD	ZTR	BLS
LNH	PGC	WPN	BLF	HRP	NCT	RHN		BMD
LPG	PJG	WQN	BLZ	HRX	NFR	RLT		BNQ
LPT	PKM	WRC	BNH	HSX	NGC	RLZ		BNX
LPZ	PLR	WRH	BPL	HTM	NGP	RMG		BNZ
LQS	PMJ	WRZ	BQT	HTQ	NGS	RPC		BPD
LQT	PSZ	WSD	BQX	HTZ	NHC	RTM		BRP
LRW	PTF	WTG	BSM	JGD	NHK	RTX		BSL
LSN	PWL	XBR	BTN	JPT	NJZ	RWT		BSQ
LTG	QCT	XCR	BWK	JRM	NKG	RZD		BWD
LTP	QFT	XGR	BWN	JRT	NPD	SBL		BZR
LXR	QHT	XHT	BXR	JRW	NQT	SCL		CGR
LXZ	QKS	XLD	CGN	JSH	NRD	SDL		CKS
LZN	QNK	XPN	CHG	JTG	NRT	SGM		CHK
MFD	RBG	XRK	CHX	JWT	NTJ	SHL		CHT
MGC	RDN	XSP	CHZ	KCH	NTK	SKG		CKT
MGK	RDX	ZHN	CLH	KCN	NTX	SLF		CLG
MJG	RDZ	ZHS	CNK	KCT	NWR	SLN		CLT
MJS	RHM	ZJR	CNL	KNH	PCG	SLQ		CLQ
MPK	RKF	ZMP	DGL	KNW	PCL	SNC		CLX
MRB	RNH	ZMR	DKN	KNX	PCS	SQH		CMR
MSW	RNL	ZMT	DLR	KRB	PCW	SQX		CMS
MTB	RNX	ZPD	DMT	KRD	PDN	SWB		CNG
MTK	RPG	ZPR	DNP	KRN	PDS	TBP		CNT
MTP	RWN	ZPS	DNR	KRX	PHC	TBQ		CPR
MTX	RXD	ZPT	DNW	KTN	PHR	TCL		CTH
MWR	SCG	ZRT	DSL	KWH	PKB	THC		CTM
MXC	SDM		DSM	LBS	PKZ	THZ		CZN
MXP	SGL		DWH	LCR	PNH	TKC		DGM
MZH	SHC		DXN	LGC	PNL	TLR		DGX
MZS	SKX		DZT	LNB	PSN	TMB		DNH
NBQ	SLX		FBS	LNC	PRH	TPK		DPN
NBW	SMH		FCL	LPH	PSD	TPN		DRX
NBZ	SNH		FDJ	LQC	PSF	TPW		DWG
NDR	SPF		FLH	LWD	PSG	TRF		DWT
NGL	SZN		FMP	LXD	PSN	TWD		FBR
NHD	TBF		FNH	LXN	PTD	TWK		FKD
NHJ	TBK		FPT	LZT	PTJ	TWP		FLB
NJC	TBW		FRJ	MDB	PTK	TXB		FLC
NJG	TDW		FRW	MDF	PTX	TXR		FNC
NLS	TDX		FTC	MDK	PWD	WCT		FSL
NPG	TGD		FTR	MFT	PWS	WDG		FSN
NPH	TJR		FWD	MGS	PXS	WFL		FWT
NRC	TKX		FXD	MGT	PZD	WKR		GCT
NSB	TMG		FXR	MHQ	QLD	WMG		GDN
NSG	TMR		GCL	MJC	QMD	WMH		GDR
NSJ	TNX		GDB	MKG	QTC	WMP		GMR
NSP	TNZ		GDL	MKX	QTL	WPG		GWR
	TPM		GMD	MPC	QTN	WPR		GZL
NTD	TWQ		GQT	MPG	QWL	WTM		HMT
NTZ	TXL		GSL	MPH	QWN	WTN		HPM
NXC	TXQ		GZS	MQS				HPN

63% (cont.)			67%			71%		
HPR	PGD	WCK	BGS	LWS	TND	BDL	KPT	TNR
HRW	PGK	WGL	BKW	LZD	TNG	BGN	KSP	TPD
HRZ	PGL	WGR	BLH	MCK	TNP	BRF	LDG	TPH
HSM	PGR	WGT	BLX	MDH	TPF	BRL	LDN	TPL
HSP	PHM	WJZ	BMS	MDX	TPZ	BRX	LGD	TRJ
JBS	PHW	WKM	BNT	MKT	TWL	BRZ	LPD	TRL
JDR	PKN	WMR	BRH	MPR	TWR	BSN	LWR	TRW
JFR	PKX	WNR	BZD	MPZ	TXN	BTR	LZR	WCH
JLP	PMB	WPS	CFT	MSB	WDR	BZN	MCR	WFR
JMS	PMR	WSC	CHP	MSP	WHS	CGS	MDR	WGS
JNP	PSL	WTZ	CHW	MSX	WKG	CHM	MDW	WHF
JPD	PTB	WZD	CLN	MTG	WLS	CMT	MRG	WHL
JTD	PTN	XMD	CRH	MTZ	WPD	CPT	MSD	WHM
KDN	PXD	XMR	CSH	MWS	WRL	CRT	MTC	WHR
KFR	QMT	XPL	CSK	MXD	WSK	CRX	MTD	WHZ
KNB	QNS	XSK	CTN	MXR	WTR	CWN	MTJ	WKN
KNP	QTB	ZHP	DBR	NFT	XMP	DGR	NCL	WPT
KRG	QTH	ZTH	DFR	NPS	XPD	DMB	NDG	WRT
KRT	RBD		DGN	PBL	XRT	DPH	NHR	XCT
KTH	RBL		DHR	PDK	ZNG	DPL	NHT	XLT
KWN	RCT		DHT	PGM	ZNS	DRJ	NHW	XPR
KWT	RDG		DMR	PGN	ZPL	DRZ	NHZ	ZNK
LDQ	RDH		DMS	PGS		DSP	NSC	ZRK
LFD	RDT		DNS	PHN		DTN	NTL	
LNZ	RKT		DPW	PHZ		FDR	NTR	
LPC	RKW		DRH	PJR		FNK	NWT	
LRT	RLD		DWF	PKF		FNL	NXT	
LTF	RLX		DWR	PKT		FRC	PCH	
LTN	RTC		DWS	PKW		FRK	PDL	
LTW	SCX		FLZ	PLD		FRL	PDW	
LTZ	SHD		FMS	PLH		FTB	PFL	
LXT	SKH		FTD	PMT		FTW	PKC	
MCX	SKZ		FTN	PNC		GLB	PRB	
MDP	SMQ		FTX	PRW		GLZ	PRL	
MDT	SMW		FTZ	PTG		GMS	PRN	
MHS	SPJ		GLT	PTZ		GNR	PSW	
MKD	SPM		GMC	PWN		GPR	QSH	
MPD	SPW		GND	QCK		GRC	QTZ	
MRF	SPZ		GNK	QTD		GRZ	QWT	
MRH	SQD		GPT	RGN		GWK	RFL	
MRP	SQM		GSD	RGT		HDS	RFT	
MTQ	SWD		HDR	RKC		HFT	RTH	
NBK	SWH		HSC	RLF		HLS	RWD	
NCR	TBN		HTD	RPL		HQS	SCK	
NDS	TBZ		JNS	RTG		HRK	SCM	
NHB	TCN		JPN	RTL		HRL	SCN	
NHF	TFN		JRZ	SCF		HRM	SLC	
NHQ	TFR		JSP	SCP		HWL	SMX	
NHX	THQ		KDS	SCW		HWT	SPG	
NKD	TKG		KPS	SHM		JGL	SQW	
NLT	TMK		KTZ	SLB		JMB	SWF	
NPK	TNC		LBN	SMC		JNR	SWL	
NTF	TNH		LCT	SMP		JRD	SWZ	
NTG	TNQ		LDS	SNL		JWL	TBG	
NWH	TPG		LGN	SPC		KGR	TBL	
PDG	TRC		LGR	SPH		KGS	TBR	
PDT	TRG		LPR	SPX		KMP	TDL	
PFD	TRZ		LSH	TFL		KNF	THF	
PFT	TXC		LTX	TLP		KNT	THP	

75%		79%		83%		88%	92%
BKG	NBL	BDG	NHP	BGR	PRM	BLT	BKD
BKN	NCK	BDR	NHS	BKR	PSH	BRG	BNK
BKS	NGR	BDS	NTH	BLW	QLT	BRT	BRN
BMP	NKS	BLN	PHX	BMT	RHT	BTL	CHL
BRM	NPT	BNG	PKR	BRK	RMP	BXT	DBT
BSK	NWS	BNS	PKS	BSH	RPD	CHF	DRT
BXD	PKD	BRW	PLB	BTH	RPT	CRN	DSK
CHN	PLG	BWL	PLC	CHR	SCH	CRW	FLT
CLR	PLZ	BWR	PMS	CLF	SHK	DMP	FND
CMP	PMD	CHS	PRG	CLP	SKF	DRG	FRD
CPS	PNG	CRL	PRT	CLS	SKM	DRP	GRD
CRG	PRX	CRP	PRZ	CLW	SNZ	FDL	GRL
CSP	PSM	CWT	PTR	CRK	SPD	FLD	GRT
CTR	PTH	CZR	PWR	CRM	SWP	FLW	HLT
CWL	PWT	DBL	RBT	DFT	SXN	FNT	HRT
DRB	QNT	DBS	RFC	DGT	TGR	FSH	JMP
DRF	RBN	DGS	RND	DPR	THK	GLW	KNG
DRL	RCH	DKS	RPM	DRM	TLD	GRB	LNG
DTR	RDM	DLT	SGN	DRW	TMD	GRP	LRD
FLN	RGD	DNG	SLG	DZN	TXG	HRN	LTD
FLS	RGL	DNK	SMG	FCT	WDN	HZL	MBR
FNS	RMD	DPS	SMK	FLR	WLD	JCT	MSH
FRN	RMT	DRN	SND	FLX	WNS	KND	MSK
FRT	RTD	DTH	SNF	FTH	WRD	LNT	PKG
GDS	RTN	FHT	SPK	FWN	WRK	LWN	PND
GLN	SDN	FRZ	SPL	GLR	WSH	MCH	RFD
GLP	SHF	FWL	SQB	GNT		NSH	RNG
GNS	SHW	GBR	SWK	HMP		PHD	RNK
GNW	SKW	GBS	THW	HMS		PLS	SHN
GRM	SMD	GLS	TRB	HND		PLT	SHP
GWD	SNB	GMP	TRD	HNT		PNT	SKN
HBR	SQL	GRK	TRM	HTL		PRD	SKP
HCK	TCH	GRW	TXD	JLT		RCK	SLP
HDN	THB	GSP	WDS	JNT		RNT	TCK
HKS	THM	GTR	WHN	JRN		RTZ	THN
HLP	THX	GWN	WHT	LBR		SKD	THR
HNR	TKN	HCL	WLT	LGT		SLD	TNK
HPS	TPR	HDL	WSP	MDS		SNG	TRK
HSB	TRH	HNK	WTH	MFR		SNP	TRP
HTN	TRX	HQT	XMS	MGR		SPN	WND
JDG	TWG	HRB	XTR	MJR		SWG	WNG
JHN	TXP	HSK	ZBR	MRJ		SWN	WNK
JNC	WFT	HWK		MRK		THD	WRP
JNX	WGN	JNG		MRW		TMP	
KFT	WKD	LGS		MSC		TRN	
LDR	WKS	LNX		MSQ		WNT	
LHT	WLF	LPS		MTH		WRN	
LND	WMS	LQD		NSW		ZNC	
LNS	WRG	LRN		PCK			
LRG	WRM	LSP		PCT			
LTH	WTC	MPS		PHB			
LTR		MRT		PHL			
LWT		MRX		PHS			
MDG		MTR		PLN			
MDZ		MXT		PLW			
MPT		NBR		PRC			
MRD		NBS		PRF			
MRZ		NGD		PRK			
		NGT					

96%	100%
BLD	DNT
BND	DPT
BRD	DRK
DSH	HRD
DWN	PNK
FLP	SLW
FRM	SNK
FSK	SNW
GLD	SWM
GRN	WHP
HLD	
LFT	
TWN	

These values were determined by Noble. (Noble, C. E. An analysis of meaning. *Psychol. Rev.*, 1952, 59, 421–430. Courtesy, The American Psychological Association, Inc.)

Dissyllable	M	Dissyllable	M	Dissyllable	M
GOJEY	0.99	GAMIN	1.95	YEOMAN	4.60
NEGLAN	1.04	FEMUR	2.09	QUOTA	4.68
MEARDON	1.05	LOZENGE	2.09	QUARRY	5.10
BYSSUS	1.13	FERRULE	2.13	EFFORT	5.13
BALAP	1.22	STOMA	2.14	UNIT	5.32
VOLVAP	1.22	GRAPNEL	2.15	FATIGUE	5.33
TAROP	1.24	FLOTSAM	2.19	KEEPER	5.47
XYLEM	1.24	CAROM	2.26	KENNEL	5.52
LATUK	1.26	NIMBUS	2.26	MALLET	5.61
QUIPSON	1.26	LEMUR	2.28	LEADER	5.94
GOKEM	1.27	CAPSTAN	2.41	QUARTER	5.98
NARES	1.28	PERCEPT	2.43	REGION	5.98
ZUMAP	1.28	LICHENS	2.48	HUNGER	6.02
POLEF	1.30	JETSAM	2.54	ZERO	6.15
SAGROLE	1.33	ENDIVE	2.59	INCOME	6.24
NOSTAW	1.34	TARTAN	2.63	UNCLE	6.57
BODKIN	1.39	OVUM	2.69	YOUNGSTER	6.75
ULNA	1.50	ROSTRUM	2.73	TYPHOON	6.83
WELKIN	1.53	VERTEX	2.76	CAPTAIN	6.88
ICON	1.54	BODICE	2.80	ZEBRA	7.12
KUPOD	1.55	TANKARD	2.89	GARMENT	7.17
DELPIN	1.60	PALLOR	3.06	VILLAGE	7.28
ATTAR	1.71	SEQUENCE	3.21	INSECT	7.39
MATRIX	1.73	ARGON	3.34	JEWEL	7.58
DAVIT	1.74	RAMPART	3.36	JELLY	7.70
WIDGEON	1.78	JITNEY	3.51	HEAVEN	7.91
BRUGEN	1.79	ENTRANT	3.55	OFFICE	7.95
KAYSEN	1.82	PALLET	3.62	WAGON	8.12
MAELSTROM	1.84	NAPHTHA	3.64	DINNER	8.33
TUMBRIL	1.84	PIGMENT	3.77	MONEY	8.98
RENNET	1.86	ORDEAL	3.91	ARMY	9.43
ROMPIN	1.90	ZENITH	4.44	KITCHEN	9.61

Bigram frequencies are given for two different counts, and trigram frequencies for three different counts (see Chapter 4).

T-L: Based on a random sample from the Thorndike-Lorge word list.

U: Based on 15,000 words of running text.

P: Trigram frequencies as given by Pratt and based on 20,000 words of running text. (Pratt, F. *Secret and urgent.* Indianapolis: Bobbs-Merrill, 1939. Courtesy of Mrs. Fletcher Pratt.)

Bigrams

	T-L	U	Total		T-L	U	Total		T-L	U	Total
AA	2	1	3	CT	431	176	607	FI	568	153	721
AB	518	121	639	CU	416	43	459	FL	113	35	148
AC	1031	187	1218	CY	60	17	77	FN	—	3	3
AD	619	128	747					FO	482	228	710
AE	1	5	6	DA	251	91	342	FR	192	111	303
AF	114	61	175	DB	1	—	1	FS	6	—	6
AG	475	113	588	DD	56	19	75	FT	133	67	200
AH	18	7	25	DE	1127	349	1476	FU	284	65	349
AI	631	198	829	DF	54	4	58	FY	90	2	92
AJ	137	10	147	DG	80	18	98				
AK	364	75	439	DH	2	3	5	GA	326	72	398
AL	1235	455	1690	DI	493	213	706	GB	1	—	1
AM	582	177	759	DK	35	—	35	GD	7	—	7
AN	2048	1134	3182	DL	113	27	140	GE	682	201	883
AO	—	1	1	DM	93	6	99	GF	2	1	3
AP	601	102	703	DN	38	18	56	GG	73	28	101
AQ	—	1	1	DO	261	136	397	GH	519	165	684
AR	1793	596	2389	DP	—	2	2	GI	366	90	456
AS	997	543	1540	DR	415	57	472	GL	160	32	192
AT	1643	720	2363	DS	10	85	95	GM	58	1	59
AU	301	61	362	DT	—	1	1	GN	30	17	47
AV	346	133	479	DU	96	69	165	GO	67	97	164
AW	73	37	110	DV	72	11	83	GP	2	3	5
AX	55	7	62	DW	25	4	29	GR	397	93	490
AY	54	144	198	DY	115	37	152	GS	21	43	64
AZ	17	13	30					GT	102	10	112
				EA	2051	465	2516	GU	81	46	127
BA	317	96	413	EB	19	7	26	GY	52	7	59
BB	12	8	20	EC	551	178	729				
BD	—	1	1	ED	535	641	1176	HA	838	558	1396
BE	472	289	761	EE	817	229	1046	HB	—	5	5
BI	170	64	234	EF	142	59	201	HD	—	2	2
BJ	—	7	7	EG	237	58	295	HE	1238	1659	2897
BK	1	—	1	EH	44	10	54	HF	—	4	4
BL	627	120	747	EI	310	87	397	HG	—	1	1
BN	—	1	1	EJ	—	1	1	HI	555	448	1003
BO	249	155	404	EK	50	20	70	HL	14	4	18
BR	123	74	197	EL	1271	308	1579	HM	47	3	50
BS	40	18	58	EM	527	164	691	HN	4	7	11
BT	—	2	2	EN	2487	716	3203	HO	826	303	1129
BU	392	130	522	EO	51	38	89	HP	—	1	1
BV	—	2	2	EP	241	79	320	HR	141	52	193
BW	5	—	5	EQ	146	13	159	HS	—	12	12
BY	1	67	68	ER	2921	1113	4034	HT	392	104	496
				ES	1543	679	2222	HU	411	67	478
CA	758	297	1055	ET	1040	228	1268	HV	—	1	1
CC	199	26	225	EU	25	7	32	HW	—	6	6
CE	1334	262	1596	EV	225	152	377	HY	36	10	46
CG	—	2	2	EW	222	90	312				
CH	1010	287	1297	EX	505	98	603	IA	310	111	421
CI	472	131	603	EY	45	108	153	IB	45	35	80
CK	587	89	676	EZ	33	2	35	IC	998	311	1309
CL	582	66	648					ID	331	164	495
CO	772	345	1117	FA	328	92	420	IE	496	174	670
CQ	—	1	1	FB	1	1	2	IF	398	115	513
CR	356	76	432	FE	589	123	712	IG	785	140	925
CS	—	5	5	FF	261	67	328	IK	18	31	49

	T-L	U	Total		T-L	U	Total		T-L	U	Total
IL	796	287	1083	LW	—	13	13	OM	448	292	740
IM	262	179	441	LY	846	254	1100	ON	2321	786	3107
IN	2637	1265	3902					OO	510	206	716
IO	1366	249	1615	MA	921	289	1210	OP	149	119	268
IP	198	36	234	MB	232	56	288	OQ	—	1	1
IQ	12	1	13	ME	761	400	1161	OR	1605	655	2260
IR	857	204	1061	MF	—	5	5	OS	442	150	592
IS	1467	584	2051	MI	548	172	720	OT	492	246	738
IT	680	654	1334	ML	1	3	4	OU	1428	690	2118
IU	7	4	11	MM	12	40	52	OV	693	73	766
IV	442	152	594	MN	3	1	4	OW	446	230	676
IW	1	—	1	MO	648	204	852	OX	27	11	38
IX	110	14	124	MP	273	109	382	OY	89	22	111
IZ	17	33	50	MR	1	10	11	OZ	1	4	5
				MS	8	41	49				
JA	66	17	83	MT	—	1	1	PA	917	181	1098
JE	70	23	93	MU	73	75	148	PB	4	—	4
JI	—	2	2	MY	17	60	77	PE	1033	230	1263
JO	157	47	204					PF	14	—	14
JU	133	30	163	NA	505	132	637	PH	125	32	157
				NB	16	—	16	PI	206	75	281
KA	47	4	51	NC	661	134	795	PK	—	1	1
KB	5	2	7	ND	870	780	1650	PL	342	156	498
KD	1	1	2	NE	1242	447	1689	PM	9	3	12
KE	673	155	828	NF	105	19	124	PN	—	1	1
KF	4	2	6	NG	1369	629	1998	PO	685	133	818
KG	—	1	1	NH	8	10	18	PP	359	92	451
KH	1	2	3	NI	422	152	574	PR	659	181	840
KI	132	73	205	NJ	—	8	8	PS	6	26	32
KL	25	9	34	NK	105	37	142	PT	250	33	283
KN	37	51	88	NL	31	42	73	PU	172	48	220
KO	13	—	13	NM	10	15	25	PY	65	7	72
KP	—	1	1	NN	201	34	235				
KR	8	1	9	NO	471	257	728	QU	369	61	430
KS	24	31	55	NP	1	2	3				
KT	—	1	1	NQ	65	4	69	RA	1183	305	1488
KU	5	—	5	NR	23	3	26	RB	53	17	70
KY	26	8	34	NS	263	203	466	RC	458	57	515
				NT	2341	511	2852	RD	266	88	354
LA	1068	239	1307	NU	223	46	269	RE	2877	914	3791
LB	7	7	14	NV	137	18	155	RF	116	10	126
LC	52	3	55	NW	13	—	13	RG	125	40	165
LD	504	178	682	NX	2	1	3	RH	1	8	9
LE	2299	495	2794	NY	14	71	85	RI	1190	325	1515
LF	43	32	75	NZ	—	5	5	RK	191	59	250
LG	15	2	17					RL	209	68	277
LH	—	1	1	OA	32	34	66	RM	303	62	365
LI	925	346	1271	OB	85	36	121	RN	175	107	282
LK	11	13	24	OC	508	70	578	RO	1288	433	1721
LL	907	391	1298	OD	194	110	304	RP	19	9	28
LM	163	18	181	OE	69	24	93	RR	157	60	217
LN	3	6	9	OF	239	498	737	RS	228	242	470
LO	854	200	1054	OG	184	33	217	RT	529	158	687
LP	160	15	175	OH	—	6	6	RU	69	71	140
LR	1	5	6	OI	74	39	113	RV	104	33	137
LS	168	59	227	OJ	—	3	3	RW	47	4	51
LT	84	56	140	OK	360	46	406	RX	2	—	2
LU	237	53	290	OL	757	193	950	RY	326	133	459
LV	113	14	127								

	T-L	U	Total		T-L	U	Total		T-L	U	Total
SA	433	133	566	UA	119	52	171	WS	8	15	23
SB	3	18	21	UB	61	29	90	WT	3	3	6
SC	260	69	329	UC	120	85	205	WY	10	6	16
SD	—	1	1	UD	110	29	139				
SE	1444	421	1865	UE	251	69	320	XA	90	12	102
SF	14	6	20	UF	163	8	171	XC	44	18	62
SG	48	1	49	UG	153	96	249	XE	56	15	71
SH	953	250	1203	UI	196	48	244	XF	15	2	17
SI	812	245	1057	UK	1	2	3	XH	—	3	3
SK	72	39	111	UL	631	186	817	XI	107	13	120
SL	311	38	349	UM	131	157	288	XL	9	1	10
SM	36	54	90	UN	904	243	1147	XM	2	—	2
SN	34	13	47	UO	37	—	37	XO	—	1	1
SO	745	175	920	UP	236	75	311	XP	205	32	237
SP	624	83	707	UR	1018	286	1304	XT	107	18	125
SQ	—	12	12	US	825	254	1079	XU	13	2	15
SR	—	1	1	UT	860	277	1137				
SS	833	204	1037	UV	1	5	6	YA	83	13	96
ST	2865	608	3473	UX	9	1	10	YB	1	5	6
SU	470	128	598	UY	2	4	6	YC	4	8	12
SW	75	25	100	UZ	6	1	7	YD	17	2	19
SY	148	32	180					YE	31	74	105
				VA	338	41	379	YG	8	—	8
TA	672	241	913	VE	1549	491	2040	YH	—	2	2
TB	—	5	5	VI	492	121	613	YI	44	20	64
TC	130	33	163	VO	93	29	122	YL	77	7	84
TD	—	2	2	VR	1	—	1	YM	18	15	33
TE	2316	583	2899	VU		1	1	YN	4	6	10
TF	15	4	19	VY	9	3	12	YO	65	186	251
TG	3	—	3					YP	25	9	34
TH	1084	1795	2879	WA	421	302	723	YR	20	3	23
TI	1984	513	2497	WB	6	—	6	YS	1	55	56
TJ	—	1	1	WC	—	2	2	YT	1	16	17
TL	566	73	639	WD	114	3	117	YV	—	1	1
TM	41	22	63	WE	511	268	779	YW	14	5	19
TN	12	4	16	WH	441	259	700	YX	4	—	4
TO	846	367	1213	WI	216	122	338				
TP	—	1	1	WK	3	1	4	ZA	1	9	10
TR	810	218	1028	WL	5	12	17	ZE	56	32	88
TS	150	192	342	WM	—	1	1	ZI	6	4	10
TT	279	139	418	WN	165	47	212	ZL	1	3	4
TU	358	114	472	WO	143	145	288	ZO	5	3	8
TW	24	41	65	WP	1	—	1	ZY	3	4	7
TY	618	107	725	WR	51	13	64	ZZ	2	7	9
TZ	4	—	4								

Trigrams

	T-L	U	Pratt	Total		T-L	U	Pratt	Total
AAC	—	1	—	1	AFE	54	5	2	61
AAM	—	—	1	1	AFF	60	13	9	82
AAR	2	—	—	2	AFN	—	3	—	3
					AFR	—	3	—	3
ABA	45	1	6	52	AFT	—	34	30	64
ABB	2	5	—	7					
ABD	—	1	1	2	AGA	10	16	16	42
ABE	5	3	1	9	AGD	6	—	—	6
ABI	—	7	3	10	AGE	193	56	20	269
ABL	230	48	39	317	AGG	—	4	3	7
ABO	223	40	28	291	AGI	68	4	3	75
ABR	2	1	1	4	AGN	14	4	2	20
ABS	—	6	1	7	AGO	4	15	6	25
ABU	7	3	—	10	AGP	1	1	—	2
ABY	—	4	—	4	AGR	21	3	8	32
					AGS	—	2	—	2
ACA	86	4	3	93	AGU	8	6	2	16
ACC	50	8	20	78					
ACE	228	29	20	277	AHA	3	1	—	4
ACF	—	—	1	1	AHE	—	2	2	4
ACG	—	2	—	2	AHO	—	2	1	3
ACH	187	26	21	234	AHU	—	—	1	1
ACI	38	9	8	55	AHY	—	—	1	1
ACK	161	31	18	210					
ACL	—	3	—	3	AIA	1	1	—	2
ACO	1	2	—	3	AIC	2	—	—	2
ACQ	—	1	1	2	AID	5	45	24	74
ACR	9	8	4	21	AIG	—	5	3	8
ACT	218	61	41	320	AII	—	—	3	3
ACU	17	—	2	19	AIL	119	22	16	157
ACY	31	2	3	36	AIM	1	3	6	10
					AIN	235	65	60	360
ADA	17	4	4	25	AIR	163	31	16	210
ADD	16	9	10	35	AIS	—	5	5	10
ADE	177	40	32	249	AIT	3	18	3	24
ADF	50	2	—	52	AIV	2	—	—	2
ADG	—	2	—	2					
ADH	—	1	—	1	AJA	6	—	—	6
ADI	4	21	15	40	AJE	31	—	1	32
ADJ	—	—	5	5	AJO	100	10	5	115
ADL	—	3	3	6					
ADM	82	3	10	95	AKA	—	1	—	1
ADN	—	1	—	1	AKD	—	1	—	1
ADO	24	7	3	34	AKE	20	47	35	102
ADR	2	—	—	2	AKI	—	10	5	15
ADS	—	8	4	12	AKN	37	—	1	38
ADU	—	5	3	8	AKR	—	—	1	1
ADV	72	11	4	87	AKS	—	1	1	2
ADW	—	2	—	2	AKY	4	—	—	4
ADY	3	9	7	19					
					ALA	162	12	5	179
AEO	—	1	—	1	ALB	—	4	1	5
AER	—	2	—	2	ALC	—	—	1	1
AES	—	—	1	1	ALD	8	1	2	11
AET	1	—	—	1	ALE	62	14	14	90
AEV	—	1	—	1	ALF	—	7	3	10
					ALI	61	37	17	115

	T-L	U	Pratt	Total		T-L	U	Pratt	Total
ALK	—	6	2	8	APS	3	7	1	11
ALL	243	156	99	498	APT	103	2	7	112
ALM	151	15	10	176					
ALO	7	8	9	24	AQU	—	1	—	1
ALP	—	1	—	1					
ALR	—	3	2	5	ARA	16	32	16	64
ALS	—	15	19	34	ARB	—	4	—	4
ALT	49	18	16	83	ARC	28	5	12	45
ALU	29	3	7	39	ARD	129	53	53	235
ALV	24	1	1	26	ARE	190	137	105	432
ALW	—	13	5	18	ARF	12	—	—	12
ALY	1	1	—	2	ARG	33	14	34	81
					ARI	55	29	29	113
AMA	23	8	2	33	ARK	132	20	6	158
AMB	49	6	4	59	ARL	128	22	18	168
AME	158	64	53	275	ARM	163	21	13	197
AMH	—	—	1	1	ARN	55	11	8	74
AMI	8	16	6	30	ARO	4	13	7	24
AML	—	1	1	2	ARP	—	1	1	2
AMM	—	5	—	5	ARR	13	24	19	56
AMN	—	—	1	1	ARS	—	35	46	81
AMO	109	6	8	123	ART	338	63	48	449
AMP	11	11	10	32	ARV	—	4	3	7
AMR	1	—	—	1	ARY	139	23	34	196
AMS	1	5	6	12					
AMU	—	1	—	1	ASA	—	2	1	3
AMY	—	1	1	2	ASB	1	—	—	1
					ASC	—	6	3	9
ANA	20	11	6	37	ASE	120	19	20	159
ANC	217	47	39	303	ASH	109	12	14	135
AND	368	548	154	1070	ASI	5	23	9	37
ANE	127	15	15	157	ASK	13	22	6	41
ANF	—	1	—	1	ASL	—	1	1	2
ANG	78	35	17	130	ASM	—	1	1	2
ANH	—	2	—	2	ASN	—	2	—	2
ANI	110	25	21	156	ASO	103	6	6	115
ANK	98	15	10	123	ASP	29	5	1	35
ANL	1	—	—	1	ASQ	—	—	1	1
ANN	63	19	13	95	ASS	153	33	31	217
ANO	7	17	10	34	AST	352	59	36	447
ANQ	—	—	1	1	ASU	1	6	6	13
ANS	36	40	25	101	ASY	3	4	—	7
ANT	370	85	55	510					
ANU	67	1	4	72	ATA	8	3	1	12
ANV	—	—	1	1	ATB	—	—	1	1
ANX	—	1	1	2	ATC	37	13	9	59
ANY	4	61	54	119	ATE	527	127	139	793
					ATH	140	27	17	184
AOR	—	—	1	1	ATI	539	132	128	799
AOW	—	1	—	1	ATL	—	5	4	9
					ATM	41	3	1	45
APA	11	7	10	28	ATN	—	1	—	1
APB	1	—	—	1	ATO	35	13	22	70
APE	44	13	16	73	ATR	10	6	5	21
APH	38	2	1	41	ATS	—	14	2	16
API	—	11	5	16	ATT	4	41	41	86
APO	4	2	5	11	ATU	1	18	19	38
APP	238	50	40	328	ATY	50	—	1	51
APR	—	2	2	4					

	T-L	U	Pratt	Total		T-L	U	Pratt	Total
AUC	50	1	1	52	BAJ	—	—	1	1
AUD	—	2	4	6	BAK	—	1	—	1
AUF	—	1	2	3	BAL	6	15	6	27
AUG	34	10	4	48	BAN	71	26	12	109
AUK	—	1	—	1	BAR	60	12	7	79
AUL	9	3	4	16	BAS	39	8	7	54
AUM	—	—	1	1	BAT	18	3	8	29
AUN	11	—	—	11	BAU	1	—	—	1
AUR	14	4	2	20	BAV	—	1	—	1
AUS	106	19	17	142					
AUT	18	18	17	53	BBE	—	5	1	6
AUX	9	—	—	9	BBI	—	2	2	4
AUZ	6	—	—	6	BBL	12	—	—	12
					BBO	—	1	—	1
AVA	60	4	11	75	BBY	—	—	3	3
AVE	254	104	60	418					
AVI	21	16	12	49	BDO	—	1	—	1
AVO	3	5	5	13	BDU	—	—	1	1
AVY	8	3	6	17					
					BEA	192	24	7	223
AWA	7	10	8	25	BEC	—	18	15	33
AWD	1	—	—	1	BED	8	19	2	29
AWE	7	1	—	8	BEE	80	37	32	149
AWI	—	1	1	2	BEF	—	15	8	23
AWK	3	1	—	4	BEG	—	13	5	18
AWL	—	—	1	1	BEH	—	3	2	5
AWN	53	3	—	56	BEI	100	12	19	131
AWS	—	1	3	4	BEL	12	13	14	39
AWY	—	6	—	6	BEN	11	4	3	18
					BEQ	—	—	4	4
AXE	—	2	1	3	BER	48	27	35	110
AXI	33	4	1	38	BES	—	12	6	18
AXL	9	—	—	9	BET	16	16	13	45
AXM	1	—	—	1	BEV	—	1	—	1
AXO	—	1	—	1	BEX	—	—	1	1
AXP	5	—	—	5	BEY	—	1	2	3
AYB	—	2	1	3	BIA	2	4	4	10
AYE	5	12	6	23	BIC	—	—	1	1
AYH	—	1	—	1	BID	43	—	2	45
AYI	—	4	—	4	BIE	—	—	1	1
AYL	7	1	—	8	BIG	1	15	4	20
AYR	—	1	—	1	BIL	118	15	13	146
AYS	—	35	17	52	BIM	—	—	5	5
AYT	—	1	—	1	BIN	—	7	—	7
					BIO	1	2	—	3
AZA	—	1	1	2	BIQ	1	—	—	1
AZE	6	2	—	8	BIR	—	6	—	6
AZI	3	2	1	6	BIS	—	—	3	3
AZO	5	—	—	5	BIT	2	12	12	26
AZY	3	4	—	7	BIV	1	1	—	2
AZZ	—	4	—	4	BIZ	1	2	—	3
BAB	—	6	4	10	BJE	—	7	7	14
BAC	2	16	7	25					
BAD	—	3	1	4	BKI	1	—	—	1
BAF	—	1	3	4					
BAG	119	3	1	123	BLA	112	5	1	118
BAH	—	1	—	1	BLE	269	70	43	382

	T-L	U	Pratt	Total		T-L	U	Pratt	Total
BLI	207	14	36	257	CAD	36	2	5	43
BLL	—	—	1	1	CAE	—	—	1	1
BLO	—	14	—	14	CAG	—	9	2	11
BLU	33	5	—	38	CAI	8	1	—	9
BLY	6	12	12	30	CAK	—	1	—	1
					CAL	80	62	28	170
BNE	—	1	—	1	CAM	—	26	15	41
					CAN	105	71	40	216
BOA	16	4	6	26	CAP	66	19	5	90
BOB	—	1	—	1	CAR	24	36	18	78
BOD	4	14	8	26	CAS	58	13	13	84
BOL	56	20	5	81	CAT	186	35	28	249
BOM	—	2	3	5	CAU	123	16	24	163
BON	5	4	1	10	CAY	—	—	1	1
BOO	4	11	11	26					
BOP	5	—	—	5	CCA	—	2	2	4
BOR	23	24	8	55	CCE	8	13	8	29
BOS	—	3	1	4	CCI	—	1	—	1
BOT	—	13	8	21	CCO	—	2	13	15
BOU	129	33	2	164	CCU	191	8	6	205
BOV	100	4	—	104					
BOW	—	5	2	7	CDO	—	—	1	1
BOX	1	5	2	8					
BOY	6	12	5	23	CEA	12	1	3	16
					CED	1	17	15	33
BRA	48	15	12	75	CEE	—	1	1	2
BRE	14	14	—	28	CEF	5	1	—	6
BRI	34	12	—	46	CEI	1	8	13	22
BRO	18	27	8	53	CEL	2	8	10	20
BRU	9	6	7	22	CEM	4	2	2	8
					CEN	163	28	34	225
BSC	—	1	1	2	CEP	9	9	8	26
BSE	—	4	2	6	CER	18	15	21	54
BSI	—	1	—	1	CES	166	46	42	254
BSO	1	3	1	5	CET	—	1	—	1
BST	39	2	1	42	CEU	—	1	—	1
BTA	—	—	3	3	CGR	—	2	—	2
BTS	—	—	8	8					
					CHA	210	32	29	271
BUC	—	3	—	3	CHD	—	1	—	1
BUF	13	—	—	13	CHE	160	49	27	236
BUG	18	3	—	21	CHG	—	1	—	1
BUI	3	6	11	20	CHI	134	44	22	200
BUL	7	8	3	18	CHL	9	—	1	10
BUM	—	4	—	4	CHM	22	—	3	25
BUN	—	3	1	4	CHN	4	1	1	6
BUR	105	6	4	115	CHO	1	23	6	30
BUS	106	17	7	130	CHR	62	12	—	74
BUT	140	76	54	270	CHS	—	2	3	5
BUY	—	4	3	7	CHT	3	—	1	4
					CHU	50	8	8	66
BVI	—	2	—	2	CHY	1	1	—	2
BWE	5	—	—	5	CIA	22	28	23	73
					CIB	2	1	1	4
BYL	1	—	—	1	CID	1	4	6	11
					CIE	158	11	17	186
CAB	14	4	3	21	CIF	—	2	2	4
CAC	2	—	1	3					

	T-L	U	Pratt	Total		T-L	U	Pratt	Total
CIG	—	3	—	3	CTA	13	3	8	24
CIL	1	2	6	9	CTE	9	19	22	50
CIM	—	—	1	1	CTF	13	1	—	14
CIN	17	23	5	45	CTI	78	61	31	170
CIO	82	2	4	88	CTL	50	7	3	60
CIP	29	6	13	48	CTO	21	17	13	51
CIR	133	9	—	142	CTR	—	7	5	12
CIS	4	10	7	21	CTS	—	12	5	17
CIT	23	25	13	61	CTU	104	16	17	137
CIV	—	4	5	9					
					CUA	3	—	—	3
CKA	—	—	2	2	CUB	—	1	1	2
CKB	5	2	—	7	CUD	—	—	1	1
CKE	73	17	22	112	CUE	—	—	1	1
CKG	—	1	—	1	CUF	—	2	—	2
CKI	—	4	6	10	CUI	22	1	—	23
CKL	10	2	—	12	CUL	116	12	16	144
CKN	—	2	2	4	CUM	1	2	3	6
CKO	—	—	1	1	CUO	18	—	—	18
CKP	—	1	1	2	CUP	100	8	2	110
CKS	1	11	8	20	CUR	138	10	10	158
CKT	—	1	—	1	CUS	9	2	10	21
CKY	14	3	1	18	CUT	19	5	12	36
					CUU	—	—	1	1
CLA	44	14	9	67					
CLE	232	28	10	270	CYC	2	5	—	7
CLI	—	2	5	7	CYP	2	—	—	2
CLO	261	12	8	281	CYR	8	—	—	8
CLU	39	10	16	65	CYS	1	—	—	1
					CYT	—	—	1	1
COA	3	6	5	14					
COB	7	1	1	9	CZA	—	—	1	1
COC	41	3	2	46					
COD	—	1	—	1	DAB	2	2	—	4
COF	—	1	2	3	DAC	10	1	—	11
COG	—	3	4	7	DAD	6	1	—	7
COI	—	1	1	2	DAG	15	1	—	16
COL	8	24	23	55	DAH	—	—	2	2
COM	149	96	56	301	DAI	—	3	1	4
CON	265	89	104	458	DAL	20	1	—	21
COO	117	7	5	129	DAM	1	2	5	8
COP	—	4	3	7	DAN	121	13	7	141
COR	114	26	17	157	DAP	—	1	1	2
COS	2	8	2	12	DAR	1	15	2	18
COT	—	3	1	4	DAT	14	3	5	22
COU	14	56	36	106	DAU	—	5	1	6
COV	—	9	9	18	DAV	24	2	1	27
COW	15	2	—	17	DAW	9	1	—	10
COX	—	3	—	3	DAY	—	36	64	100
COY	3	—	—	3	DAZ	—	—	1	1
CQU	—	1	2	3	DBI	1	—	—	1
CRA	2	18	17	37	DDE	16	6	11	33
CRE	118	24	20	162	DDI	31	5	2	38
CRI	59	17	10	86	DDL	3	3	1	7
CRO	163	15	7	185	DDR	—	1	4	5
CRU	4	1	3	8	DDS	—	1	—	1
CRY	—	1	—	1	DDY	6	—	—	6

	T-L	U	Pratt	Total		T-L	U	Pratt	Total
DEA	6	32	13	51	DLA	—	1	—	1
DEB	7	1	10	18	DLE	64	11	4	79
DEC	51	13	10	74	DLI	—	2	—	2
DED	16	40	24	80	DLL	—	—	1	1
DEE	—	4	—	4	DLO	—	—	1	1
DEF	12	10	12	34	DLY	49	13	9	71
DEG	—	2	4	6					
DEL	72	14	11	97	DMA	5	3	—	8
DEM	27	8	10	45	DME	—	—	1	1
DEN	173	31	37	241	DMI	82	3	9	94
DEO	2	—	—	2	DMO	1	—	—	1
DEP	64	12	10	86	DMU	5	—	—	5
DEQ	—	1	1	2					
DER	299	79	60	438	DNA	—	—	4	4
DES	73	31	31	135	DNE	38	1	2	41
DET	11	3	4	18	DNI	—	2	—	2
DEV	—	11	9	20	DNT	—	15	1	16
DEW	—	1	—	1					
					DOC	1	6	2	9
DFA	—	—	2	2	DOD	—	2	—	2
DFI	1	1	—	2	DOE	—	9	4	13
DFL	1	—	—	1	DOG	108	1	1	110
DFO	3	—	—	3	DOI	—	—	1	1
DFU	49	3	1	53	DOL	—	9	22	31
					DOM	—	5	4	9
DGE	30	11	2	43	DON	77	29	17	123
DGI	—	—	1	1	DOO	40	13	1	54
DGM	8	1	1	10	DOP	—	2	4	6
					DOR	22	5	1	28
DHE	—	1	—	1	DOT	—	—	1	1
DHI	1	—	—	1	DOU	—	4	5	9
DHO	1	2	—	3	DOW	11	27	8	46
					DOZ	—	2	—	2
DIA	53	12	10	75					
DIB	—	2	—	2	DPA	—	2	—	2
DIC	95	14	8	117					
DID	—	19	4	23	DRA	52	5	10	67
DIE	—	22	7	29	DRE	298	25	45	368
DIF	14	12	13	39	DRI	—	12	2	14
DIG	43	1	4	48	DRO	64	8	3	75
DIK	—	1	—	1	DRT	—	—	2	2
DIL	3	3	9	15	DRU	1	5	—	6
DIM	—	2	2	4	DRY	—	2	2	4
DIN	55	44	60	159					
DIO	2	4	1	7	DSH	—	3	—	3
DIP	23	2	—	25	DSI	—	—	1	1
DIR	—	6	9	15	DSO	—	1	1	2
DIS	143	39	48	230	DST	5	—	10	15
DIT	57	18	12	87	DSY	—	1	—	1
DIU	1	1	1	3					
DIV	—	11	3	14	DTH	4	1	—	5
DIW	1	—	—	1	DTI	6	—	—	6
DIZ	3	—	—	3					
					DUA	—	5	6	11
DJA	—	—	1	1	DUC	29	21	20	70
DJO	—	—	1	1	DUE	—	3	6	9
DJU	—	—	3	3	DUG	—	1	—	1
					DUI	—	—	1	1
DKE	35	—	—	35	DUK	—	1	—	1

	T-L	U	Pratt	Total		T-L	U	Pratt	Total
DUL	32	8	1	41	ECT	166	68	81	315
DUM	35	—	—	35	ECU	10	3	7	20
DUN	—	1	2	3	ECW	—	—	1	1
DUO	—	—	1	1					
DUP	—	—	1	1	EDA	16	—	1	17
DUR	—	8	6	14	EDE	13	11	5	29
DUS	—	10	4	14	EDG	28	6	5	39
DUT	—	6	3	9	EDI	30	17	12	59
					EDL	14	2	1	17
DVA	—	5	2	7	EDM	6	—	—	6
DVE	72	4	—	76	EDN	—	—	2	2
DVI	—	1	—	1	EDO	1	2	—	3
DVO	—	1	1	2	EDR	—	2	—	2
					EDS	2	7	12	21
DWA	8	3	1	12	EDT	10	—	—	10
DWI	10	1	1	12	EDU	2	13	12	27
DWO	2	—	—	2	EDV	—	—	2	2
					EDW	—	1	—	1
DYE	24	—	—	24	EDY	11	5	—	16
DYI	44	1	—	45					
DYS	—	1	1	2	EEC	10	1	2	13
					EED	63	24	9	96
EAB	16	1	—	17	EEF	20	—	1	21
EAC	212	25	13	250	EEI	—	2	—	2
EAD	213	56	38	307	EEK	50	19	4	73
EAF	—	6	—	6	EEL	157	14	3	174
EAG	1	5	3	9	EEM	10	14	8	32
EAK	200	12	12	224	EEN	60	61	56	177
EAL	89	30	20	139	EEP	115	11	12	138
EAM	259	17	17	293	EER	23	15	8	46
EAN	95	23	10	128	EES	46	9	11	66
EAP	132	5	1	138	EET	100	23	10	133
EAR	250	110	63	423	EEV	2	1	—	3
EAS	175	50	35	260	EEW	—	1	—	1
EAT	246	84	37	367	EEZ	33	2	1	36
EAU	51	16	6	73					
EAV	137	9	12	158	EFE	3	8	10	21
					EFF	—	6	20	26
EBA	2	—	—	2	EFI	29	6	4	39
EBB	—	—	1	1	EFL	1	2	2	5
EBC	—	—	2	2	EFO	11	15	12	38
EBI	1	—	—	1	EFS	—	—	1	1
EBL	1	—	—	1	EFT	—	8	5	13
EBO	1	4	—	5	EFU	17	12	5	34
EBR	3	1	5	9					
EBT	—	—	10	10	EGA	31	12	11	54
EBU	—	1	—	1	EGD	—	8	—	8
EBY	—	1	2	3	EGE	39	—	6	45
					EGG	8	4	—	12
ECA	—	19	13	32	EGH	1	—	—	1
ECC	—	2	—	2	EGI	42	7	20	69
ECD	—	—	1	1	EGL	—	3	2	5
ECE	156	23	30	209	EGN	—	3	—	3
ECH	25	3	6	34	EGO	—	5	5	10
ECI	20	20	15	55	EGR	—	5	4	9
ECK	112	4	4	120	EGS	—	2	—	2
ECL	3	3	6	12	EGU	—	7	6	13
ECO	14	27	24	65	EGY	24	—	3	27
ECR	45	4	3	52					

	T-L	U	Pratt	Total		T-L	U	Pratt	Total
EHA	—	3	1	4	ENF	2	2	—	4
EHE	32	1	1	34	ENG	80	22	14	116
EHI	—	4	2	6	ENH	—	1	—	1
EHO	—	2	3	5	ENI	37	19	11	67
EHU	—	—	1	1	ENJ	—	5	2	7
					ENL	16	5	4	25
EIA	2	—	—	2	ENM	—	1	—	1
EIC	—	—	1	1	ENN	1	5	3	9
EIG	192	15	22	229	ENO	18	10	9	37
EIL	3	1	—	4	ENP	—	1	—	1
EIN	103	16	19	138	ENR	7	1	2	10
EIP	—	—	4	4	ENS	45	24	35	104
EIR	—	38	36	74	ENT	1318	226	234	1778
EIS	—	4	—	4	ENU	13	2	2	17
EIT	9	5	7	21	ENV	32	4	3	39
EIV	1	7	9	17	ENZ	—	1	—	1
EIZ	—	1	—	1					
					EOF	—	—	2	2
EJO	—	1	—	1	EOI	5	—	—	5
					EOL	—	1	1	2
EKE	—	3	—	3	EON	2	3	1	6
EKI	—	2	2	4	EOP	3	23	13	39
EKL	—	1	—	1	EOR	—	5	1	6
EKS	—	4	—	4	EOT	—	1	—	1
					EOU	5	3	2	10
ELA	6	13	4	23	EOV	36	2	—	38
ELC	51	1	1	53					
ELD	5	16	5	26	EPA	10	16	9	35
ELE	93	35	40	168	EPE	5	4	8	17
ELF	43	24	13	80	EPH	—	7	8	15
ELG	—	—	4	4	EPI	14	2	1	17
ELI	137	35	17	189	EPL	35	5	2	42
ELL	221	80	43	344	EPO	6	5	5	16
ELO	22	13	19	54	EPP	—	1	1	2
ELP	162	12	1	175	EPR	—	8	12	20
ELR	1	1	1	3	EPS	1	2	2	5
ELS	136	12	7	155	EPT	50	15	10	75
ELT	—	7	6	13	EPU	15	—	9	24
ELU	1	2	1	4					
ELV	87	7	4	98	EQU	96	13	16	125
ELY	84	22	29	135					
					ERA	78	33	45	156
EMA	118	12	14	144	ERB	1	1	—	2
EMB	30	19	13	62	ERC	64	11	13	88
EME	61	32	24	117	ERD	1	5	6	12
EMI	33	6	6	45	ERE	360	193	162	715
EMM	—	—	1	1	ERF	86	9	7	102
EMN	—	1	2	3	ERG	9	8	5	22
EMO	141	10	10	161	ERH	1	6	4	11
EMP	103	22	20	145	ERI	213	51	36	300
EMS	—	14	5	19	ERK	3	2	2	7
EMU	—	2	—	2	ERL	74	5	3	82
EMY	17	2	1	20	ERM	77	16	23	116
					ERN	55	34	34	123
ENA	6	11	16	33	ERO	39	4	7	50
ENB	—	—	4	4	ERP	4	1	3	8
ENC	258	30	49	337	ERR	36	7	16	59
END	29	46	44	119	ERS	56	115	124	295
ENE	36	39	29	104	ERT	14	24	25	63

	T-L	U	Pratt	Total		T-L	U	Pratt	Total
ERU	12	—	17	29	EWM	—	1	—	1
ERV	103	27	2	132	EWO	3	3	—	6
ERW	17	—	—	17	EWS	—	2	4	6
ERX	2	—	—	2	EWV	—	—	1	1
ERY	49	50	36	135	EWT	3	2	—	5
					EWY	—	—	6	6
ESA	12	—	1	13					
ESC	1	11	12	24	EXA	89	12	11	112
ESD	—	—	5	5	EXC	44	18	6	68
ESE	48	40	35	123	EXE	—	4	6	10
ESH	—	6	5	11	EXH	—	3	3	6
ESI	1	17	14	32	EXI	58	5	4	67
ESK	—	3	2	5	EXP	200	32	26	258
ESL	4	—	—	4	EXT	100	16	8	124
ESM	5	1	2	8	EXU	13	2	1	16
ESN	—	1	—	1					
ESO	9	5	5	19	EYA	—	3	—	3
ESP	110	8	9	127	EYC	1	—	—	1
ESQ	—	1	—	1	EYD	—	1	—	1
ESS	537	123	77	737	EYE	—	10	4	14
EST	537	109	96	742	EYO	—	1	1	2
ESU	—	5	3	8	EYR	—	—	1	1
					EYS	—	1	4	5
ETA	5	8	6	19	EYV	—	1	1	2
ETB	—	2	1	3					
ETC	33	5	2	40	EZE	33	2	1	36
ETE	14	17	14	45					
ETH	17	22	7	46	FAB	—	2	—	2
ETI	73	19	15	107	FAC	52	22	21	95
ETL	27	—	—	27	FAD	—	1	1	2
ETO	32	1	1	34	FAI	191	15	9	215
ETR	—	3	2	5	FAL	—	4	5	9
ETS	—	12	17	29	FAM	—	10	6	16
ETT	258	31	20	309	FAN	27	5	4	36
ETU	4	4	3	11	FAR	25	8	14	47
ETW	9	9	10	28	FAS	1	12	1	14
ETY	5	5	7	17	FAT	31	11	3	45
					FAU	—	1	1	2
EUG	—	—	1	1	FAV	1	1	4	6
EUM	—	1	1	2					
EUN	1	—	—	1	FBE	—	1	—	1
EUP	21	—	—	21	FBO	1	—	—	1
EUR	3	5	8	16					
EUT	—	1	1	2	FEA	—	5	5	10
EUV	—	—	4	4	FEB	—	—	4	4
					FEC	2	6	13	21
EVA	12	4	5	21	FED	—	6	2	8
EVE	81	131	107	319	FEE	254	11	9	274
EVI	118	12	7	137	FEG	—	1	—	1
EVO	14	4	3	21	FEI	9	—	—	9
					FEL	3	16	7	26
EWA	10	2	3	15	FEN	8	6	4	18
EWB	—	—	2	2	FER	95	23	28	146
EWC	—	1	—	1	FES	113	7	2	122
EWE	4	6	—	10	FET	105	3	—	108
EWH	80	—	1	81	FEU	—	1	2	3
EWI	25	7	2	34	FEW	—	13	7	20
EWJ	—	—	4	4					
EWL	—	1	—	1	FFA	—	2	1	3
					FFB	1	1	—	2

	T-L	U	Pratt	Total		T-L	U	Pratt	Total
FFD	—	—	4	4	FUL	170	45	27	242
FFE	42	23	34	99	FUM	16	1	—	17
FFI	93	24	24	141	FUN	86	3	2	91
FFL	7	2	4	13	FUR	—	7	5	12
FFO	51	3	6	60	FUS	12	3	1	16
FFR	3	—	—	3	FUT	—	3	1	4
FFS	—	—	1	1					
FFU	10	—	—	10	FYI	—	—	2	2
FIA	—	1	—	1	GAB	8	1	—	9
FIB	—	—	5	5	GAC	3	—	—	3
FIC	119	1	36	156	GAD	5	—	—	5
FID	16	—	—	16	GAG	58	2	1	61
FIE	—	14	12	26	GAI	—	15	13	28
FIF	101	7	23	131	GAL	3	5	4	12
FIG	133	3	4	140	GAM	—	4	1	5
FIL	2	8	7	17	GAN	66	18	—	84
FIN	64	25	28	117	GAP	1	—	—	1
FIR	1	40	25	66	GAR	17	16	12	45
FIS	2	9	4	15	GAS	1	1	10	12
FIT	—	9	3	12	GAT	8	5	7	20
FIV	—	7	21	28	GAU	24	—	—	24
FIX	110	5	—	115	GAV	1	3	2	6
					GAY	—	—	1	1
FLA	—	3	2	5	GAZ	—	2	—	2
FLE	68	7	6	81					
FLI	4	4	5	13	GBE	1	—	—	1
FLO	37	14	10	61					
FLU	1	5	7	13	GDA	7	—	—	7
FLY	1	2	8	11					
					GEA	1	3	—	4
FNE	—	3	—	3	GEC	3	—	—	3
					GED	8	20	6	34
FOC	—	1	—	1	GEE	—	2	—	2
FOE	2	—	—	2	GEL	53	2	2	57
FOG	4	2	3	9	GEM	30	—	3	33
FOI	8	—	—	8	GEN	202	19	30	251
FOL	65	14	8	87	GEO	5	3	1	9
FOO	1	7	6	14	GER	48	25	31	104
FOR	402	194	177	773	GES	2	20	13	35
FOU	—	10	27	37	GET	—	33	7	40
FRA	87	15	12	114	GFI	2	1	—	3
FRE	78	18	17	113					
FRI	11	18	7	36	GGA	11	2	1	14
FRO	16	58	43	117	GGE	31	16	2	49
FRU	—	2	—	2	GGI	11	5	—	16
					GGL	—	2	2	4
FSA	6	—	—	6	GGO	3	1	—	4
					GGR	—	—	2	2
FTE	104	43	34	181	GGS	—	1	—	1
FTH	—	1	2	3	GGY	17	1	—	18
FTI	2	1	—	3					
FTL	—	1	—	1	GHB	—	5	1	6
FTS	—	3	—	3	GHE	—	4	2	6
FTT	1	—	—	1	GHI	—	1	—	1
FTY	105	2	8	115	GHL	—	—	2	2
					GHO	9	3	1	13
FUE	—	1	1	2	GHT	389	104	41	534
FUG	—	2	—	2	GHW	—	6	—	6

	T-L	U	Pratt	Total			T-L	U	Pratt	Total
GIA	—	4	5	9		GUA	29	5	2	36
GIB	8	—	2	10		GUE	22	13	4	39
GIC	42	4	—	46		GUI	1	13	10	24
GID	7	—	—	7		GUL	—	7	5	12
GIE	18	3	—	21		GUN	3	1	1	5
GIF	—	4	—	4		GUR	9	1	5	15
GIL	5	1	2	8		GUS	17	6	2	25
GIM	—	—	4	4						
GIN	123	22	21	166		GYM	—	1	—	1
GIO	69	7	1	77		GYO	—	—	1	1
GIR	—	15	2	17		GYP	22	—	—	22
GIS	54	5	5	64		GYR	—	—	5	5
GIT	28	1	1	30						
GIV	17	24	8	49		HAB	—	3	1	4
						HAC	—	1	—	1
GLA	62	7	5	74		HAD	—	63	26	89
GLE	50	12	9	71		HAE	1	1	—	2
GLI	1	6	2	9		HAF	—	1	—	1
GLO	—	2	2	4		HAI	11	8	5	24
GLU	6	—	1	7		HAK	3	1	—	4
GLY	41	5	2	48		HAL	176	18	14	208
						HAM	7	7	5	19
GME	58	1	1	60		HAN	133	73	32	238
						HAP	—	23	11	34
GNA	14	5	3	22		HAR	188	26	22	236
GNE	7	4	7	18		HAS	207	50	52	309
GNI	—	4	5	9		HAT	100	199	134	333
GNM	1	—	—	1		HAU	—	3	5	8
GNO	6	1	2	9		HAV	—	76	47	123
GNS	—	1	2	3		HAW	3	1	3	7
						HAY	—	3	1	4
GOA	—	—	1	1		HAZ	9	1	—	10
GOB	—	—	1	1						
GOD	—	1	2	3		HBO	—	3	1	4
GOE	—	2	1	3		HBY	—	2	—	2
GOI	1	8	2	11						
GOL	1	4	4	9		HCO	—	—	3	3
GON	4	5	1	10						
GOO	57	23	13	93		HDA	—	1	—	1
GOR	1	4	1	6		HDO	—	1	—	1
GOS	—	2	—	2						
GOT	3	16	9	28		HEA	268	68	28	364
GOV	—	6	15	21		HEB	1	—	—	1
						HEC	—	2	2	4
GPI	1	1	—	2		HED	49	29	38	116
GPL	1	—	—	1		HEE	109	5	1	115
GPO	—	2	—	2		HEI	—	38	36	74
						HEF	2	23	—	25
GRA	280	29	18	327		HEL	170	—	11	181
GRE	72	43	34	149		HEM	5	40	30	75
GRI	45	4	5	54		HEN	39	101	31	171
GRO	—	17	8	25		HEO	—	1	3	4
GRU	—	—	1	1		HEP	—	1	—	1
						HER	258	276	145	679
GSB	1	—	—	1		HES	28	49	25	102
GST	—	1	—	1		HET	12	8	5	25
						HEV	30	—	—	30
GTH	—	2	2	4		HEW	—	2	1	3
GTO	102	8	2	112		HEY	2	72	39	113

	T-L	U	Pratt	Total		T-L	U	Pratt	Total
HFU	—	4	3	7	HRO	2	24	13	39
					HRU	—	1	—	1
HGO	—	1	—	1	HRY	—	2	—	2
HIA	—	1	—	1	HSC	—	—	3	3
HIB	3	2	6	11	HST	—	—	2	2
HIC	106	62	53	221					
HID	2	—	—	2	HTE	88	13	5	106
HIE	69	3	6	78	HTF	—	2	2	4
HIF	2	1	—	3	HTI	—	3	—	3
HIG	105	19	10	134	HTL	—	1	—	1
HIL	67	51	16	134	HTM	—	1	—	1
HIM	1	49	15	65	HTN	—	2	—	2
HIN	162	93	38	293	HTS	—	5	1	6
HIO	—	1	—	1	HTY	8	3	6	17
HIP	56	7	7	70					
HIR	—	11	17	28	HUB	3	—	1	4
HIS	150	138	105	393	HUD	—	—	2	2
HIT	28	9	12	49	HUE	12	1	1	14
HIV	—	1	—	1	HUF	—	1	—	1
HIZ	3	—	—	3	HUG	82	2	3	87
					HUM	—	11	7	18
HLA	—	—	1	1	HUN	165	7	39	211
HLE	5	1	2	8	HUP	—	1	—	1
HLI	—	—	1	1	HUR	110	22	8	140
HLY	9	3	2	14	HUS	37	18	5	60
					HUT	—	3	1	4
HME	33	3	4	40	HUX	—	1	—	1
HMO	14	—	—	14	HUY	2	—	—	2
HNE	4	—	1	5	HVI	—	1	—	1
HNO	—	1	1	2					
HNS	—	1	—	1	HWA	—	6	—	6
					HWE	—	—	2	2
HOA	—	—	1	1					
HOB	1	1	—	2	HYD	17	—	1	18
HOC	—	3	—	3	HYE	2	—	—	2
HOD	1	3	—	4	HYG	7	—	—	7
HOE	15	2	—	17	HYN	3	—	—	3
HOG	—	1	—	1	HYP	—	2	—	2
HOI	—	—	1	1	HYR	1	—	—	1
HOK	1	3	1	5	HYS	—	2	3	5
HOL	142	27	11	180					
HOM	59	20	13	92	IAB	1	1	4	6
HON	1	13	11	25	IAD	3	—	—	3
HOO	51	26	8	85	IAE	—	2	—	2
HOP	—	11	6	17	IAG	21	9	—	30
HOR	6	15	8	29	IAH	—	—	1	1
HOS	85	24	9	118	IAL	64	34	30	128
HOT	48	7	2	57	IAM	6	3	4	13
HOU	311	69	70	450	IAN	160	28	14	202
HOV	—	1	1	2	IAO	—	1	—	1
HOW	—	35	26	61	IAR	9	1	1	11
					IAS	—	4	1	5
HPO	—	1	—	1	IAT	28	11	15	54
HRA	—	1	—	1	IBA	6	—	—	6
HRE	—	8	19	27	IBB	8	1	—	9
HRI	139	16	—	155	IBE	13	7	10	30

	T-L	U	Pratt	Total		T-L	U	Pratt	Total
IBI	2	7	12	21	IGA	1	7	1	9
IBL	12	15	11	38	IGE	47	2	4	53
IBR	2	2	7	11	IGG	4	3	1	8
IBS	1	—	—	1	IGH	461	98	49	608
IBU	—	3	7	10	IGI	113	8	6	127
IBY	1	—	—	1	IGN	6	7	21	34
					IGO	—	2	—	2
ICA	167	61	55	283	IGR	27	—	—	27
ICC	—	1	—	1	IGU	21	—	3	24
ICE	19	48	33	100					
ICH	154	58	54	266	IKE	—	30	13	43
ICI	116	19	26	161	IKI	—	—	1	1
ICK	111	19	24	154					
ICL	100	2	4	106	ILA	33	6	4	43
ICO	34	2	1	37	ILB	—	2	2	4
ICR	—	2	—	2	ILD	89	26	12	127
ICS	—	5	6	11	ILE	250	38	33	321
ICT	5	18	18	41	ILF	—	2	2	4
ICU	122	8	11	141	ILH	—	1	—	1
ICY	—	2	3	5	ILI	28	25	21	74
					ILK	—	3	1	4
IDA	34	8	4	46	ILL	297	111	110	518
IDB	1	—	—	1	ILM	—	1	—	1
IDD	21	4	2	27	ILO	—	6	4	10
IDE	210	63	51	324	ILR	—	3	4	7
IDG	2	1	1	4	ILS	—	4	3	7
IDI	5	3	4	12	ILT	3	6	6	15
IDL	1	2	2	5	ILU	—	1	2	3
IDN	—	8	5	13	ILV	—	1	1	2
IDO	—	2	2	4	ILY	45	23	9	77
IDS	—	1	—	1					
IDT	—	1	—	1	IMA	2	8	15	25
IDU	—	5	2	7	IMB	—	—	1	1
					IME	44	57	48	149
IEC	—	1	3	4	IMI	72	8	8	88
IED	7	18	15	40	IML	—	1	—	1
IEF	59	3	9	71	IMM	6	4	4	14
IEG	6	—	—	6	IMO	—	1	1	2
IEH	—	—	1	1	IMP	78	28	15	121
IEK	—	1	—	1	IMS	—	10	8	18
IEL	2	12	4	18	IMU	—	1	—	1
IEM	1	—	29	30					
IEN	185	34	—	219	INA	124	24	31	179
IER	47	13	11	71	INC	91	29	41	161
IES	2	51	26	79	IND	191	75	30	296
IET	10	16	4	30	INE	288	64	68	420
IEU	—	—	4	4	INF	42	6	12	60
IEV	7	10	8	25	ING	844	512	317	1673
IEW	28	5	3	36	INH	—	5	1	6
					INI	92	20	27	139
IFE	—	18	6	24	INJ	—	3	1	4
IFF	65	15	14	94	INK	5	20	9	34
IFI	50	9	13	72	INL	4	5	2	11
IFL	26	1	1	28	INM	—	2	1	3
IFO	50	5	—	55	INN	77	7	4	88
IFT	114	17	13	144	INO	10	3	4	17
IFU	—	6	2	8	INQ	—	—	3	3
IFY	90	2	4	96	INR	—	—	35	35
					INS	96	43	—	139

	T-L	U	Pratt	Total
INT	445	81	62	588
INU	3	19	8	30
INV	93	7	10	110
INX	2	—	—	2
INY	—	3	1	4
IOA	—	1	—	1
IOD	111	5	—	116
IOL	118	5	—	123
IOM	2	—	—	2
ION	923	215	232	1370
IOR	25	1	4	30
IOS	1	—	—	1
IOT	2	2	—	4
IOU	168	17	10	195
IPA	3	2	6	11
IPB	3	—	—	3
IPE	5	1	—	6
IPI	—	—	1	1
IPL	52	5	5	62
IPM	9	1	1	11
IPO	3	—	—	3
IPP	45	12	5	62
IPR	2	—	—	2
IPS	2	4	3	9
IPT	13	2	6	21
IPU	—	—	1	1
IQU	12	1	1	14
IRA	54	4	6	64
IRB	—	2	—	2
IRC	133	9	3	145
IRD	—	5	2	7
IRE	280	39	33	352
IRG	—	1	—	1
IRI	110	3	5	118
IRK	4	—	—	4
IRL	—	21	3	24
IRM	—	5	7	12
IRO	6	5	2	13
IRP	1	—	—	1
IRR	—	5	—	5
IRS	—	33	22	55
IRT	6	7	14	27
IRW	—	1	—	1
IRY	7	—	—	7
ISA	13	1	10	24
ISC	101	7	15	123
ISE	32	21	14	67
ISF	6	1	2	9
ISG	24	1	—	25
ISH	182	42	34	258
ISI	89	19	16	124
ISK	—	1	1	2
ISL	133	4	12	149
ISM	18	22	10	50

	T-L	U	Pratt	Total
ISN	—	3	—	3
ISO	18	4	2	24
ISP	39	5	—	44
ISR	—	1	—	1
ISS	120	16	14	150
IST	609	84	41	734
ISU	6	1	—	7
ISY	—	—	1	1
ITA	67	29	14	110
ITC	38	13	1	52
ITE	29	34	41	104
ITH	54	125	90	269
ITI	24	53	48	125
ITL	—	4	4	8
ITN	—	—	1	1
ITO	35	8	6	49
ITR	1	1	—	2
ITS	—	52	26	78
ITT	12	48	15	75
ITU	47	8	17	72
ITW	—	2	—	2
ITY	266	48	44	358
ITZ	3	—	1	4
IUM	2	2	—	4
IUR	1	—	—	1
IUS	4	2	1	7
IVA	90	6	12	108
IVE	293	114	90	497
IVI	50	32	14	96
IVO	9	—	—	9
IVU	—	—	1	1
IWO	1	—	—	1
IXA	1	—	—	1
IXE	52	5	—	57
IXT	7	2	5	14
IZA	—	7	5	12
IZE	9	22	16	47
IZI	3	—	—	3
IZO	—	3	1	4
IZZ	2	1	1	4
JAC	—	4	2	6
JAM	11	4	1	16
JAN	105	3	—	108
JAP	—	—	9	9
JAR	—	1	1	2
JAS	—	1	—	1
JAW	—	1	—	1
JAZ	—	3	—	3
JEA	—	1	4	5
JEC	—	10	9	19
JEE	—	1	—	1

	T-L	U	Pratt	Total		T-L	U	Pratt	Total
JEF	—	1	—	1	KES	6	10	4	20
JEH	—	—	1	1	KET	194	8	17	219
JER	39	4	4	47	KEW	—	1	—	1
JES	32	—	1	33	KEY	—	2	2	4
JET	—	2	—	2					
JEW	—	4	—	4	KFU	4	2	—	6
JIM	—	1	3	4	KGR	—	1	—	1
JOA	—	1	—	1	KHA	1	2	—	3
JOB	—	3	2	5					
JOC	—	2	—	2	KID	—	3	4	7
JOE	—	4	—	4	KIE	7	4	—	11
JOH	—	6	3	9	KIL	1	2	4	7
JOI	2	3	1	6	KIM	—	1	9	10
JOK	34	—	—	34	KIN	4	48	15	67
JOL	22	—	1	23	KIP	2	1	—	3
JON	—	7	—	7	KIR	8	2	—	10
JOR	200	10	4	214	KIS	100	3	3	106
JOS	—	3	—	3	KIT	10	8	2	20
JOU	—	1	—	1	KIV	—	—	1	1
JOW	—	1	—	1					
JOY	—	5	2	7	KLA	9	2	—	11
					KLE	3	—	1	4
JUD	112	1	2	115	KLI	2	3	—	5
JUL	—	3	—	3	KLY	11	4	2	17
JUM	—	3	—	3					
JUN	—	1	—	1	KMA	—	—	1	1
JUR	—	4	1	5					
JUS	113	18	5	136	KNE	37	11	1	49
JUT	6	—	—	6	KNI	—	2	—	1
					KNO	—	38	18	56
KAB	—	—	2	2					
KAG	—	1	—	1	KOB	—	—	1	1
KAL	—	—	1	1	KOR	5	—	—	5
KAM	—	—	1	1	KOU	8	—	1	9
KAN	2	2	—	4					
KAR	1	—	1	2	KPI	—	—	1	1
KAT	33	1	—	34	KPO	—	1	—	1
KBE	5	—	—	5	KRA	7	1	—	8
KBR	—	2	—	2	KRI	1	—	—	1
					KRO	—	—	1	1
KCA	—	—	1	1					
					KSB	1	—	—	1
KDE	1	—	—	1	KSC	1	—	—	1
KDO	—	1	—	1	KSG	17	—	—	17
					KSH	—	4	—	4
KEA	1	—	1	2	KSK	—	1	—	1
KED	35	33	14	82	KSM	1	—	—	1
KEE	2	6	4	12	KSO	2	—	—	2
KEF	3	1	—	4	KSP	1	—	—	1
KEG	—	1	—	1	KST	—	—	1	1
KEI	2	—	—	2					
KEL	13	2	4	19	KTA	—	1	—	1
KEM	—	—	8	8					
KEN	52	17	—	69	KUR	1	—	—	1
KEP	—	2	1	3	KUT	—	—	1	1
KER	130	6	11	147					

	T-L	U	Pratt	Total		T-L	U	Pratt	Total
KYS	—	1	—	1	LEW	42	2	—	44
					LEX	—	3	2	5
LAB	40	9	7	56	LEY	21	12	4	37
LAC	198	15	15	228					
LAD	13	8	3	24	LFA	26	—	1	27
LAG	—	3	1	4	LFI	—	1	3	4
LAH	—	1	—	1	LFR	—	—	1	1
LAI	4	12	8	24	LFS	6	—	—	6
LAK	—	3	5	8	LFT	—	—	1	1
LAM	61	4	1	66	LFU	—	—	1	1
LAN	355	54	45	454					
LAP	86	3	1	90	LGA	—	—	1	1
LAR	149	35	56	240	LGE	15	—	—	15
LAS	61	19	16	96	LGI	—	—	5	5
LAT	55	35	28	118	LGR	—	2	—	2
LAU	26	5	2	33					
LAV	25	1	4	30	LHA	—	1	—	1
LAW	—	11	5	16					
LAX	—	3	—	3	LIA	11	12	10	33
LAY	4	16	9	29	LIB	—	—	8	8
LAZ	—	—	1	1	LIC	10	25	43	78
					LID	18	7	2	27
LBA	—	2	—	2	LIE	114	25	19	158
LBE	5	—	4	9	LIF	2	20	3	25
LBO	2	1	—	3	LIG	81	24	10	115
LBU	—	3	—	3	LIK	—	28	11	39
					LIL	—	1	—	1
LCA	—	1	2	3	LIM	86	2	11	99
LCH	2	1	—	3	LIN	205	62	42	309
LCO	50	1	2	53	LIO	9	13	14	36
					LIP	8	7	2	17
LDE	142	9	7	158	LIQ	5	—	1	6
LDF	1	—	—	1	LIR	5	—	—	5
LDH	—	2	1	3	LIS	262	30	19	311
LDI	3	7	—	10	LIT	45	56	39	140
LDL	16	1	—	17	LIU	2	—	—	2
LDN	2	5	—	7	LIV	60	23	4	87
LDO	—	1	—	1	LIZ	1	11	10	22
LDR	—	11	2	13					
LDS	3	12	7	22	LKE	—	—	1	1
					LKI	1	3	—	4
LEA	148	48	29	225	LKS	—	2	—	2
LEB	1	1	1	3	LKY	—	1	—	1
LEC	5	20	24	49					
LED	64	46	35	145	LLA	20	12	21	53
LEE	—	9	4	13	LLB	1	—	—	1
LEF	—	10	5	15	LLE	30	43	22	95
LEG	76	19	7	102	LLI	8	43	30	81
LEH	5	—	—	5	LLM	1	2	1	4
LEI	2	2	—	4	LLN	—	1	—	1
LEJ	—	1	—	1	LLO	29	23	22	74
LEM	119	13	4	136	LLS	—	14	7	21
LEN	309	20	10	339	LLU	76	1	8	85
LEO	4	—	—	4	LLY	193	47	44	284
LEP	—	6	7	13					
LER	62	7	10	79	LMA	—	—	2	2
LES	148	55	52	255	LME	6	3	—	9
LET	270	26	16	312	LMI	13	—	—	13
LEV	—	10	3	13	LML	—	1	—	1

	T-L	U	Pratt	Total		T-L	U	Pratt	Total
LMO	108	9	8	125	LUD	13	4	11	28
LMS	7	1	—	8	LUE	3	6	6	15
					LUG	—	2	1	3
LNE	3	5	1	9	LUI	—	1	1	2
LNS	—	1	—	1	LUL	—	—	5	5
					LUM	32	8	4	44
LOA	2	—	1	3	LUN	33	7	2	42
LOB	—	—	5	5	LUR	8	1	2	11
LOC	80	8	11	99	LUS	95	8	10	113
LOD	—	1	1	2	LUT	43	8	5	56
LOE	—	1	—	1	LUX	—	—	1	1
LOF	—	—	1	1					
LOG	10	8	4	22	LVA	16	—	—	16
LOM	23	2	—	25	LVE	93	12	—	105
LON	3	35	26	64	LVI	3	2	—	5
LOO	133	22	7	162					
LOP	72	10	10	92	LWA	—	13	5	18
LOQ	—	1	—	1					
LOR	46	11	3	60	LYA	—	1	—	1
LOS	17	14	19	50	LYC	1	—	—	1
LOT	260	18	6	284	LYE	—	—	1	1
LOU	10	12	12	34	LYI	—	2	7	9
LOV	162	11	2	175	LYM	—	2	—	2
LOW	29	37	28	94	LYN	—	6	2	8
LOY	—	8	9	17	LYP	1	1	—	2
					LYR	—	1	—	1
LPA	—	1	—	1	LYS	—	—	1	1
LPE	12	1	—	13	LYW	14	2	—	16
LPF	14	—	—	14	LYX	1	—	—	1
LPH	—	1	1	2					
LPI	—	1	1	2	MAA	—	—	1	1
LPL	34	1	—	35	MAB	5	—	—	5
LPS	—	1	—	1	MAC	43	9	5	57
LPY	—	—	1	1	MAD	5	23	16	44
					MAG	59	6	7	72
LRE	—	2	2	4	MAH	3	—	—	3
LRO	—	3	4	7	MAI	5	6	8	19
LRY	1	2	1	4	MAJ	131	10	5	146
					MAK	127	18	13	158
LSA	1	—	—	1	MAL	—	23	10	33
LSE	129	7	1	137	MAM	8	3	—	11
LSH	25	—	—	25	MAN	220	82	93	395
LSI	3	—	1	4	MAP	—	1	2	3
LSO	—	6	6	12	MAR	110	35	20	165
LST	7	—	—	7	MAS	123	16	8	147
					MAT	27	24	23	74
LTA	9	2	—	11	MAU	—	1	—	1
LTE	—	1	9	10	MAW	1	—	—	1
LTH	8	12	7	27	MAX	23	1	—	24
LTI	—	8	3	11	MAY	—	19	27	46
LTO	—	1	1	2	MAZ	8	2	—	10
LTR	—	—	1	1					
LTS	—	6	—	6	MBA	39	1	1	41
LTU	—	2	3	5	MBE	26	24	18	68
LTY	13	3	4	20	MBI	1	6	8	15
					MBK	1	—	—	1
LUA	1	—	3	4	MBL	51	6	2	59
LUB	—	6	1	7	MBN	—	1	—	1
LUC	9	1	—	10	MBO	31	11	4	46

	T-L	U	Pratt	Total		T-L	U	Pratt	Total
MBR	7	1	1	9	MOM	—	4	4	8
MBS	—	—	1	1	MON	70	31	22	123
MBU	1	2	1	4	MOO	—	9	—	9
					MOP	—	—	2	2
MEA	—	21	11	32	MOR	74	51	39	164
MEB	—	2	—	2	MOS	102	39	31	172
MEC	14	—	3	17	MOT	100	22	6	128
MED	18	18	22	58	MOU	105	18	19	142
MEE	—	5	2	7	MOV	119	9	7	135
MEF	—	1	—	1					
MEH	—	1	1	2	MPA	26	21	11	58
MEL	—	6	4	10	MPE	73	14	8	95
MEM	35	10	11	56	MPH	4	3	2	9
MEN	296	84	70	450	MPI	—	1	1	2
MEO	—	1	—	1	MPL	—	34	22	56
MER	83	26	31	140	MPO	16	10	9	35
MES	35	34	16	85	MPR	95	2	4	101
MET	3	24	12	39	MPS	—	2	—	2
MEW	59	3	1	63	MPT	35	8	10	53
MEX	58	1	—	59	MPU	—	6	1	7
					MPY	—	—	1	1
MFO	—	5	—	5					
					MRO	1	—	—	1
MHE	—	—	1	1	MRS	—	8	8	16
MIA	5	1	—	6	MSA	1	—	—	1
MIC	9	10	6	25	MSE	—	10	6	16
MID	—	3	—	3	MSH	1	—	—	1
MIE	—	2	3	5	MSO	—	1	—	1
MIG	30	8	5	43	MST	—	1	—	1
MIL	56	47	26	129					
MIN	308	61	42	411	MTH	—	1	—	1
MIR	10	3	4	17					
MIS	41	23	17	81	MUA	1	—	—	1
MIT	84	10	18	112	MUC	—	14	7	21
MIX	—	2	—	2	MUD	—	1	—	1
					MUG	—	—	1	1
					MUI	2	—	—	2
MLE	1	1	1	3	MUK	1	—	—	1
MLY	—	2	2	4	MUL	35	5	2	42
					MUM	—	3	—	3
MMA	1	3	2	6	MUN	9	14	3	26
MME	2	11	8	21	MUR	—	6	1	7
MMI	4	—	5	9	MUS	24	26	16	66
MMO	—	5	3	8	MUT	1	6	1	8
MMU	5	17	1	23					
MMY	—	4	—	4	MYS	—	2	4	6
MNA	1	—	2	3	NAB	12	3	3	18
MNI	1	1	—	2	NAC	3	3	1	7
MNY	1	—	—	1	NAD	2	2	2	6
					NAF	—	1	—	1
MOA	—	1	—	1	NAG	2	1	3	6
MOB	—	4	2	6	NAH	—	1	—	1
MOC	—	5	7	12	NAI	56	1	1	58
MOD	—	6	8	14	NAK	32	2	—	34
MOI	37	1	—	38	NAL	156	33	30	219
MOK	9	3	—	12	NAM	—	7	1	8
MOL	33	1	—	34	NAN	5	12	10	27

	T-L	U	Pratt	Total		T-L	U	Pratt	Total
NAP	3	4	5	12	NEW	8	50	30	88
NAR	5	10	11	26	NEX	110	10	2	122
NAS	—	5	1	6	NEY	—	7	7	14
NAT	181	38	40	259					
NAU	2	1	—	3	NFA	10	1	3	14
NAV	8	—	13	21	NFE	37	2	5	44
NAW	7	1	—	8	NFI	42	2	7	51
NAZ	—	—	1	1	NFL	—	—	4	4
					NFO	—	8	6	14
NBA	—	—	1	1	NFR	2	2	—	4
NBE	12	—	3	15	NFU	14	3	1	18
NBU	1	—	1	2					
NBV	3	—	—	3	NGA	92	2	2	96
					NGE	100	43	26	169
NCA	13	—	1	14	NGF	—	1	—	1
NCE	488	77	96	661	NGG	—	1	—	1
NCH	29	12	15	56	NGH	8	—	—	8
NCI	15	10	19	44	NGI	5	12	10	27
NCL	3	8	15	26	NGL	87	18	8	113
NCO	66	9	3	78	NGN	2	—	—	2
NCR	1	4	4	9	NGO	1	—	2	3
NCS	—	—	1	1	NGP	1	2	—	3
NCT	36	6	6	48	NGR	—	4	—	4
NCY	10	8	5	23	NGS	20	34	11	65
					NGT	102	10	4	116
NDA	25	11	6	42	NGU	1	6	6	13
NDE	145	63	45	253					
NDF	3	1	3	7	NHA	—	4	1	5
NDH	1	—	—	1	NHE	2	1	—	3
NDI	112	41	30	183	NHI	2	3	—	5
NDK	35	—	—	35	NHO	2	2	—	4
NDL	60	12	5	77	NHU	2	—	—	2
NDM	3	3	1	7					
NDO	41	17	9	67	NIA	9	7	6	22
NDP	—	2	—	2	NIB	13	—	—	13
NDR	104	3	36	143	NIC	36	15	5	56
NDS	—	40	30	70	NIE	18	8	—	26
NDU	44	8	11	63	NIF	53	4	2	59
NDW	—	1	1	2	NIG	14	13	5	32
NDY	4	6	2	12	NIK	—	1	—	1
					NIL	5	—	—	5
NEA	—	13	9	22	NIM	—	4	2	6
NEC	267	13	8	288	NIN	47	42	40	129
NED	14	53	46	113	NIO	39	3	4	46
NEE	—	17	6	23	NIP	4	1	—	5
NEF	—	2	1	3	NIS	128	15	16	159
NEG	4	3	5	12	NIT	45	25	22	92
NEH	—	1	—	1	NIU	—	1	1	2
NEI	2	3	2	7	NIV	1	5	6	12
NEL	20	6	7	33	NIW	—	—	7	7
NEM	17	2	1	20	NIZ	2	8	—	10
NEN	—	—	4	4					
NEO	1	1	1	3	NJA	—	1	2	3
NEP	—	—	1	1	NJO	—	4	—	4
NER	153	38	21	212	NJU	—	3	1	4
NES	203	58	32	293					
NET	38	7	11	56	NKA	1	—	—	1
NEU	—	2	—	2	NKE	3	1	4	8
NEV	4	18	14	36	NKF	4	2	—	6

	T-L	U	Pratt	Total		T-L	U	Pratt	Total
NKI	—	4	4	8	NSA	—	2	8	10
NKL	2	3	1	6	NSC	27	2	—	29
NKN	—	—	1	1	NSE	35	16	8	59
NKS	18	4	5	27	NSF	1	2	1	4
					NSG	7	—	—	7
NLA	3	1	—	4	NSH	3	—	—	3
NLE	1	4	—	5	NSI	95	19	20	134
NLI	—	1	—	1	NSK	1	—	1	2
NLO	2	—	—	2	NSL	—	1	—	1
NLS	—	—	4	4	NSM	—	1	—	1
NLU	8	—	—	8	NSO	5	5	1	11
NLY	17	36	26	79	NSP	39	3	4	46
					NST	9	25	29	63
NMA	9	2	1	12	NSU	36	8	2	46
NME	1	13	7	21	NSW	—	9	2	11
NMO	—	—	1	1	NSY	—	—	2	2
NNA	3	2	3	8	NTA	23	24	33	80
NNE	31	7	8	46	NTE	485	73	53	611
NNI	61	5	7	73	NTH	14	19	8	41
NNK	2	—	—	2	NTI	225	52	44	321
NNO	82	11	8	101	NTL	326	14	12	352
NNS	—	—	2	2	NTM	—	—	1	1
NNU	15	4	3	22	NTN	15	—	—	15
NNY	5	3	1	9	NTO	10	27	19	56
					NTR	30	28	33	91
NOA	6	—	—	6	NTS	—	42	28	70
NOB	14	3	2	19	NTU	65	7	3	75
NOC	55	2	2	59	NTV	—	—	5	5
NOE	—	—	5	5	NTY	10	6	32	48
NOG	—	1	1	2					
NOI	8	4	1	13	NUA	16	3	3	22
NOK	—	1	—	1	NUB	2	—	—	2
NOL	2	2	2	6	NUC	—	2	—	2
NOM	—	6	6	12	NUD	—	1	—	1
NON	30	4	5	39	NUE	5	11	5	21
NOO	6	6	3	15	NUF	61	1	2	64
NOP	14	—	—	14	NUG	9	1	—	10
NOR	121	11	23	154	NUI	12	—	3	15
NOS	4	2	6	12	NUL	7	—	—	7
NOT	71	99	67	237	NUM	1	8	8	17
NOU	27	7	12	46	NUN	—	—	4	4
NOV	—	3	1	4	NUR	1	3	—	4
NOW	11	61	31	103	NUS	1	2	4	7
NOX	1	—	—	1	NUT	1	14	2	17
NOY	—	—	1	1					
NOZ	—	1	—	1	NVA	—	1	2	3
					NVE	127	9	14	150
NPL	—	—	1	1	NVI	10	7	2	19
NPO	1	1	1	3	NVO	1	1	3	5
NPR	—	1	—	1					
					NWA	2	—	2	4
NQU	65	4	7	76	NWI	11	—	—	11
NRA	2	1	—	3	NXI	—	1	1	2
NRI	4	1	—	5					
NRO	17	1	1	19	NYB	—	1	—	1
NRY	—	—	2	2	NYI	—	—	1	1
					NYL	—	1	—	1

	T-L	U	Pratt	Total		T-L	U	Pratt	Total
NYO	—	5	3	8	OET	—	1	—	1
NYT	—	5	2	7	OEU	—	—	4	4
NYW	—	2	—	2	OEV	15	1	—	16
NZE	—	2	—	2	OFE	111	6	—	117
NZI	—	1	—	1	OFF	—	24	26	50
					OFI	—	2	2	4
OAC	8	5	2	15	OFL	—	1	—	1
OAD	2	11	10	23	OFO	8	—	—	8
OAH	6	—	—	6	OFT	119	8	4	131
OAL	—	—	1	1					
OAM	—	—	2	2	OGA	6	—	—	6
OAN	—	3	1	4	OGD	1	—	—	1
OAR	2	3	7	12	OGE	17	11	2	30
OAS	—	5	—	5	OGF	2	—	—	2
OAT	14	6	1	21	OGG	1	—	—	1
					OGI	1	4	1	6
OBA	—	1	6	7	OGL	1	—	—	1
OBB	2	2	4	8	OGN	8	3	5	16
OBE	1	2	2	5	OGR	38	8	2	48
OBI	13	7	2	22	OGS	—	2	3	5
OBJ	—	2	3	5	OGU	—	1	—	1
OBL	58	9	4	71	OGY	1	2	6	9
OBO	—	1	2	3					
OBR	1	—	1	2	OHI	—	—	5	5
OBS	—	7	7	14	OHN	—	6	—	6
OBT	—	—	3	3					
OBU	4	—	—	4	OIB	1	—	—	1
OBV	—	2	—	2	OIC	—	7	2	9
OBW	5	—	—	5	OID	3	3	1	7
					OIL	8	5	7	20
OCA	103	8	8	119	OIN	11	18	10	39
OCC	142	9	5	156	OIR	5	—	—	5
OCE	45	7	8	60	OIS	46	6	1	53
OCH	9	—	1	10					
OCI	7	9	5	21	OJE	—	3	2	5
OCK	191	22	15	128					
OCL	—	1	—	1	OKA	1	—	—	1
OCO	—	3	2	5	OKE	204	17	4	225
OCR	—	3	5	8	OKI	8	7	2	17
OCT	1	8	2	11	OKL	—	2	2	4
					OKO	8	—	—	8
ODA	—	7	28	35	OKS	—	3	7	10
ODD	—	3	—	3	OKY	7	—	—	7
ODE	1	13	6	20					
ODF	—	1	—	1	OLA	45	5	—	50
ODG	—	2	—	2	OLC	—	—	2	2
ODI	11	5	8	24	OLD	194	54	22	270
ODL	16	2	—	18	OLE	240	15	6	261
ODM	2	—	—	2	OLG	8	—	1	9
ODN	34	—	—	34	OLI	27	30	31	88
ODO	—	2	—	2	OLK	10	3	—	13
ODS	—	7	4	11	OLL	97	28	41	166
ODU	—	11	4	15	OLM	7	—	1	8
ODY	8	12	5	25	OLN	—	2	—	2
					OLO	12	13	7	32
OEF	6	—	—	6	OLP	—	1	—	1
OER	—	2	—	2	OLS	31	4	2	37
OES	—	14	6	20	OLT	—	4	—	4

	T-L	U	Pratt	Total		T-L	U	Pratt	Total
OLU	3	8	9	20	OPO	13	5	8	26
OLV	—	4	5	9	OPP	1	15	2	18
OLY	16	5	—	21	OPR	28	1	1	30
					OPS	—	5	4	9
OMA	122	23	7	152	OPT	7	4	6	17
OMB	59	8	5	72	OPU	1	6	3	10
OME	108	81	52	241					
OMF	—	5	—	5	OQU	—	1	—	1
OMI	2	17	22	41					
OML	1	—	1	2	ORA	64	12	8	84
OMM	6	27	14	47	ORB	44	5	3	52
OMN	—	—	5	5	ORC	121	19	14	154
OMO	35	7	—	42	ORD	83	22	32	137
OMP	55	37	25	117	ORE	122	70	63	255
OMS	—	2	10	12	ORF	19	—	—	19
OMY	—	3	1	4	ORG	21	13	5	39
					ORH	—	1	—	1
ONA	82	28	18	128	ORI	259	17	15	291
ONC	19	17	23	59	ORK	52	36	18	106
OND	59	27	32	118	ORL	6	16	13	35
ONE	142	126	78	346	ORM	65	19	31	115
ONF	51	6	10	67	ORN	53	31	9	93
ONG	241	38	27	306	ORO	8	2	1	11
ONI	34	13	5	52	ORP	14	1	—	15
ONK	1	—	1	2	ORR	39	12	12	63
ONL	1	28	21	50	ORS	10	31	17	58
ONM	—	1	—	1	ORT	65	59	60	184
ONN	12	3	8	23	ORU	3	—	1	4
ONO	34	7	14	55	ORV	—	—	6	6
ONP	—	—	1	1	ORW	30	13	—	43
ONQ	57	4	2	63	ORY	117	14	—	131
ONR	10	2	1	13					
ONS	69	67	78	214	OSA	12	4	—	16
ONT	69	59	30	158	OSB	—	3	—	3
ONU	—	—	3	3	OSC	2	1	2	5
ONV	12	6	6	24	OSE	72	43	41	156
ONY	4	2	1	7	OSH	—	3	—	3
ONZ	—	2	—	2	OSI	17	6	10	33
					OSL	—	—	2	2
OOD	74	55	25	154	OSN	—	—	1	1
OOF	—	2	2	4	OSO	—	3	—	3
OOG	—	1	—	1	OSP	3	6	3	12
OOK	160	30	23	213	OSS	3	27	18	48
OOL	164	15	6	185	OST	321	49	34	404
OOM	—	24	8	32	OSU	11	1	—	12
OON	17	15	5	37	OSY	1	—	—	1
OOP	8	6	—	14					
OOR	40	20	2	62	OTA	—	2	10	12
OOS	3	5	1	9	OTB	—	1	1	2
OOT	2	9	8	19	OTE	33	22	22	77
OOV	35	—	2	37	OTF	—	—	1	1
OOZ	2	—	—	2	OTG	3	—	—	3
					OTH	225	89	40	354
OPA	3	2	1	6	OTI	54	10	10	74
OPE	80	25	30	135	OTL	—	1	—	1
OPH	2	4	3	9	OTO	131	7	2	140
OPI	—	2	1	3	OTS	—	5	4	9
OPL	1	24	13	38	OTT	—	7	4	11
OPM	—	2	5	7	OTY	—	1	1	2

	T-L	U	Pratt	Total		T-L	U	Pratt	Total
OUA	1	—	—	1	PAR	317	72	36	425
OUB	—	5	6	11	PAS	14	16	21	51
OUC	—	3	1	4	PAT	265	25	12	302
OUD	—	7	1	8	PAU	—	3	2	5
OUG	5	56	28	89	PAW	4	1	—	5
OUI	—	2	4	6	PAY	5	7	5	17
OUL	203	72	38	313					
OUN	201	89	60	350	PEA	328	19	20	367
OUP	—	12	1	13	PEC	153	25	16	194
OUR	177	105	56	338	PED	1	29	7	37
OUS	317	61	66	444	PEE	13	4	2	19
OUT	623	106	54	783	PEG	17	1	—	18
OUV	1	5	—	6	PEL	—	1	—	1
					PEN	109	30	22	161
OVA	29	—	1	30	PEO	—	24	11	35
OVE	566	64	65	695	PER	329	71	79	479
OVI	96	9	5	110	PES	—	3	1	4
					PET	27	11	2	40
OWA	—	7	1	8	PEW	—	1	—	1
OWB	6	—	1	7					
OWC	—	1	—	1	PHA	6	7	2	15
OWD	113	3	2	118	PHE	22	6	5	33
OWE	162	40	32	234	PHI	7	4	8	19
OWF	—	—	1	1	PHO	53	9	8	70
OWH	1	—	1	2	PHR	—	1	—	1
OWI	—	10	6	16	PHS	—	2	—	2
OWL	5	12	—	17	PHY	2	2	3	7
OWN	110	44	24	178					
OWP	1	—	—	1	PIA	—	1	—	1
OWS	8	12	8	28	PIC	19	10	11	40
OWT	—	1	2	3	PID	1	—	4	5
OWY	10	—	—	10	PIE	35	5	3	43
					PIG	44	—	—	44
OXE	—	4	1	5	PIK	—	1	1	2
OXF	15	2	—	17	PIL	—	8	7	15
OXI	13	3	8	24	PIM	—	—	12	12
					PIN	49	14	—	63
OYA	65	5	1	71	PIO	—	1	—	1
OYC	—	—	1	1	PIP	1	—	—	1
OYD	—	1	—	1	PIQ	6	—	—	6
OYE	—	7	8	15	PIR	48	5	3	56
OYH	—	1	—	1	PIS	3	1	—	4
OYI	—	1	1	2	PIT	—	28	8	36
OYM	—	—	1	1	PIZ	—	1	—	1
OYS	—	7	3	10					
					PKE	—	1	—	1
OZE	2	3	—	5					
OZZ	—	1	—	1	PLA	194	52	46	292
					PLE	98	62	37	197
PAB	9	2	—	11	PLI	23	15	16	54
PAC	6	3	2	11	PLO	24	11	9	44
PAD	—	2	1	3	PLU	—	6	1	7
PAG	—	9	2	11	PLY	3	10	6	19
PAI	188	11	12	211					
PAJ	6	—	—	6	PMA	—	—	1	1
PAL	58	5	6	69	PME	9	3	6	18
PAN	85	20	21	126					
PAP	—	5	12	17	PNE	—	1	—	1
PAQ	—	—	1	1					

	T-L	U	Pratt	Total		T-L	U	Pratt	Total
POA	2	—	—	2	PWA	—	—	1	1
POC	50	3	2	55					
POD	3	—	—	3	PYA	—	—	1	1
POE	3	1	—	4	PYT	1	—	—	1
POI	3	9	5	17					
POK	43	1	1	45	QUA	11	18	13	42
POL	41	12	25	78	QUE	209	21	25	255
PON	2	10	16	28	QUI	149	22	10	181
POO	9	4	1	14	QUO	—	—	2	2
POP	—	8	6	14					
POR	60	29	27	116	RAA	—	1	—	1
POS	189	28	26	243	RAB	22	21	4	47
POT	2	8	—	10	RAC	147	37	16	200
POU	1	2	1	4	RAD	124	16	11	151
POW	157	18	10	185	RAF	—	11	7	18
					RAG	23	12	4	39
PPA	90	4	2	96	RAH	8	1	1	10
PPE	116	32	23	171	RAI	19	28	17	64
PPI	26	12	4	42	RAK	—	3	1	4
PPL	25	13	11	49	RAL	40	23	38	101
PPM	—	—	1	1	RAM	80	13	2	95
PPO	—	13	6	19	RAN	185	44	40	269
PPR	88	11	12	111	RAP	135	4	5	144
PPT	—	—	1	1	RAR	16	4	3	23
PPY	14	7	—	21	RAS	35	8	6	49
					RAT	273	49	54	376
PRA	5	14	4	23	RAU	—	2	1	3
PRE	116	48	52	216	RAV	3	10	5	18
PRI	123	31	23	177	RAW	49	3	4	56
PRO	412	86	67	565	RAX	2	—	—	2
PRU	2	2	1	5	RAY	2	6	3	11
PRY	1	—	—	1	RAZ	—	5	—	5
PSC	—	1	—	1	RBA	4	2	—	6
PSE	—	3	—	3	RBE	1	3	—	4
PSI	1	—	—	1	RBI	43	5	4	52
PSU	2	1	—	3	RBO	4	2	1	7
PSY	2	3	—	5	RBS	—	1	—	1
					RBU	1	1	—	2
PTA	100	3	1	104	RBY	—	2	—	2
PTE	—	8	7	15					
PTH	49	1	—	50	RCA	7	—	18	25
PTI	45	5	8	58	RCE	181	16	—	197
PTO	7	1	1	9	RCH	126	16	14	156
PTS	—	1	1	2	RCI	6	12	7	25
PTU	13	1	1	15	RCL	108	5	1	114
PTY	—	3	1	4	RCS	—	—	12	12
					RCU	28	5	1	34
PUB	15	7	26	48	RCY	2	3	1	6
PUC	4	—	—	4					
PUD	17	—	—	17	RDA	—	3	3	6
PUL	17	10	11	38	RDE	60	15	14	89
PUN	12	1	1	14	RDH	1	—	—	1
PUP	19	1	—	20	RDI	19	6	15	40
PUR	89	5	5	99	RDL	—	1	1	2
PUS	—	3	1	4	RDO	37	1	—	38
PUT	15	20	5	40	RDS	2	9	12	23
PUZ	—	1	—	1	RDU	—	1	1	2

	T-L	U	Pratt	Total		T-L	U	Pratt	Total
RDW	15	—	—	15	RIS	145	24	23	192
RDY	15	2	1	18	RIT	135	24	23	182
					RIU	2	2	—	4
REA	540	111	82	733	RIV	133	21	15	169
REB	5	2	2	9	RIZ	3	3	3	9
REC	36	43	45	124					
RED	114	70	101	285	RKA	—	2	2	4
REE	228	47	45	320	RKE	101	8	5	114
REF	29	6	20	55	RKH	1	1	—	2
REG	112	12	19	143	RKI	2	4	2	8
REH	27	3	1	31	RKM	—	—	2	2
REI	35	6	8	49	RKN	—	1	—	1
REL	77	27	12	116	RKS	5	9	1	15
REM	140	24	20	184	RKY	1	—	—	1
REN	158	47	39	244					
REO	36	5	2	43	RLA	4	3	—	7
REP	45	21	28	94	RLB	1	—	—	1
REQ	126	7	—	133	RLD	5	13	13	31
RER	19	6	8	33	RLE	109	14	5	128
RES	226	106	114	446	RLI	7	4	6	17
RET	76	19	18	113	RLO	27	1	1	29
REU	22	—	—	22	RLS	—	7	—	7
REV	155	12	14	181	RLY	55	15	8	78
REW	39	6	—	45					
REY	1	—	—	1	RMA	17	10	26	53
					RME	3	12	12	27
RFA	—	1	—	1	RMI	24	10	8	42
RFE	43	2	4	49	RML	—	—	1	1
RFL	—	1	—	1	RMO	7	5	8	20
RFO	10	1	—	11	RMS	—	4	6	10
RFU	51	5	3	59	RMT	—	1	1	2
					RMU	—	3	—	3
RGA	18	8	5	31					
RGE	88	18	26	132	RNA	14	4	9	27
RGH	—	2	—	2	RNE	44	33	19	96
RGI	—	3	—	3	RNF	—	1	—	1
RGL	3	—	—	3	RNI	—	14	10	24
RGO	—	3	1	4	RNM	—	6	8	14
RGS	—	—	1	1	RNO	7	6	7	20
RGU	2	1	1	4	RNS	—	7	—	7
RGY	10	4	—	14	RNT	1	17	1	19
RHA	—	5	—	5	ROA	3	17	13	33
RHE	1	1	—	2	ROB	4	12	10	26
RHO	—	2	—	2	ROC	118	11	14	143
					ROD	1	11	5	17
RIA	93	23	13	129	ROE	10	1	1	12
RIB	4	12	10	26	ROF	111	8	2	121
RIC	86	38	33	157	ROG	23	8	2	33
RID	32	7	3	42	ROH	—	—	5	5
RIE	28	41	29	98	ROI	1	—	—	1
RIF	37	3	1	41	ROJ	—	3	2	5
RIG	119	24	19	162	ROK	—	7	—	7
RIK	—	1	2	3	ROL	25	9	9	43
RIL	61	10	3	74	ROM	41	63	65	169
RIM	52	19	6	77	RON	255	21	10	286
RIN	45	53	39	137	ROO	—	25	3	28
RIO	147	14	13	174	ROP	37	24	15	76
RIP	63	6	4	73	ROR	15	3	1	19

	T-L	U	Pratt	Total		T-L	U	Pratt	Total
ROS	38	16	14	68	RUN	17	9	6	32
ROT	—	16	3	19	RUP	23	1	1	25
ROU	86	146	28	260	RUR	—	—	1	1
ROV	208	6	10	224	RUS	21	8	2	31
ROW	218	19	11	248	RUT	—	8	1	9
ROX	—	—	7	7					
ROY	80	5	5	90	RVA	6	4	4	14
ROZ	—	1	—	1	RVE	7	18	8	33
					RVI	44	9	9	62
RPA	2	—	—	2	RVO	47	2	—	49
RPE	—	1	2	3					
RPH	1	—	—	1	RWA	31	4	2	37
RPI	2	—	1	3	RWE	7	—	—	7
RPL	—	3	2	5	RWO	9	—	2	11
RPO	14	2	1	17					
RPR	—	2	1	3	RXE	2	—	—	2
RRA	—	3	5	8	RYA	2	—	—	2
RRE	23	10	16	49	RYB	—	2	2	4
RRI	28	25	13	66	RYI	—	11	2	13
RRO	66	8	8	82	RYL	—	1	—	1
RRU	21	—	1	22	RYM	—	1	—	1
RRY	19	14	3	36	RYO	—	3	2	5
					RYS	—	2	3	5
RSA	6	2	—	8	RYT	—	10	—	10
RSB	—	1	—	1					
RSD	—	1	—	1	SAA	—	1	—	1
RSE	197	32	11	240	SAC	46	3	—	49
RSH	15	1	4	20	SAD	21	3	2	26
RSI	—	5	8	13	SAF	52	5	2	59
RSO	10	5	8	23	SAG	12	3	2	17
RSP	9	—	2	11	SAI	8	40	15	63
RST	6	36	21	63	SAL	69	11	8	88
RSU	—	1	—	1	SAM	7	8	4	19
RSY	—	—	1	1	SAN	49	14	33	96
					SAP	—	1	5	6
RTA	2	23	16	41	SAR	103	7	7	117
RTE	1	10	10	21	SAS	—	2	1	3
RTF	2	—	—	2	SAT	9	7	11	27
RTH	100	13	22	135	SAU	48	1	—	49
RTI	227	21	32	280	SAV	—	9	1	10
RTL	1	—	3	4	SAW	—	7	3	10
RTM	—	10	2	12	SAY	1	11	3	15
RTN	11	—	—	11					
RTO	17	2	1	20	SBA	—	12	—	12
RTR	18	—	1	19	SBO	—	3	—	3
RTS	5	14	8	27	SBU	3	2	—	5
RTU	27	6	4	37	SBY	—	1	—	1
RTY	—	11	17	28					
					SCA	27	8	7	42
RUA	4	—	4	8	SCE	1	8	3	12
RUB	—	—	1	1	SCH	62	16	13	91
RUC	21	18	11	50	SCI	138	13	11	162
RUD	—	—	1	1	SCL	15	1	—	16
RUE	—	8	2	10	SCO	3	11	—	14
RUG	1	8	1	10	SCR	14	11	9	34
RUI	1	2	2	5	SCU	—	1	9	10
RUL	—	4	4	8					
RUM	2	5	4	11	SDA	—	—	5	5

	T-L	U	Pratt	Total		T-L	U	Pratt	Total
SEA	108	10	12	130	SIT	88	23	17	128
SEC	7	15	15	37	SIU	2	—	—	2
SED	14	26	13	53	SIV	45	11	3	59
SEE	151	33	15	199	SIX	—	7	10	17
SEF	—	2	—	2	SIZ	1	3	2	6
SEG	—	—	2	2					
SEH	—	—	2	2	SKA	45	—	6	51
SEI	—	1	29	30	SKE	14	16	6	36
SEL	187	50	—	237	SKI	5	10	1	16
SEM	11	6	2	19	SKR	8	—	—	8
SEN	36	31	50	117	SKS	—	—	1	1
SEP	2	7	3	12	SKY	—	4	2	6
SEQ	—	1	5	6					
SER	26	33	20	79	SLA	151	7	11	169
SES	7	36	23	66	SLE	35	7	7	49
SET	247	14	10	271	SLI	7	6	4	17
SEU	3	10	1	14	SLO	57	4	2	63
SEV	—	1	21	22	SLU	—	3	—	3
SEW	32	7	1	40	SLY	61	11	3	75
SEX	1	3	1	5					
SEY	21	1	4	26	SMA	6	18	4	28
					SME	—	1	1	2
SFA	1	1	2	4	SMI	—	7	6	13
SFE	—	1	1	2	SMO	12	8	1	21
SFI	5	—	—	5	SMS	—	1	—	1
SFO	—	1	3	4	SMU	—	1	1	2
SFU	8	3	—	11					
					SNA	—	4	—	4
SGI	17	1	—	18	SNE	4	—	1	5
SGO	1	—	—	1	SNI	—	2	—	2
SGR	30	—	—	30	SNO	10	—	1	11
					SNP	—	—	1	1
SHA	159	13	8	180	SNT	—	6	—	6
SHC	—	—	1	1	SNU	20	1	—	21
SHE	142	109	33	284					
SHI	157	33	19	209	SOA	—	1	2	3
SHM	25	3	1	29	SOB	—	1	—	1
SHN	—	—	1	1	SOC	—	8	4	12
SHO	307	50	12	369	SOD	—	—	1	1
SHR	1	4	—	5	SOL	149	14	—	163
SHS	—	1	—	1	SOM	55	40	—	95
SHU	—	4	1	5	SON	313	28	—	341
SHV	—	1	—	1	SOO	—	2	2	4
SHY	3	—	1	4	SOP	—	2	—	2
					SOR	60	14	—	74
SIA	1	6	4	11	SOT	—	—	1	1
SIB	9	15	12	36	SOU	167	17	—	184
SIC	1	20	6	27	SOV	—	2	—	2
SID	104	36	23	163					
SIE	15	4	5	24	SPA	90	9	6	105
SIF	—	4	1	5	SPE	223	36	25	284
SIG	2	7	9	18	SPH	30	—	1	31
SIL	173	8	7	188	SPI	53	15	14	82
SIM	1	13	3	17	SPL	2	3	1	6
SIN	129	35	34	198	SPO	153	7	13	173
SIO	157	22	33	212	SPR	1	9	4	14
SIP	3	—	1	4	SPS	—	1	—	1
SIR	—	13	2	15	SPU	44	3	1	48
SIS	81	18	12	111					

	T-L	U	Pratt	Total		T-L	U	Pratt	Total
SQU	—	12	9	21	TAD	—	1	3	4
					TAF	—	1	1	2
SRE	—	—	1	1	TAG	106	12	4	122
SRU	—	1	—	1	TAI	101	23	26	150
					TAK	2	22	16	40
SSA	172	11	4	187	TAL	18	37	18	73
SSE	32	31	38	101	TAM	—	2	1	3
SSF	7	3	2	12	TAN	55	43	26	124
SSI	154	38	33	225	TAP	—	2	1	3
SSL	7	3	—	10	TAR	124	28	21	173
SSM	—	1	1	2	TAS	11	5	2	18
SSO	59	8	2	69	TAT	103	29	44	176
SSU	—	10	8	18	TAU	2	1	1	4
SSW	—	1	—	1	TAW	—	2	—	2
SSY	9	2	—	11	TAX	9	2	1	12
					TAY	7	2	1	10
STA	374	91	67	532					
STE	558	72	50	680	TBA	—	3	1	4
STH	1	—	—	1	TBO	—	2	—	2
STI	542	57	61	660	TBR	—	—	1	1
STL	11	8	4	23					
STM	—	8	—	8	TCA	—	1	—	1
STO	309	46	13	368	TCH	130	29	11	170
STP	—	1	1	2	TCO	—	1	—	1
STR	319	72	57	448	TCR	—	1	—	1
STS	—	21	18	39					
STU	25	19	6	50	TDO	—	2	—	2
STY	87	5	—	92					
					TEA	256	18	16	290
SUA	2	7	6	15	TEB	—	—	2	2
SUB	39	10	6	55	TEC	2	5	5	12
SUC	7	18	16	41	TED	17	98	104	219
SUD	—	3	4	7	TEE	66	15	17	98
SUE	—	5	6	11	TEF	6	2	1	9
SUF	111	3	2	116	TEG	—	4	4	8
SUG	—	10	2	12	TEI	1	1	—	2
SUI	2	2	1	5	TEL	18	28	28	74
SUL	28	8	5	41	TEM	104	23	22	149
SUM	6	9	6	21	TEN	318	52	46	416
SUN	116	10	5	131	TEO	3	2	1	6
SUP	73	15	11	99	TEP	6	7	—	13
SUR	79	25	20	124	TER	758	193	143	1094
SUS	7	—	4	11	TES	25	50	46	121
					TET	—	—	4	4
SWA	—	1	1	2	TEU	—	1	—	1
SWE	75	17	10	102	TEV	—	2	—	2
SWI	—	5	2	7	TEW	6	—	3	9
SWO	—	2	—	2	TEX	—	2	1	3
SYB	1	—	—	1	TFA	—	—	1	1
SYC	—	3	—	3	TFI	1	1	—	2
SYG	1	—	—	1	TFO	1	1	—	2
SYL	14	2	3	19	TFU	15	2	2	19
SYM	18	11	4	33					
SYN	1	—	—	1	THA	124	199	143	466
SYR	6	—	—	6	THC	—	—	2	2
SYS	—	6	5	11	THD	—	1	1	2
					THE	257	1201	1054	2512
TAB	128	23	13	164	THF	—	4	2	6
TAC	1	4	14	19					

	T-L	U	Pratt	Total		T-L	U	Pratt	Total
THI	85	130	83	298	TOU	4	7	2	13
THL	5	4	3	12	TOW	4	10	10	24
THO	72	41	60	173	TOX	3	1	—	4
THP	—	1	—	1	TOY	—	2	1	3
THR	78	34	33	145					
THS	—	7	7	14	TPH	—	1	—	1
THU	100	11	5	116					
THW	—	—	2	2	TRA	307	62	40	409
THY	4	3	3	10	TRE	225	33	23	281
					TRI	92	44	31	167
TIA	105	9	7	121	TRO	167	23	17	207
TIB	5	1	1	7	TRU	5	36	20	61
TIC	363	57	61	481	TRY	—	—	21	21
TID	57	1	1	59					
TIE	1	21	15	37	TSB	—	2	—	2
TIF	189	11	12	212	TSE	—	7	1	8
TIG	20	4	—	24	TSH	1	—	—	1
TIL	50	26	17	93	TSI	100	7	—	107
TIM	18	51	40	109	TSK	5	1	—	6
TIN	144	102	64	310	TSM	—	—	1	1
TIO	678	170	177	1025	TSO	—	—	1	1
TIP	9	3	2	14	TSP	1	—	—	1
TIQ	—	1	—	1	TST	—	3	3	6
TIR	157	6	8	171					
TIS	29	9	12	50	TTA	4	7	9	20
TIT	52	8	20	80	TTE	118	59	40	217
TIV	143	28	30	201	TTI	10	26	6	42
TIZ	—	4	1	5	TTL	106	30	16	152
					TTO	2	5	3	10
TJU	—	1	—	1	TTR	1	3	—	4
					TTS	37	4	—	41
TLA	—	—	4	4	TTY	1	4	2	7
TLE	323	39	23	385					
TLI	—	2	1	3	TUA	52	12	7	71
TLY	243	32	20	295	TUB	—	—	8	8
					TUC	—	4	—	4
TMA	—	9	—	9	TUD	13	10	7	30
TME	41	13	3	57	TUE	—	—	4	4
TMO	—	—	2	2	TUI	4	—	—	4
					TUL	13	—	—	13
TNE	1	2	1	4	TUM	36	1	1	38
TNI	11	2	—	13	TUN	23	12	3	38
					TUO	18	—	1	19
TOA	—	—	1	1	TUR	147	71	49	267
TOB	—	2	—	2	TUS	6	1	1	8
TOC	—	2	—	2	TUT	45	3	12	60
TOD	—	8	25	33					
TOE	7	4	—	11	TWA	24	1	1	26
TOF	8	—	—	8	TWE	—	14	45	59
TOG	38	8	7	53	TWI	—	3	1	4
TOI	7	—	—	7	TWO	—	23	40	63
TOL	17	7	1	25					
TOM	116	18	19	153	TYL	53	2	—	55
TON	265	24	12	301	TYP	—	6	—	6
TOO	11	38	12	61	TYR	5	1	—	6
TOP	2	13	3	18	TYX	3	—	—	3
TOR	339	52	40	431					
TOS	—	2	—	2	UAB	—	—	3	3
TOT	—	—	6	6	UAC	7	—	—	7

	T-L	U	Pratt	Total		T-L	U	Pratt	Total
UAD	—	1	3	4	UGS	1	3	—	4
UAG	—	2	—	2	UGU	—	1	2	3
UAL	66	28	20	114					
UAN	4	1	1	6	UIC	—	2	—	2
UAP	4	—	—	4	UID	—	6	2	8
UAR	22	14	13	49	UIE	2	3	1	6
UAT	6	6	4	16	UIL	4	12	15	31
UAV	3	—	—	3	UIM	1	—	3	4
					UIN	1	—	—	1
UBB	—	—	1	1	UIP	—	3	2	5
UBE	4	—	10	14	UIR	118	8	4	130
UBI	1	—	1	2	UIS	10	4	10	24
UBJ	—	5	4	9	UIT	48	10	4	62
UBL	15	12	25	52	UIV	13	—	—	13
UBO	—	1	—	1					
UBS	39	4	2	45	UKD	1	—	—	1
UBT	—	2	2	4	UKE	—	2	4	6
UBU	—	1	—	1	UKI	—	—	1	1
UCA	—	6	3	9	ULA	128	20	19	167
UCC	7	6	4	17	ULB	5	1	—	6
UCE	82	10	8	100	ULC	1	2	—	3
UCH	1	29	19	49	ULD	203	67	27	297
UCI	6	1	—	7	ULE	33	9	7	49
UCK	12	14	4	30	ULF	—	1	2	3
UCL	—	2	1	3	ULG	15	—	2	17
UCO	—	1	—	1	ULI	12	1	2	15
UCR	1	—	1	2	ULK	—	1	—	1
UCT	5	16	15	36	ULL	27	18	14	59
UCY	6	—	—	6	ULM	5	—	—	5
					ULN	3	4	1	8
UDA	—	—	1	1	ULO	1	2	4	7
UDD	19	3	6	28	ULP	—	1	6	7
UDE	25	12	12	49	ULS	—	3	1	4
UDG	50	1	1	52	ULT	32	21	12	65
UDI	16	4	10	30	ULU	2	—	—	2
UDL	—	1	—	1	ULY	9	3	1	13
UDY	—	3	1	4					
					UMA	1	5	4	10
UEA	—	1	2	3	UMB	76	11	13	100
UED	—	11	8	19	UME	8	6	6	20
UEE	—	3	1	4	UMI	9	3	—	12
UEL	2	1	1	4	UMM	—	4	3	7
UEN	3	2	9	14	UMN	3	—	—	3
UEP	—	2	—	2	UMO	—	1	—	1
UER	67	—	2	69	UMP	26	12	2	40
UES	133	23	18	174	UMS	—	6	2	8
UEY	—	—	1	1	UMU	—	1	2	3
UFA	52	1	2	55	UNA	44	10	3	57
UFF	133	7	4	144	UNB	16	—	1	17
					UNC	75	13	13	101
UGA	1	2	1	4	UND	221	85	78	384
UGB	1	—	—	1	UNE	12	8	3	23
UGE	52	3	5	60	UNF	14	3	2	19
UGG	7	15	3	25	UNG	57	18	8	83
UGH	50	66	40	156	UNH	5	1	—	6
UGI	—	1	—	1	UNI	54	31	20	105
UGM	7	—	—	7	UNK	—	2	3	5

	T-L	U	Pratt	Total
UNL	9	4	3	16
UNM	9	—	—	9
UNN	48	5	3	56
UNO	—	1	—	1
UNP	—	1	1	2
UNQ	8	—	1	9
UNR	2	—	—	2
UNS	14	7	8	29
UNT	138	41	31	210
UNU	—	2	—	2
UNW	13	—	—	13
UOS	1	—	—	1
UOT	—	—	1	1
UOU	36	—	1	37
UPA	42	4	2	48
UPE	20	2	2	24
UPI	8	1	1	10
UPK	—	1	—	1
UPL	—	5	2	7
UPO	21	7	10	38
UPP	75	15	10	100
UPS	—	1	—	1
UPT	20	1	2	23
UPW	—	—	1	1
UPY	50	—	1	51
URA	37	13	7	57
URB	8	5	2	15
URC	212	13	8	233
URD	103	4	2	109
URE	211	59	55	325
URF	—	1	—	1
URG	64	5	4	73
URI	1	11	13	25
URK	—	—	1	1
URL	—	4	1	5
URM	—	1	—	1
URN	12	31	13	56
URO	9	3	4	16
URP	—	5	3	8
URR	69	13	7	89
URS	212	20	7	239
URT	9	6	3	18
URV	1	3	1	5
URY	2	4	7	13
USA	21	2	27	50
USB	—	12	—	12
USC	—	1	2	3
USE	169	61	37	267
USH	10	9	7	26
USI	31	33	13	77
USK	7	1	1	9
USL	60	10	3	73
USN	4	—	—	4
USP	—	—	2	2
USS	11	7	10	28

	T-L	U	Pratt	Total
UST	148	52	38	238
USU	—	5	5	10
USY	101	3	2	106
UTA	7	5	2	14
UTB	—	2	—	2
UTC	22	2	—	24
UTD	—	2	—	2
UTE	75	15	15	105
UTF	—	1	—	1
UTH	104	16	19	139
UTI	26	23	21	70
UTJ	—	1	—	1
UTL	18	1	—	19
UTM	—	—	1	1
UTN	—	1	—	1
UTO	10	6	9	25
UTR	—	4	—	4
UTS	107	15	3	125
UTT	4	12	2	18
UTU	1	4	1	6
UTW	—	—	1	1
UTY	13	10	4	27
UUM	—	—	1	1
UVA	—	—	1	1
UVE	—	5	—	5
UVR	1	—	4	5
UXI	3	—	—	3
UXL	2	1	—	3
UXU	—	—	1	1
UYE	—	—	1	1
UYI	—	1	—	1
UYS	—	—	1	1
UZE	6	—	—	6
UZZ	—	1	—	1
VAB	4	—	2	6
VAC	70	2	1	73
VAD	7	1	1	9
VAG	3	1	—	4
VAI	42	3	4	49
VAL	51	5	22	78
VAN	78	10	6	94
VAP	—	1	3	4
VAR	—	9	7	16
VAS	—	3	3	6
VAT	75	6	10	91
VAU	—	—	1	1
VEA	—	1	4	5
VED	7	27	18	52
VEE	—	—	3	3
VEG	—	1	—	1
VEH	—	2	—	2

	T-L	U	Pratt	Total		T-L	U	Pratt	Total
VEI	1	—	—	1	WBE	—	—	1	1
VEL	130	30	17	177	WBO	6	—	—	6
VEM	—	4	5	9	WBR	—	—	2	2
VEN	326	59	63	448					
VER	248	150	147	545	WCA	—	1	—	1
VES	62	29	30	121	WCO	—	1	—	1
VET	35	1	—	36					
VEY	—	—	2	2	WDE	13	—	1	14
					WDL	1	—	—	1
VIA	6	1	—	7					
VIC	29	13	12	54	WEA	73	9	6	88
VID	1	15	9	25	WEB	5	—	—	5
VIE	28	7	7	42	WED	17	13	9	39
VIF	—	1	—	1	WEE	58	26	15	99
VIG	—	1	1	2	WEI	—	2	1	3
VIK	18	—	—	18	WEL	185	31	14	230
VIL	33	7	6	46	WEN	1	12	27	40
VIM	—	—	14	14	WEP	—	2	1	3
VIN	73	39	—	112	WER	165	84	60	309
VIO	175	7	—	182	WES	7	6	4	17
VIR	2	3	2	7	WET	—	—	3	3
VIS	96	16	9	121	WEV	—	9	11	20
VIT	2	8	7	17					
VIV	26	3	2	31	WFL	—	—	1	1
VIZ	3	—	—	3					
					WHA	17	33	11	61
VOC	21	3	1	25	WHE	81	93	51	225
VOI	2	10	2	14	WHI	117	74	67	258
VOK	—	—	1	1	WHO	226	57	33	316
VOL	14	7	6	27	WHY	—	2	—	2
VOR	1	1	5	7					
VOT	—	4	5	9	WIC	—	2	2	4
VOU	55	2	—	57	WID	—	4	8	12
VOW	—	1	—	1	WIF	—	2	4	6
VOY	—	1	—	1	WIG	1	—	2	3
					WIL	58	49	54	161
VRE	1	—	4	5	WIN	125	38	19	182
					WIR	—	3	1	4
VUL	—	1	—	1	WIS	6	10	1	17
VUS	—	—	1	1	WIT	26	114	75	215
					WIV	—	—	1	1
VYS	—	—	1	1					
					WJE	—	—	1	1
WAB	1	—	—	1					
WAD	19	—	—	19	WLA	—	1	3	4
WAF	4	—	—	4	WLE	—	7	2	9
WAG	—	2	—	2	WLI	—	1	1	2
WAI	5	14	5	24	WLY	—	3	1	4
WAK	—	2	—	2					
WAL	—	10	7	17	WME	—	1	—	1
WAM	—	—	1	1					
WAN	82	16	1	99	WNE	1	5	3	9
WAR	23	28	32	83	WNH	3	1	—	4
WAS	246	166	74	486	WNI	1	—	—	1
WAT	—	17	19	36	WNP	1	—	—	1
WAU	—	1	—	1	WNR	4	—	—	4
WAV	—	2	2	4	WNS	3	3	—	6
WAY	35	44	16	95	WNW	—	—	2	2
					WNY	—	1	—	1

	T-L	U	Pratt	Total		T-L	U	Pratt	Total
WOB	1	—	—	1	XIL	4	—	—	4
WOE	32	—	—	32	XIM	19	1	7	27
WOK	14	—	—	14	XIN	—	4	1	5
WOL	—	—	1	1	XIO	1	2	1	4
WOM	3	13	4	20	XIS	9	2	3	14
WON	—	13	2	15	XIX	3	—	—	3
WOO	81	12	5	98					
WOR	9	50	40	99	XLE	9	1	—	10
WOU	—	34	23	57					
WOV	2	—	—	2	XMA	1	—	—	1
					XMI	1	—	—	1
WPE	1	—	—	1					
					XON	—	1	—	1
WRA	51	—	—	51					
WRE	—	2	2	4	XPA	39	2	—	41
WRI	—	7	4	11	XPE	109	21	11	141
WRO	—	3	—	3	XPL	2	6	7	15
WRY	—	1	—	1	XPO	55	1	—	56
					XPR	—	2	7	9
WSE	5	—	—	5	XPU	—	—	1	1
WSI	3	—	—	3					
WSP	—	1	3	4	XTE	—	5	5	10
WSU	—	—	1	1	XTH	—	1	2	3
					XTI	—	1	—	1
WTE	3	—	—	3	XTR	—	1	2	3
WTH	—	1	2	3	XTU	7	1	—	8
WTO	—	2	—	2	XTY	—	—	3	3
WYE	—	6	—	6	XUA	—	2	1	3
WYO	—	—	7	7	XUB	1	—	—	1
					XUD	1	—	—	1
XAC	89	2	3	94	XUL	11	—	—	11
XAM	—	8	7	15	XUR	—	—	2	2
XAN	—	—	1	1					
XAS	—	2	—	2	YAB	—	1	—	1
XAT	1	—	—	1	YAC	2	—	1	3
					YAH	1	—	—	1
XCE	—	7	5	12	YAL	78	4	3	85
XCH	—	2	—	2	YAN	—	1	1	2
XCI	—	7	—	7	YAR	2	5	6	13
XCL	44	2	2	48	YAT	—	1	—	1
					YAW	—	1	—	1
XEC	—	1	2	3					
XED	52	6	—	58	YBE	—	2	—	2
XEM	—	—	1	1	YBO	1	3	1	5
XER	2	3	3	8	YBR	—	—	1	1
XES	2	2	2	6					
XEY	—	3	—	3	YCE	1	—	—	1
					YCH	—	3	—	3
XFO	15	2	—	17	YCL	2	5	—	7
					YCO	1	—	1	2
XHA	—	1	2	3					
XHI	—	—	1	1	YDR	17	—	1	18
XHO	—	1	—	1					
XHU	—	1	—	1	YEA	—	34	19	53
					YED	—	15	8	23
XIB	—	1	1	2	YEE	—	3	3	6
XIC	61	2	—	63	YEL	—	3	1	4
XID	10	—	—	10	YEN	2	—	—	2

	T-L	U	Pratt	Total		T-L	U	Pratt	Total
YER	6	7	3	16	YRO	—	1	—	1
YES	—	14	11	25	YRU	5	—	5	10
YET	—	5	7	12	YRY	1	—	—	1
YGI	7	—	—	7	YSA	—	2	—	2
YGO	1	—	—	1	YSC	—	1	—	1
					YSE	—	1	2	3
YHE	—	1	—	1	YSH	—	—	1	1
YHO	—	1	—	1	YSI	—	2	5	7
					YSO	—	—	1	1
YIN	44	20	15	79	YST	1	6	7	14
YLA	—	1	—	1	YTH	1	15	2	18
YLE	51	2	—	53	YTI	—	1	—	1
YLI	3	—	—	3					
YLK	1	—	—	1	YVE	—	1	—	1
YLL	12	1	—	13					
YLO	7	2	—	9	YWA	—	1	—	1
YLP	—	—	1	1	YWH	—	1	—	1
YLV	2	1	—	3	YWI	1	—	—	1
YLY	—	—	2	2	YWO	13	3	—	16
YMA	—	1	1	2	ZAB	—	1	—	1
YMB	18	11	4	33	ZAN	—	1	—	1
YME	—	—	1	1	ZAR	1	1	3	5
YMO	—	3	—	3	ZAT	—	6	3	9
YNC	1	—	—	1	ZED	2	17	11	30
YND	—	1	—	1	ZEL	6	—	—	6
YNE	3	—	—	3	ZEN	—	7	1	8
					ZER	1	2	1	4
YOM	—	—	1	1	ZES	—	1	—	1
YON	33	9	5	47					
YOR	32	12	8	52	ZIC	—	1	—	1
YOS	—	1	—	1	ZIE	3	1	—	4
YOU	—	164	33	197	ZIN	3	2	1	6
					ZIS	—	—	1	1
YPE	—	7	5	12					
YPH	1	—	—	1	ZLE	1	2	—	3
YPO	—	1	—	1	ZLI	—	1	1	2
YPR	2	—	—	2					
YPS	—	—	1	1	ZON	5	3	2	10
YPT	22	1	—	23					
					ZZA	1	—	1	2
YRA	1	—	—	1	ZZI	—	1	—	1
YRE	4	1	1	6	ZZL	1	3	1	5
YRI	11	1	—	12					

APPENDIX E
PRONUNCIABILITY RATINGS FOR 239
THREE-LETTER UNITS

A low value indicates "easy to pronounce," a high value, "hard to pronounce." See details of scaling procedure in Chapters 2 and 7.

ABL	5.57 *	GAW	3.35	MPT	7.56
ALI	3.57 *	GEL	2.82	MUL	2.35
AND	2.15	GHT	7.63		
ART	1.97	GIH	5.18	NCE	7.60 *
ATI	4.34 *	GOI	4.60 *	NDE	7.63 *
		GUD	4.36	NDF	8.31
BAD	1.50	GVS	8.04	NDR	8.14 *
BAL	2.33			NIQ	5.33
BLE	4.23 *	HAT	1.77 *	NOP	2.63
BLI	3.37 *	HAZ	3.27	NUW	5.56
BON	2.11 *	HEG	3.27		
BOT	2.64	HER	2.06 *	OMP	3.99
BOY	2.26 *	HFG	8.40	OUS	3.84
BUT	1.91	HOB	2.29		
BUV	4.37	HOV	3.01	PAR	1.74 *
		HTF	8.40 *	PEH	5.04
CAK	4.10	HUM	1.80	PEX	3.51
CAT	1.60			PID	3.16
CES	3.35	IDW	7.92	PIM	2.62
CED	3.07	IFO	4.34	PLO	3.11 *
CFL	7.38	ING	2.36	POH	3.64
CHA	2.95	ISH	2.23 *	PUF	2.92
CHI	3.29 *	ITE	3.41	PUS	2.82
CIB	3.44	ITS	2.69 *		
CKB	8.39			QAD	4.89
COH	5.22	JAD	3.35	QAZ	5.99
COM	2.31 *	JEC	3.66 *	QOH	6.78
COU	3.14 *	JOK	4.89	QOW	6.29
CQU	8.23 *	JOP	3.78	QUE	4.23
CRS	7.42	JOR	3.51 *	QUW	7.08
CUB	1.80 *	JPV	8.47	QZP	8.28
CYR	5.44	JUM	3.11 *		
		JUS	3.29 *	RAJ	5.25
DAL	2.62	JUX	5.08	RAT	1.81
DAP	2.65			RCE	6.83 *
DFL	7.66	KBR	8.34 *	RCH	7.27
DGM	8.42	KBV	8.51	REC	2.43
DIH	5.04	KIM	2.24	REL	2.50
DIR	2.81	KIT	2.15	ROC	3.18
DOK	3.54	KIV	3.86 *	ROP	3.46 *
DYI	6.11 *	KIX	2.44	ROQ	4.25
		KNO	4.40 *	ROX	3.49
EIG	5.86			ROZ	3.48
EKL	6.59	LAR	2.23 *	RTI	7.43 *
ELK	2.81	LED	1.91 *	RZQ	8.59
ENT	3.17 *	LIR	4.03 *		
EQR	7.80	LOX	2.86	SAY	1.82
EST	2.46	LTY	7.03 *	SCI	3.60 *
		LZW	8.53	SLO	2.20 *
FAC	2.63			SOG	2.65
FAI	3.83 *	MAK	3.29	SOM	2.36
FEM	1.95	MAN	1.66	SOU	4.15
FEN	2.17	MBE	7.80 *	STI	2.49
FET	2.49 *	MBK	8.18	STY	3.19
FIB	1.92	MEF	3.28	SUB	1.72
FID	2.66	MEL	1.99	SUD	1.99
FJQ	8.73	MOG	3.06	SUK	3.24
FOC	3.56	MOP	2.04	SUL	3.03
FOD	2.65	MPA	7.34 *		
FON	2.83	MPO	7.23 *	TIO	3.94 *
FRO	2.40 *	MPR	7.94 *	TIS	2.09
FUS	2.51			TIV	3.43

TJU	7.74 *	WAM	2.92	XPO	7.81
TLY	5.75	WAS	2.19	XYH	8.51
TOZ	3.36	WFI	7.93	XYZ	8.75
TRC	6.49	WHA	3.23 *		
TUD	3.49	WHE	4.09 *	YAL	3.67
TUW	6.48	WHO	2.29	YAG	3.60
		WIB	3.90	YIN	3.17 *
ULD	5.00	WIF	3.40	YIR	4.69
UND	3.83 *	WIH	5.93	YLV	8.37 *
UNH	7.10	WIS	3.40	YOQ	6.37
URN	2.40 *	WOM	3.60	YOX	4.57
		WSE	7.06 *	YQG	8.77
VAD	2.06	WUQ	6.83	YUK	4.27
VAS	2.88	WUX	4.15	YUQ	6.60
VEN	2.66 *	WXY	8.59	YUW	6.82
VER	2.60				
VGJ	8.73	XAN	5.58	ZAM	2.67
VIF	3.83 *	XAT	6.35	ZAV	4.27
VIL	3.14 *	XET	6.22	ZED	3.39
VIT	3.16	XFH	8.72	ZIN	2.63
VIZ	3.03	XIK	7.52	ZJM	8.34
VOL	2.98	XOL	5.91	ZOJ	6.60
VOM	3.22	XOM	5.76	ZON	3.15
VOZ	4.08	XOQ	7.71	ZOX	4.76
VUF	5.36	XPE	8.05	ZUN	3.29
VXK	8.64	XPL	8.43 *		

* Based on ratings of 35 subjects; all others based on ratings of 181 subjects.

A total of 273 subjects was presented with all single-letter and all possible two-letter combinations and were asked to write down for each the first letter they thought of. These tables give the number of subjects responding with each letter to each stimulus. For example, to the single-letter stimulus B, 47 subjects responded with A, 3 with B, 8 with C, and so on. To the two-letter stimulus AB, 9 subjects responded with A, 2 with B, 135 with C, and so on. The sum of each column equals 273. See Chapter 9 for details of the procedure.

Responses to Single-Letter Stimulus

Response						Stimulus Letter							
	A	B	C	D	E	F	G	H	I	J	K	L	M
A	6	47	32	17	19	28	25	19	8	42	34	30	22
B	50	3	5	4	6	9	4	5	9	8	4	4	4
C	7	8	3	4	3	6	8	5	3	3	2	3	10
D	7	12	20	4	21	10	5	6	15	12	12	6	3
E	5	31	9	16	12	17	12	26	5	12	6	11	34
F	4	2	0	4	25	0	4	0	23	4	1	1	0
G	0	2	2	6	2	5	2	2	0	2	9	1	4
H	4	1	2	2	5	5	11	2	2	0	1	1	3
I	5	13	13	15	11	32	10	107	1	16	31	15	9
J	1	0	3	0	2	0	1	1	6	1	2	2	0
K	2	4	4	2	9	3	3	6	3	26	7	2	0
L	6	7	7	7	19	11	5	5	6	7	24	2	3
M	10	4	7	4	16	5	4	11	31	3	12	64	3
N	19	3	2	3	26	3	5	3	31	2	2	6	49
O	11	71	86	130	14	64	132	42	19	61	53	69	70
P	8	5	5	3	5	3	3	6	4	21	3	9	4
Q	1	0	7	2	0	6	2	1	5	3	2	1	0
R	11	5	8	2	14	9	5	7	5	15	10	6	12
S	39	8	2	1	13	11	2	1	10	4	3	6	4
T	61	12	15	12	31	16	13	8	64	2	21	14	6
U	1	19	17	17	3	18	11	2	7	15	13	6	7
V	2	1	5	2	4	2	0	1	5	3	5	4	2
W	3	0	3	2	1	3	0	1	4	2	1	2	0
X	5	1	1	1	5	2	2	0	3	3	1	4	1
Y	1	9	10	1	0	2	2	3	0	3	7	2	19
Z	2	4	3	7	3	0	2	1	2	2	2	0	1
Omit	2	1	2	5	4	3	0	2	2	1	5	2	3

Responses to Single-Letter Stimulus

Response	Stimulus Letter												
	N	O	P	Q	R	S	T	U	V	W	X	Y	Z
A	11	4	24	22	38	11	14	2	34	33	15	22	29
B	3	5	7	5	6	0	11	9	7	2	2	3	3
C	3	1	6	1	1	3	1	3	4	3	4	5	1
D	5	12	6	4	1	6	3	5	22	4	4	5	12
E	5	5	7	4	19	10	9	4	14	40	8	16	21
F	3	8	2	2	3	3	2	4	0	1	0	1	3
G	0	3	1	1	3	2	2	2	0	1	2	0	1
H	2	8	1	1	2	2	1	6	1	5	3	2	2
I	7	4	16	13	20	9	16	8	33	15	50	11	19
J	2	4	3	1	3	1	3	0	1	2	1	0	0
K	1	7	1	2	1	2	1	3	0	1	0	3	4
L	5	8	11	8	4	4	4	8	2	2	10	5	3
M	9	29	4	6	6	8	10	7	10	3	6	6	3
N	2	34	2	5	7	4	3	13	3	3	5	10	10
O	170	8	99	15	63	110	128	7	51	54	41	100	70
P	11	54	0	14	3	8	1	62	1	1	6	2	5
Q	1	0	19	2	1	2	1	1	2	1	1	2	2
R	4	15	8	57	15	9	7	15	6	6	9	3	5
S	5	13	7	16	33	4	18	19	7	7	3	6	4
T	7	32	12	28	15	50	6	41	19	8	18	10	25
U	13	7	20	49	9	10	21	7	12	29	5	18	16
V	1	0	0	4	2	4	7	35	7	12	0	5	4
W	0	3	1	1	2	4	1	0	22	8	1	2	1
X	1	2	6	6	8	2	1	5	3	13	11	13	7
Y	0	2	4	1	3	2	1	3	7	6	51	4	11
Z	1	3	3	5	0	1	0	3	3	8	16	16	9
Omit	1	2	3	0	5	2	1	1	2	5	1	3	3

Responses to Two-Letter Combinations

A   First Stimulus Letter

Response	Second Stimulus Letter												
	A	B	C	D	E	F	G	H	I	J	K	L	M
A	127	9	7	12	3	10	16	38	4	19	13	3	23
B	25	2	8	10	10	22	10	7	8	10	10	21	12
C	10	135	29	17	12	9	19	4	7	17	6	7	6
D	4	29	48	80	17	12	8	8	18	11	5	11	6
E	0	19	47	31	6	24	61	26	27	11	38	27	28
F	3	5	2	2	16	11	6	3	6	4	2	7	19
G	2	1	14	2	1	6	8	3	0	3	1	2	3
H	1	1	0	0	2	1	7	37	4	5	2	0	2
I	2	0	2	6	22	5	8	18	11	8	14	5	10
J	2	1	0	0	1	1	2	2	5	6	2	2	1
K	8	2	16	2	1	5	10	3	3	71	16	7	2
L	4	11	4	4	15	24	3	19	12	9	42	54	2
M	4	3	4	12	2	4	9	18	45	6	4	21	6
N	5	4	2	7	7	10	4	6	7	5	9	3	25
O	9	9	18	13	18	12	32	8	18	14	22	14	19
P	5	5	3	13	55	6	4	6	11	4	8	9	39
Q	1	0	5	1	2	5	1	0	1	7	2	0	3
R	7	7	5	6	13	6	12	14	10	9	18	4	8
S	6	9	6	12	18	13	14	11	10	8	19	9	5
T	22	8	41	12	31	67	8	21	50	18	13	47	32
U	12	2	2	8	5	3	11	1	2	0	3	2	5
V	2	0	2	9	2	1	6	6	3	1	4	6	6
W	7	0	1	1	3	2	3	4	2	1	9	4	1
X	0	3	2	2	1	3	1	3	2	15	2	3	3
Y	0	2	1	3	4	1	6	3	1	5	3	1	0
Z	2	4	1	8	3	5	3	1	3	3	3	1	2
Omit	3	2	3	0	3	5	1	3	3	3	3	3	5

Responses to Two-Letter Combinations

	A	First Stimulus Letter											
Response					Second Stimulus Letter								
	N	O	P	Q	R	S	T	U	V	W	X	Y	Z
A	12	4	19	13	12	8	16	9	20	14	7	18	30
B	13	18	15	14	6	7	11	9	7	6	9	9	20
C	2	2	13	10	8	8	4	4	7	7	7	3	0
D	110	9	14	4	9	18	2	25	32	3	11	6	13
E	10	14	55	11	66	10	45	5	95	63	73	111	41
F	2	3	5	3	6	3	3	7	4	9	4	3	4
G	1	2	3	1	2	2	2	15	4	1	2	1	1
H	2	2	1	2	2	5	4	1	4	2	0	2	3
I	1	5	5	5	11	3	6	2	9	4	13	4	7
J	1	0	0	1	0	2	1	2	1	0	4	1	0
K	2	4	0	3	5	24	3	7	2	7	7	1	7
L	3	3	4	4	8	2	12	12	6	16	7	7	3
M	6	6	8	4	11	4	9	5	2	9	6	3	10
N	29	4	4	7	5	7	4	4	7	6	2	5	8
O	20	2	34	22	11	10	57	6	21	12	18	15	14
P	10	99	19	15	4	7	5	9	5	5	3	4	11
Q	0	1	2	7	1	2	0	1	1	1	4	1	1
R	1	4	16	45	10	6	9	17	5	5	6	9	9
S	9	5	19	12	14	55	16	11	2	47	10	14	10
T	22	63	21	25	63	76	44	72	11	19	25	6	39
U	1	7	3	46	4	6	3	4	6	3	5	2	5
V	4	4	1	7	5	0	4	14	2	7	3	5	6
W	2	4	2	1	1	3	2	11	5	7	2	14	2
X	1	2	2	3	2	0	2	17	2	6	13	8	3
Y	7	3	1	4	3	0	1	2	8	6	23	3	10
Z	1	2	5	3	0	2	4	2	3	5	6	17	11
Omit	1	1	2	1	4	3	4	0	2	3	3	1	5

Responses to Two-Letter Combinations

	B	First Stimulus Letter										

Response					Second Stimulus Letter							
	A	B	C	D	E	F	G	H	I	J	K	L	M
A	7	14	34	42	14	24	26	35	7	18	14	32	26
B	24	54	6	7	15	7	6	6	8	17	18	6	4
C	7	39	28	11	7	14	11	12	8	19	6	11	21
D	37	18	39	9	43	14	12	16	14	24	7	18	11
E	1	10	16	50	25	24	13	13	3	20	20	12	7
F	2	1	5	8	12	7	10	7	6	2	3	2	3
G	1	15	2	1	10	18	15	1	11	3	6	1	2
H	1	1	4	2	0	1	8	7	0	8	0	0	0
I	1	6	9	26	1	11	29	25	2	12	12	32	40
J	1	0	1	3	0	4	0	1	4	2	3	2	2
K	7	1	10	3	4	8	1	4	2	19	6	2	4
L	10	10	10	2	11	10	7	11	23	6	19	9	8
M	13	34	13	12	7	6	22	10	17	2	15	9	13
N	16	3	4	7	18	11	7	10	7	6	10	6	15
O	1	11	26	28	4	21	40	40	8	14	48	45	25
P	4	2	3	3	8	6	2	8	11	14	1	11	6
Q	1	1	6	2	1	1	0	2	1	6	3	3	5
R	15	4	8	10	12	21	10	13	4	13	16	4	5
S	23	13	11	8	9	13	19	11	10	16	11	7	25
T	91	17	17	9	62	28	8	14	107	23	23	34	25
U	1	0	5	5	1	2	7	3	5	10	3	12	0
V	1	3	2	11	3	2	2	9	3	3	2	1	5
W	1	1	2	2	2	5	4	3	1	8	8	3	6
X	1	4	2	4	0	3	5	3	4	0	3	3	7
Y	3	7	2	5	1	5	2	6	3	2	9	6	2
Z	0	2	5	2	2	5	4	1	2	1	4	1	5
Omit	3	2	3	1	1	2	3	2	2	5	3	1	1

Responses to Two-Letter Combinations

Response	B First Stimulus Letter												
	Second Stimulus Letter												
	N	O	P	Q	R	S	T	U	V	W	X	Y	Z
A	23	4	22	17	43	27	32	4	15	23	18	14	32
B	5	46	9	7	3	15	3	8	3	5	4	8	5
C	16	8	6	6	13	11	2	11	3	17	7	8	9
D	11	13	11	6	6	8	5	17	99	10	5	9	25
E	8	5	11	10	21	8	55	2	20	25	7	101	15
F	4	1	6	1	2	5	2	1	3	4	4	1	5
G	0	7	4	0	3	6	1	9	4	4	3	2	4
H	5	0	5	1	1	9	1	4	0	2	0	1	2
I	15	0	20	13	19	5	14	0	11	9	22	8	15
J	5	0	3	1	2	1	0	1	0	3	2	0	2
K	1	0	2	3	3	2	1	7	2	9	2	2	2
L	7	6	14	4	1	10	10	12	4	6	12	10	13
M	13	4	6	5	5	5	2	9	4	15	5	7	1
N	0	6	9	4	6	2	5	7	3	11	8	6	4
O	70	15	50	38	57	18	48	3	28	35	35	8	36
P	10	31	8	10	5	8	3	5	3	9	7	7	4
Q	6	6	8	3	1	3	8	1	0	3	3	1	9
R	10	9	19	48	23	7	14	14	12	10	12	8	10
S	7	10	9	17	10	23	10	31	7	13	18	11	5
T	25	68	23	17	24	81	7	113	16	16	36	29	38
U	5	3	7	31	9	9	36	1	8	4	2	7	9
V	7	2	3	0	1	4	2	0	2	7	2	1	1
W	2	3	2	4	2	2	0	2	11	8	5	1	1
X	5	14	3	10	3	2	2	2	6	12	8	6	6
Y	7	11	4	4	5	2	7	2	2	7	34	9	9
Z	6	0	6	9	4	0	2	4	5	2	9	8	8
Omit	0	1	3	4	1	0	1	3	2	4	3	0	3

Responses to Two-Letter Combinations

Response	C	First Stimulus Letter											
						Second Stimulus Letter							
	A	B	C	D	E	F	G	H	I	J	K	L	M
A	4	48	18	30	15	10	34	36	6	24	21	16	26
B	7	6	7	9	9	10	8	4	7	12	1	10	8
C	5	11	72	10	6	13	20	5	8	12	5	5	12
D	19	18	16	7	33	24	24	3	20	16	6	10	13
E	0	6	4	40	11	29	7	24	4	7	31	18	12
F	6	2	3	9	14	10	14	5	10	5	3	8	2
G	1	4	11	3	2	11	7	5	2	7	4	1	11
H	1	1	0	3	0	2	8	1	0	7	5	1	3
I	1	9	8	24	4	9	9	47	2	16	17	12	14
J	1	2	1	1	2	2	4	1	5	8	4	0	5
K	4	0	3	3	3	3	2	4	2	18	15	4	2
L	9	11	8	4	15	19	4	9	21	16	36	6	9
M	6	4	5	7	10	8	6	3	17	7	12	15	7
N	14	9	13	6	13	2	3	3	9	7	4	9	18
O	5	23	26	46	4	25	41	49	20	25	20	59	45
P	20	1	8	10	15	5	3	6	28	7	7	10	13
Q	1	4	1	5	3	2	5	1	1	5	1	2	2
R	19	6	15	6	7	10	17	10	6	9	16	5	5
S	3	65	6	11	13	9	12	5	14	16	16	8	4
T	139	23	14	11	76	39	23	10	75	23	15	26	42
U	2	0	9	9	2	11	3	29	5	6	6	24	3
V	1	2	3	4	5	3	4	1	7	3	6	5	6
W	1	5	5	0	5	3	3	2	1	3	3	2	1
X	2	8	5	5	0	5	5	2	0	3	6	3	5
Y	0	0	9	8	1	0	3	3	1	4	4	9	3
Z	1	3	1	1	4	5	1	2	1	3	6	2	1
Omit	1	2	2	1	1	4	3	3	1	4	3	3	1

Responses to Two-Letter Combinations

C   First Stimulus Letter

Second Stimulus Letter

Response	N	O	P	Q	R	S	T	U	V	W	X	Y	Z
A	14	5	87	17	34	18	88	3	29	28	14	10	36
B	9	10	4	7	8	29	3	20	12	8	6	7	10
C	9	8	4	7	6	6	6	2	7	11	9	11	7
D	14	46	9	11	10	14	6	15	17	21	11	21	7
E	17	6	9	5	28	4	15	7	17	21	11	25	13
F	3	3	4	4	5	2	0	6	3	4	5	8	9
G	1	2	1	2	5	7	2	3	0	3	5	2	3
H	5	1	3	6	4	6	1	3	1	2	3	1	5
I	11	2	20	9	16	6	18	3	11	7	10	6	8
J	3	0	1	2	1	4	1	0	3	2	2	1	3
K	3	1	2	5	3	7	0	2	4	8	1	1	3
L	6	11	11	9	8	10	6	28	14	3	16	10	8
M	7	17	4	3	10	11	7	10	13	13	6	3	6
N	6	15	4	5	8	7	3	8	6	7	1	14	8
O	69	10	46	30	29	22	42	6	37	55	26	29	28
P	8	37	3	5	6	8	2	31	6	7	5	10	5
Q	5	3	2	7	2	3	2	0	3	3	2	2	6
R	12	13	12	57	7	9	10	8	6	14	10	27	21
S	11	6	10	17	21	9	12	5	20	20	4	11	13
T	31	51	15	22	27	60	5	91	31	4	25	46	25
U	8	1	16	22	9	6	29	2	11	10	8	4	9
V	4	4	1	2	2	7	3	8	5	11	14	4	2
W	6	4	0	2	3	4	0	2	6	4	4	3	2
X	3	11	1	5	1	3	3	2	7	9	10	5	7
Y	5	0	2	4	12	4	4	3	2	6	48	5	15
Z	1	2	2	6	6	4	3	6	1	6	17	4	11
Omit	2	4	0	2	2	3	2	3	3	2	1	3	3

Responses to Two-Letter Combinations

D First Stimulus Letter

Second Stimulus Letter

Response	A	B	C	D	E	F	G	H	I	J	K	L	M
A	7	21	35	13	12	15	22	23	6	21	20	22	34
B	15	8	15	1	22	10	15	11	4	5	3	5	10
C	4	12	22	6	4	29	10	15	5	19	6	21	19
D	56	9	15	43	25	9	7	4	45	8	5	5	3
E	1	23	11	12	14	33	16	11	10	16	75	13	12
F	6	4	7	4	20	12	7	9	3	3	3	4	5
G	8	1	2	5	10	18	19	8	9	3	2	3	2
H	1	2	1	2	1	5	3	4	3	7	2	4	4
I	1	14	7	8	0	10	10	31	2	22	25	14	22
J	2	2	1	4	1	4	2	3	3	8	2	3	5
K	4	4	5	1	20	4	2	4	6	18	6	7	2
L	12	7	17	4	15	5	5	19	19	9	27	7	9
M	25	5	3	5	19	8	14	8	11	10	14	26	8
N	14	3	3	1	29	7	2	5	13	11	9	16	28
O	4	50	36	26	2	16	82	43	8	13	13	32	29
P	20	7	4	6	14	11	4	12	19	5	4	7	7
Q	4	8	2	0	0	3	1	2	5	6	0	2	1
R	11	20	11	6	8	23	3	12	4	12	13	10	4
S	8	28	8	15	12	7	26	6	7	31	14	15	18
T	28	18	11	91	15	21	5	15	58	13	9	28	15
U	4	7	11	4	4	2	4	8	5	13	3	4	5
V	11	6	8	2	6	2	1	6	5	3	2	4	6
W	4	2	31	2	4	7	2	4	2	3	8	4	5
X	3	1	2	2	6	1	2	1	9	3	5	7	4
Y	15	2	3	2	0	4	4	5	1	4	1	4	6
Z	4	4	1	1	6	4	2	4	9	5	1	4	7
Omit	1	5	1	7	4	3	3	0	2	2	1	2	3

Responses to Two-Letter Combinations

Response	D	First Stimulus Letter											
						Second Stimulus Letter							
	N	O	P	Q	R	S	T	U	V	W	X	Y	Z
A	20	10	22	11	32	14	25	1	28	30	13	25	49
B	5	9	0	8	6	1	2	17	5	3	2	5	2
C	12	6	21	8	2	9	6	12	3	7	9	20	2
D	4	27	5	5	6	12	28	21	12	7	5	10	4
E	10	13	11	8	9	12	14	16	20	36	26	54	13
F	5	3	7	3	1	4	6	17	3	2	1	3	3
G	4	13	11	5	3	6	6	3	5	3	12	4	4
H	1	0	4	0	1	4	2	4	1	1	1	2	2
I	14	1	8	7	92	12	13	4	33	13	54	4	15
J	0	0	4	1	0	2	1	3	3	1	2	2	1
K	2	0	1	4	5	7	1	11	0	2	5	7	5
L	5	7	20	11	2	10	13	7	8	9	20	13	13
M	12	14	6	9	7	13	3	14	9	10	6	5	10
N	4	42	2	8	2	4	6	15	16	6	8	10	6
O	94	15	35	23	10	19	22	8	40	54	17	20	28
P	9	12	14	17	6	4	3	11	2	5	9	5	2
Q	4	2	29	3	0	3	2	0	1	0	3	1	2
R	8	10	20	48	7	15	12	5	10	10	15	6	6
S	8	2	13	18	26	16	20	9	14	18	7	20	25
T	22	59	10	24	18	83	28	34	20	8	14	13	33
U	8	5	5	19	8	4	22	4	9	5	4	9	16
V	6	4	2	4	12	3	3	18	1	4	3	4	1
W	4	12	7	4	0	3	2	2	10	10	2	0	1
X	2	1	6	6	3	1	3	4	9	15	4	8	4
Y	5	3	3	5	12	1	13	4	4	5	19	6	14
Z	3	2	4	11	2	8	16	28	2	7	11	15	10
Omit	2	1	3	3	1	3	1	1	5	2	1	2	2

Responses to Two-Letter Combinations

Response	E	First Stimulus Letter											
					Second Stimulus Letter								
	A	B	C	D	E	F	G	H	I	J	K	L	M
A	3	16	27	14	11	7	16	18	10	19	13	15	10
B	16	19	11	4	14	4	12	7	5	8	9	5	45
C	27	29	18	14	6	9	7	7	5	19	5	4	2
D	5	19	24	31	10	19	10	6	21	7	5	10	13
E	1	21	6	23	50	15	9	13	5	16	52	26	10
F	6	6	10	13	40	27	12	14	14	10	14	19	4
G	2	0	10	0	2	49	76	3	9	3	2	1	4
H	2	0	4	3	0	5	8	24	2	9	3	3	1
I	6	7	11	18	6	5	2	30	7	21	11	11	6
J	2	4	1	2	4	3	3	4	10	4	4	0	3
K	0	1	15	3	17	5	5	5	5	25	21	10	2
L	10	8	4	3	12	6	11	14	34	11	38	48	8
M	5	16	4	9	11	3	5	11	13	11	6	34	14
N	4	14	4	17	7	4	3	7	11	8	4	4	36
O	5	24	33	13	7	12	23	17	13	11	12	5	15
P	8	2	9	10	13	8	6	5	3	12	6	12	28
Q	0	0	7	3	1	3	4	3	0	3	1	0	0
R	35	17	10	5	15	9	7	20	13	14	20	9	7
S	6	19	6	22	6	6	18	10	7	14	11	6	8
T	111	24	37	32	21	60	12	34	63	25	22	27	46
U	0	3	5	19	1	1	3	3	3	5	2	2	0
V	8	1	2	0	7	3	5	0	3	2	1	10	2
W	4	4	2	4	2	3	5	1	4	4	2	3	0
X	3	5	3	2	2	3	5	7	6	3	0	2	1
Y	2	6	8	7	3	2	3	4	3	5	6	6	3
Z	2	7	1	2	3	2	0	2	3	3	3	0	3
Omit	0	1	1	0	2	0	3	4	1	1	0	1	2

Responses to Two-Letter Combinations

	E	First Stimulus Letter										
		Second Stimulus Letter										
Response	N	O	P	Q	R	S	T	U	V	W	X	Y	Z
A	5	19	18	14	39	3	51	9	30	20	19	7	32
B	3	17	8	5	9	1	8	14	3	4	13	4	5
C	10	15	4	4	7	1	16	22	6	11	16	5	0
D	97	19	17	11	13	9	5	23	8	11	7	13	12
E	10	4	11	9	17	8	33	2	87	47	10	82	30
F	2	11	2	6	9	1	2	6	2	7	8	3	4
G	4	6	3	3	3	5	1	16	5	2	3	2	1
H	3	1	3	3	4	1	7	2	1	1	1	5	4
I	6	3	15	5	4	5	11	4	5	8	16	4	13
J	2	0	1	2	2	1	2	3	2	4	3	0	1
K	5	5	7	3	5	0	0	3	2	6	6	13	6
L	0	12	23	8	4	4	11	10	3	10	8	12	5
M	6	21	3	4	6	5	5	13	10	5	13	9	8
N	1	23	5	4	15	4	8	16	7	8	5	6	7
O	23	3	21	16	6	11	28	7	15	19	13	15	18
P	10	30	17	5	11	7	4	30	2	10	18	7	6
Q	2	1	11	2	0	3	2	0	2	1	1	3	4
R	3	17	16	33	20	9	12	19	19	16	8	7	11
S	15	10	27	41	23	20	24	7	9	25	12	13	6
T	42	39	25	22	64	164	21	41	17	18	42	17	30
U	8	7	7	50	2	1	8	4	8	6	6	3	7
V	6	5	3	4	1	2	1	6	6	5	2	2	1
W	1	0	1	3	0	0	1	2	5	10	0	8	3
X	4	1	13	3	3	0	1	3	8	3	10	15	1
Y	2	2	2	4	2	5	6	3	7	1	24	7	45
Z	1	1	5	6	3	0	4	5	3	14	7	8	12
Omit	2	1	5	3	1	3	1	3	1	1	2	3	1

Responses to Two-Letter Combinations

Response	F	First Stimulus Letter											
					Second Stimulus Letter								
	A	B	C	D	E	F	G	H	I	J	K	L	M
A	5	11	27	22	4	15	15	56	2	19	17	9	24
B	21	7	7	7	14	1	5	7	32	12	6	5	15
C	15	31	39	24	4	7	13	4	3	16	4	14	7
D	26	17	21	6	25	14	12	5	18	19	11	26	10
E	1	7	7	16	26	21	7	17	6	8	19	9	5
F	4	6	5	3	6	50	3	2	5	2	4	1	11
G	6	7	13	3	4	14	6	8	14	12	4	4	2
H	4	1	1	1	3	3	31	6	2	8	0	3	2
I	1	50	12	12	10	10	22	44	0	20	20	11	6
J	1	3	1	3	2	2	1	3	7	4	4	3	1
K	4	10	7	0	3	4	3	6	1	21	3	8	4
L	8	10	7	11	13	7	6	2	9	8	37	8	12
M	8	9	3	4	8	2	4	5	8	4	7	19	13
N	21	29	6	7	22	6	8	4	18	8	6	13	30
O	1	7	16	32	5	14	58	31	3	26	24	41	14
P	6	3	3	11	10	5	4	10	7	13	8	7	14
Q	0	12	6	5	3	4	2	4	0	1	0	3	4
R	10	8	19	46	21	11	18	13	3	12	19	16	31
S	9	14	6	9	9	20	9	11	8	3	20	4	6
T	104	6	38	26	51	29	14	14	99	28	13	43	26
U	3	2	12	10	1	9	14	4	1	9	30	1	8
V	3	4	3	3	8	12	2	7	7	5	3	4	21
W	7	7	3	3	4	1	0	1	1	2	0	1	1
X	0	2	2	2	7	2	5	2	9	5	1	2	2
Y	3	2	4	3	1	2	5	4	1	5	6	11	2
Z	0	5	3	3	8	6	5	2	5	2	6	4	0
Omit	2	3	2	1	1	2	1	1	4	1	1	3	2

Responses to Two-Letter Combinations

F   First Stimulus Letter

Response

Second Stimulus Letter

	N	O	P	Q	R	S	T	U	V	W	X	Y	Z
A	15	3	11	23	36	16	29	3	20	31	14	9	15
B	4	36	9	9	6	4	13	10	9	4	7	6	16
C	2	8	18	9	11	5	10	40	10	6	10	10	7
D	8	14	16	8	20	16	10	23	8	5	14	14	13
E	12	5	17	8	44	10	13	1	18	30	11	35	16
F	2	3	6	1	1	4	6	1	8	2	4	5	1
G	6	19	6	8	3	5	1	15	3	6	4	6	4
H	2	0	4	5	2	1	1	1	7	1	2	2	2
I	15	1	18	5	19	15	17	6	14	8	32	12	15
J	8	0	3	1	2	5	2	9	2	0	2	3	0
K	2	1	2	1	1	4	0	11	2	9	2	3	3
L	5	15	3	14	5	7	11	15	7	5	14	25	11
M	14	4	2	12	8	7	11	5	13	12	8	3	9
N	6	3	4	8	9	7	6	23	29	10	9	8	10
O	51	9	33	12	33	16	46	5	16	27	31	15	26
P	3	29	8	13	3	8	12	12	9	10	6	2	11
Q	3	1	4	2	2	2	3	0	1	1	4	3	2
R	7	59	29	41	8	18	12	17	8	19	6	12	13
S	8	7	12	7	8	23	19	7	4	9	3	9	4
T	22	31	31	19	24	78	10	45	32	13	30	28	47
U	17	3	18	37	9	11	14	1	14	9	1	3	12
V	43	4	1	3	3	0	5	5	5	19	5	3	3
W	3	3	1	4	1	2	6	2	18	8	3	2	3
X	3	7	2	8	3	1	3	2	5	6	4	10	5
Y	3	1	2	4	8	0	2	1	2	9	16	3	14
Z	5	2	10	10	3	6	10	10	7	12	27	41	10
Omit	4	5	3	1	1	2	1	3	2	2	4	1	1

Responses to Two-Letter Combinations

	G	First Stimulus Letter											
Response					Second Stimulus Letter								
	A	B	C	D	E	F	G	H	I	J	K	L	M
A	18	27	42	17	8	22	17	14	11	17	23	35	26
B	11	3	17	11	8	6	6	6	20	18	3	6	6
C	2	17	15	12	13	25	24	6	5	14	4	29	72
D	22	19	23	5	14	10	11	2	25	13	10	15	7
E	2	13	11	15	19	18	13	9	4	11	29	7	6
F	5	4	12	5	12	11	7	5	6	10	2	9	4
G	19	3	6	2	1	9	63	3	16	9	7	2	2
H	3	1	3	4	2	8	10	4	4	6	6	3	2
I	6	22	11	32	3	23	9	71	3	13	21	15	13
J	1	2	5	3	1	2	1	1	10	5	3	2	2
K	0	2	6	1	7	5	8	3	4	23	9	12	1
L	18	13	18	15	15	15	11	11	16	11	41	8	2
M	16	6	10	7	32	4	4	11	3	12	12	4	16
N	7	8	1	3	23	10	6	7	15	4	6	3	19
O	3	34	17	75	10	29	32	27	10	30	23	40	34
P	36	3	8	6	16	3	2	10	26	10	8	6	7
Q	0	1	2	1	0	3	0	6	1	4	2	5	4
R	23	22	8	6	11	18	10	15	11	16	17	5	3
S	18	42	9	12	7	7	15	10	21	15	11	14	6
T	44	8	27	16	60	26	7	26	40	12	9	16	22
U	1	7	6	8	0	4	3	10	2	4	6	16	9
V	4	4	3	2	2	0	2	3	8	5	5	2	1
W	3	2	1	0	3	7	2	2	4	1	5	1	2
X	1	7	3	5	1	3	6	0	1	3	4	2	0
Y	6	0	5	4	2	3	3	6	1	2	4	6	4
Z	2	2	1	5	0	0	1	2	3	4	2	7	1
Omit	2	1	3	3	3	2	0	3	3	1	1	3	2

Responses to Two-Letter Combinations

G   First Stimulus Letter

Second Stimulus Letter

Response	N	O	P	Q	R	S	T	U	V	W	X	Y	Z
A	20	6	22	15	61	31	53	10	55	43	26	12	39
B	8	12	8	10	11	9	5	21	4	3	5	8	8
C	18	4	7	7	8	11	8	4	5	17	19	30	7
D	9	47	16	9	5	6	4	6	12	6	7	7	10
E	12	9	9	5	44	15	12	3	12	12	9	13	15
F	7	3	2	9	2	3	6	0	1	4	1	4	5
G	3	8	5	3	2	3	1	10	2	2	2	4	2
H	3	3	4	9	1	5	2	0	3	11	4	6	4
I	14	1	15	14	14	6	12	4	34	8	16	5	21
J	1	0	2	3	0	0	2	1	1	0	0	3	2
K	2	3	0	3	2	2	2	3	2	7	7	5	2
L	6	0	16	15	8	10	16	18	13	6	14	14	20
M	8	8	4	8	10	10	4	10	6	7	11	11	6
N	6	25	11	11	7	10	1	34	12	15	9	5	6
O	69	24	66	19	30	34	54	7	45	48	36	32	25
P	12	20	8	9	9	12	4	21	4	6	3	21	9
Q	4	0	4	2	1	4	0	1	2	1	3	0	4
R	9	4	24	30	8	10	18	7	9	13	11	16	7
S	7	6	15	20	6	15	23	22	13	10	9	18	12
T	20	73	9	19	13	49	9	72	13	12	17	8	19
U	19	3	6	23	8	11	18	1	3	10	6	8	15
V	7	4	2	9	7	7	5	2	4	1	4	5	5
W	2	4	1	3	3	2	2	3	1	9	4	6	1
X	1	3	2	7	2	2	5	0	8	13	9	11	9
Y	2	1	9	2	7	1	4	8	4	1	28	10	13
Z	3	1	3	4	2	2	2	4	2	5	12	8	6
Omit	1	1	3	5	2	3	1	1	3	3	1	3	1

Responses to Two-Letter Combinations

	H First Stimulus Letter												
Response	Second Stimulus Letter												
	A	B	C	D	E	F	G	H	I	J	K	L	M
A	15	17	15	7	11	16	16	14	1	13	23	10	7
B	27	10	7	21	7	2	15	5	2	6	4	10	6
C	3	12	12	6	0	72	7	5	4	5	5	15	7
D	29	10	19	9	20	6	5	3	11	4	5	9	5
E	0	7	10	23	17	17	5	14	6	8	10	25	4
F	4	4	7	3	4	6	5	3	4	5	4	7	2
G	1	2	2	0	1	15	8	16	13	8	3	0	2
H	8	5	9	3	8	8	10	53	6	5	4	2	4
I	3	34	25	31	5	22	30	47	5	51	38	27	33
J	2	4	1	2	0	1	3	3	9	9	8	2	1
K	2	6	5	3	3	2	4	6	7	43	5	7	2
L	6	10	31	19	18	6	5	13	27	7	59	12	9
M	24	9	6	17	19	3	12	15	18	8	13	23	10
N	8	16	7	5	8	4	11	5	3	4	13	5	55
O	1	37	46	45	10	14	44	22	4	18	23	31	27
P	13	2	4	4	10	2	5	0	18	12	4	17	10
Q	2	7	2	9	0	4	4	6	3	18	0	1	1
R	13	28	9	18	44	12	9	11	6	9	11	4	11
S	10	13	10	2	18	11	15	8	8	6	5	10	37
T	75	23	25	21	55	30	21	8	102	11	10	27	15
U	0	4	5	5	1	6	14	4	2	5	4	1	4
V	19	3	5	2	3	3	2	4	5	1	3	6	4
W	2	1	1	2	3	1	9	0	1	2	2	5	3
X	0	3	1	3	4	1	5	2	3	2	1	4	1
Y	1	1	1	8	2	0	5	2	5	7	5	5	9
Z	3	3	5	3	1	8	1	3	0	2	7	7	0
Omit	2	2	3	2	1	1	3	1	0	4	4	1	4

Responses to Two-Letter Combinations

Response	H First Stimulus Letter Second Stimulus Letter												
	N	O	P	Q	R	S	T	U	V	W	X	Y	Z
A	18	4	9	11	8	6	16	6	33	16	11	13	20
B	5	34	6	8	11	13	4	26	7	8	5	13	5
C	10	5	9	7	12	9	12	4	8	20	7	10	7
D	19	10	12	9	6	4	4	13	23	4	5	16	7
E	19	8	10	11	29	7	20	8	16	19	16	27	13
F	2	2	3	4	6	2	2	2	2	5	1	5	8
G	1	2	4	4	3	2	4	11	3	2	1	3	2
H	1	12	4	8	10	9	10	4	3	1	2	6	3
I	30	4	52	11	11	53	41	4	11	17	27	16	32
J	2	1	0	2	3	2	3	2	2	3	1	1	2
K	3	4	2	3	3	0	4	7	1	14	11	4	11
L	10	7	15	5	2	9	6	5	20	15	16	5	11
M	10	27	8	9	12	12	4	36	13	11	16	16	5
N	3	9	5	7	7	3	2	15	6	11	7	9	6
O	65	8	47	23	30	10	56	2	43	27	23	16	18
P	6	31	7	5	5	10	5	12	6	8	5	19	16
Q	6	1	15	7	5	1	6	1	3	1	5	2	7
R	14	4	20	57	13	12	9	13	11	12	12	7	10
S	5	4	6	10	37	26	25	5	11	22	6	10	5
T	18	76	20	21	32	70	9	74	11	10	23	23	44
U	6	2	5	26	8	3	8	2	15	6	1	6	2
V	8	3	1	3	4	4	5	6	2	3	5	5	9
W	0	6	0	3	0	2	1	3	9	3	4	8	2
X	0	2	5	4	4	1	2	2	6	15	8	3	7
Y	4	2	2	4	3	3	2	5	7	8	35	9	9
Z	5	3	4	9	5	0	10	3	0	9	17	20	8
Omit	3	2	2	2	4	0	3	2	1	3	3	1	4

Responses to Two-Letter Combinations

Response	I First Stimulus Letter												
	Second Stimulus Letter												
	A	B	C	D	E	F	G	H	I	J	K	L	M
A	7	19	44	25	11	8	96	35	2	14	11	7	20
B	9	9	10	5	13	2	6	6	4	2	6	7	71
C	4	23	44	39	7	43	7	7	2	4	7	3	11
D	16	11	13	16	21	6	7	6	4	10	4	13	7
E	4	13	26	44	12	10	13	26	3	5	52	7	12
F	12	2	3	9	15	37	5	5	5	4	3	4	3
G	9	0	2	3	1	9	14	3	1	9	4	1	4
H	2	0	6	3	1	7	11	11	3	8	3	0	3
I	0	7	6	5	3	10	2	16	71	6	4	5	7
J	3	1	1	0	4	4	4	4	13	2	13	2	2
K	4	0	10	3	14	3	6	3	4	86	6	11	2
L	12	3	8	1	11	12	7	21	46	15	46	100	9
M	37	103	13	15	15	2	14	21	8	13	9	22	13
N	30	4	6	11	12	13	13	22	7	9	23	8	15
O	26	16	10	16	15	7	7	4	6	10	7	8	10
P	7	2	4	5	11	4	9	8	8	18	3	5	29
Q	5	4	1	4	1	4	2	1	1	4	5	3	1
R	11	4	16	7	19	4	8	4	1	8	8	4	2
S	10	11	7	16	19	16	12	20	5	2	17	6	15
T	37	23	25	31	44	49	11	39	53	25	23	33	23
U	6	3	9	5	5	6	10	2	8	4	2	4	5
V	12	2	2	5	8	1	0	1	4	6	2	3	5
W	6	0	1	0	4	4	0	2	4	1	1	5	0
X	2	3	1	4	4	1	2	2	1	4	3	1	0
Y	0	3	3	0	1	2	5	1	5	2	7	2	2
Z	1	3	0	0	2	6	1	0	2	0	3	6	1
Omit	1	4	2	1	0	3	1	3	2	2	1	3	1

Responses to Two-Letter Combinations

Response	I	First Stimulus Letter										
					Second Stimulus Letter							
	N	O	P	Q	R	S	T	U	V	W	X	Y	Z
A	10	6	24	23	18	8	13	10	24	28	9	12	36
B	6	7	2	7	6	7	2	3	7	3	12	8	4
C	2	3	9	9	12	4	4	12	11	6	5	14	1
D	24	17	8	10	12	4	2	10	9	2	6	12	7
E	9	3	24	8	30	9	35	10	47	24	10	25	20
F	6	3	3	1	5	2	4	7	3	4	8	3	2
G	1	4	0	0	5	2	2	1	1	2	3	3	4
H	0	3	4	5	2	10	4	1	1	8	0	4	5
I	3	2	11	3	0	5	14	7	14	10	16	7	7
J	2	5	0	4	1	1	0	4	3	1	2	2	4
K	10	5	6	0	11	5	2	4	4	5	3	5	6
L	3	11	17	2	7	12	8	6	8	6	20	20	16
M	7	15	26	14	10	11	9	19	9	12	38	1	5
N	41	21	7	10	4	14	4	18	5	17	12	3	5
O	17	2	11	28	11	9	16	44	11	19	14	9	14
P	8	20	19	10	13	4	3	10	3	6	10	12	10
Q	4	12	10	6	4	2	0	1	3	2	4	3	5
R	3	8	11	24	16	7	3	8	15	14	6	10	1
S	32	6	30	23	26	16	91	11	8	23	6	15	9
T	72	37	29	34	56	131	39	44	17	19	35	31	54
U	5	67	3	29	3	5	3	8	3	9	5	10	9
V	3	2	2	2	6	0	3	13	5	5	6	14	2
W	0	6	1	3	1	1	1	9	2	18	4	5	2
X	0	2	2	6	3	0	3	5	8	16	12	12	4
Y	0	4	7	1	2	1	3	1	44	6	19	17	20
Z	4	1	4	8	5	2	2	6	6	7	3	13	16
Omit	1	1	3	3	4	1	3	1	2	1	5	3	5

Responses to Two-Letter Combinations

Response	J First Stimulus Letter												
					Second Stimulus Letter								
	A	B	C	D	E	F	G	H	I	J	K	L	M
A	6	17	10	27	9	11	24	19	6	7	27	5	11
B	12	9	16	6	7	3	16	16	4	8	4	15	10
C	14	31	34	14	9	29	16	6	5	6	6	10	10
D	15	26	22	8	20	23	7	7	17	29	2	6	11
E	1	12	9	21	3	38	13	15	3	7	21	9	16
F	1	9	6	7	9	9	3	6	3	4	1	10	5
G	11	5	5	7	3	9	6	9	17	13	2	3	2
H	4	2	4	3	2	1	4	6	4	5	4	3	4
I	0	9	9	14	1	18	21	24	3	7	9	29	49
J	5	2	3	3	2	1	9	5	2	54	2	4	2
K	20	9	14	6	10	7	6	17	11	43	7	27	9
L	11	22	17	11	14	14	20	18	28	6	98	11	6
M	31	9	9	12	12	1	13	7	26	4	15	20	14
N	15	6	7	1	18	2	5	7	16	3	6	11	29
O	0	26	26	16	3	10	32	26	6	17	25	20	24
P	58	6	19	12	13	13	6	10	58	8	5	11	14
Q	2	4	2	2	2	3	3	3	1	5	1	3	3
R	10	12	11	11	15	14	14	8	5	10	8	9	10
S	6	21	8	12	22	16	18	8	5	12	5	8	8
T	28	14	19	12	78	32	7	23	40	8	12	17	17
U	1	5	6	41	4	5	9	16	3	7	3	20	5
V	7	2	4	7	0	0	5	4	1	3	4	5	2
W	4	5	3	4	10	4	1	6	2	1	2	3	0
X	3	6	1	4	2	3	6	3	2	4	1	1	6
Y	3	1	4	11	1	3	3	2	0	1	1	9	3
Z	4	3	2	0	3	3	1	2	3	0	1	4	1
Omit	1	0	3	1	1	1	5	0	2	1	1	0	2

Responses to Two-Letter Combinations

J   First Stimulus Letter

Response

Second Stimulus Letter

	N	O	P	Q	R	S	T	U	V	W	X	Y	Z
A	19	11	19	23	9	11	22	2	14	23	17	21	34
B	10	64	6	1	5	9	14	11	6	11	6	5	6
C	4	10	14	2	16	9	7	5	8	14	12	18	3
D	11	10	11	12	6	10	7	36	25	6	15	19	12
E	13	32	17	8	11	13	43	7	11	33	14	21	16
F	2	1	3	7	6	4	4	3	3	3	4	4	13
G	3	2	3	2	7	1	0	14	2	3	3	5	4
H	1	1	2	2	3	4	5	1	1	3	1	0	1
I	7	3	20	13	8	11	8	2	13	13	25	8	13
J	5	2	3	2	3	5	4	6	2	3	5	0	5
K	9	15	2	10	9	9	3	10	5	9	7	7	9
L	9	5	17	27	15	7	15	15	16	4	33	15	8
M	19	10	27	6	15	11	13	11	6	6	3	8	5
N	5	14	13	6	10	4	6	15	12	4	8	9	2
O	56	4	25	13	19	7	34	5	35	12	12	40	23
P	32	23	7	10	15	9	4	17	4	27	10	14	5
Q	4	1	8	1	2	0	1	2	4	5	3	1	10
R	9	3	21	49	12	9	12	8	15	12	12	9	13
S	9	1	13	19	49	9	22	18	14	28	5	10	9
T	18	23	10	15	27	102	10	59	14	11	25	17	29
U	6	0	13	23	7	18	20	2	19	4	5	8	6
V	7	7	0	7	1	4	6	9	8	9	2	2	7
W	2	2	5	1	4	4	0	3	19	7	2	2	6
X	0	1	3	10	3	1	4	3	5	10	2	7	7
Y	3	22	4	0	4	0	2	1	3	1	32	2	12
Z	6	2	6	3	3	0	5	5	6	11	9	20	15
Omit	4	4	1	1	4	2	2	3	3	1	1	1	0

Responses to Two-Letter Combinations

| | K First Stimulus Letter | | | | | | | | | | | | |
| | Second Stimulus Letter | | | | | | | | | | | | |
Response	A	B	C	D	E	F	G	H	I	J	K	L	M
A	5	25	20	14	8	17	22	34	2	30	13	11	15
B	6	6	7	2	18	6	5	5	0	4	2	6	5
C	2	22	20	5	8	12	5	5	2	4	1	4	8
D	12	14	19	10	26	10	7	12	26	9	12	17	8
E	0	7	8	16	5	27	18	10	0	5	3	3	6
F	7	1	1	10	6	6	7	2	2	6	2	9	3
G	3	4	9	5	4	17	17	4	14	3	59	8	1
H	3	4	3	2	1	2	8	6	2	3	2	1	1
I	4	12	13	49	3	15	28	38	3	18	11	10	23
J	0	2	12	2	3	1	2	3	9	8	1	4	2
K	8	8	3	7	6	2	21	7	13	8	54	3	1
L	17	28	24	16	20	21	31	28	11	57	31	2	14
M	25	13	18	14	13	9	10	6	19	17	4	78	4
N	14	9	6	6	30	7	8	3	11	8	5	14	57
O	2	20	30	21	10	23	37	24	10	20	21	36	49
P	35	2	4	10	21	7	5	9	18	9	4	4	16
Q	1	5	1	0	0	0	2	2	1	2	1	3	0
R	14	14	17	8	11	13	10	21	10	10	10	7	9
S	4	23	9	26	7	9	6	1	11	3	7	6	9
T	92	33	19	19	38	44	10	19	89	19	16	22	17
U	0	2	5	3	0	3	2	5	0	7	0	5	4
V	2	1	3	5	3	1	1	3	2	1	1	5	5
W	7	1	3	3	6	1	0	4	4	4	4	3	2
X	3	9	6	9	3	4	0	3	5	5	2	3	4
Y	4	4	3	4	13	8	5	12	2	4	2	3	4
Z	3	3	5	5	5	7	1	6	3	6	4	4	5
Omit	0	1	5	2	5	1	5	1	4	3	1	2	1

Responses to Two-Letter Combinations

K First Stimulus Letter

Response

	Second Stimulus Letter												
	N	O	P	Q	R	S	T	U	V	W	X	Y	Z
A	12	4	22	17	44	20	29	3	24	15	13	13	17
B	8	12	3	5	8	5	6	8	3	1	4	3	4
C	8	2	9	7	5	8	8	4	4	4	4	10	1
D	12	8	27	10	10	11	11	11	27	2	4	7	20
E	13	1	16	7	23	3	8	2	8	22	8	45	7
F	2	4	1	3	2	3	8	3	3	6	3	3	5
G	4	3	6	7	5	4	0	2	2	3	11	4	1
H	6	1	4	2	0	2	3	3	2	4	0	0	2
I	7	4	15	8	17	34	26	6	21	15	21	3	18
J	2	0	4	2	2	1	1	1	1	3	3	1	4
K	2	22	2	5	3	4	7	13	7	5	13	6	4
L	8	27	22	14	20	7	28	27	16	17	19	18	18
M	13	27	7	8	5	12	14	21	13	12	7	4	12
N	4	12	5	6	5	9	6	14	12	21	8	9	10
O	83	5	37	32	12	14	35	7	33	34	23	8	30
P	8	36	8	8	12	10	5	25	4	6	7	0	12
Q	2	2	3	3	2	0	1	1	1	0	4	1	3
R	11	10	30	45	3	18	8	15	13	13	17	6	7
S	6	7	9	14	30	24	13	7	14	14	4	21	6
T	20	56	31	15	20	62	15	68	20	22	20	56	43
U	8	4	2	21	10	3	9	7	17	5	3	6	6
V	18	7	2	3	4	3	3	3	4	4	7	4	5
W	5	4	2	8	4	3	1	2	9	13	3	8	5
X	2	6	0	10	5	2	2	10	4	14	7	6	6
Y	1	5	3	5	7	8	15	4	5	6	45	4	18
Z	8	3	2	6	13	2	9	5	5	7	11	25	7
Omit	0	1	1	2	2	1	2	1	1	5	4	2	2

Responses to Two-Letter Combinations

Response	L First Stimulus Letter												
	Second Stimulus Letter												
	A	B	C	D	E	F	G	H	I	J	K	L	M
A	7	29	28	9	17	18	26	23	5	14	12	16	10
B	36	10	6	7	13	6	6	9	10	11	6	8	4
C	14	24	13	10	4	9	24	4	5	6	2	2	16
D	12	21	24	12	12	8	11	9	7	13	8	25	6
E	0	10	9	10	33	37	5	15	6	8	15	3	7
F	2	5	5	8	4	12	1	3	3	4	5	1	15
G	6	5	8	2	3	10	4	2	2	4	3	10	0
H	1	3	6	4	1	2	5	10	0	7	0	0	0
I	5	10	10	20	0	17	12	41	3	26	31	29	5
J	2	0	2	2	0	4	3	3	2	5	6	3	3
K	0	4	6	3	4	2	7	5	4	42	5	2	0
L	4	4	5	12	2	8	3	0	10	9	12	54	0
M	38	16	17	12	25	21	18	16	34	18	42	38	8
N	14	14	5	4	22	13	12	9	15	1	13	8	98
O	4	22	49	36	7	14	72	17	5	18	22	10	23
P	27	4	11	6	12	7	5	14	45	14	12	8	18
Q	1	3	2	1	3	2	2	4	1	5	0	4	1
R	12	13	8	14	3	11	8	17	3	6	10	8	3
S	36	28	11	8	12	12	11	12	7	11	15	7	19
T	21	22	21	56	69	37	15	32	81	21	14	6	20
U	1	3	7	8	2	6	10	4	2	6	6	5	2
V	9	2	4	12	4	3	2	12	10	6	6	14	1
W	3	2	3	3	8	2	2	3	4	3	4	3	1
X	5	5	1	7	5	2	1	1	5	7	6	0	2
Y	3	4	6	0	4	3	6	1	1	5	5	7	3
Z	6	5	3	4	3	6	0	3	2	3	8	1	4
Omit	4	5	3	3	1	1	2	4	1	0	5	1	4

Responses to Two-Letter Combinations

Response	L First Stimulus Letter											
	Second Stimulus Letter											
	N	O	P	Q	R	S	T	U	V	W	X	Y	Z
A	8	1	27	11	24	7	9	5	29	34	14	4	27
B	8	14	3	6	3	4	3	12	4	3	9	6	9
C	7	7	5	10	6	2	12	18	6	12	13	10	1
D	13	9	19	20	11	9	29	16	28	6	6	16	16
E	18	4	7	1	12	5	19	3	23	24	13	48	17
F	2	4	2	3	6	6	2	5	3	7	4	5	6
G	2	7	4	3	3	0	2	7	4	2	1	0	1
H	1	1	1	1	1	2	1	1	3	4	0	2	3
I	27	3	19	24	10	10	12	3	35	16	18	16	43
J	1	0	2	1	1	3	3	6	3	1	0	0	6
K	4	4	1	0	6	2	0	9	2	1	5	4	5
L	0	1	5	6	5	5	9	20	5	4	4	11	4
M	33	26	25	23	11	32	40	27	14	12	15	2	5
N	9	8	20	6	14	4	13	16	13	20	10	18	4
O	55	6	39	15	15	14	39	7	31	22	17	18	19
P	18	29	5	11	4	4	8	17	1	13	10	11	10
Q	1	3	3	1	6	4	3	0	3	2	4	0	7
R	9	9	34	41	6	9	11	6	9	12	12	7	11
S	4	10	13	19	52	9	15	6	4	12	7	11	4
T	20	55	17	30	40	121	8	40	23	18	16	27	35
U	2	6	7	14	5	6	12	1	4	9	27	7	6
V	11	21	0	7	6	4	6	22	4	13	12	6	4
W	0	36	5	5	0	3	3	3	11	8	4	5	4
X	3	3	7	0	5	1	2	14	2	11	5	7	5
Y	6	2	0	4	7	3	6	1	7	3	29	6	8
Z	6	1	3	9	12	4	5	5	1	2	15	25	11
Omit	5	3	0	2	2	0	1	3	1	2	3	1	2

Responses to Two-Letter Combinations

M First Stimulus Letter

Second Stimulus Letter

Response	A	B	C	D	E	F	G	H	I	J	K	L	M
A	8	11	37	20	12	11	34	21	2	11	13	12	7
B	10	7	8	5	2	12	9	10	2	10	8	10	4
C	4	17	26	10	9	11	41	8	11	15	2	12	6
D	17	24	23	26	12	21	8	7	5	10	5	9	4
E	2	12	10	22	26	11	7	13	6	4	16	9	6
F	1	1	5	7	2	5	4	4	2	4	3	7	3
G	4	2	6	3	1	17	5	4	4	10	6	1	3
H	3	0	1	2	0	0	4	8	0	7	3	1	1
I	2	6	28	18	8	3	21	45	2	16	43	18	7
J	2	3	4	2	1	6	4	2	2	4	5	3	3
K	3	0	2	2	1	2	3	3	4	26	3	13	1
L	7	17	15	13	14	12	9	7	12	19	35	9	6
M	21	6	8	5	7	8	16	4	10	6	5	11	62
N	54	38	5	17	57	14	2	20	27	7	24	30	46
O	1	34	19	17	8	18	23	22	15	20	37	34	47
P	24	5	10	4	5	8	9	9	10	16	3	13	8
Q	2	3	1	1	1	0	1	1	1	2	1	3	5
R	13	14	9	17	6	15	18	20	3	17	12	7	7
S	20	10	13	33	11	21	14	20	4	16	11	16	10
T	53	42	14	11	62	32	17	12	131	23	13	28	13
U	2	2	8	7	4	6	7	7	2	7	2	4	3
V	2	4	7	13	2	14	2	6	6	8	8	6	5
W	8	1	2	2	6	10	4	1	0	0	6	4	5
X	2	4	3	9	6	0	4	2	4	4	2	2	4
Y	7	5	6	2	6	7	2	9	4	3	4	5	2
Z	1	3	2	4	2	6	2	4	1	4	3	1	2
Omit	0	2	1	1	2	3	3	4	3	4	0	5	3

Responses to Two-Letter Combinations

Response	M First Stimulus Letter												
	Second Stimulus Letter												
	N	O	P	Q	R	S	T	U	V	W	X	Y	Z
A	18	6	27	20	10	12	23	9	23	24	17	13	25
B	3	8	4	8	5	5	2	2	8	7	4	4	4
C	4	13	22	7	7	7	8	5	5	20	8	13	4
D	7	8	11	7	8	8	5	21	40	7	10	11	16
E	16	5	3	5	4	4	16	7	9	17	20	47	28
F	2	1	0	4	2	2	2	3	0	9	1	8	4
G	1	1	1	0	3	3	0	1	3	3	2	1	1
H	4	3	2	2	0	1	4	5	1	5	0	1	3
I	4	0	12	8	9	6	47	7	16	5	39	8	9
J	1	1	0	2	7	5	3	2	0	3	2	0	1
K	2	1	5	0	6	3	5	3	3	6	3	2	10
L	10	7	9	9	5	9	7	9	8	9	16	7	11
M	3	28	8	8	10	6	1	22	3	12	0	9	4
N	4	45	10	14	9	8	18	39	13	5	13	29	12
O	129	8	54	29	21	13	39	13	45	27	27	16	37
P	13	33	13	15	6	7	10	10	14	10	11	10	10
Q	2	1	5	2	2	4	5	0	0	2	2	3	2
R	8	19	15	59	6	47	12	4	10	14	11	7	12
S	5	10	33	13	112	29	14	34	11	23	10	30	6
T	12	57	17	14	18	65	13	45	27	15	18	27	31
U	5	3	5	20	3	8	10	9	7	9	5	2	6
V	12	6	1	11	3	7	12	7	4	8	8	3	2
W	0	0	1	0	1	1	3	6	13	9	3	1	5
X	2	2	3	3	4	1	3	3	5	12	9	6	10
Y	0	3	1	5	6	6	7	2	4	4	29	3	13
Z	5	3	5	7	4	3	4	4	1	7	4	8	5
Omit	1	1	6	1	2	3	0	1	0	1	1	4	2

Responses to Two-Letter Combinations

Response	N First Stimulus Letter												
					Second Stimulus Letter								
	A	B	C	D	E	F	G	H	I	J	K	L	M
A	10	42	49	20	18	15	36	21	3	14	11	15	17
B	51	6	4	3	19	10	10	11	11	10	9	8	4
C	5	51	8	8	7	13	6	5	8	18	2	9	3
D	8	16	13	5	16	9	13	5	11	19	11	6	6
E	2	15	11	17	6	14	7	12	4	8	23	14	6
F	2	2	1	4	4	5	4	3	2	6	8	9	3
G	4	2	4	3	0	9	5	5	1	3	5	6	3
H	1	2	2	4	3	1	2	10	1	4	0	3	7
I	0	8	16	15	3	10	10	31	4	21	18	20	7
J	2	2	1	3	1	5	1	3	2	5	2	1	3
K	5	3	3	0	4	4	2	4	9	32	5	5	7
L	6	13	14	10	13	19	7	10	28	5	18	9	8
M	28	6	4	6	12	7	1	16	14	3	12	7	9
N	18	5	2	5	13	4	6	4	11	6	8	1	20
O	2	28	55	61	15	29	71	29	12	22	46	65	90
P	35	4	12	11	12	16	10	12	41	9	10	14	31
Q	1	3	1	2	3	0	5	4	1	6	2	6	7
R	9	23	8	12	12	18	26	19	4	6	19	14	8
S	8	11	9	15	20	14	6	15	6	16	9	14	2
T	51	15	27	33	41	38	19	18	79	27	16	12	9
U	3	3	10	17	2	12	6	11	3	5	11	5	5
V	7	1	6	8	6	3	7	2	4	8	12	18	6
W	5	0	2	1	34	1	3	6	1	1	2	0	4
X	2	7	1	3	4	1	2	1	9	6	2	3	3
Y	3	1	7	3	2	3	5	11	0	9	10	5	1
Z	2	2	0	3	0	10	3	2	3	2	1	3	3
Omit	3	2	3	1	3	3	0	3	1	2	1	1	1

Responses to Two-Letter Combinations

Response	N	First Stimulus Letter											
					Second Stimulus Letter								
	N	O	P	Q	R	S	T	U	V	W	X	Y	Z
A	11	2	40	19	33	22	20	8	30	17	13	10	26
B	8	10	2	9	7	7	5	7	4	8	7	2	8
C	4	2	12	2	10	10	3	8	2	10	3	68	3
D	3	14	9	4	7	7	16	9	22	1	14	8	12
E	5	4	12	9	10	13	7	8	14	40	13	19	16
F	3	3	3	6	4	4	5	6	2	3	2	4	9
G	1	1	6	2	7	2	2	4	2	5	1	4	2
H	1	0	1	2	1	5	6	1	2	3	2	4	0
I	5	3	12	9	7	18	20	5	6	7	40	2	14
J	3	1	1	1	0	3	2	0	1	2	1	2	2
K	1	4	3	3	7	1	1	1	4	6	3	9	2
L	4	4	5	7	9	2	2	3	8	4	10	6	4
M	23	11	15	5	7	7	3	7	7	13	5	4	8
N	50	21	9	4	4	4	10	13	5	9	6	10	3
O	84	7	55	36	52	33	83	11	69	25	42	15	47
P	17	43	4	26	13	22	5	18	4	5	10	6	16
Q	3	2	11	2	9	3	1	1	6	2	3	1	5
R	3	10	22	60	9	17	17	19	19	17	4	6	10
S	5	3	12	12	20	10	13	18	6	15	4	21	3
T	16	97	20	13	32	59	15	55	17	13	20	21	40
U	6	3	4	21	7	11	21	27	16	31	4	15	5
V	3	3	1	3	4	4	2	15	3	1	11	7	4
W	3	15	1	5	2	3	2	21	10	7	4	5	4
X	3	1	4	6	5	0	6	4	6	12	12	5	6
Y	3	2	1	2	3	3	1	2	4	7	26	6	11
Z	4	4	5	5	2	1	4	1	1	7	13	7	10
Omit	1	3	3	0	2	2	1	1	3	3	0	6	3

Responses to Two-Letter Combinations

O   First Stimulus Letter

Second Stimulus Letter

Response	A	B	C	D	E	F	G	H	I	J	K	L	M
A	3	14	25	8	17	7	33	17	7	12	27	11	13
B	20	16	10	8	19	8	6	10	4	31	2	7	12
C	9	15	35	11	10	9	12	3	5	6	2	5	2
D	11	11	20	68	29	8	27	16	10	12	31	56	4
E	3	20	9	46	5	10	13	12	10	24	37	26	32
F	4	3	4	6	14	116	3	6	3	2	5	11	1
G	0	4	5	6	2	4	28	0	2	7	4	1	1
H	5	1	1	0	2	1	8	22	9	2	2	1	10
I	7	4	5	4	2	1	11	31	10	19	6	16	10
J	1	3	1	1	4	1	1	2	0	4	12	2	3
K	8	7	9	3	2	3	3	0	4	24	19	4	1
L	6	8	5	9	12	5	21	15	32	9	17	16	7
M	10	1	8	14	20	7	4	13	13	12	3	27	7
N	9	2	8	1	21	5	7	8	11	13	4	9	67
O	6	15	10	17	6	3	17	38	7	14	12	8	8
P	17	7	20	7	22	3	8	13	18	11	10	15	24
Q	0	10	2	3	2	1	1	0	3	5	1	1	1
R	16	12	8	2	13	5	6	14	5	12	7	5	10
S	18	63	21	16	16	7	19	6	8	6	15	12	11
T	102	33	36	24	33	56	22	27	63	25	21	16	31
U	4	3	16	5	2	1	4	6	34	3	17	1	2
V	0	1	4	2	2	1	4	6	5	3	1	7	5
W	5	2	2	0	6	0	0	1	3	3	4	5	2
X	1	7	3	2	4	1	2	1	2	4	1	0	0
Y	1	5	4	3	4	5	8	3	3	4	12	3	3
Z	3	5	0	4	2	5	3	2	1	1	0	2	2
Omit	4	1	2	3	2	0	2	1	1	5	1	6	4

Responses to Two-Letter Combinations

	O	First Stimulus Letter										
Response				Second Stimulus Letter								
	N	O	P	Q	R	S	T	U	V	W	X	Y	Z
A	8	4	37	11	9	10	22	3	35	9	4	6	26
B	7	3	2	11	15	13	6	2	5	6	9	9	2
C	1	6	5	3	2	4	8	20	3	9	1	9	2
D	15	11	7	5	23	5	6	2	14	4	4	15	11
E	66	1	29	8	32	16	28	8	64	55	92	47	35
F	2	2	5	5	1	6	0	3	1	3	7	1	2
G	1	5	2	2	6	0	4	2	1	0	0	2	3
H	3	18	1	1	2	1	4	4	1	3	1	2	1
I	11	1	5	4	6	7	6	20	7	14	12	11	7
J	0	1	3	1	0	2	1	1	0	1	0	1	0
K	1	5	1	4	4	2	1	8	2	1	0	7	0
L	9	8	3	5	3	0	10	5	8	16	12	11	6
M	9	9	13	7	2	4	9	7	7	7	9	8	1
N	18	5	8	7	5	3	7	3	11	21	14	11	5
O	14	80	12	11	8	7	23	3	13	12	6	11	16
P	13	33	20	39	15	17	7	15	10	8	5	5	11
Q	1	2	15	7	4	2	5	1	6	1	1	1	2
R	3	7	20	46	10	7	14	18	8	10	6	5	9
S	14	8	37	11	26	43	40	9	12	16	13	25	14
T	59	40	19	27	79	100	30	112	27	19	19	30	43
U	2	7	14	35	2	17	18	3	12	7	1	9	5
V	5	1	4	3	5	1	3	4	7	6	4	4	1
W	4	4	1	1	0	1	5	6	5	21	2	3	11
X	0	2	4	6	3	0	3	2	4	8	13	12	7
Y	2	2	2	4	7	3	5	5	2	5	33	16	8
Z	2	8	3	8	1	1	5	4	7	7	2	10	44
Omit	3	0	1	1	3	1	3	3	1	4	3	2	1

Responses to Two-Letter Combinations

Response	P First Stimulus Letter												
	Second Stimulus Letter												
	A	B	C	D	E	F	G	H	I	J	K	L	M
A	14	26	33	18	10	13	27	18	4	30	47	46	53
B	8	9	1	3	7	2	10	8	12	4	5	7	14
C	4	12	22	9	8	24	8	2	10	6	6	9	14
D	22	12	18	11	16	16	8	55	13	14	7	9	8
E	6	10	9	19	5	11	16	18	21	8	30	22	9
F	0	0	12	5	6	19	3	23	3	4	1	1	1
G	5	2	7	5	4	9	9	1	9	6	6	3	0
H	0	1	2	12	3	4	5	3	2	16	2	3	2
I	3	12	10	14	1	11	32	43	3	13	37	6	7
J	3	5	9	3	1	4	2	0	4	5	3	0	3
K	4	1	5	0	3	9	4	4	7	19	8	2	4
L	12	10	3	5	13	7	8	5	8	4	27	1	8
M	20	8	8	2	4	6	15	1	4	14	2	21	9
N	32	8	2	4	32	8	7	3	7	9	4	10	26
O	2	29	35	25	10	14	40	20	7	12	12	31	56
P	41	4	3	6	20	7	3	3	25	8	3	5	6
Q	1	13	17	47	4	6	7	1	18	17	1	2	1
R	13	21	18	21	13	6	13	10	7	16	20	8	8
S	9	18	10	16	14	15	14	3	5	26	9	12	11
T	50	29	24	18	76	55	13	21	77	15	21	14	14
U	3	9	10	10	3	4	7	11	7	11	0	38	2
V	5	5	4	3	1	8	2	2	3	0	3	2	4
W	4	3	5	1	9	3	4	3	1	4	7	2	2
X	1	7	5	8	1	2	8	3	5	2	4	4	4
Y	9	16	0	5	1	3	6	11	2	5	2	11	1
Z	0	3	0	3	6	4	1	0	5	2	5	4	3
Omit	2	0	1	0	2	3	1	1	4	3	1	0	3

Responses to Two-Letter Combinations

P   First Stimulus Letter

Response					Second Stimulus Letter								
	N	O	P	Q	R	S	T	U	V	W	X	Y	Z
A	22	4	10	14	19	10	46	4	26	31	17	11	22
B	4	8	5	3	5	3	29	6	4	4	14	8	3
C	10	5	6	4	5	7	8	6	4	11	4	8	2
D	12	30	9	16	6	7	5	23	20	2	14	3	4
E	19	0	5	6	17	11	14	4	7	16	7	38	10
F	5	1	0	4	4	3	4	2	5	6	1	5	5
G	5	1	3	1	0	1	3	8	2	3	3	9	2
H	1	0	2	2	2	3	2	3	3	1	2	2	3
I	18	1	12	11	38	26	14	9	17	6	19	6	18
J	3	4	2	1	1	0	1	3	2	2	1	2	2
K	4	3	4	0	0	1	1	9	3	7	5	3	6
L	4	11	11	7	8	4	9	9	11	2	2	9	11
M	8	18	5	3	11	7	4	8	5	5	6	5	9
N	5	13	7	3	9	5	3	19	6	2	1	5	7
O	65	6	42	17	31	11	29	4	29	48	20	32	32
P	8	30	51	6	2	5	1	20	3	3	4	6	4
Q	7	12	24	3	9	19	11	2	11	6	24	4	18
R	9	9	18	116	8	9	17	17	21	21	6	14	18
S	5	4	11	16	40	32	17	8	7	20	17	33	15
T	16	95	20	8	31	79	14	91	43	10	14	28	39
U	18	1	8	10	6	11	17	6	17	13	9	5	5
V	6	3	1	3	6	5	6	2	2	3	3	0	2
W	4	8	0	2	2	3	2	3	11	7	4	2	4
X	3	0	4	8	3	2	5	0	5	33	17	11	5
Y	6	2	9	4	6	5	7	4	6	4	47	7	16
Z	4	1	4	4	3	3	3	1	2	6	11	15	8
Omit	2	3	0	1	1	1	1	2	1	1	1	2	3

Responses to Two-Letter Combinations

Q First Stimulus Letter

Response	Second Stimulus Letter												
	A	B	C	D	E	F	G	H	I	J	K	L	M
A	6	17	21	14	2	13	31	15	8	15	20	17	24
B	22	10	10	6	11	8	6	10	7	6	8	6	8
C	16	19	8	14	5	12	19	9	10	9	7	10	18
D	12	12	18	5	36	17	9	12	18	6	8	15	11
E	4	11	11	16	9	12	13	10	3	9	14	6	11
F	8	13	3	8	9	7	2	5	4	5	7	2	0
G	2	2	4	0	1	11	7	3	2	4	2	2	0
H	0	3	0	4	0	0	9	8	0	4	1	0	0
I	5	10	11	16	4	14	9	39	4	14	16	13	16
J	0	2	1	1	1	5	2	1	4	1	2	1	3
K	5	3	9	2	4	3	4	1	5	14	8	4	6
L	19	5	6	12	4	8	7	13	11	16	24	6	3
M	14	5	6	8	13	3	2	6	13	9	9	42	4
N	18	11	4	4	17	1	6	8	10	5	7	9	25
O	9	18	25	36	5	10	12	15	10	7	14	23	13
P	5	3	10	24	8	5	9	5	26	18	7	12	14
Q	0	5	3	4	2	2	1	10	4	1	4	4	0
R	14	42	44	39	28	42	47	42	28	53	35	15	25
S	17	20	10	14	27	22	21	9	13	15	11	18	15
T	61	28	27	14	39	39	20	14	65	28	19	32	29
U	17	9	10	7	17	13	15	15	12	9	22	12	12
V	3	2	8	4	7	3	3	3	1	2	8	6	15
W	5	0	4	2	8	2	2	3	4	4	3	2	0
X	3	5	8	9	5	10	9	4	3	5	2	4	5
Y	2	4	6	4	1	4	5	6	0	7	5	1	5
Z	4	7	5	4	6	6	2	4	7	7	9	8	7
Omit	2	7	1	2	4	1	1	3	1	0	1	3	4

Responses to Two-Letter Combinations

Response	Q First Stimulus Letter												
	Second Stimulus Letter												
	N	O	P	Q	R	S	T	U	V	W	X	Y	Z
A	12	10	16	6	18	8	27	17	17	17	17	6	31
B	12	6	3	5	11	5	15	6	5	7	9	4	13
C	7	7	6	2	6	7	5	4	10	14	9	10	6
D	7	12	19	2	7	4	4	8	14	3	8	5	6
E	11	3	10	4	6	6	13	21	9	15	12	11	9
F	3	1	1	4	3	3	2	3	3	3	3	3	3
G	1	2	2	2	1	2	0	1	1	0	2	3	1
H	1	2	2	1	2	1	3	1	4	2	3	1	1
I	8	4	13	3	8	8	14	21	11	12	17	6	20
J	2	0	0	2	0	2	0	1	1	0	3	1	0
K	2	4	0	0	4	3	3	3	0	3	2	3	1
L	3	8	12	4	6	10	5	6	10	6	7	14	10
M	5	6	3	8	14	7	7	11	5	10	8	15	19
N	6	16	11	7	6	6	2	11	4	5	6	11	10
O	51	10	32	9	12	15	21	24	26	19	15	21	12
P	20	42	1	9	14	10	13	13	8	8	10	7	10
Q	3	4	2	59	2	2	4	1	3	1	2	2	6
R	33	35	49	67	11	53	70	24	39	23	16	30	21
S	18	9	35	15	61	7	16	14	23	33	9	26	8
T	30	38	23	13	44	80	12	45	21	18	27	21	30
U	10	30	6	23	11	13	13	5	9	18	5	14	14
V	10	5	5	5	8	6	7	14	5	5	11	2	2
W	3	5	1	0	0	4	2	3	17	3	3	7	8
X	5	3	7	3	5	0	1	5	13	15	8	14	11
Y	4	3	3	5	7	2	6	0	6	2	31	3	13
Z	6	7	8	9	3	5	7	9	6	29	25	29	6
Omit	0	1	3	6	3	4	1	2	3	2	5	4	2

Responses to Two-Letter Combinations

| Response | R First Stimulus Letter | | | | | | | | | | | | |
| | Second Stimulus Letter | | | | | | | | | | | | |
	A	B	C	D	E	F	G	H	I	J	K	L	M
A	4	28	37	19	10	21	39	14	1	15	15	19	23
B	20	12	9	4	12	3	13	8	8	6	10	8	12
C	3	20	34	6	10	14	8	5	7	9	6	12	7
D	14	14	20	4	25	40	14	11	21	9	4	14	12
E	5	12	6	32	5	22	15	16	3	13	18	7	21
F	3	4	11	22	18	11	7	27	5	6	6	3	5
G	7	1	3	1	4	22	6	1	8	8	1	2	2
H	12	1	1	3	3	0	11	7	2	4	0	3	5
I	5	26	7	21	2	7	12	42	2	19	14	12	10
J	5	1	5	3	5	2	1	1	4	9	8	1	2
K	4	2	5	1	5	1	2	1	6	32	4	5	1
L	3	16	9	8	6	10	11	10	9	14	22	9	11
M	14	8	7	9	20	5	9	9	12	12	9	23	3
N	10	1	7	5	14	6	8	22	10	11	4	10	32
O	1	18	29	46	4	10	25	22	4	11	61	37	38
P	25	4	8	2	16	6	9	9	54	5	7	13	12
Q	2	4	5	6	0	2	10	3	2	10	0	5	1
R	2	9	9	13	2	6	4	4	4	5	8	6	5
S	3	33	8	15	45	14	21	7	15	23	25	21	15
T	95	29	21	9	30	48	19	27	76	19	13	33	27
U	3	10	5	10	2	8	8	7	1	8	7	6	6
V	5	2	12	3	14	4	2	5	1	3	10	6	10
W	6	0	2	1	0	1	1	1	4	8	3	2	2
X	1	11	2	18	13	2	5	6	4	2	4	3	0
Y	11	2	2	4	3	1	6	4	4	5	6	9	3
Z	10	2	4	5	4	6	3	2	4	4	5	3	6
Omit	0	3	5	3	1	1	4	2	2	3	3	1	2

Responses to Two-Letter Combinations

Response	R First Stimulus Letter											
	Second Stimulus Letter											
	N	O	P	Q	R	S	T	U	V	W	X	Y	Z
A	23	10	29	16	10	11	24	4	11	23	18	16	42
B	4	16	7	4	8	5	7	16	4	8	7	6	7
C	6	7	4	4	17	2	11	4	12	15	11	10	2
D	19	27	6	6	6	7	4	12	12	6	26	3	12
E	10	5	14	10	3	8	10	3	29	22	20	70	13
F	5	3	1	5	2	3	1	7	2	9	6	2	3
G	4	3	3	3	3	1	0	6	2	1	1	4	3
H	3	4	3	0	3	2	2	1	2	2	5	1	3
I	5	2	43	12	4	5	16	3	12	6	8	8	16
J	1	0	1	3	1	1	2	2	0	2	4	1	0
K	2	10	2	3	0	3	0	4	1	2	1	4	6
L	4	11	16	1	6	6	6	8	3	7	6	12	5
M	11	9	13	21	3	2	5	17	1	7	9	7	9
N	15	5	9	12	5	3	6	23	3	1	12	9	7
O	49	4	26	29	11	12	45	6	24	27	23	7	32
P	11	19	10	7	13	9	1	12	15	15	17	3	8
Q	0	3	9	1	0	2	0	2	4	0	2	0	2
R	2	3	15	9	65	1	5	10	5	11	4	11	4
S	21	11	18	50	42	7	66	31	44	37	7	26	18
T	22	94	15	22	41	160	10	84	32	15	29	16	40
U	27	1	7	24	3	4	12	2	19	7	7	8	4
V	12	6	5	6	5	7	3	2	2	10	5	2	3
W	2	7	5	3	1	4	2	2	16	5	2	1	6
X	8	3	4	5	13	2	9	3	7	17	5	19	11
Y	2	4	4	1	2	1	12	3	7	10	22	5	10
Z	2	5	2	12	3	2	13	3	2	5	15	20	6
Omit	3	1	2	4	3	3	1	3	2	3	1	2	1

Responses to Two-Letter Combinations

Response	S First Stimulus Letter												
	Second Stimulus Letter												
	A	B	C	D	E	F	G	H	I	J	K	L	M
A	3	17	32	24	18	17	11	14	3	10	19	28	41
B	13	5	16	7	10	11	117	2	7	25	7	6	5
C	6	12	16	3	5	8	2	4	6	7	1	7	4
D	20	8	17	3	14	8	6	1	14	19	7	10	5
E	23	10	11	12	44	19	6	58	5	15	20	10	9
F	4	2	1	5	11	22	0	3	10	8	3	2	1
G	6	64	3	4	5	17	2	1	8	7	6	1	3
H	2	0	7	2	2	2	1	22	2	3	4	1	0
I	2	8	16	18	0	8	9	64	1	15	47	14	19
J	5	3	3	3	0	2	3	1	6	5	6	2	4
K	1	7	4	2	1	4	4	3	3	19	5	3	6
L	11	1	8	5	18	8	5	4	17	8	23	3	8
M	25	0	5	3	6	10	8	3	16	13	4	18	3
N	7	5	6	6	13	10	3	3	13	4	3	20	16
O	0	20	53	32	4	12	25	35	4	12	25	50	54
P	21	3	7	11	4	9	10	3	17	15	1	12	12
Q	0	5	1	6	0	1	0	1	1	0	2	0	3
R	9	4	16	5	5	13	10	6	7	16	15	5	3
S	10	5	8	10	9	22	6	4	20	10	8	5	5
T	67	30	18	89	77	40	27	15	88	30	22	41	32
U	2	2	12	6	3	9	0	14	5	10	17	7	23
V	3	3	2	6	3	3	7	1	5	8	7	10	4
W	8	0	3	0	8	2	0	0	3	3	1	2	4
X	5	57	1	2	3	4	3	1	5	3	3	4	1
Y	12	1	2	3	4	4	2	9	2	3	15	11	2
Z	3	0	4	4	5	5	1	0	3	1	2	0	4
Omit	5	1	1	2	1	3	5	1	2	4	0	1	2

Responses to Two-Letter Combinations

| Response | S First Stimulus Letter | | | | | | | | | | | | |
	N	O	P	Q	R	S	T	U	V	W	X	Y	Z
					Second Stimulus Letter								
A	19	6	33	15	24	10	30	5	26	31	2	6	24
B	8	33	3	17	10	4	8	20	8	6	44	9	14
C	2	6	10	4	3	2	5	2	2	3	7	7	4
D	5	14	10	4	8	8	25	13	26	6	4	16	9
E	9	4	39	3	23	4	16	29	16	39	39	27	23
F	5	3	2	3	1	16	4	4	7	4	10	1	5
G	5	0	4	2	2	0	0	2	4	3	7	5	0
H	1	4	1	0	1	2	2	6	1	2	1	5	1
I	16	0	11	11	28	9	10	4	14	24	14	8	14
J	16	1	1	1	1	3	2	3	1	6	1	2	1
K	2	1	1	2	0	2	1	3	4	4	7	10	6
L	5	19	10	2	11	2	4	7	6	3	8	31	9
M	9	11	5	6	5	1	3	24	5	10	4	12	3
N	3	11	8	3	3	3	1	22	14	13	1	8	5
O	76	16	36	13	19	14	39	5	21	35	10	11	25
P	8	28	6	9	12	6	0	35	4	7	11	4	13
Q	6	2	8	2	4	0	4	1	2	4	2	5	4
R	8	9	21	57	3	18	26	10	7	4	9	9	12
S	5	31	9	10	16	68	9	23	7	12	6	15	9
T	25	50	20	23	61	71	12	35	52	13	27	29	43
U	13	7	9	57	10	5	40	4	8	8	4	8	12
V	12	2	3	9	9	10	7	5	3	4	9	5	7
W	6	10	1	3	4	1	1	2	19	4	4	1	3
X	1	3	6	4	3	2	3	3	4	11	16	14	7
Y	3	0	6	3	5	6	8	2	5	8	22	7	12
Z	4	1	7	6	2	4	10	4	5	5	3	15	7
Omit	1	1	3	4	5	2	3	0	2	4	1	3	1

Responses to Two-Letter Combinations

	T	First Stimulus Letter											
Response					Second Stimulus Letter								
	A	B	C	D	E	F	G	H	I	J	K	L	M
A	3	54	34	20	15	21	29	8	5	22	37	20	17
B	40	9	0	11	2	8	12	2	14	6	1	3	13
C	7	10	9	12	8	17	6	5	9	11	2	15	17
D	12	11	23	15	16	9	8	2	19	9	1	3	8
E	1	4	7	18	19	17	15	158	8	16	50	31	21
F	9	6	1	4	10	10	18	6	15	9	3	3	1
G	9	3	6	3	2	17	6	0	1	2	5	1	0
H	5	1	0	0	13	3	6	1	2	3	7	3	1
I	1	17	10	27	3	22	29	23	3	24	15	16	33
J	0	2	4	1	2	5	2	0	3	6	3	6	6
K	10	2	4	1	12	6	1	0	4	13	9	4	5
L	11	9	11	16	17	6	7	4	17	17	14	11	5
M	25	6	7	6	21	9	11	4	37	10	1	27	5
N	16	4	5	7	25	10	4	6	17	6	7	11	22
O	3	27	25	44	1	17	41	13	12	48	49	42	43
P	44	3	29	14	19	4	5	0	40	5	3	8	14
Q	0	5	4	0	0	3	1	0	1	2	0	4	1
R	13	16	8	10	15	24	11	14	1	10	16	9	7
S	9	26	6	13	13	17	22	6	7	12	11	17	9
T	25	11	6	22	31	18	6	6	31	6	8	8	15
U	3	36	54	7	4	11	17	8	7	14	8	8	2
V	9	0	4	0	2	3	5	1	9	7	5	3	7
W	5	1	8	2	4	4	2	0	1	1	2	3	2
X	6	3	0	2	9	1	2	2	3	5	3	4	6
Y	1	4	3	11	3	7	3	2	1	2	8	8	6
Z	2	2	2	1	6	3	2	1	3	5	3	5	3
Omit	4	1	3	6	1	1	1	1	3	2	2	0	4

Responses to Two-Letter Combinations

Response	T First Stimulus Letter												
	Second Stimulus Letter												
	N	O	P	Q	R	S	T	U	V	W	X	Y	Z
A	10	2	35	18	27	19	14	9	65	76	60	11	38
B	8	4	3	2	8	5	3	27	5	2	5	7	7
C	3	7	19	7	11	5	1	14	6	7	5	9	5
D	3	18	7	3	7	4	9	6	3	7	5	15	3
E	10	7	25	13	15	28	4	9	15	20	23	48	17
F	3	1	3	1	4	8	5	12	0	6	5	1	5
G	1	3	0	1	1	3	2	9	4	2	1	8	2
H	4	0	1	1	1	8	0	0	3	1	3	3	2
I	16	1	23	10	25	16	32	3	14	11	19	8	29
J	15	0	0	2	1	3	1	1	2	1	4	3	0
K	3	4	3	0	1	5	3	4	3	2	5	1	5
L	6	5	9	7	9	6	10	4	7	3	7	15	15
M	3	31	5	10	5	5	4	20	7	6	6	8	10
N	6	16	7	3	5	5	14	9	8	6	2	13	9
O	34	50	28	24	33	24	32	4	20	45	27	17	24
P	6	38	4	13	5	9	5	15	5	3	0	10	5
Q	1	0	13	5	3	8	1	1	3	0	3	2	8
R	1	10	26	68	8	39	10	10	14	7	8	15	14
S	7	5	24	26	41	16	19	10	22	16	14	18	7
T	88	49	6	3	10	33	62	36	14	6	12	8	15
U	10	2	12	32	13	12	22	5	21	11	10	3	13
V	13	2	1	2	1	3	3	39	9	5	4	5	8
W	4	10	2	2	3	3	4	2	9	2	5	6	2
X	6	1	8	7	4	1	2	12	3	17	5	9	5
Y	5	2	3	2	28	2	5	0	3	4	30	5	13
Z	3	3	4	8	2	1	4	11	4	4	5	23	8
Omit	4	2	2	3	2	2	2	1	4	3	0	0	4

Responses to Two-Letter Combinations

Response	U First Stimulus Letter												
					Second Stimulus Letter								
	A	B	C	D	E	F	G	H	I	J	K	L	M
A	8	29	24	11	12	17	18	22	6	21	15	18	14
B	15	9	0	6	4	5	8	5	7	8	7	8	17
C	8	17	16	6	6	7	6	3	6	6	4	31	13
D	11	10	14	32	14	5	7	3	12	9	6	19	13
E	2	33	26	39	8	16	18	9	4	14	43	17	16
F	10	5	6	8	14	18	4	36	7	3	4	4	1
G	2	3	4	1	5	11	24	10	2	5	3	1	2
H	8	5	5	8	4	31	57	15	3	12	9	1	10
I	3	12	5	14	11	8	11	27	11	13	14	3	10
J	2	0	1	7	1	1	4	1	1	8	4	1	1
K	7	1	12	2	6	2	3	5	4	37	13	7	1
L	13	6	56	12	17	13	18	10	27	20	44	10	8
M	13	15	7	5	8	8	4	17	30	2	7	25	4
N	21	7	3	12	14	7	9	17	20	5	13	5	33
O	10	12	14	18	6	10	12	27	15	12	14	10	10
P	10	5	2	4	9	9	8	5	25	10	3	19	27
Q	2	2	0	2	3	0	1	0	4	4	2	2	0
R	16	19	7	15	26	18	14	12	4	11	18	6	5
S	12	28	13	13	25	9	14	6	6	4	12	9	8
T	47	24	38	27	46	53	10	16	38	14	16	45	61
U	4	3	5	10	3	2	4	6	7	7	2	5	2
V	14	3	6	5	10	7	5	11	16	23	3	13	6
W	28	2	4	4	11	6	3	4	4	3	4	3	3
X	4	10	2	1	3	2	3	3	6	4	3	3	2
Y	2	4	1	3	2	2	3	1	1	10	2	4	0
Z	0	8	1	5	2	6	3	1	3	3	6	3	3
Omit	1	1	1	3	3	0	2	1	4	5	2	1	3

Responses to Two-Letter Combinations

Response	U First Stimulus Letter												
	Second Stimulus Letter												
	N	O	P	Q	R	S*	T	U	V	W	X	Y	Z
A	30	10	34	16	12	—	42	8	17	25	8	11	18
B	7	8	7	5	9	—	5	5	3	6	4	6	6
C	4	12	5	7	9	—	11	3	4	11	4	12	7
D	15	13	20	5	13	—	3	8	12	1	8	2	6
E	17	5	13	6	29	—	25	0	11	16	13	16	30
F	2	2	1	2	3	—	5	2	0	4	5	10	8
G	2	4	5	3	0	—	2	2	1	3	1	6	1
H	4	2	2	5	6	—	6	4	5	3	5	6	6
I	20	12	12	9	11	—	11	5	13	11	19	7	10
J	1	2	1	3	1	—	0	0	4	1	1	0	1
K	1	4	0	5	3	—	2	1	2	6	5	7	9
L	8	8	2	3	9	—	9	4	10	6	19	10	6
M	5	12	2	10	4	—	3	12	16	11	10	7	7
N	15	9	3	9	13	—	6	12	23	22	11	17	6
O	30	9	17	28	7	—	31	13	16	11	9	13	17
P	11	46	27	19	13	—	11	15	5	12	9	7	9
Q	1	3	4	10	2	—	1	1	0	0	1	4	1
R	11	15	25	39	12	—	22	8	15	12	13	6	8
S	14	7	23	19	40	—	21	13	6	18	4	15	14
T	33	51	46	26	53	—	27	34	18	12	29	23	38
U	4	5	7	14	1	—	9	64	4	6	8	3	3
V	25	16	4	5	4	—	11	45	2	24	26	8	12
W	5	8	6	6	1	—	2	5	64	15	5	11	7
X	2	1	3	7	2	—	1	1	11	19	5	20	13
Y	2	6	1	4	5	—	3	2	3	8	35	6	15
Z	3	2	2	7	7	—	3	5	7	7	15	37	15
Omit	1	1	1	1	4	—	1	1	1	3	1	3	0

* U S missing in original gathering of data.

Responses to Two-Letter Combinations

V   First Stimulus Letter

Second Stimulus Letter

Response	A	B	C	D	E	F	G	H	I	J	K	L	M
A	7	20	19	28	9	17	18	24	8	21	15	19	21
B	6	9	4	7	7	2	6	3	6	6	6	6	5
C	7	8	10	4	3	10	12	1	6	10	5	4	9
D	13	29	29	13	18	13	22	18	10	39	8	16	14
E	3	17	11	22	2	9	14	21	5	16	16	10	9
F	1	3	1	10	8	3	7	6	2	3	4	3	2
G	19	2	2	4	4	7	4	2	2	3	3	2	2
H	0	2	4	2	2	13	3	6	2	3	3	1	0
I	7	22	36	43	10	10	26	33	5	15	37	25	48
J	2	2	2	1	0	2	0	3	1	5	7	1	1
K	2	3	3	7	3	3	5	4	5	11	9	6	1
L	18	6	7	8	19	9	10	16	16	10	33	5	2
M	17	12	6	12	17	11	6	21	27	9	11	44	9
N	36	7	4	7	30	15	8	16	6	8	6	8	21
O	4	35	53	25	7	20	70	23	3	38	22	47	39
P	5	7	4	7	9	4	1	6	45	14	2	10	16
Q	0	5	4	3	4	5	2	3	3	0	2	0	2
R	21	20	6	8	13	14	10	9	12	13	12	2	10
S	14	13	4	18	11	8	18	10	9	13	14	5	5
T	65	23	32	20	67	21	9	18	68	19	15	23	29
U	5	5	11	4	1	5	7	5	1	3	10	8	4
V	3	2	0	4	5	1	2	6	9	3	6	4	4
W	7	4	3	4	6	57	6	8	4	2	7	8	9
X	3	7	10	5	13	5	1	2	12	4	6	4	7
Y	4	2	5	5	1	5	4	5	1	3	6	5	3
Z	2	4	2	2	1	3	0	3	4	1	4	4	0
Omit	2	4	1	0	3	1	2	1	1	1	4	3	1

Responses to Two-Letter Combinations

V   First Stimulus Letter

Response	Second Stimulus Letter											
	N	O	P	Q	R	S	T	U	V	W	X	Y	Z
A	17	3	12	20	19	18	32	4	12	16	9	18	25
B	6	10	0	3	6	8	1	6	3	6	5	6	7
C	7	11	5	7	6	9	5	6	9	13	9	11	8
D	14	16	6	4	7	10	7	12	11	2	6	8	6
E	16	3	15	10	14	12	21	8	8	11	12	28	17
F	6	3	1	8	2	2	7	5	2	8	2	2	5
G	3	5	0	1	3	6	1	2	3	0	2	2	0
H	1	2	1	4	0	4	4	1	1	9	2	5	1
I	16	4	91	16	28	31	29	4	22	9	22	16	30
J	2	0	1	2	1	1	0	0	3	0	2	3	1
K	4	5	0	3	2	4	0	3	2	1	4	4	3
L	8	22	12	12	10	11	12	14	11	4	13	10	11
M	12	21	11	14	15	10	16	27	7	11	8	6	8
N	8	8	7	8	11	5	7	16	4	14	8	3	7
O	66	4	35	21	29	18	38	8	23	29	16	11	30
P	11	23	18	10	7	5	6	42	1	10	2	12	4
Q	0	1	5	2	6	3	2	2	0	2	3	3	5
R	22	14	9	51	10	7	13	8	4	15	13	11	9
S	6	7	11	17	17	9	12	9	16	7	4	19	12
T	13	64	9	15	34	71	14	42	12	19	30	26	24
U	10	7	8	20	10	12	19	4	12	13	3	5	5
V	4	7	2	4	4	3	3	9	71	5	10	4	2
W	11	19	3	6	4	5	5	21	23	10	25	13	9
X	2	9	0	8	8	1	7	9	4	44	3	25	11
Y	2	1	6	0	12	1	5	2	4	4	44	3	23
Z	3	0	2	5	5	4	6	6	4	9	12	16	7
Omit	3	4	3	2	3	3	1	3	1	2	4	3	3

Responses to Two-Letter Combinations

Response	W First Stimulus Letter

Response	A	B	C	D	E	F	G	H	I	J	K	L	M
A	19	20	37	23	16	23	38	42	2	25	32	11	20
B	8	20	10	4	5	8	6	4	3	3	8	17	13
C	12	21	5	10	3	24	8	5	20	7	4	15	13
D	13	3	8	8	25	10	4	3	9	17	2	9	10
E	0	18	2	19	20	14	13	27	2	12	22	9	9
F	5	2	8	2	6	13	3	1	3	1	6	6	2
G	5	4	6	3	2	6	7	0	2	8	7	2	1
H	2	5	2	4	2	1	9	7	4	4	1	2	5
I	3	8	16	33	4	27	21	52	11	30	25	29	24
J	1	1	1	4	1	4	0	0	1	21	1	2	2
K	4	3	3	1	3	3	10	5	9	24	10	2	2
L	15	3	7	3	7	9	11	4	38	8	24	12	9
M	38	15	5	7	17	6	3	1	11	4	8	14	24
N	24	12	8	20	30	8	29	0	31	10	11	12	50
O	2	25	41	29	3	22	31	48	10	16	27	25	25
P	13	15	5	5	8	8	5	1	10	2	8	6	9
Q	0	8	2	2	0	1	1	1	1	5	4	0	1
R	14	12	7	12	12	15	16	3	3	19	17	7	3
S	16	13	8	11	17	10	13	4	9	17	13	30	8
T	40	20	56	32	68	27	17	8	57	6	11	25	17
U	6	4	20	13	6	7	7	7	3	5	8	4	6
V	9	5	2	3	5	5	1	4	7	1	1	3	5
W	11	1	5	5	4	4	3	1	2	8	3	6	4
X	8	17	4	6	4	2	8	2	10	11	8	4	3
Y	2	4	3	8	0	4	4	39	3	3	5	6	2
Z	0	11	1	5	3	11	4	2	7	6	4	11	4
Omit	3	3	1	1	2	1	1	2	5	0	3	4	2

Responses to Two-Letter Combinations

W   First Stimulus Letter

Response

Second Stimulus Letter

Response	N	O	P	Q	R	S	T	U	V	W	X	Y	Z
A	15	7	47	21	32	33	45	6	16	20	35	8	36
B	11	9	6	6	3	3	4	13	3	4	4	4	9
C	6	12	7	2	10	8	9	8	18	8	8	6	2
D	11	8	3	3	3	5	7	9	11	5	6	4	11
E	6	7	8	3	19	10	12	4	10	10	9	23	16
F	3	2	5	5	0	3	7	4	6	3	3	5	1
G	8	1	1	2	3	4	4	4	3	3	4	4	1
H	2	3	3	4	4	6	6	1	3	2	1	10	3
I	18	2	23	9	20	28	23	4	25	9	16	2	18
J	2	3	1	2	1	1	0	0	5	2	1	2	4
K	3	8	3	2	1	3	1	9	3	1	2	7	9
L	4	14	11	8	2	8	9	6	5	13	6	6	15
M	11	47	8	9	5	4	4	18	8	17	5	11	4
N	7	23	7	18	28	13	7	22	5	10	9	7	11
O	62	11	36	28	28	15	42	6	27	18	28	19	21
P	17	15	6	2	5	6	5	17	6	5	6	6	3
Q	2	0	3	1	2	2	1	0	1	4	2	1	4
R	15	16	19	50	4	8	16	21	18	10	7	13	10
S	7	6	24	15	42	11	15	23	14	8	9	18	7
T	14	29	9	14	9	68	11	43	17	18	12	14	27
U	13	11	15	24	10	8	25	5	11	9	5	3	12
V	10	4	5	5	5	6	4	21	4	11	8	7	5
W	7	22	6	4	4	5	4	4	15	63	2	5	2
X	4	5	2	14	9	6	3	11	19	9	11	30	16
Y	5	4	4	4	13	6	1	1	5	6	56	7	18
Z	7	3	11	16	9	3	5	10	14	4	16	50	4
Omit	3	1	0	2	2	0	3	3	1	1	2	1	4

Responses to Two-Letter Combinations

Response	X First Stimulus Letter												
	Second Stimulus Letter												
	A	B	C	D	E	F	G	H	I	J	K	L	M
A	3	26	20	26	11	18	33	14	5	9	13	11	27
B	19	9	12	12	11	7	26	6	3	5	5	9	1
C	3	21	15	15	7	10	7	7	7	13	7	9	10
D	10	17	28	3	5	4	3	6	7	9	7	6	7
E	4	8	9	19	4	18	9	9	2	10	12	4	7
F	3	2	2	9	6	9	6	4	3	4	4	2	2
G	3	6	7	3	2	14	3	3	3	9	8	0	4
H	1	4	3	0	1	0	6	3	0	2	2	1	2
I	0	12	17	29	4	14	15	47	6	23	21	18	11
J	1	2	3	6	0	4	1	6	5	4	2	2	2
K	0	2	5	6	2	2	8	6	7	30	5	3	4
L	15	9	10	7	6	13	11	11	28	14	35	2	24
M	60	11	11	11	28	12	9	10	10	9	9	35	4
N	14	4	4	4	30	7	7	6	9	4	10	9	38
O	2	22	23	14	9	7	36	19	11	22	18	20	28
P	23	5	11	8	18	8	8	4	24	7	10	8	13
Q	2	4	2	2	1	6	3	2	0	7	0	5	4
R	10	16	19	9	16	7	17	13	1	13	21	17	8
S	4	15	11	14	6	22	7	6	10	6	6	6	11
T	38	20	12	27	40	28	22	24	58	18	16	23	20
U	2	6	5	4	4	9	7	6	2	8	12	9	1
V	13	0	4	4	6	8	3	8	10	5	2	19	6
W	2	4	0	2	3	5	2	1	5	4	2	3	5
X	15	15	11	6	18	4	7	13	21	8	8	9	6
Y	20	17	21	22	17	15	10	28	11	17	29	26	15
Z	5	13	7	8	16	19	3	10	23	11	7	17	10
Omit	1	3	1	3	2	3	4	1	2	2	2	0	3

Responses to Two-Letter Combinations

Response	X First Stimulus Letter Second Stimulus Letter												
	N	O	P	Q	R	S	T	U	V	W	X	Y	Z
A	20	14	18	10	22	23	16	7	14	17	3	8	21
B	5	18	8	11	13	6	9	11	4	5	2	3	10
C	5	7	10	5	14	2	7	14	2	10	1	6	6
D	12	10	11	3	11	7	8	5	15	2	7	5	10
E	19	3	8	7	8	10	13	3	5	11	4	3	1
F	4	2	8	9	4	3	2	5	1	2	3	5	3
G	3	2	3	1	1	2	1	2	2	1	3	4	2
H	0	1	1	1	1	2	1	1	2	3	3	0	1
I	7	3	17	11	7	15	25	3	13	6	19	4	4
J	3	2	3	1	1	2	1	1	2	3	1	3	1
K	4	2	0	4	3	1	3	3	2	2	3	6	3
L	8	6	15	8	18	16	13	13	11	10	9	7	6
M	9	21	3	13	12	23	13	17	7	17	6	4	0
N	7	17	2	7	9	5	9	16	7	7	3	10	3
O	54	7	28	15	18	7	27	6	11	34	12	12	17
P	14	31	9	17	8	9	10	10	9	11	5	9	3
Q	5	0	12	6	5	1	4	1	6	0	6	3	2
R	11	10	25	49	9	8	12	13	9	6	9	5	7
S	3	4	14	7	21	17	14	12	7	8	7	2	5
T	18	41	16	19	44	51	8	47	37	15	10	5	31
U	6	6	12	18	8	5	10	1	20	3	4	3	3
V	13	8	1	5	3	3	12	25	3	15	3	3	1
W	2	6	4	9	4	2	3	3	30	8	2	6	8
X	7	16	7	6	5	12	3	19	10	10	93	7	9
Y	20	22	18	16	12	20	36	11	30	30	41	3	99
Z	12	12	17	14	11	17	13	23	11	36	12	141	15
Omit	2	2	3	1	1	4	0	1	3	1	2	6	2

Responses to Two-Letter Combinations

Y   First Stimulus Letter

Response

Second Stimulus Letter

	A	B	C	D	E	F	G	H	I	J	K	L	M
A	3	37	42	31	18	26	44	38	7	21	37	18	19
B	12	4	12	9	5	12	8	10	7	7	3	10	13
C	4	19	8	19	3	21	14	11	8	16	5	10	36
D	9	12	18	7	11	5	7	11	20	13	8	12	5
E	2	26	16	26	3	31	13	13	3	6	17	12	13
F	4	7	0	7	5	4	5	3	5	4	1	3	2
G	4	2	7	2	0	15	9	1	5	4	1	2	3
H	5	1	1	4	1	1	8	9	1	5	2	2	1
I	0	13	9	28	1	16	8	28	6	11	8	12	5
J	1	1	1	2	1	4	0	4	4	5	0	2	1
K	6	5	8	0	1	2	5	3	7	32	8	8	3
L	16	4	23	5	6	10	9	13	9	21	41	10	5
M	39	25	10	10	5	3	23	14	11	4	11	23	5
N	20	2	8	4	11	7	12	7	13	6	9	9	34
O	7	20	40	45	5	22	19	33	9	25	44	27	62
P	40	7	6	6	7	6	5	13	71	17	6	9	7
Q	0	3	1	1	0	1	1	6	4	0	4	0	0
R	19	11	3	12	6	14	10	5	4	12	9	9	4
S	11	21	8	23	131	16	19	8	5	9	8	6	6
T	44	10	26	17	31	15	16	11	45	17	17	21	16
U	8	5	7	4	3	9	15	19	8	5	8	16	11
V	5	2	0	2	1	2	3	1	4	5	7	8	5
W	4	3	6	0	5	6	0	0	4	5	4	2	2
X	4	14	5	3	3	5	7	2	2	9	3	11	2
Y	3	6	3	1	4	8	6	2	7	5	3	11	2
Z	2	8	2	4	4	11	5	6	3	7	7	19	7
Omit	1	5	3	1	2	1	2	2	1	2	2	1	4

Responses to Two-Letter Combinations

Response	Y First Stimulus Letter												
						Second Stimulus Letter							
	N	O	P	Q	R	S	T	U	V	W	X	Y	Z
A	26	4	22	12	26	6	36	8	20	26	12	7	43
B	8	7	6	3	4	6	5	6	5	5	10	4	11
C	13	3	4	7	8	7	5	5	6	25	7	3	4
D	10	9	11	10	9	10	7	17	9	2	7	5	8
E	18	2	22	5	34	91	25	3	12	12	8	5	15
F	5	1	2	3	2	4	7	2	1	4	3	4	6
G	1	6	3	2	2	1	0	4	0	1	2	2	2
H	0	2	1	1	0	5	0	0	3	1	1	3	2
I	2	3	49	9	6	3	20	2	14	4	5	13	7
J	1	0	2	2	2	0	1	2	5	0	2	2	3
K	3	6	1	3	0	2	3	7	4	4	1	0	2
L	9	5	8	16	5	2	9	15	12	10	14	7	7
M	13	6	6	8	5	8	24	15	8	6	2	5	10
N	5	13	8	9	5	6	10	13	6	15	2	2	6
O	61	2	39	35	15	19	33	49	32	40	10	23	23
P	8	10	8	9	8	5	7	30	2	11	14	2	12
Q	2	0	3	1	2	0	2	1	3	2	4	2	2
R	5	9	15	43	5	10	9	19	6	5	13	3	8
S	9	9	11	22	51	11	23	9	8	10	6	17	8
T	23	25	17	11	39	45	10	28	19	15	20	28	34
U	9	119	6	30	16	9	9	4	16	9	5	3	6
V	5	5	3	5	3	3	6	12	6	10	4	6	1
W	3	4	6	2	2	4	2	6	34	6	9	5	6
X	2	1	3	11	10	1	4	5	20	20	7	16	29
Y	7	18	9	1	5	3	6	5	10	5	9	59	7
Z	20	3	8	12	9	12	9	4	9	24	92	44	9
Omit	5	1	1	0	0	0	1	2	3	1	4	3	2

Responses to Two-Letter Combinations

Response	Z First Stimulus Letter												
	Second Stimulus Letter												
	A	B	C	D	E	F	G	H	I	J	K	L	M
A	2	33	34	39	14	18	41	24	7	28	21	29	24
B	35	4	7	6	19	15	10	4	12	5	10	3	8
C	6	8	6	6	5	12	6	4	4	7	0	8	8
D	15	11	16	6	18	12	5	7	2	10	6	8	8
E	3	10	8	19	5	22	12	16	3	10	26	5	15
F	1	0	3	7	11	9	7	7	2	6	3	5	6
G	2	5	7	3	1	10	3	3	8	2	3	1	4
H	0	0	6	4	2	4	5	6	3	8	2	0	1
I	2	15	19	16	4	10	28	44	3	15	21	7	19
J	0	0	0	2	0	4	2	0	2	4	3	2	1
K	6	3	15	2	3	9	4	11	9	22	4	13	6
L	7	13	13	8	19	15	18	17	17	21	39	3	9
M	18	7	1	8	12	13	5	5	19	9	6	28	8
N	12	8	5	8	15	14	4	10	5	8	4	11	19
O	4	31	18	43	11	18	32	35	8	19	31	51	25
P	39	1	9	4	30	12	8	4	65	13	9	11	11
Q	0	4	5	4	2	7	2	4	0	2	3	9	2
R	11	11	21	10	6	11	8	9	9	13	12	7	9
S	6	13	14	8	7	6	11	10	4	10	12	7	7
T	75	66	27	36	71	27	15	23	63	28	19	32	52
U	0	4	7	9	1	3	10	4	3	7	8	5	7
V	2	3	6	0	4	2	3	3	6	5	5	3	4
W	3	0	4	1	6	1	3	4	3	3	5	5	1
X	6	12	13	7	2	5	15	2	4	10	3	3	7
Y	4	4	5	5	1	3	7	12	3	4	11	7	4
Z	11	6	4	9	3	9	5	4	7	4	3	7	7
Omit	3	1	0	3	1	2	4	1	2	0	4	3	1

Responses to Two-Letter Combinations

Response	Z First Stimulus Letter												
						Second Stimulus Letter							
	N	O	P	Q	R	S	T	U	V	W	X*	Y	Z
A	19	3	29	29	28	13	85	5	32	33	—	20	24
B	8	17	2	5	7	7	13	10	4	9	—	5	6
C	5	3	2	2	3	9	5	0	7	6	—	9	1
D	3	5	15	5	4	5	5	21	12	3	—	9	5
E	15	2	14	5	20	17	16	3	14	12	—	19	7
F	6	6	0	4	7	5	4	2	2	4	—	8	5
G	3	2	0	2	3	1	2	3	2	0	—	4	2
H	3	2	1	3	2	1	2	0	1	1	—	3	0
I	14	1	73	9	7	9	19	2	26	18	—	5	14
J	3	0	1	3	1	1	0	0	1	2	—	3	0
K	10	4	6	2	8	1	0	7	3	3	—	6	1
L	9	0	9	11	12	7	5	25	8	7	—	13	10
M	10	10	3	8	4	5	7	11	12	10	—	4	4
N	10	9	13	6	5	6	7	10	9	12	—	8	4
O	42	107	32	33	24	30	29	8	20	28	—	19	22
P	12	26	3	9	13	15	6	29	4	12	—	16	9
Q	6	3	2	2	4	2	0	0	4	2	—	3	0
R	11	6	13	43	5	6	5	13	14	8	—	8	7
S	8	2	6	22	23	10	15	9	9	15	—	11	9
T	36	41	26	14	57	106	6	77	15	26	—	42	43
U	4	3	6	28	12	5	21	4	12	7	—	4	2
V	2	1	1	3	2	1	2	11	5	6	—	5	5
W	6	6	3	4	5	1	1	4	26	6	—	3	0
X	14	0	3	8	3	2	1	6	14	20	—	28	10
Y	10	2	6	2	7	4	5	2	11	15	—	6	13
Z	2	9	3	10	4	2	10	11	3	6	—	10	66
Omit	2	3	1	1	3	2	2	0	3	2	—	2	4

* Z X missing in original gathering of data.

Author Index